Organizations with Incomplete Information

ESSAYS IN ECONOMIC ANALYSIS

A Tribute to Roy Radner

There have been systematic attempts over the last twenty-five years to explore the implications of decision making with incomplete information and to model an "economic man" as an information processing organism. These efforts are associated with the work of Roy Radner, who joins other analysts in this collection to offer accessible overviews of the existing literature on topics such as Walrasian equilibrium with incomplete markets, rational expectations equilibrium, learning, Markovian games, dynamic game-theoretic models of organization, and experimental work on mechanism selection. Some essays also take up relatively new themes related to bounded rationality, complexity of decisions, and economic survival. The collection overall introduces models that add to the toolbox of economists, expand the boundaries of economic analysis, and enrich our understanding of the inefficiencies and complexities of organizational design in the presence of uncertainty.

Mukul Majumdar is H. T. Warshow and Robert Irving Warshow Professor of Economics at Cornell University, and Co-Editor of *Economic Theory*. He has also taught at Stanford University, the University of Wisconsin, Madison, and the London School of Economics. Professor Majumdar has been a Guggenheim Fellow, a Ford Rotating Research Professor at the University of California, Berkeley, an Erskine Fellow at the University of Canterbury, an Oskar Morgenstern Visiting Professor at New York University, and a lecturer at the Collège de France. Elected Fellow of the Econometric Society in 1976 and the author of many research articles, he is well known for his research on dynamic economic models.

T0339884

Organizations with Incomplete Information

ESSAYS IN ECONOMIC ANALYSIS

A Tribute to Roy Radner

Edited by
Mukul Majumdar

CAMBRIDGE
UNIVERSITY PRESS

CAMBRIDGE UNIVERSITY PRESS
Cambridge, New York, Melbourne, Madrid, Cape Town, Singapore, São Paulo, Delhi

Cambridge University Press
The Edinburgh Building, Cambridge CB2 8RU, UK

Published in the United States of America by Cambridge University Press, New York

www.cambridge.org
Information on this title: www.cambridge.org/9780521553001

First published 1998
This digitally printed version 2008

A catalogue record for this publication is available from the British Library

ISBN 978-0-521-55300-1 hardback
ISBN 978-0-521-08466-6 paperback

Contents

v

Contributors

Beth Allen, University of Minnesota and Federal Reserve Bank of Minneapolis

Lawrence E. Blume, Cornell University

Prajit K. Dutta, Columbia University

David Easley, Cornell University

James S. Jordan, University of Minnesota

Kenneth R. Mount, Northwestern University

Roy Radner, New York University

Stanley Reiter, Northwestern University

Andrew Schotter, New York University

Wayne Shafer, University of Illinois

Rangarajan K. Sundaram, New York University

Timothy Van Zandt, Princeton University

Preface

This collection of essays grew out of a conference that I organized at Cornell University in June 1992 to honor Professor Roy Radner on his sixty-fifth birthday: it is a pleasure to note that some of the distinguished alumni of Cornell (Professors Beth Allen, Prajit Dutta, James Jordan, Andrew Schotter, Raghu Sundaram) were able to contribute to this volume. Generous financial support from the Center for Applied Mathematics, the Center for Analytic Economics, and the Department of Economics is gratefully acknowledged. In this context, I am particularly grateful to David Easley, Don Randel, John Guckenheimer, Karl Shell, and Tapan Mitra for their encouragement. The success of the conference owed much to the organizational skills of Ann Stiles.

I would like to thank Professors C. D. Aliprantis, A. Banerjee, J. Benhabib, J. Boyd, M. Datta, M. El-Gamal, R. Ericson, L. Fernandez, J. K. Ghosh, T. Groves, L. Hurwicz, M. Ali Khan, P. Linhart, E. Malinvaud, E. Maskin, C. B. McGuire, L. McKenzie, M. Meurer, L. Miller, K. Nishimura, Y. Nyarko, A. Radunskaya, R. Rosenthal, M. Rothschild, A. Rubinstein, G. Sorger, S. Williams, K. Yun, and E. Zajac for their help and advice at various stages of the project.

This volume does not adequately reflect Roy Radner's impressive range of interests and contributions, and it is not meant to be a *Festschrift*. Productive as ever, Roy is keenly exploring new areas and searching for new paradigms. But time and again, he has returned to topics involving decisions and organizations with incomplete information, and we feel that a set of essays on these themes is a fitting tribute to his creativity.

Ithaca, New York

ix

Introduction: Searching for Paradigms

Mukul Majumdar

1   Introduction

Problems of decision making with incomplete information about all the "payoff relevant" variables have been posed and studied in depth from several angles. At one extreme are models that focus on an *individual* agent (e.g., the literature building on the "Savage paradigm"[1]). At the other extreme – in the Walrasian tradition – are models that highlight the role of prices in coordinating independent decisions made by *many* agents. In between, there are models – in the Cournot tradition – with a *small number of interacting agents*, often with divergent interests. Problems of characterizing optimal decisions of individual agents, mutual consistency of such decisions in the larger context of an organization or an entire economy, and the possibility of achieving efficiency through appropriate design of organizations have been among the themes of enduring interest. Some of the essays in this collection review recent developments on several fronts while others stress the need for new directions.

2   Equilibrium

We begin with a review of a substantial literature on economic equilibrium under uncertainty. Chapters 1 and 2 are very much in the Walrasian tradition in the sense that the decision makers participate in markets and accept the terms of transactions as given. It has been pointed out that Walrasian equilibrium theory embodies a number of ideas. Such an equilibrium portrays a balance of the forces of supply and demand

I am particularly grateful to Professor Prajit Dutta for his detailed advice and criticism on an earlier version. Thanks are due to Professors Kaushik Basu, Manjira Datta, David Easley, Uri Possen, Roy Radner, and Jennifer Wissink for their comments.
[1] See the recent critical assessment of Radner (1997, pp. 326–8).

1

simultaneously in all the markets. Thus, the question of existence of an equilibrium was often reduced to the study of conditions under which a certain set of equations had a solution. And John Hicks in his *Value and Capital* (1939, p. 60), after an exposition of the existence question by counting the number of equations and unknowns, felt that it was a great achievement of Walras "to have shown, even so schematically, the mechanism of the interrelation of markets." Developments in the fifties included a re-examination of the existence question with a striking allegiance to mathematical rigor, often in an axiomatic framework. There was also a reinterpretation of the problem (perhaps made possible by the availability of new tools) as one of proving that a number of decentralized decisions (derived as solutions to independent optimization exercises) can be carried out simultaneously.[2] When one dispensed with the demand and supply *functions* as basic ingredients of the models of individual choice, *mutual consistency of independent plans* became a key element of the equilibrium concept. Hicks had earlier noted a consistency requirement as follows (1939, p. 58, footnote 1):

A market is in equilibrium, statically considered, if every person is acting in such a way as to reach his most preferred position, subject to the opportunities open to him. This implies that the actions of different persons trading must be consistent.

This definition of equilibrium remains meaningful even when one rejects the "price taking" behavior of Walrasian agents, and is consistent with other equilibrium concepts explored in several chapters and discussed in more detail in the later sections of this chapter.

The connection between a Walrasian equilibrium and Pareto optimal allocation of resources had engaged the attention of economic theorists for quite some time, and a calculus treatment of the problem had been given by Lange (1942) and others; see the review in Samuelson (1947, Chap. 8). But, with arguments that led to some gains in generality, elegant versions of the two fundamental theorems of the *new* welfare economics were obtained in the fifties, and these were viewed by some as a "specification of conditions under which a decentralization of economic decisions through a price system is compatible with efficient utilization of resources" (Koopmans 1957). These welfare propositions have figured prominently in policy debates on the role of markets and government intervention, even in contexts that are far removed from the models in which they were rigorously established. They also stimulated a program of research on the more general question of attaining efficiency or Pareto

---

[2] This point of view was cogently offered by Koopmans (1957).

optimality through *any* informationally decentralized system of decision making that takes account of *dispersal of information* and *limits on communication and information processing* in an economy (and may "work" in environments where markets fail; see Hurwicz 1986 for a formal review of the literature). In the chapters by Van Zandt, Schotter, and Radner, the reader will be exposed to various facets of the problems of organizational design and possible conflicts between decentralization and attainment of efficiency.

3   Sterility?

It is not difficult to find, even in the writings of acknowledged masters of microeconomics, a sense of unease with the Walrasian theory. One does not have to go back beyond *Value and Capital* (1939, pp. 60–1), where it was pointed out that "many economists (perhaps most, even of those who have studied Walras seriously)" would say that

Walras does give one a picture of the whole system; but it is a very distant picture, and hardly amounts to more than an assurance that things will work themselves out somehow, though it is not very clear how they will work themselves out. Other economists are theoretically less ambitious, but they at least give us results which are applicable to actual problems. Now the reason for the sterility of the Walrasian system is largely, I believe, that he did not go on to work out the laws of change for his system of General Equilibrium.

A careful reading of Hicks's comments takes us out of the immediate bounds of the static Walrasian theory and prompts us to set some general criteria (that have figured prominently in many a methodological debate!) for evaluating formal economic models. First, does the model provide explanations of economic relationships and/or insights into the functioning of specific institutions? Secondly, does the model enable us to predict economic events (and prepare us better to meet contingencies)? Finally, does the model provide advice on improving the performance of an individual, an organization, or perhaps an economy? My subsequent remarks are primarily motivated by such criteria.

A significant volume of research in the last thirty years has thrown further light on the points raised by Hicks regarding the scope of Walrasian analysis. Early efforts to identify conditions under which a Walrasian equilibrium is *unique* led to the recognition that the property holds

under strong assumptions, and, ... economies with multiple equilibria must be allowed for. Such economies still seem to provide a satisfactory explanation of equilibrium as well as a satisfactory foundation for the study of stability provided that all the equilibria of the economy are locally unique. But if the set of equilibria is compact (a common situation), local uniqueness is equivalent to finiteness. One is thus led to investigate conditions under which an economy has a *finite set of equilibria*. (Debreu 1970)

One of Debreu's influential contributions was to point out that such finiteness holds generically over an appropriate set of models,[3] and that the set of equilibrium price vectors varies continuously with the characteristics of the economy. Although no general result involving a bound on the number of equilibria was obtained, this continuity property is obviously important in the context of predicting the equilibria from the characteristics of an economy: "otherwise, the slightest error of observation on the data of the economy might lead to an entirely different set of predicted equilibria. This consideration, which is common in the study of physical systems, applies with even greater force to the study of social systems" (Debreu 1974, p. 71). This formal way of looking at the "typical" case has no doubt enriched economic theory (see e.g. Chapter 2). It is sometimes argued that multiplicity of equilibria is not necessarily bad since it holds out the possibility that there are many possible outcomes consistent with a general scenario (and enables us to catch glimpses of many worlds in a given universe!). The point is well taken and perhaps comforting. But, in the absence of some understanding of how things will work themselves out and how a particular equilibrium is likely to emerge (depending on the historical evolution) or how we can drive an economy to a "better" equilibrium, I am still left with a sense of sterility.

In the Walrasian setting, the difficulties of making progress in Samuelsonian comparative statics[4] have long been clear to the experts, but the limited prospects for qualitative economics was subsequently made even clearer by a class of results obtained by Sonnenschein, Mantel, Debreu, Mas-Colell, and others. We now know that *any* (non-

---

[3] Informally, finiteness was shown to be "typical": in Debreu's formulation (1970), the "exceptional" class of economies is identified with a "closed set of Lebesgue measure zero" in a finite-dimensional Euclidean space.

[4] "The usefulness of our theory emerges from the fact that by our analysis we are often able to determine the nature of changes in our unknown variables resulting from a designated change in one or more parameters. Our theory is meaningless unless it does imply some restrictions upon empirically observable quantities by which it could conceivably be refuted. This in brief is the method of *comparative statics*, meaning by this the investigation of changes in a system from one position of equilibrium to another without regard to the transitional process involved in adjustment" (Samuelson 1947, pp. 7–8). The difficulties in deriving comparative static results are summarized in Arrow and Hahn (1971).

empty) compact (sub)set of the (relative interior of the) price simplex can be viewed as the set of Walrasian equilibria of *some* economy in which agents have continuous strictly convex and monotone preferences; see Shafer and Sonnenschein (1982, Sec. 4) for a more formal and precise discussion of such results. The challenge posed by Hicks and Samuelson on predicting the movement of variables in response to changes in parameters can be accepted only through less ambitious models with "more concrete" structures on preferences and technologies or through numerical specification of the relationships, or through drastic simplifications on the number of commodities and/or agents. Not surprisingly, all these routes have been followed in applications of Walrasian equilibrium theory, and it can be hoped that – with the dramatic advances of our computational ability – comparative statics and dynamics will be carried out through a combination of theory and computer experiments.

4 Time

Some of the themes that appear repeatedly in this volume – learning and expectation formation, for example – are essentially linked to the passage of time. Here, I would like to recall that an interesting aspect of Debreu's exposition (1959) was his emphasis on a unified treatment of time and location by defining a commodity appropriately (as long as markets are complete and the behavior assumptions hold). But how significant is such an interpretation? I am more inclined to argue that a model with "once-and-for-all" decision making (which makes it formally equivalent to a static counterpart) is inadequate to yield genuinely dynamic analysis involving intertemporal allocation and welfare.[5] In order to make significant progress on the road toward a combination of welfare theory over time and the theory of capital, "it is necessary to begin from the first principles with due attention to the peculiarities of capital" (Dorfman, Samuelson, and Solow 1958, p. 416). The transition from (essentially) static to dynamic models has been attempted in several ways, with some startling conclusions, even without a recognition

---

[5] One can ask a similar question about the role of the very general Walrasian equilibrium model with regard to international trade. It has been argued that "if there is any one thing that could legitimately be demanded of a theory of international trade, it is that it should be capable of explaining observed patterns and flows of trade among countries" (Chipman 1987). The Walrasian model in its *general* form is not particularly illuminating in this direction. In order to make headway, economists have turned to the development of systems with special structures, addressing specific issues.

of uncertainty. One can look at a sequence of momentary or temporary equilibria, where each equilibrium is defined by some consistency conditions and behavioral rules. From Malinvaud (1953) and Samuelson (1958) we learn that even in the classical convex environment, a (neverending) sequence of competitive equilibria need not be efficient in the long run. Furthermore, the "verification scenario" (Hurwicz 1986) describing the decentralized allocation in a static Walrasian economy runs into obvious difficulties, even if the correct equilibrium messages are proposed (by the mechanism designer), when no action is taken until *all* the verifications of intertemporal equilibrium conditions over the entire life span of the economy are completed (see Bala, Mitra, and Majumdar 1991 for details). And going beyond prices, when the agents are not clairvoyant, it may not be possible to design *any* intertemporally decentralized resource allocation mechanism that assures long-run Pareto efficiency.[6]

As a digression, I would like to recall that there was a prominent theme involving economic dynamics that came out of the Walrasian *tâtonnement* through Samuelson. Although the conceptual difficulties of such a framework are well known,[7] the particularly appealing feature was the attempt to present an explicitly dynamic process that captured the working of markets and to look at an equilibrium as a rest point of such a process (although little was known about the efficiency or decentralizability of an economy out of equilibrium!). There was a resurgence of interest in the late fifties in such dynamics, but the mainstream of research in Walrasian economics seemed to veer away from this direction after Scarf's example of instability (1960).[8] However, it seems to me that we will not meet the concerns of Hicks about understanding the working of an economy – how it evolves and how things work out – by looking exclusively at a chain of sophisticated static equilibrium concepts.

---

[6] "How can Pareto efficiency be achieved by a decentralized price system which operates through time with no terminal date? After forty years of research, the problems raised by this question are not exhausted. . . . We are facing one of those cases in which scientists have to feel uncomfortable because the validity of some central propositions in their disciplines remains exposed to doubt with respect to some not fully negligible circumstances" (Malinvaud 1992). For an elaboration of these issues, see the collection of articles edited by Majumdar (1992).

[7] See Nikaido (1968), Arrow and Hahn (1971), and Hahn (1982) for analytical results and a discussion of the difficulties in interpreting the process. More recently, Saari (1985) and Bala and Majumdar (1992) have explored the possibility of chaotic trajectories even in a two-commodity model.

[8] See, however, Uzawa (1961b, 1962b), Hurwicz, Radner, and Reiter (1975), Dierker (1982), Bala et al. (1991), and the references cited in these papers.

5 Uncertainty

In the last chapter of his book, Debreu (1959) provided a succinct account of how his analysis can be further extended to "the case where uncertain events determine the consumption sets, the production sets, and the resources of the economy." The basic idea[9] is that

a contract for the transfer of a commodity now specifies, in addition to its physical properties, its location and its date, an event on the occurrence of which the transfer is conditional. This new definition of a commodity allows one to obtain a theory of uncertainty free from any probability concept and formally identical with the theory of certainty.

In short, *uncertainty* is modeled in terms of an expanded set of commodities (with a corresponding expansion of the number of markets), and results on the existence and optimality of an equilibrium parallel to the case of certainty are then obtained with the same analytical apparatus. Of course, taken literally, this expansion of the list of markets raises skepticism about the plausibility of having many participants in *all* these markets, the usual justification of price-taking behavior.

Radner (1968, 1970) was the first to provide a comprehensive assessment of the scope and explanatory power of the Arrow–Debreu model of uncertainty.[10] First, note that there are some interesting features of the optimization exercise confronting the agents. For a given price system, there is no uncertainty about the value of any production plan, and there is no ambiguity in defining the concept of a profit-maximizing firm. Secondly, given a price system and production plans, there is no uncertainty about an individual consumer i's net worth (determining i's budget constraint). It follows that *beliefs and attitudes towards risk play no role in the assumed behavior of producers* (although a consumer i's preference among plans will reflect not only i's tastes but also i's subjective beliefs about the likelihoods of different events and attitudes towards risk). Next, we note that:

If the Arrow-Debreu model is given a literal interpretation, then it clearly requires that the economic agents possess capabilities of imagination and calculation that exceed reality by many orders of magnitude. Related to this is the observation that the theory requires in principle a complete system of insurance and futures markets, which appears to be too complex, detailed, and refined to have practical significance. (Radner 1970, p. 457)

---

[9] See Arrow (1970, pp. 121–33) for the English translation of his earlier 1953 paper.
[10] In what follows in this section, I have drawn directly from Radner's beautiful exposition (1970).

Both of these points – complexity of computation and complexity in the design of institutions for dealing with resource allocation and risk bearing – figure prominently in several chapters of this volume (especially the last three).

Limitations on agents' capacities for observation, communication, and computation (as well as other transactions costs) make it intuitively clear why markets are not complete, and hence why there are active but incomplete markets at every date. Once this is made explicit, certain phenomena and institutions not accounted for in the Arrow–Debreu model can be brought within the range of theoretical analysis. In particular, one achieves a better understanding of

(i)   a theory of demand for money;
(ii) stock markets and speculation;
(iii) the difficulties of formulating a satisfactory theory of the expected profit maximization by a firm owned partially by agents not involved in management; and
(iv) the difficulties of formulating a satisfactory theory of intertemporal consumption and investment of a consumer having an uncertain net worth.

Radner's search for paradigms that could enhance the scope of the Arrow–Debreu theory under uncertainty led him to explore a number of equilibrium concepts and to raise new questions about the role of prices in information processing and the efficiency of the market mechanism. The concept of an equilibrium of plans, prices, and price expectations developed by Radner (1972a) became a landmark in the literature on incomplete markets, reviewed by Shafer in Chapter 1. In Radner's view, this definition came closest to the notion of "equilibrium over time" described in Hicks (1939, Chap. X). His study of the existence question led to a new twist: a bound on the size of trades in the *asset* markets. This was not just an ad hoc element in a particular *method* of proof, as Hart's example (1975) revealed. Shafer points out that it "makes sense that for markets to remain competitive, no individual agent should participate with a significant share of the market. From this point of view, a priori bounds on the size of trades an individual can make seems reasonable. ... For many assets, however, there is no such natural bound." This "annoying" property has been one of the themes in a new literature primarily aimed at the existence question. However, the questions of local uniqueness and Pareto efficiency have called for a sophisticated exploration. It is particularly important to remember that an equilibrium need *not* be locally unique, and *may not be* Pareto optimal (even viewing models generically). Indeed, there are some subtle issues involving the notion of Pareto optimality, but the robust examples highlight a fundamental break in the link between equilibrium and efficiency as one moves into paradigms of incomplete markets.

6   Heterogeneity of Information

A part of Radner's pioneering paper (1968) dealt with the issue of *heterogeneity of information*. In the Arrow–Debreu model of uncertainty, each agent has incomplete information about the environment, "but all agents have the same information. This . . . assumption is not tenable if we are to take good account of the effects of uncertainty in an economy." His first task was to construct a formal extension of the model in order to derive a theory of existence and optimality of competitive equilibrium with fixed (but possibly divergent) structures of information. In the context of attaining optimality through markets, Radner noted that "the limits on the information available to the agents . . . and the differences among the information structures of several agents will typically have the effect of drastically reducing the number of markets." First, there is no need for contracts that depend on information that is not available in the economy. Second, the net trade between any group of agents and the rest of the economy can at most depend upon information that is common to both groups (see the example in Radner 1968, Sec. 7).

Once one allows for such heterogeneity, yet another concept of "equilibrium" emerges. When traders enter markets with different nonprice information (i.e., information about the economic environment other than prices), there is an opportunity for agents to learn *about* the environment *from* prices because market prices "pool," in a possibly complicated manner, the nonprice information signals received by various agents. These inferences are derived, explicitly or implicitly, from individuals' own models of the relationship between the nonprice information received by market participants and the market prices. On the other hand, the true relationship is determined by the individual agents' behavior and hence jointly by their individual models. An equilibrium of this system, in which the individuals' models are identical with the true model, is called a *rational expectations equilibrium* (see Radner 1967, 1979, 1982). This is the subject of Chapter 2 by Allen and Jordan. The early literature offered little toward understanding any process of information communication and focused primarily on the existence of such an equilibrium – one that reveals *all* the initial information possessed by all the traders (a positive generic answer was the principal accomplishment of Radner 1979). Subsequent research on efficiency properties is particularly fascinating, as it enables us to deal more precisely with a number of themes on the "efficiency" of competitive markets in pooling private information (see the fifth section of Chapter 2). "Only for three special parametric classes of utility functions – linear, logarithmic, and exponential – do we find informationally efficient rational expectations equilibria. Moreover, these economies obviously constitute 'knife-edge' examples; they are not generic in any reasonable sense."

7   Learning

In Chapter 3, Blume and Easley review a number of issues in the burgeoning literature on learning, covering single-agent models, dynamic games, and rational expectations equilibria. Economic theorists interested in models of decision making under uncertainty have repeatedly stressed the need to incorporate the process of expectation formation into the "model of an economic man" viewed "as a learning, estimating, searching, information-processing organism" (Simon 1959, Sec. 5; 1972). And it is surely trite to observe that learning is an important element in the improvement of economic efficiency. The theory of stochastic dynamic programming with discounting (Blackwell 1965) has been a basic tool in modeling optimization under uncertainty; the framework allows agents to choose actions in a particular period on the basis of their "experience" or history of the system: the evolution of the states and actions. A notable advance was to extend dynamic programming techniques to the situation where a decision maker has incomplete information about the state (if the "true" state is only partially observable, or if the agent is said to receive a "signal" or "message" about the true state). By explicitly introducing beliefs (as probability distributions over true states or the unobservable components), the decision-making problem was shown (Rhenius 1974) to be logically equivalent to a (Bayesian) dynamic programming problem in which the agent chooses an action on the basis of observed history and beliefs, which are revised or updated according to the rules of the calculus of conditional probabilities.

These developments set the stage for a study of the appropriate functional equation of the problem and for deriving some optimal stationary policy. But one faces formidable difficulties in deriving (analytically) any property that can be invoked to offer practical advice. This is true even in the class of deceptively innocuous "bandit" models that have quite concrete structures (see Berry and Fristedt 1985). These models have a particularly attractive feature, since they embody a widespread conflict: acquisition of information has an immediate cost, but may enhance future prospects. However, the numerical computations needed to approximate an optimal policy (calculating the Gittins–Jones index, for example) in even special examples seem to require a combination of programming skills and exceptionally powerful machines that most decision makers do not have at this stage.[11]

Naturally, analytical complexity is more formidable in the case of a choice of more than one variable and when the decision maker is exposed to more than one source of uncertainty. It is not difficult to understand why we have achieved only modest progress in carrying out the following program of research on the long-run dynamics of an economy suggested by Radner (1970):

The evolution of the economy will depend upon the rules or processes of expectation formation and revision used by the agents. In particular, there might be interesting conditions under which such a sequence of momentary equilibria would converge, in some sense, to a (stochastic) steady state. This steady state ... would constitute a second concept of equilibrium.

It would take me too far from the central theme of this volume to reflect on the advances in understanding the long-run dynamics of economies. The interested reader can turn to the selective review by Radner (1991), which has an extended list of references. Some of the deterministic, highly aggregated ("match box") Walrasian models – in the tradition of Uzawa (1961a, 1963) – do not deal with optimizing agents explicitly; see Wan (1971) for a survey. But these models do provide insights into questions of convergence of momentary equilibria to a long-run steady state. On the other hand, in Samuelson's (1958) framework of overlapping generations, or in David Gale's "dual" competitive economies supporting optimal allocations, trajectories of momentary equilibria may be chaotic.[12] There is certainly room for considerable work on the stochastic steady states of nonlinear dynamical systems that are subject to random shocks.

8   Games and Organizations: Incentives and Efficiency

It is fair to say that, for many writers, the Walrasian mechanism is the canonical model of decentralized decision making in which (Pareto) efficiency is achieved through agents acting in their own self-interest. There is now an impressive literature that challenges the appropriate-

---

[11] At least this is my impression from the admittedly limited look at the relevant literature when I was involved in the preparation of Majumdar and Radner (1993), and from talking to Professors M. El-Gamal and V. Bala. See also Basu, Bose, and Ghosh (1996), which contains an extensive list of references.

[12] See the references in Majumdar and Mitra (1994).

ness of utility and profit maximization assumptions from a number of perspectives,[13] and the need to examine the issue of "self-interest" in the presence of public goods was raised over forty years ago by Samuelson.

If one considers "decentralization" to mean "a special case of division of labor, where the 'labor' in question is that of making decisions,"[14] it is natural to study it in the general context of an organization with many decision makers, each having limited information and limited control of all the activities and each acting in self interest as perceived. The outcome to the organization typically depends jointly on these decisions, and perhaps on some stochastic environmental variables. If one recognizes that the rules of organizations are not immutable, then the broad question that one can pose is the following: How can the rules be designed so as to provide agents with proper incentives to make decisions that will promote the objectives (efficiency, long-run survival, equity, etc.) of the organization? Chapter 4 by Radner is an introduction to what is now a vast literature dealing with such issues by using the tools of dynamic games with incomplete information. Again, one is led to the study of equilibria (in the tradition of Cournot–Nash) and their Pareto efficiency properties. In such a framework, two types of problems arise: *hidden actions* and *hidden information* (to use the terminology of Arrow 1986), and these are viewed by Radner through "partnership" and "principal–agent" games. A particularly interesting point is that when one considers a relationship that is repeated over time, new opportunities for incentives and efficiency open up because the evolution of the system provides evidence as to the role of hidden elements. An elegant example is provided in Radner (1981), where the law of the iterated logarithm is used in the context of a repeated principal–agent game.

A few interesting points that emerge from such a game-theoretic approach have a bearing on some of the mathematical modeling issues listed in Section 2. First, the approach continues to face the same problem of multiplicity of equilibria (here, Cournot–Nash equilibria and many of the subsequent variations), which significantly weakens the incisiveness of prediction (to be sure, repeated or stochastic games do not offer any help in this direction). Secondly, the decentralization of information, when combined with a divergence of interests of the agents, leads to inefficiencies that go beyond what can be attributed to incompleteness of information in itself. Finally, it is not easy to formalize "how things will work themselves out" and how a particular equilibrium is

---

[13] A summary of the voluminous literature is in Scherer and Ross (1990). See also Dutta and Radner (1994, 1995) and Radner (1996).

[14] See Radner (1972b, p. 88).

attained (if one thinks of an equilibrium as a rest point of some dynamic process).

It should be clear that, in most realistic settings, the organized decision problems are not even approximately repeated. The essay by Dutta and Sundaram (Chapter 5) deals with the question of existence of equilibria in Markovian games. In these games there is a "payoff-relevant" state variable moving through time in response to actions taken in the game (i.e., a stationary stochastic law of motion that, in principle, depends on the actions of the players). Thus, a player's current actions could affect his future rewards in two ways: (i) through the effect on the evolution of the state variable, and (ii) through the impact on the behavior of other players, who choose their actions on the basis of observed histories of evolutions of states and *all* actions. One should recall that, in the Arrow–Debreu paper (1954), the existence of a Walrasian equilibrium was formulated as a problem of existence of a Cournot–Nash equilibrium in a "generalized game" – a problem solved by applying a fixed-point theorem.[15] But in many Markovian games the existence question turns out to be particularly subtle, and the discussion is of import as these games arise naturally in the analysis of some questions that figure prominently in public-policy debates (for example, the management of renewable and exhaustible resources). I should add here that even in relatively simple formulations, however, the trajectory of states in an equilibrium can behave in a chaotic manner (see Dutta and Sundaram 1993).

There is no doubt that the game-theoretic approach leads to a better understanding of "a good many economic relations inexplicable in previously standard analysis," since "contractual relations are frequently a good deal more complicated than the simple models of exchange of commodities and services at fixed prices would suggest" (Arrow 1986). Arrow did note the gap between the complexity of some solutions and their real-life counterparts, and felt that bridging this gap would involve modeling such elements as costs of communication, variety and vagueness of monitoring, and socially mediated rewards – elements that "go beyond the usual boundaries of economic analysis." The last three chapters of the volume can be regarded as attempts to do just that.

In Chapter 6, Schotter notes that, although the literature on "mechanisms" inspired by Hurwicz (1972, 1986) has become rich in detail, it has tended to remain somewhat abstract and theoretical. His focus is a real-

---

[15] Subsequent research generated a literature (reviewed in Border 1985) on logical interconnections and equivalences among these equilibrium concepts and fixed-point theorems; see Uzawa (1962a) and Peleg (1967).

world *mechanism selection problem* that typically confronts the leaders of an organization (e.g., a corporate CEO or government official). Of course, this question of choosing *among* mechanisms leads to formidable analytical difficulties (one of the earliest contributions is Marschak 1972). Schotter stresses the point that a real-world decision maker may judge mechanisms on the basis of criteria that disqualify many that are "theoretically elegant." A part of the review uses the allocation problem in the baseball industry as a motivating example: here the problem is one of allocating a number of heterogeneous indivisible goods (baseball players) among a set of consumers (baseball teams). Schotter proposes a list of seven criteria that are likely to be appealing to real-world decision makers. "Some of the criteria I have discovered by speaking to corporate leaders, while others I have simply dreamed myself"; it is particularly important to note that equity is one of the criteria (one hopes that the theoretical literature on mechanism design will attempt to incorporate such issues). He goes on to review experimental results, relying on his previous studies and those of Linhart, Nalbantian, Radner, and others. For the baseball industry, three mechanisms are compared, including a laboratory version of the current free-agency system.

9   Bounded Rationality

If one thinks of an individual decision maker "as a learning, estimating, searching, information-processing organism," then it is obvious that management of a large organization will inevitably lead to some form of decentralized decision making, particularly when delays involving decision making prove costly to the organization. "Information processing" includes not only the routine gathering and storage of information but also, and perhaps more importantly, studying the implications of the information and coming to a judgment on the basis of some explicit and/or implicit calculations. Moreover, extending beyond a single individual involves a process of communication or transmission of payoff-relevant information. Within an organization, it is often the case that the process of choosing an action following "a meeting of the managers" involves some or all of these activities. The costs of decision making are considerable: when an adequate performance of these tasks is beyond the capabilities of the individuals responsible, there develops an urge to rely on a supporting "staff" of humans and machines.[16] Of course, given

---

[16] Radner (1992) notes that in U.S. firms a significant fraction of employees – one third to one half – are directly or indirectly engaged in "information processing."

decentralization, hidden information, and imperfect monitoring, it is possible for a subgroup of managers to engage in activities that serve themselves better, perhaps in conflict with the overall objective of the organization; the game-theoretic approach is a natural tool for addressing this issue. But this is only one aspect of the study of costs and benefits of decentralization. A second aspect involves looking into the best structure or design of a decentralized organization, and determining endogenously the number and arrangement of information processing agents that can promote efficiency. These and other issues involving returns to scale have figured prominently in the literature surveyed by Van Zandt in Chapter 7. The formal modeling of decentralization has a resemblance to networks of computers, and parts of his essay and the analysis of Mount and Reiter (Chapter 8) explore related ideas.[17] Mount and Reiter also face up to the issue of "computational complexity." The motivating applications they present, however, are mostly not to problems of economics, and – as they concede – the value of their particular formalism will eventually depend on whether new *economic* insights come out of it.

10 Concluding Comments

The models reviewed in the chapters of this volume add to the toolbox of economic theorists and expand the boundaries of economic analysis, or at least leave us with a deeper understanding of the complexities involved in developing theories of households and firms acting under uncertainty. We are in a better position to explain a large number of economic relations that have a direct bearing on the working and efficiency of an economy. On the other hand, some approaches, whether Walrasian or game-theoretic, have yet to resolve the problems posed by bounded rationality and indeterminacy of equilibria. Perhaps there is an inexorable difficulty with these formal models having their emphasis on optimization and consistency among relations, particularly among relations that are not observable or easily refutable. Economics, according to Hicks (1968),

surely, is a social science. It is concerned with the operations of human beings, who are not omniscient, and not wholly rational; who (perhaps because they are not wholly rational) have diverse, and not wholly consistent, ends. As such, it cannot be reduced to a pure technics; for we can then say that its concern is with the use that can be made of pure technics by man in society.

[17] Radner (1997) pointed out that the idea of representing human bounded rationality with a model of a computer was due to T. A. Marschak and C. B. McGuire (1971).

Can we predict the outcome of events in a "not wholly rational" world through tractable formal models?

And, yes, it is not easy for us to offer good advice on how to choose the best action in promoting individual or social welfare. This is understandable: Rushdie (1996) persuades us easily – without formal definitions and theorems – that good advice is rarer than rubies.

The Spirit of the Road smiled on Apu and said, "Silly boy, the road never ends . . . it stretches forward from the familiar to the unfamiliar, . . . I have made you homeless to share the strange pleasures of the journey. . . . Let us move on." (Bibhuti Banerji in *Pather Panchali*, The Song of the Road)

References

Arrow, K. J. (1970): *Essays in the Theory of Risk Bearing*, North-Holland, Amsterdam.

(1986): "Agency and the Market," in *Handbook of Mathematical Economics*, vol. 3 (eds. K. J. Arrow and M. D. Intrilligator), North-Holland, Amsterdam, pp. 1183–95.

Arrow, K. J., and G. Debreu (1954): "Existence of Equilibrium for a Competitive Economy," *Econometrica*, 22, pp. 265–90.

Arrow, K. J., and F. Hahn (1971): *General Competitive Analysis*. Holden-Day, San Francisco.

Bala, V., and M. Majumdar (1992): "Chaotic Tatonnement," *Economic Theory*, 2, pp. 437–45.

Bala, V., T. Mitra, and M. Majumdar (1991): "Resource Allocation in Non-Walrasian Environments," *Journal of Economic Behavior and Organization*, 15, pp. 1–28.

Basu, A., A. Bose, and J. K. Ghosh (1996): "Sequential Design and Allocation Rules," in *Handbook of Sequential Analysis* (eds. B. K. Ghosh and P. K. Sen), Marcel Dekker, New York, pp. 475–502.

Berry, D. A., and B. Fristedt (1985): *Bandit Problems: Sequential Allocation of Experiments*, Chapman and Hall, London.

Blackwell, D. (1965): "Discounted Dynamic Programming," *Annals of Mathematical Statistics*, 36, pp. 226–35.

Border, K. C. (1985): *Fixed Point Theorems with Applications to Economics and Game Theory*, Cambridge University Press.

Chipman, J. S. (1987): "International Trade," in *The New Palgrave* (eds. J. Eatwell, M. Milgate, and P. Newman), MacMillan, London, pp. 922–54.

Debreu, G. (1959): *Theory of Value*, Wiley, New York.

(1970): "Economies with a Finite Set of Equilibria," *Econometrica*, 38, pp. 387–92.

(1974): "Four Aspects of the Mathematical Theory of Economic Equilibrium," in *Proceedings of the International Congress of Mathematicians* (Vancouver); reprinted as Chapter 18 in *Mathematical Economics: Twenty Papers of Gerard Debreu*, Cambridge University Press, 1983.

Dierker, E. (1982): "Regular Economies," in *Handbook of Mathematical Economics*, vol. 2 (eds K. J. Arrow and M. D. Intrilligator), North-Holland, Amsterdam, pp. 795–830.

Dorfman, R., P. A. Samuelson, and R. Solow (1958): *Linear Programming and Economic Analysis*, McGraw-Hill, New York.

Dutta, P., and R. Radner (1994): "Profit Maximization and the Market Selection Hypothesis," Working Paper, Stern School of Business, New York University (revised 1997).

(1995): "Moral Hazard," in *Handbook of Game Theory*, vol. 2 (eds. R. J. Aumann and S. Hart), North-Holland, Amsterdam, pp. 869–903.

Dutta, P., and R. Sundaram (1993): "How Different Can Strategic Models Be?" *Journal of Economic Theory*, 60, pp. 42–61.

Hahn, F. (1982): "Stability," in *Handbook of Mathematical Economics*, vol. 2 (eds. K. J. Arrow and M. D. Intriligator), North-Holland, Amsterdam, pp. 744–93.

Hart, O. D. (1975): "On the Optimality of Equilibrium When the Market Structure Is Incomplete," *Journal of Economic Theory*, 11, pp. 418–43.

Hicks, J. R. (1939): *Value and Capital: An Enquiry into Some of the Fundamental Principles of Economic Theory*, 2nd ed., Oxford University Press, London.

(1968): "Linear Theory," *Economic Journal*, 70, pp. 671–709.

Hurwicz, L. (1972): "On Informationally Decentralized Systems," in *Decision and Organization* (eds. C. B. McGuire and R. Radner), North-Holland, Amsterdam.

(1986): "On Informational Decentralization and Efficiency in Resource Allocation Mechanisms," in *Studies in Mathematical Economics* (ed. S. Reiter), MAA Studies in Mathematics, vol. 25, Mathematical Association of America, Washington, DC.

Hurwicz, L., R. Radner, and S. Reiter (1975): "A Stochastic Decentralized Resource Allocation Process Parts (i) and (ii)," *Econometrica*, 43, pp. 187–221 and pp. 363–93.

Koopmans, T. C. (1957): *Three Essays on the State of Economic Science*, McGraw-Hill, New York.

Lange, O. (1942): "The Foundations of Welfare Economics," *Econometrica*, 10, pp. 215–18.

Majumdar, M. (ed.) (1992): *Decentralization in Infinite Horizon Economies*, Westview, Boulder, CO.

Majumdar, M., and T. Mitra (1994): "Some Lessons from the Theory of Chaotic Dynamical Systems: An Overview," presented at the ASSA Annual Meeting (Boston).

Majumdar, M., and R. Radner (1993): "When to Switch to a New Technology: Learning about the Learning Curve," AT&T Bell Laboratories, Murray Hill, NJ.

Malinvaud, E. (1953): "Capital Accumulation and Efficient Allocation of Resources," *Econometrica*, 21, pp. 233–68.

(1992): "Foreword," in *Decentralization in Infinite Horizon Economies* (ed. M. Majumdar), Westview, Boulder, CO.

Marschak, T. A. (1972): "Computation in Organizations: The Comparison of

Price Mechanisms and Other Adjustment Processes," in *Decision and Organization* (eds. C. B. McGuire and R. Radner), North-Holland, Amsterdam, pp. 237–83.

Marschak, T. A., and C. B. McGuire (1971): *Lecture Notes on Economic Models for Organizational Design*, Unpublished manuscript, University of California, Berkeley.

Nikaido, H. (1968): *Convex Structures and Economic Theory*, Academic Press, New York.

Peleg, B. (1967): "Equilibrium Points for Open Acyclic Relations," *Canadian Journal of Mathematics*, 19, pp. 366–9.

Radner, R. (1967): "Équilibre des marchés à terme et au comptant en cas d'incertitude" *Cahiers d'Econométrie* (C.N.R.S., Paris) 4, pp. 35–42.

(1968): "Competitive Equilibrium under Uncertainty," *Econometrica*, 36, pp. 31–58.

(1970): "Problems in the Theory of Markets under Uncertainty," *American Economic Review*, 60, pp. 454–60.

(1972a): "Existence of Equilibrium of Plans, Prices and Price Expectations in a Sequence of Markets," *Econometrica*, 40, pp. 289–304.

(1972b): "Normative Theories of Organization: An Introduction," in *Decision and Organization* (eds. C. B. McGuire and R. Radner), North-Holland, Amsterdam, pp. 177–88.

(1979): "Rational Expectations Equilibrium: Generic Existence and the Information Revealed by Prices," *Econometrica*, 47, pp. 655–78.

(1981): "Monitoring Cooperative Agreements in a Repeated Principal–Agent Relationship," *Econometrica*, 49, pp. 1127–48.

(1982): "Equilibrium Under Uncertainty," in *Handbook of Mathematical Economics*, vol. 2 (eds. K. J. Arrow and M. D. Intriligator), North-Holland, Amsterdam, pp. 973–1006.

(1991): "Intertemporal General Equilibrium," in *Value and Capital: Fifty Years Later* (eds. L. W. McKenzie and S. Zamagni), MacMillan, London.

(1992): "Hierarchy: The Economics of Managing," *Journal of Economic Literature*, 30, pp. 1382–1415.

(1996): "Economic Survival," Nancy Schwartz Memorial Lecture, Northwestern University, Evanston, IL.

(1997): "Bounded Rationality, Indeterminacy and the Managerial Theory of the Firm," in *Organizational Decision Making* (ed. Z. Shapira), Cambridge University Press, pp. 324–52.

Rhenius, D. (1974): "Incomplete Information in Markovian Decision Models," *Annals of Statistics*, 2, pp. 1327–34.

Rushdie, S. (1996): "Good Advice is Rarer than Rubies," in *East, West*, Vintage, New York.

Saari, D. G. (1985): "Iterative Price Mechanism," *Econometrica*, 53, pp. 1117–31.

Samuelson, P. A. (1947): *Foundations of Economic Analysis*, Harvard University Press, Cambridge, MA.

(1958): "An Exact Consumption-Loan Model of Interest With or Without the Social Contrivance of Money," *Journal of Political Economy*, 66, pp. 467–82.

Scarf, H. (1960): "Some Examples of Global Instability of Competitive Equilibrium," *International Economic Review*, 1, pp. 157–72.

Scherer, F. M., and D. Ross (1990): *Industrial Market Structure and Economic Performance*, 3rd ed., Houghton-Mifflin, Boston.

Shafer, W., and H. Sonnenschein (1982): "Market Demand and Excess Demand Functions," in *Handbook of Mathemtical Economics*, vol. 2 (eds. K. J. Arrow and M. D. Intriligator), North-Holland, Amsterdam, pp. 671–96.

Simon, H. A. (1959): "Theories of Decision-Making in Economics and Behavioral Science," *American Economic Review*, 49, pp. 253–83.

(1972): "Theories of Bounded Rationality," in *Decision and Organization* (eds. C. B. McGuire and R. Radner), North-Holland, Amsterdam.

Uzawa, H. (1961a): "On a Two Sector Model of Economic Growth, I," *Review of Economic Studies*, 29, pp. 40–7.

(1961b): "The Stability of Dynamic Processes," *Econometrica*, 29, pp. 617–31.

(1962a): "Walras' Existence Theorem and Brouwer's Fixed Point Theorem," *Economic Studies Quarterly*, 13, pp. 59–62.

(1962b): "On the Stability of Edgeworth's Barter Process," *International Economic Review*, 3, pp. 218–32.

(1963): "On a Two Sector Model of Economic Growth, II," *Review of Economic Studies*, 30, pp. 105–18.

Wan, H. Y. (1971): *Economic Growth*, Harcourt Brace Jovanovich, New York.

CHAPTER 1

Equilibrium with Incomplete Markets in a Sequence Economy

Wayne Shafer

I   Introduction

In the now classical extension of the general competitive model to include time and uncertainty, it was observed that if at time 0 (today) there are markets for future delivery of all goods contingent on the date and state of nature, then the resulting equilibrium allocation will be Pareto efficient. Moreover, in such an equilibrium future spot markets would not need to be active; the future would simply consist of agents fulfilling their promises (see Debreu 1959). In the event that there is not a complete system of contingent commodity contracts at time 0, then a new problem arises; there will be reason for future spot markets to be active, so that agents making decisions at the current data need to make expectations about what future prices will be. Thus a new equilibrium concept is required, and that is the topic of this essay. Following the basic paper of Arrow (1964), Roy Radner, in a fundamental series of papers (1967, 1968, 1972), developed the concept of an equilibrium of plans, prices, and price expectations for the sequence of markets that will arise when there is not a complete set of contingent contracts at time 0 – a concept that has led to a substantial amount of research in the last two decades. It is the purpose of this essay in honor of Roy Radner to review this research program that his pioneering work has spawned, and to assess its future. A substantial number of interesting issues arise if all uncertainty is not resolved at the initial date. First, in order to investigate efficiency properties of markets, a new notion of completeness of markets is required, since in this context markets are never complete in the sense of a complete system of contingent contracts available at the initial date. Another development is that a firm's decision problem is now a nontrivial optimization problem in the face of uncertainty, and this has led to an extensive literature on how to model firm behavior. Whether or not returns to assets are denominated in terms of goods or in a unit

20

of account becomes important in certain situations, and there is in general no longer a clear dichotomy between the real side of the economy and the financial side, in terms of determining the allocation of resources in equilibrium. We will look at these and other issues in this essay.

This paper is organized as follows. In order to have an explicit point of reference, we first describe a canonical model that has become standard in most of the literature on this subject. Then the equilibrium concept is defined, and basic results on existence, determinacy, and efficiency are described. This part of the paper is intended to be an overview, not a comprehensive survey of the area, and in particular we do not discuss the rather substantial technical apparatus that has been developed to deal with this model. For a comprehensive bibliography and a more detailed analysis of the technical problems, the reader is referred to the survey by Magill and Shafer (1991) and the special 1990 issue on incomplete markets of the *Journal of Mathematical Economics*. The emphasis of this essay is on the conceptual modeling issues that arise, and the final section is devoted to discussing these as well as suggesting some interesting open problems of a conceptual nature.

II A Canonical Model

We begin by describing a canonical model for sequential trading. There will be two time periods, 0 and 1, with S states of nature in time period 1. In each of the two time periods, ℓ commodities are traded, with the trades at time 1 being contingent on the realized state s. Thus the commodity space is $\Re^{\ell(S+1)}$. We have $I \geq 2$ agents, each characterized by a utility function $u_i: \Re_{++}^{\ell(S+1)} \to \Re$ and an endowment vector $w_i \in \Re_{++}^{\ell(S+1)}$. Denote by $w = (w_1, \ldots, w_I) \in \Re^{I\ell(S+1)}$ the list of endowment vectors; this will parameterize the agents. The utility functions are assumed to be smooth, differentiably strictly monotone, and strictly quasiconcave, with the usual boundary conditions. Each agent is supposed to know his own characteristics and each observes the true state when it occurs at time 1. We write a vector $y \in \Re^{\ell(S+1)}$ in the form $y = (y(0), y(1), \ldots, y(S))$ with each $y(s) \in \Re^{\ell}$. A spot price system is a vector $p \in \Re_{++}^{\ell(S+1)}$.

We first review the standard competitive equilibrium in this model in which all trades and prices are decided at time 0. We will denote the competitive equilibrium prices by P; $P(0)$ is the vector of prices for goods consumed at period 0, and $P(s)$ ($s \geq 1$) is the price vector at time 0 for delivery of goods in period 1 contingent on state s being the realized state. An agent's optimization problem is

$$\max_{x} u_i(x)$$

subject to: $P(0)(x(0) - w_i(0)) + \sum_{s \geq 1} P(s)(x(s) - w_i(s)) = 0.$

A *competitive equilibrium* is a collection $((\bar{x}_i)_{i=1,\dots,I}, \bar{P})$ such that

(i) $\bar{x}_i$ solves agent i's optimization problem at $\bar{P}$; and
(ii) $\Sigma_i(\bar{x}_i(s) - w_i(s)) = 0$ for $s = 0, \dots, S$.

To introduce the Radner model, we suppose there are J assets which are traded at time 0 and which return dividends at time 1. These are to be viewed as publicly traded assets on competitive markets; this simple model will not include other types of assets that may hedge against risk, such as insurance contracts or labor contracts. A unit of asset j will cost q_j units of account payable at time 0 ($q = (q_1, \dots, q_J) \in \mathfrak{R}^J$) and return $v_j(s)$ units of account at time 1 in state s. The asset is called *nominal* if the returns are given exogenously; an asset is called *real* if the return at state s is the market value of commodity vector, that is, if $v_j(s) = p(s)a_j(s)$ for a vector $a_j(s) \in \mathfrak{R}^\ell$. Of course, mixtures are possible. However, for our simple model we shall consider only the pure real asset case or the pure nominal asset case. One may also consider nonlinear assets such as options, with either real or nominal strike prices. In any case we denote by V the $S \times J$ returns matrix that has in row s and column j the dividend of asset j in state s, $v_j(s)$, and let $v(s)$ denote the vector of the returns in state s. In the real asset case, the list of vectors $a = (a_j(s)) \in \mathfrak{R}^{S\ell J}$ parameterizes the asset structure, and the returns matrix is a function of p, $V(p)$. For example, suppose each $a_j(s)$ is the unit vector with a 1 in coordinate j and 0 elsewhere; that is, asset j promises delivery of one unit of good j in every state. With these commodity forward contracts, $v_j(s) = p(s)a_j(s) = p_j(s)$ and V is just the matrix of period-1 prices. In the nominal case the returns matrix V itself parameterizes the asset structure. Denote by z_j the amount purchased of asset j, with $z = (z_1, \dots, z_J) \in \mathfrak{R}^J$. The amount z_j may be positive or negative; the assets are considered to be in zero net supply.

We now apply to this model Radner's concept of an equilibrium of plans, prices, and price expectations. At a spot price system p and an asset price system q, define an agent's optimization problem as

$$\max_{x,z} u_i(x)$$

subject to: $p(0)(x(0) - w_i(0)) = -qz,$

$$p(s)(x(s) - w_i(s)) = \sum_j v_j(s)z_j, \quad s = 1, \dots, S.$$

The first constraint listed is that the net expenditure on goods plus the cost of the portfolio of assets must sum to zero. The constraints for $s \geq 1$ indicate that if s is the realized state in period 1, the net expenditure on goods must equal the dividends of the asset portfolio. The purchase of the assets in period 0 and their dividends in period 1 provides a means both for transferring income between period 0 and period 1 and for transferring income across the potential states in period 1. Note that these constraints preclude the agent from planning bankruptcy in any state; implicit in the constraints is an infinite penalty for bankruptcy.

An *equilibrium of plans, prices, and price expectations* is a list $((\bar{x}_i, \bar{z}_i)_{i \geq 1}, (\bar{p}, \bar{q}))$ such that:

(i) $(\bar{x}_i, \bar{z}_i)$ solves agent i's optimization problem at $(\bar{p}, \bar{q})$;
(ii) $\Sigma_i(\bar{x}_i(s) - w_i(s)) = 0, s = 0, \ldots, S$; and
(iii) $\Sigma_i \bar{z}_i = 0$.

The interpretation of this equilibrium concept is as follows. At time 0, each agent i observes the current spot prices $\bar{p}(0)$ and the asset prices $\bar{q}$, the "prices." Then, based on some beliefs or "price expectations" about spot prices at time 1, say $p^e(s), s = 1, \ldots, S$, the agent solves the optimization problem, forming the "plans" $(\bar{x}_i, \bar{z}_i)$. If it turns out that the price expectations of every agent are the same and the common expectation $\bar{p}(s) \ (s = 1, \ldots, S)$ is such that, together with the observed prices $\bar{p}(0)$ and q, all markets clear, then we are in an equilibrium. In effect, every agent is correctly predicting the spot prices that would clear the market in each state s if that state occurs. We shall discuss this concept critically later on in this essay. This equilibrium concept will also be referred to as a *Radner equilibrium*. Note that the same concept appears in the literature under other names as well, including "GEI equilibrium," "perfect foresight equilibrium", and "rational expectations equilibrium."

Although this is a model with uncertainty, probabilities have not yet been mentioned. Presumably, if agents have Savage-like assessments of probability of states, then these are incorporated into their preferences via their utility functions. The assumption of monotonicity then implies that they give a strictly positive probability to each state, for otherwise they would be indifferent to planning consumption in a state they feel would not occur. However, the model viewed in this way allows agents to have different probability assessments of states.

The information requirements of this model are quite strict. As mentioned previously, each agent is fully informed in the sense that he or she will be able to verify the true state once it occurs. In addition, each agent knows exactly the distribution of returns of each asset across the states (i.e., each agent knows each $a_j(\cdot)$ in the real asset case and each $v_j(\cdot)$ in the nominal case). Thus there is no "inside information." For assets such as corporate stocks, this is a strong requirement.

To a great extent, interpretation of both the informational requirements in this model and the equilibrium concept depend on what is meant by a "state of nature," and this will be discussed later.

We now define what is meant by completeness of markets in this model. The formal definition is that, for any possible vector of units of account across the S states of nature, an agent can form a portfolio of assets that gives this distribution of returns. That is, for any S-vector y of net expenditures on goods at period 1 ($y_s = p(s)(x(s) - w(s))$), there is some portfolio z such that $y = V_z$. In our model, for the nominal case this is equivalent to the returns matrix V having rank $= S$, so that the column vectors of V span all of $\Re^S$. In particular, there must be $J \geq S$ assets. In the case of real assets, there is a problem. The rank of the returns matrix $V(p)$ is a function of p, and is thus endogenous to the model. However, since $V(\cdot)$ is linear in p, it has a "generic" rank – that is, the rank of $V(p)$ is constant on an open set of full measure in the domain of p – and this rank is the maximum rank the returns matrix can take on at any p. For the preceding example of commodity forward contracts in which $V(p)$ is the matrix of period-1 spot prices, $V(p)$ is just an arbitrary positive matrix as p ranges over all positive prices, and this just says that most matrices have maximum rank. Thus we say that the real asset structure is complete if this generic rank is S. Again this requires $J \geq S$. We note for later reference that if one imposes restrictions on the size of trades an agent can make in the asset market then these markets cannot be complete regardless of the number of assets, since by restricting asset trades z we cannot in general expect to express every vector in $\Re^S$ in the form V_z.

We will frequently have to make "generic" statements. If B is a subset of some Euclidean space, then the statement "for almost all $b \in B$" will mean "for all b in some open subset of B whose complement in B has Lebesgue measure 0."

A very useful way of developing an understanding for this model, and for the relationship between the Radner model and the classical competitive model, is to evaluate the Kuhn–Tucker conditions (hereafter KTCs) for the agent's optimization problem. We proceed with this now.

The KTCs for an agent in the classical competitive model, with θ_i the multiplier, are:

$$D_{x(s)} u_i(x_i) = \theta_i P(s), \quad s = 0, \ldots, S;$$

$$P(0)(x_i(0) - w_i(0)) + \sum_{s \geq 1} P(s)(x_i(s) - w_i(s)) = 0.$$

The KTC for the consumer's problem in the Radner model is as follows, with $\lambda_i(s)$ the Lagrangian multipliers for the constraints $s = 0, \ldots, S$:

$$D_{x(s)}u_i(x_i) = \lambda_i(s)p(s), \quad s = 0, \ldots, S;$$

$$-\lambda_i(0)q + \sum_{s \geq 1}\lambda_i(s)v(s) = 0;$$

$$p(0)(x_i(0) - w_i(0)) = -qz_i;$$

$$p(s)(x_i(s) - w_i(s)) = v(s)z_i, \quad s = 1, \ldots, S.$$

Suppose we have a competitive equilibrium allocation x with prices P and Lagrangian multipliers θ. In order to obtain this as a Radner equilibrium with the same allocation, one can proceed as follows.

Fix positive numbers $\beta(s)$ $(s = 0, \ldots, S)$ with $\beta(0) = 1$. Define $\lambda_i(s) = \theta_i\beta(s)$ for all i and s. Define $p(s) = 1/\beta(s)P(s)$, and define $q = \Sigma_{s \geq 1}\beta(s)v(s)$. Then all of the KTCs except possibly the budget constraints will be satisfied. For the budget constraints, choose z_i such that the constraints for $s = 1, \ldots, S$ will be satisfied for each agent, and let y_i be the S-vector whose sth coordinate is $p(s)(x_i(s) - w_i(s))$; then these S-constraints can be written $y_i = Vz_i$. Provided that V has rank S, such a solution will exist (as noted previously), and since $\Sigma y_i = 0$, the z_i can be chosen so that $\Sigma z_i = 0$. Finally, we need to show that the constraint for period 0 is satisfied. We have $\beta(s)p(s)(x_i(s) - w_i(s)) = \beta(s)v(s)z_i$ for $s \geq 1$; summing over s gives

$$\sum_{s \geq 1}P(s)(x_i(s) - w_i(s)) = \sum_{s \geq 1}\beta(s)p(s)(x_i(s) - w_i(s))$$

$$= \sum_{s \geq 1}\beta(s)v(s)z_i = qz_i.$$

Since $p(0) = P(0)$ from the competitive budget constraint, we thus obtain the period-0 constraint for the Radner model.

Now suppose we have a Radner equilibrium allocation x with spot prices p, asset prices q, asset trades z, and Lagrangian multipliers λ. We will try to construct a competitive equilibrium. First, note that if V has rank S then $q = \Sigma_{s \geq 1}(\lambda_i(s)/\lambda_i(0))v(s)$ has a unique solution given q for the multiplier ratios $\lambda_i(s)/\lambda_i(0)$; in particular, they must be independent of i. (These ratios are sometimes referred to as "personalized state prices"). Thus we can define $\beta(s) = \lambda_i(s)/\lambda_i(0)$ for $s \geq 1$ and, as before, let $\beta(0) = 1$. Then define $P(s) = \beta(s)p(s)$ for $s \geq 0$, and set $\theta_i = \lambda_i(0)$. With this construction, the KTCs for the competitive consumer will be satisfied except possibly the budget constraint. To show the budget is satisfied also, note that

$$P(0)\big(x_i(0) - w_i(0)\big) + \sum_{s \geq 1} P(s)\big(x_i(s) - w_i(s)\big)$$

$$= p(0)\big(x_i(0) - w_i(0)\big) + \sum_{s \geq 1} \beta(s)p(s)\big(x_i(s) - w_i(s)\big)$$

$$= p(0)\big(x_i(0) - w_i(0)\big) + qz_i = 0.$$

Observe that, in both directions, the condition that V have rank S was what allowed us to proceed. In particular, in the second case it guaranteed that the personal state prices $\lambda_i(s)/\lambda_i(0)$ were the same for all agents. As is easily checked, this is precisely the additional condition needed in order to show that if the agents all satisfy the KTCs then we will have equality of all marginal rates of substitution between goods, which is equivalent to Pareto efficiency with our assumptions. In the incomplete markets case, where V has rank less than S, these personal state prices need no longer be the same.

III   Existence of Equilibrium

Radner (1972) demonstrated that equilibrium exists in a model more general than the one just described, provided we impose bounds on the size of trades in the asset markets. (The size of the bound is irrelevant; it is necessary only that there be one.)

Theorem 1. *In the model described in Section II, if each agent's optimization problem is modified with an additional constraint of the form $z \geq b$, then an equilibrium of plans, prices, and price expectations exists.*

It makes sense that, for markets to remain competitive, no individual agent should participate with a significant share of the market. From this point of view, a priori bounds on the size of trades an individual can make seems reasonable. However, the same reasoning applies to the commodity markets, and no such bounds are necessary in this case. In fact, one could easily impose a bound on the size of trade in commodities without affecting the equilibrium; simply make the bound larger than the aggregate supply. For many assets, however, there is no such natural bound. Indeed, even for contracts for forward delivery of commodities, as long as they can be satisfied by payment in units of account of the market value of the contract, there is no requirement connecting the amount of forward trades with the actual supply of the good. Perhaps this explains a rather annoying property of the model; as Hart (1975) discovered, without exogenous bounds on the size of trades in the asset markets, equilibria may fail to exist. Put another way, if one imposes a bound on asset trades, then the bound may be binding in equilibrium no matter how large the bound. One might argue that if the data of the economy are such that agents want to make very large trades, perhaps the data are inconsistent with the hypothesis of competitive behavior. However, Hart's example can be embedded in a model with a nonatomic measure space of agents, where each agent's trades will indeed be negligible, and the same nonexistence problem will arise.

This problem of nonexistence when bounds are not imposed on the size of trades has lead, in the last fifteen years, to a substantial number of papers designed to resolve this problem. The main characteristic of Hart's example is that the returns matrix changes rank with p, and one approach has been to restrict attention to asset structures that do not exhibit this behavior. Cass (1984) and Werner (1985) showed that, if one restricts attention to pure nominal asset structures, then equilibria exist without imposing bounds. Similarly, Geanakoplos and Polemarchakis (1986) observed, in the real asset case, that if all assets are denominated in terms of the market value of a single good then the returns matrix $V(p)$ will have constant rank and – just as in the nominal case – equilibria always exist. In general, then, we have the following theorem.

Theorem 2. *In the model described in Section II, if the asset structure is such that the matrix of returns has constant rank, then an equilibrium of plans, prices, and price expectations exists.*

The mere presence of two assets that are commodity forward contracts will in general preclude the hypothesis of Theorem 2. In this case the columns of $V(p)$ corresponding to the two assets will just be the vector of prices for these goods across the states, and these will inevitably be collinear for some prices. In effect they become perfect substitutes, and the returns matrix will drop rank (unless there are at least $S - 1$ other independent assets). This results in a failure of upper hemicontinuity of the demand correspondence defined by the constraints of the agents' optimization problems, and this is the technical reason for nonexistence. In this case the best that one could hope for is that, in some reasonable sense, equilibria exist generically.

To illustrate how equilibria may fail to exist, we provide a simple example. Consider the Radner model with one state in period 1, one asset, two consumers, and two goods, with the following data. Endowments are $w_i(s) = (1, 1)$ for $s = 0, 1$. Utility functions are $u_1(x) = v_1(x(0)) + v_1(x(1))$ with $v_1(x) = (1/3)\ell n\, x_1 + (2/3)\ell n\, x_2$ for agent 1 and $u_2(x) = v_2(x(0)) + (1/2)v_2(x(1))$ with $v_2(x) = (2/3)\ell n\, x_1 + (1/3)\ell n\, x_2$ for agent 2. The competitive equilibrium prices can be easily computed in this log-linear economy; they are $P_1(0) = 11/36, P_2(0) = 10/36, P_1(1) = 7/36$, and $P_2(1) = 8/36$. Now consider a Radner version of the model, with one real asset given by $a_1 = (8, -7)$. The return on this asset in state 1 is $V = p_1(1)8 - p_2(1)7$, so investing in this asset is essentially a bet that the relative price of good 1 in terms of good 2 is greater than 7/8. Since there is one state and one asset, this is the complete markets case. Note that the 1×1 returns matrix drops rank precisely in the case the relative price is 7/8 in state 1.

We now show that this Radner model does not have an equilibrium. First, we try for an equilibrium with the return $V \neq 0$. If such an equilibrium existed, it would have to coincide with the competitive equilibrium since V has rank 1, but in the unique competitive equilibrium the period-1 price ratio is 7/8 and so $V = 0$, a contradiction. Second, consider the possibility of an equilibrium with $V = 0$. Then there would be no transfers of income between periods 0 and 1, so the period-1 equilibrium would have to coincide with the static competitive equilibrium with the utility functions v_1 and v_2. But it is easy to see from the symmetry of the functions and the equal endowments that the relative price ratio in this case would be 1, and thus $V \neq 0$, again a contradiction. Thus no equilibrium exists. Note that this example is not robust: Alter the asset a small amount so that $V \neq 0$ at the price ratio 7/8 and then the complete markets case will work; or alter endowments or utility parameters a little so that the period-1 price ratio is no longer 7/8, and the complete markets case again works.

This example gives a clue on how to proceed for the existence problem with real assets when markets are complete as defined in Section II. In this case, remember, $V(p)$ has constant rank S on an open set of full measure in the space of prices. As we have demonstrated using the KTCs, an equilibrium of plans, prices, and price expectations at which $V(p)$ has rank S is equivalent to a competitive equilibrium with a complete set of contingent commodity contracts. That is, the allocations will be the same, and there is an easy correspondence between competitive equilibrium prices and prices in a Radner equilibrium. Thus a natural strategy in this complete markets case is first to obtain a competitive equilibrium, which always exists in our model, and then to construct the corresponding Radner prices. If, at these prices, $V(p)$ has rank S, then we have an equilibrium of plans, prices, and price expectations. Kreps (1982) made the critical observation that if the rank of the returns matrix is less than S at such prices, a small perturbation of the returns structure a will restore $V(p)$ to full rank (as in our preceding example) and thus we have an equilibrium. That is, generically in a, a Radner equilibrium exists. Similarly, Magill and Shafer (1990) observed that a small perturbation of endowments would cause the competitive equilibrium prices to move in the region where $V(p)$ has full rank, and thus equilibrium exists generically in endowments.

Theorem 3. *In the model described in Section II:*

(1)   *if* $J \geq S$ *then, for each* $w \in \Re_{++}^{\ell(S+1)}$, *an equilibrium of plans, prices, and price expectations exists for almost all* a *in* $\Re^{\ell JS}$;

(2)   *for each asset structure* a *for which* $V(\cdot)$ *has generic rank* S, *an equilibrium of plans, prices, and price expectations exists for almost all endowment lists* w *in* $\Re_{++}^{\ell(S+1)}$.

In the case where both $V(p)$ can change rank with p and markets are not complete (in particular, if $J < S$), the trick of first obtaining a competitive equilibrium and then converting it to a Radner equilibrium is no longer available. Nevertheless, by defining a "pseudo" equilibrium concept that replaces the competitive equilibrium in the argument for the complete market case, Duffie and Shafer (1985) were able to show that a Radner equilibrium exists generically in both a and w.

Theorem 4. *In the model described in Section II with all real assets, an equilibrium of plans, prices, and price expectations exists for almost all* (a, w) *in* $\Re^{\ell JS} \times \Re_{++}^{\ell(S+1)}$.

This result is not as satisfactory as the complete market case, because the sense of genericity is weaker. It is still an open question, for example, whether or not equilibrium exists generically in w for any fixed asset structure. Bottazi (1995) has recently shown that this is true, for "most" asset structures, and provides criteria for checking a particular asset structure for this property.

IV   Determinacy

We now look at the issue of local uniqueness. In what follows, in "counting" equilibria we are counting the number of equilibrium allocations, since there are certain redundancies in equilibrium prices. We now look at the issue of local uniqueness. In the complete market case this is fairly straightforward, requiring only an adaptation of Debreu's (1970) seminal argument, since competitive equilibria and Radner equilibria coincide when the returns matrix has full rank. In the case of incomplete markets and all real assets, an argument similar to Debreu's applied to the "pseudo" equilibrium also works. The only difficult part of the following theorem is in the real asset case, showing that generically less than maximal rank equilibria do not exist.

Theorem 5.   *In the model described in Section II, if the asset structure is such that markets are complete, or if all assets are real, then for almost all* w *in the space of endowment lists there exist a finite number of equilibria of plans, prices, and price expectations, and each equilibrium is locally a smooth function of endowment lists* w *and asset structures* a *or* V.

The situation with nominal assets and incomplete markets is completely different, and leads to one of the most fascinating and controversial properties of the Radner model. The following result was proven by Geanakoplos and Mas-Colell (1989) and a similar result by Balasko and Cass (1989).

Theorem 6.   *In the model of Section II with nominal assets, let the returns matrix* V *be in general position,* $J < S$, *and* $I > J$. *Then, for almost all* w *in the space of endowment lists, the set of allocations of an equilibrium of plans, prices, and price expectations contains a set homeomorphic to* $\mathfrak{R}^{S-1}$.

In order to understand why this result holds, consider first the real asset case. Since each $v_j(s) = p(s)a_j(s)$, the constraints in the agent optimization problem are homogeneous in prices. Thus one may separately normalize the period-0 prices $(p(0), q)$ and each period-1 price $p(s)$ without affecting the constraints – for example, by picking good 1 to be the numeraire in every state. To most easily see this and what happens in the nominal case, let us look specifically at the agents' constraints for the one-good, two-state case, with $p(0) = 1$ as a normalization:

$$x(0) - w_i(0) = -qz;$$

$$x(s) - w_i(s) = \sum_j \left(\frac{v(s)_j}{p(s)} \right) z_j, \quad s = 1, \ldots, S.$$

Note that, in the case of all real assets where $v_j(s) = p(s)a_j(s)$, the period-1 constraints take the form

$$x(s) - w_i(s) = \sum_j a_j(s) z_j, \quad s = 1, \ldots, S,$$

and so the period-1 prices disappear completely (in the multi-good case, this corresponds to only relative prices in each state matter, not absolute price levels). As seen in the KTC analysis, if markets are complete, then the resulting equilibrium allocations will coincide with the competitive allocations, and in particular will be independent of the particular $a_j(s)$. Suppose markets are incomplete, with (say) one asset and two states.

Then, from the budget constraints alone, the period-1 consumption vector is constrained to satisfy

$$\begin{pmatrix} x(1) \\ x(2) \end{pmatrix} = \begin{pmatrix} w_i(1) \\ w_i(2) \end{pmatrix} + \begin{pmatrix} a_1(1) \\ a_1(2) \end{pmatrix} z_1$$

for some value of z_1, and this obviously is a severe constraint on what equilibrium allocations can be. Moreover, changing the relative values of $a_1(1)$ and $a_1(2)$ necessarily changes the allocation if there is any trade at all; this, in contrast to the complete markets case, implies that the exact structure of the assets now influences the equilibrium allocation.

Now consider the nominal case, where the $v_j(s)$ are denominated in the unit of account. Again, the equilibrium allocations in the complete markets case will correspond to the competitive allocations. In the incomplete markets case, however, matters are significantly different. Consider again the one-asset, two-state case, and simply define $a_1(s)$ by fixing $p(s)$ arbitrarily positive and setting $a_1(s) = v_1(s)/p(s)$. Then, for these fixed period-1 prices, the corresponding real model defined will have an equilibrium. Now, if we change the relative values of the $p(s)$, we obtain a new model with different relative $a_1(s)$ and thus a different equilibrium allocation. In the two-state case there is a one-dimensional set of relative period-1 prices, so there will be a one-dimensional set of equilibrium allocations. In other words, in this case only the common expectations of period-1 prices in a Radner equilibrium really matter and are not constrained by the equilibrium concept itself.

For the general ℓ-good case, the foregoing discussion can be interpreted as saying that one may arbitrarily fix the price level in each state, and for different relative price levels one obtains different equilibria. For example, choosing good 2 as a numeraire instead of good 1 will in general alter the resulting equilibrium. Or, with fiat money and a simple quantity equation to determine the price levels, altering the money supply across states will alter the equilibria. In any event, the term "unit of account" now becomes critical, and equilibria are not determinant unless the agents are given extra information so they can correctly predict price levels in each state. The notion of correct price expectations in the Radner equilibrium is not sufficient by itself to peg price levels in each state, but is only sufficient for pegging relative prices within each state. This leads to the conclusion that the monetary or banking system, which determines the unit of account and its purchasing power, needs to be explicitly incorporated into the model as a necessary condition for obtaining determinacy. (Whether it will be sufficient may depend on the structure of the monetary system; for example, in the simple-minded quantity theory mentioned previously, it would require that the monetary authority announce at time 0 what the supply of fiat money would be in period 1, contingent on the state, or at least that agents could infer it from the observed behavior of the authorities. It is not at all clear that this would be a reasonable hypothesis.) Magill and Quinzii (1992) have examined one such interesting model; much more work needs to be done. In a general sense, the model with an incomplete nominal asset structure provides a framework in which financial institutions can have real effects even in the absence of asymmetric information.

V   Efficiency and Comparative Statics

As mentioned in Section III, at a Radner equilibrium at which the returns matrix has rank S, the resulting equilibrium allocation will also be a competitive equilibrium allocation, and thus fully Pareto efficient. Thus we have our next theorem.

Theorem 7.   *For the model described in Section II:*

(1)   in the nominal asset case, if V *has rank* S *then every Radner equilibrium allocation is Pareto efficient;*

(2)   in the real asset case, if the asset structure is such that the generic rank of $V(\bullet)$ *is* S *then, for almost all* w *in the space of endowment lists, Radner equilibrium allocations are Pareto efficient.*

In case of incomplete markets, one certainly does not expect full allocative efficiency, for otherwise our definition of completeness would be suspect. The following result indicates this.

Theorem 8.   *For the model described in Section II, if* $J < S$ *then for (*w, a*) in an open set of full measure in* $\Re^{\ell JS} \times \Re_{++}^{\ell I(S+1)}$, *Radner equilibrium allocations are not Pareto efficient.*

One might hope that, in some suitable sense, Radner equilibria are constrained efficient. There is still no generally accepted notion of what the correct definition of "constrained efficiency" might be in this case; some argue that the concept cannot be properly defined unless the reasons for incompleteness of markets are endogenously embedded into the model. Nevertheless, we can discuss certain efficiency properties of the equilibria. First, there are robust examples of the model with multiple equilibria in which two of the Radner equilibria have the property that one Pareto dominates the second. One such example is as follows.

Consider a simple two-good, two-consumer, one-period economy (an

Edgeworth box). Suppose preferences are such that there are three equilibria, which we call A, B, and C for simplicity, with a strictly convex contract curve and relative good-1 equilibrium prices p_a, p_b, and p_c. The equilibria are labeled so that $u_1(A) < u_1(B) < u_1(C)$ and $u_2(A) > u_2(B) > u_2(C)$ for the strictly concave utility functions u_1 and u_2. In these circumstances, the line segment joining A and C in the Edgeworth box must have an open region where it lies below the indifference curves through B from the perspective of both agents; suppose $0.5A + 0.5C$ is one such point.

Now consider a Radner model with one state in period 1 and utility functions $u_i(x(0)) + u_i(x(1))$ for each agent. Suppose there are no assets, so that markets are incomplete. Then, for example, BB (B in period 0, B in period 1) is an equilibrium, as is AC. But $u_i(A) + u_i(C) < 2u_i(0.5A + 0.5C) < 2u_i(B)$ for both agents (by concavity and our assumptions), so BB Pareto dominates AC. Note this can be made a robust example; that is, if the original three-equilibrium case is regular then small perturbations of preferences and endowments will not change the Pareto dominance phenomena.

As a consequence of such robust examples, any efficiency property that the incomplete market Radner equilibria may possess must be a very weak concept. One approach to constrained efficiency is to ask the following question: If a central planner were permitted to choose the asset portfolios for the agents, and then allow agents to trade freely on competitive markets for commodities, could the planner improve upon a Radner equilibrium? The answer is, in an appropriate generic sense, Yes. For a precise statement of the result, see Geanakoplos and Polemarchakis (1986). This is, of course, not possible if markets are complete.

A natural question to ask is if there is a connection between how inefficient the Radner equilibria are and how incomplete the markets may be. One measure of incompleteness is $S - J$, assuming the J assets give the returns matrix a generic rank J. By introducing a new asset, which reduces the incompleteness in this sense, does efficiency improve? The answer is No, again due to an example of Hart (1975), in which a new asset is introduced but the new Radner equilibrium allocation is Pareto dominated by the original Radner equilibrium allocation. This suggests that perhaps this notion of "almost complete" is at fault; see the discussion of completeness in Section VI.

We briefly point out one of the more interesting distinctions between the complete and incomplete market cases. When markets are complete, the Radner equilibrium allocations generically coincide with competitive equilibrium allocations, so that the actual structure of the assets themselves (i.e., V or a) is irrelevant in determining the equilibrium allocation. Thus there is the classic dichotomy between the "real" side of the economy and the financial sector; only the real side (preferences and endowments) matter. However, if markets are incomplete then this is no longer the case. For the following, see Magill and Shafer (1991).

Theorem 9. *For the model described in Section II in the case of real assets with* $J < S$, *the set of Radner equilibrium allocations for almost all* (w, a) *is distinct from the set of Radner equilibrium allocations for* (w, a + Δa) *for almost all* Δa.

It is difficult to formulate an analogous statement for the nominal asset case, owing to indeterminacy. Theorem 9 states that a small change in the existing assets will cause the equilibrium to change. Of course, introducing a new asset would cause changes also. In any event, there is consequently a nontrivial connection between the nature of the existing assets and the resulting allocation. We return to this point in our discussion of endogenous asset formation.

VI   Central Issues

As we have remarked, there are essential differences in behavior of the model between the cases of complete versus incomplete markets. In the context of the model we are discussing, completeness is essentially defined as having at least S independent assets. Since this is generically necessary and sufficient for Pareto efficiency, it seems to be the correct definition. However, in order to apply the definition, one must count the number of states of nature, and so one must have some precise idea of what a state of nature is. More appropriately: What is the best notion for the model we are discussing? I am not sure there will ever be a good answer to this, but the definition of completeness as well as the interpretation of the equilibrium concept itself (discussed shortly) depends on it. For example, one could take a state of nature to be a description of exogenous events that affect the basic data of the model – that is, the preferences and endowments of the agents. An enumeration of such states, even assuming it would be finite, seems a hopeless task.

There is a serious problem regarding what a relevant state of nature is; "sunspot" phenomena are possible in our model. To illustrate sunspot phenomena as simply as possible, take the basic data of the ABC model in Section V and consider the case in which there is no consumption but only potential trade in assets in period 0. First suppose there is one state in period 1 and no assets; this is a complete markets case equivalent to the static one-period economy, with the three equilibria A, B, and C. Now suppose that in the face of uncertainty the utility functions u_i serve as von Neuman–Morgenstern utility functions for the agents, and that for some reason the agents believe that two observable events $s = 1, 2$ may be relevant to the equilibria. In particular, suppose $p_c > p_a$ and that agents believe $s = 1$ signals high prices and $s = 2$ signals low prices. Then the price expectations of p_c in state 1 and p_1 in state 2 can be realized as a Radner equilibrium with equilibrium allocation C in state 1 and A in state 2. Note that, since there are now two states and still no assets, this is an incomplete market equilibrium. Moreover, if the agents believe the states have equal probability, then $0.5u_i(A) + 0.5u_i(C) < u_i(0.5A + 0.5C) < u_i(B)$, so that the equilibrium of C in state 1 and A in state 2 is Pareto dominated by the equilibrium with B in both states. With these beliefs about states mattering, suppose an entrepreneur sees that introducing an asset to accomodate transfers of income across the two states would be welcome, and does so. Then we would have a complete market model, and the equilibrium allocations would have to be AA, BB, or CC across the two states. But in any of these equilibria there would be no need to trade in the asset, so the demand for the asset would be zero. If the entrepreneur correctly anticipated this demand, she would have no incentive to introduce the asset in the first place. Thus exogenous states that may not be relevant in an intrinsic sense may still have an effect on the Radner equilibria of the model, and can change the market structure from complete to incomplete.

Comparing the number of assets with the number of states seems a silly exercise, so one possibility is to alter the definition of completeness. One would like the dichotomy between complete and incomplete markets to coincide with the dichotomy of Pareto efficiency and inefficiency; the definition employed here is in one sense too strong. With our definition of completeness of the asset market, Radner equilibrium will be efficient regardless of the structure of preferences and endowments. It seems unlikely, however, that the observed asset structure arose independently from the basic data defining the economy. A more sensible definition of completeness perhaps should involve a joint condition on assets and on preferences and endowments. For example, in the standard one-good capital asset pricing model in which agent utilities depend only on the mean and variance of a portfolio, only two independent assets are required in order to achieve efficiency in a Radner equilibrium, regardless of the number of states.

An alternate approach to defining completeness – one not directly based on the number of assets versus the number of states – is the idea that some agents may be restricted from participating (or participating fully) in the markets for some assets. Such restrictions, for example, could arise if some agents could not verify states upon which the asset payment is conditional. See Balasko, Cass, and Siconolfi (1990) for such an analysis applied to the model with nominal assets.

The foregoing approach of restricted participation may be viewed as an initial attempt at studying the issue of why markets may be incomplete, whatever the definition. One needs to emphasize that the model considered here is appropriate for describing publicly traded securities, and these markets alone cannot be expected to handle all types of risk. Insurance markets handle different types of risk and there are adequate theoretical explanations (e.g., moral hazard) of why such contracts are not optimal for such risks. Our model excludes such risks; there is no moral hazard or asymmetric information in the model, for example, and one may reasonably ask why such markets may be incomplete without introducing such issues. The basic argument goes like this: If there are risks for which no existing portfolio of assets can hedge, then entrepreneurs will see this and introduce such new assets. (But remember the sunspot example, in which a new asset will not be traded in equilibrium.) In fact, new securities are issued regularly on publicly traded markets. Most of these are portfolios of existing assets, usually requiring trading strategies too complex to be carried out by individual investors. In fact, when looking at a multi-period version of our model with a maximum of (say) K branches at any node in the event tree, our version of completeness requires only K independent securities (see Kreps 1982). But the required portfolios or trading strategies can be quite complex, and one natural source of restricted participation is that most agents may not be able to implement the more complicated trading strategies, or even discover what they are. Thus computational complexity may be a source of incompleteness. Returning to newly introduced securities, occasionally they are really new, such as a futures contract on a commodity for which no such contracts previously existed. This is both evidence that entrepreneurs are looking for opportunities to introduce new assets and evidence that markets are not yet complete – that is, there are risks which can be handled by a publicly traded security and for which no such security exists. As yet we have no suitably general model of asset introduction that permits the asset structure to become endogenous (the closest is the work by Allen and Gale 1988), and until we do we cannot answer the question of whether such a model would lead to complete markets.

One major source of publicly traded assets are shares and bonds issued by corporate firms, which are absent from our canonical model. There are two main difficulties with introducing firms into the model, one conceptual and one technical. The conceptual issue is how to model the firm's objective without leaving the competitive markets framework. This is straightforward for a single-owner firm but a nontrivial problem for a corporate firm. To see this, we construct a simple example of the Radner model with a corporate firm. Take the case of one good and no assets except for the shares of a single firm. The firm uses the good in period 0 as an input ($y(0)$), and obtains a state-dependent output in period 1, $y(s)$ for $s \geq 1$ according to a production relation $f(y) = 0$. Agent i is initially endowed with share γ_i of the firm at the beginning of period 0, and her demand for share ownership in period 0 is denoted by α_i. In this case the agent optimization problem is

$$U_i(y) = \max_{x,\alpha} u_i(x)$$

subject to: $x(0) - w_i(0) + \big(q + y(0)\big)\alpha = q\gamma,$

$$x(s) - w_i(s) = y(s)\alpha, \quad s = 1, \dots, S.$$

Here U_i denotes an indirect utility function depending on the firm decision y. By Shephard's lemma, $\partial U_i(y)/\partial y(0) = -\alpha\lambda_i(0)$ and $\partial U_i(y)/\partial y(s) = \alpha\lambda_i(s)$ for $s \geq 1$, where the $\lambda_i(s)$ are multipliers for the agent optimization problem. Define $\beta_i(s) = \lambda_i(s)/\lambda_i(0)$, the "personal state prices" as in the KTC analysis of Section II. Note that, with this notation, one of the KTCs for the optimization problem is $q = -y(0) + \Sigma_{s\geq1}\beta_i(s)y(s)$.

The first-order conditions for the following problem of the agent choosing what she would like the firm to do,

$$\max_y U_i(y)$$

subject to: $f(y) = 0,$

are $\beta_i(s) = -\partial f(y)/\partial y(s)$ for $s \geq 1$. Now consider the general problem

$$\max_y -y(0) + \sum_{s\geq1} \beta(s)y(s)$$

subject to: $f(y) = 0.$

The KTC for this problem, eliminating the multiplier, is $\beta(s) = -\partial f(y)/\partial y(s)$. This means that agent i would like the firm to maximize a weighted sum of dividends, the "market value," using her personal state prices as the weights. Thus, if the personal state prices β_i are the same for all i (the complete markets case), then all agents agree that the firm should maximize the market value according to the common β. However, if the β_i are different then the agents want different objective functions for the firm (see Radner 1974).

A number of proposals have been made to overcome this problem. One type of proposal is for the firm to use, as state prices in its objective function, a weighted average of shareholders' personal state prices across the S states (these will be generically different if markets are incomplete). These weights could be the posttrade fractions of shares held (Dreze 1974) or the initial fractions of shares held (Grossman and Hart 1979). Both papers give arguments to the reasonableness of their proposal, and one may argue about which is better, but in the end the choice is somewhat arbitrary. Regardless of how one chooses state prices for the firm to use, the choice will affect the firm's behavior and thus the equilibrium allocations that come about.

Since there seems to be no natural way to define a competitive objective function for a corporate firm when markets are incomplete, it may be most appropriate to model the firm as a strategic player. Even if the data of the model are such that it is a reasonable approximation to suppose the firm behaves as a perfect competitor in the commodity markets, it is another matter to suppose that it is a perfect competitor in the asset markets. The shares issued by the firm need have no perfect substitutes if the asset markets are incomplete, and the firm should recognize that its market value will depend not only on its own production decision but also on the production decisions of all other corporate firms. Modulo difficulties associated with multiple equilibria, one can readily describe the market value of each firm as a function of the decisions of all firms, and in this context a Nash equilibrium seems appropriate. There are, however, serious technical difficulties associated with such a setup, and it is not clear if such a research program can be successfully carried out.

Even if one chooses one of the competitive objective functions, there is a serious technical problem associated with production sets. Existing theorems providing existence of Radner equilibria impose strong smoothness assumptions on production sets, and such smoothness assumptions are absolutely essential. Consider the simple case of a constant-returns technology with a capacity constraint. There will typically be an open set of prices p at which the firm would have negative market value if it chose to produce, and so chooses not to produce at all, and another open set of prices at which the firm will choose to produce and its shares will have positive market value. In effect, the number of assets available will be a function of p, and in this example the corresponding returns matrix will no longer have a generic rank. This precludes any generic existence theorem.

Finally, we look at the notion of an equilibrium of plans, prices, and price expectations in more detail. One may seriously question whether this is a reasonable solution concept; the requirements are really quite strong. When states of nature are interpreted as exogenous events affecting the data of the economy, the requirement of common and correct price expectations seems inordinately strong. In a literal sense, it requires the agent to know all the data of the economy – not just his own characteristics – and to compute the general equilibrium. However, one may also view the solution concept as an idealization of the idea that agents active on the markets for assets learn the relationship between states and prices. For example, if the state of nature represents adverse conditions for growing a commodity, thus predicting a small harvest, agents understand that the price will be higher than normal. In other words, there is certainly knowledge gained from experience about the relationship between states of nature and prices, and the Radner equilibrium concept recognizes this. It is, however, a great leap of faith to suppose that agents know the relationship exactly. On the other hand, the notion of temporary equilibrium does not suppose the agents know anything about how future prices are related to states of nature, and this seems too extreme in the opposite direction. A more reasonable solution concept would seem to be one in which agents are presumed to have partial knowledge about future prices, and I think this is a useful direction for future research. It is important to remember, and a positive aspect of the equilibrium concept, that agents are not required to have the same probability beliefs about states of nature. That is, one agent may view a particular state as having a small probability of occurring, while another believes the same state has a high probability of occurrence.

One way to seemingly avoid the assumption that agents know $p(\bullet)$ is to view a state of nature as including endogenous outcomes of the model. One could, for example, define a state of nature s in the form $s = (e, p, w_1, \ldots, w_l)$, where e represents an exogenous observable event, p a price vector for the ℓ commodities, and w_i an endowment ℓ-vector for agent i. In this case the period-1 price function is just the appropriate projection map on this new set of states and hence trivial to compute. Likewise, the agent's period-1 endowment will be a projection map and hence trivial. It would appear that with this interpretation the strong informational requirement of the Radner equilibria disappears. However, the problem has simply shifted. In this setup, the agents must form preferences over consumption plans contingent on states, and we may suppose that agents achieve this by forming subjective probability measures over states with a common support and plans that are consistent. For example, consider our sunspot example with one relevant state e. Enlarge the state space to the new definition. Then the equilibrium B, for example, would be the outcome if the subjective probability distributions of the agents give probability 1 to the state $s = (e, p_b, w_1, \ldots, w_I)$. However, if their subjective probabilities assign 0.5 to the state $(e, p_a, w_1, \ldots, w_I)$ and 0.5 to the state $(e, p_c, w_1, \ldots, w_I)$ then the sunspot equilibrium will be the outcome. Thus, defining the state space in this new way – so as to avoid the informational requirements of the Radner equilibrium – introduces all possible sunspot equilibria as well as the original equilibria. And since agents must have similar probability assessments in the sense of agreeing which states have positive probability, it does not remove the "common" requirement from the expectations assumption of a Radner equilibrium.

Whatever one's view of the Radner equilibrium concept, it is difficult to conceive of how one could change it and still have a framework for studying problems involving the efficient allocation of resources under uncertainty. It seems to be the correct concept in this context, in particular because it yields outcomes equivalent to the standard competitive equilibrium with complete contingent contracts when markets are complete in a natural way. Radner's equilibrium concept is also central to the notion of no arbitrage pricing of assets; without the hypothesis that agents have common price expectations, agents will not have common beliefs about the returns of real assets and thus will have different views about the presence of arbitrage opportunities.

References

Allen, F., and D. Gale (1988), "Optimal security design," *Review of Financial Studies* 1: 229–63.

Arrow, K. (1964), "The role of securities in the optimal allocation of risk bearing," *Review of Economic Studies* 31: 91–6.

Balasko, Y., and D. Cass (1989), "The structure of financial equilibrium: I. Exogenous yields and unrestricted participation," *Econometrica* 57: 135–62.

Balasko, Y., D. Cass, and P. Siconolfi (1990), "The structure of financial equilibrium with exogenous yields: II. Endogenous yields and restricted participation," *Journal of Mathematical Economics* 19: 195–216.

Bottazi, J. (1995), "Existence of equilibrium with incomplete markets: The case of smooth returns," *Journal of Mathematical Economics* 24: 59–72.

Cass, D. (1984), "Competitive equilibria in incomplete financial markets," Working Paper no. 84–09, CARESS, University of Pennsylvania, Philadelphia.

Debreu, G. (1959), *Theory of Value*, New York: Wiley.

(1970), "Economies with a finite set of equilibria," *Econometrica* 38: 387–92.

Dreze, J. (1974), "Investment under private ownership: Optimality, equilibrium, and stability," in J. Dreze (ed.), *Allocation under Uncertainty: Equilibrium and Optimality*. New York: Wiley, pp. 129–65.

Duffie, D., and W. Shafer (1985), "Equilibrium in incomplete markets I: A basic model of generic existence," *Journal of Mathematical Economics* 14: 185–200.

Geanakoplos, J., and A. Mas-Colell (1989), "Real indeterminacy with financial assets," *Journal of Economic Theory* 47: 22–38.

Geanakoplos, J., and H. Polemarchakis (1986), "Existence, regularity, and constrained suboptimality of competitive allocations when markets are incomplete," in W. P. Heller, R. M. Starr, and D. A. Starett (eds.), *Uncertainty, Information and Communication: Essays in Honor of Kenneth Arrow*, vol. 3. Cambridge University Press.

Grossman, S., and O. Hart (1979), "A theory of competitive equilibrium in stock market economies," *Econometrica* 47: 293–330.

Hart, O. (1975), "On the optimality of equilibrium when the market structure is incomplete," *Journal of Economic Theory* 11: 418–43.

Kreps, D. (1982), "Multiperiod securities and the efficient allocation of risk: A comment on the Black–Scholes option pricing model," in J. McCall (ed.), *The Economics of Uncertainty and Information*. University of Chicago Press.

Magill, M., and W. Shafer (1990), "Characterization of generically complete real asset structures," *Journal of Mathematical Economics* 19: 167–94.

(1991), "Incomplete markets," in W. Hildenbrand and H. Sonnenschein (eds.), *Handbook of Mathematical Economics*, vol. IV. New York: Elsevier, pp. 1523–614.

Magill M., and M. Quinzii (1992), "Real effects of money in general equilibrium," *Journal of Mathematical Economics* 21: 301–42.

Radner, R. (1967), "Équilibre des marchés à terme et au comptant en cas d'incertitude," *Cahiers d'Econométrie* (C.N.R.S., Paris) 4: 35–42.

(1968), "Competitive equilibrium under uncertainty," *Econometrica* 36: 31–58.

(1972), "Existence of equilibrium of plans, prices, and price expectations in a sequence of markets," *Econometrica* 40: 289–303.

(1974), "A note on unanimity of stockholder's preferences among alternative production plans: A reformulation of the Ekern–Wilson model," *Bell Journal of Economics and Management Science* 5: 181–4.

Werner, J. (1985), "Equilibrium in economies with incomplete financial markets," *Journal of Economic Theory* 36: 110–19.

CHAPTER 2

The Existence of Rational Expectations Equilibrium: A Retrospective

Beth Allen and James S. Jordan

1 Introduction

The term "rational expectations" was introduced in the famous article of Muth (1961), but the equilibrium existence problem posed by such a concept had been recognized and addressed formally seven years earlier. Grunberg and Modigliani (1954) recognized that predictions of economic events, unlike weather forecasts, can affect predicted events. Expectations of a substantial price increase, for example, can trigger investment and production decisions that increase supply and cause the actual price increase to be smaller than expected. Weather forecasting may be difficult in practice, but even the logical possibility of economic forecasting is problematic. Although they did not model the process of price determination explicitly, Grunberg and Modigliani showed that Brouwer's fixed-point theorem implies the existence of a correct forecast, provided that the requisite continuity and boundary conditions are satisfied. Muth (1961) acknowledged the Grunberg and Modigliani article, but focused more on using the assumption of rational expectations to specify expectations in econometric models in which the equilibrium could be obtained by construction.

The dramatic advances in the mathematical theory of general equilibrium during the fifties and early sixties stimulated efforts to include expectations and uncertainty in general equilibrium models during the late sixties and early seventies. Two articles by Radner (1968 and 1972) stand out from the many notable contributions of this period for their explicit focus on the information structure underlying the formation of

Preparation of this manuscript was supported by NSF Grants SBR-9309854 and IRI-9312783. Previous financial support from the National Science Foundation for much of the research described here is also gratefully acknowledged. The views expressed herein are those of the authors and not necessarily those of the Federal Reserve Bank of Minneapolis or the Federal Reserve System.

expectations. Radner's models imposed the strong informational consistency requirement that an agent's actions could not differ across states of the world that could not be distinguished by the agent's information. This condition restricts trade among agents to events that are mutually observable. As Radner (1968, p. 50) emphasized, *"the net trade between any group of agents and the group of all other agents in the economy can at most depend upon information that is common to both groups of agents"* [italics in original]. As a result, Radner's existence theorems relied on the assumption that all agents were endowed with a common information structure. The possibility that information revealed by prices might remove incongruities in initial information was not pursued. In an earlier unpublished technical report, Radner (1967) had explicitly added the information revealed by prices to agents' information structures. However, the discussion of the existence of equilibrium was confined to the prophetic remark: "It is not clear that an equilibrium of the type defined above exists, even under the classical assumptions. The continuity of the demand functions can, in principle, be destroyed by the fact that information depends on the structure of spot prices."

The first positive and negative results on price-conditional rational expectations equilibrium were both achieved by Jerry Green (1973 and 1977, respectively). Green (1973) described a market for the exchange of state-contingent wealth claims in which some traders are privately informed of the "true" state probabilities, while other traders have no private information. Green showed that the traders' excess demand functions, when differentiated with respect to the state probabilities, have a dominant diagonal property that implies that the function from state probabilities to market-clearing prices is one-to-one. Hence there exists in this model a rational expectations equilibrium in which market prices fully reveal the state probabilities to the uninformed traders. Grossman (1981) and Handel (1980) later showed that the key property of contingent claim demand is sufficiently general that the differentiability of demand functions is unnecessary for the result. However, Green (1975, later published as Green 1977) showed that the absence of "noise" in the model is essential, not only for the full revelation property, but even for the existence of equilibrium. More specifically, Green constructed an example in which traders' endowments are subject to state-independent random noise, and showed that the example admits no rational expectations equilibrium.

The contingent claims market setting of Green's counterexample made the example necessarily complex. Subsequent authors, notably Kreps (1977), discovered much simpler examples of the nonexistence of equilibrium in spot market models. One such example will be described in the next section. Thus, while the causal influence of economic expectations that troubled Grunberg and Modigliani can be resolved, as they suggested, by conventional fixed-point methods, the informational discontinuity discovered by Radner can be fatal to the existence of rational expectations equilibrium even under classical assumptions on trader characteristics.

What follows is an exposition and review of selected aspects of the rational expectations equilibrium existence problem and its literature. We make no pretense of completeness, but refer the reader to Radner (1982) for additional references and topics. Section 2 defines the conventional concept of rational expectations equilibrium (REE), and Section 3 contains a simple example in which the equilibrium fails to exist. Section 3 also reviews the literature on the generic existence of REE. Section 4 relates the existence problem to an earlier model of informationally decentralized allocation mechanisms, and demonstrates the general existence of equilibrium when expectations are conditioned on trades as well as prices. Sections 5 and 6 contain brief discussions of the efficiency of REE and the existence of partially revealing REE, respectively.

2   Rational Expectations Equilibrium

There are n traders, indexed by the superscript i, and ℓ commodities, indexed by the subscript j. Each trader i has a set S^i of private information signals, where S^i is a finite-dimensional Euclidean space. Let $S = \Pi_{i=1}^n S^i$, with generic element $s = (s^1, \ldots, s^n)$. An element $s \in S$ will be termed a *state of information*. Let π denote a Borel probability measure on S.

Let U denote the set of smooth (infinitely continuously differentiable) functions $u: \mathbb{R}_{++}^\ell \to \mathbb{R}$ satisfying, for each $x \in \mathbb{R}_{++}^\ell$,

(i) $Du^i(x) \in \mathbb{R}_{++}^\ell$,
(ii) $D^2u^i(x)$ is negative definite, and
(iii) the closure in $\mathbb{R}^\ell$ of the upper contour set $\{x' \in \mathbb{R}_{++}^\ell : u(x') \geq u(x)\}$ is contained in $\mathbb{R}_{++}^\ell$.

The set U is topologized as a subspace of $C^\infty(\mathbb{R}_{++}^\ell, \mathbb{R})$ with the C^∞ compact-open topology.[1] Each trader i has a state-dependent utility func-

---

[1] This is the topology of C^∞ uniform convergence on compact subsets of $\mathbb{R}_{++}^\ell$, which requires that similar utility functions be uniformly close and have uniformly close mixed partial derivatives of all orders on any closed and bounded subset of strictly positive commodity bundles $x \in \mathbb{R}_{++}^\ell$. However, for all of the results described in this paper except those based on Allen (1982b) and Jordan (1982b), we could just as well have used utilities that are required only to be twice continuously differentiable; in that case, the subset

tion $v^i: S \to U$ that is Borel-measurable. The tactic of representing the utility *function* as a random variable, as opposed to viewing the utility of each commodity bundle as a separate random variable, is taken from Allen (1981a). It avoids a technical problem in the definition of conditional expected utility maximization noted by Kreps (1977).[2] In general, each trader i's endowment can also be state-dependent (but measurable with respect to s^i). However, in this exposition, we will adopt the common simplifying assumption that each trader i has a state-independent endowment $e^i \in \mathbb{R}^\ell_{++}$.

Let Δ denote the unit simplex in $\mathbb{R}^\ell_+$, and let $M = \{(p, y^1, \ldots, y^n) \in \Delta \times \mathbb{R}^{n\ell}: \Sigma_{i=1}^n y^i = 0$ and $py^i = 0$ for each $i\}$ denote the set of prices and n-tuples of net trades that satisfy the aggregate resource balance and individual budget constraints. A rational expectations equilibrium will take the form of a Borel-measurable function from S to M. The space M contains the market signals that traders can use to augment the information provided by their private signals.

In a rational expectations equilibrium, the information available to trader i will be at least s^i and at most the entire state s of information. It will be useful to define equilibria corresponding to the two extremes. A *private information equilibrium* (PIE) is a Borel measurable function $(\tilde{p}(\cdot), (\tilde{y}^i(\cdot))_i): S \to M$ satisfying, for each i,

$$\tilde{y}^i(s) \text{ maximizes } E\{v^i \mid s^i\}(e^i + y^i)$$

$$\text{subject to } \tilde{p}(s)y^i = 0 \quad \text{for a.e. } s, \tag{1}$$

where $E\{v^i \mid s^i\} \in U$ is the conditional expectation of v^i given the σ-field generated by the projection $s \to s^i$. A *full communication equilibrium* (FCE) is a Borel-measurable function $(\tilde{p}(\cdot), (\tilde{y}^i(\cdot))_i): S \to M$ satisfying, for each i,

$$\tilde{y}^i(s) \text{ maximizes } v^i(s)(e^i + y^i)$$

$$\text{subject to } \tilde{p}(s)y^i = 0 \quad \text{for a.e. } s. \tag{2}$$

U of $C^2(\mathbb{R}^\ell_{++}, \mathbb{R})$ would be given the (C^2 compact-open) topology of C^2 uniform convergence on compacta. Similarly, we could use the more complicated C^∞ Whitney topology, which imposes very strong similarity requirements "at infinity" and as we approach the boundary of the positive orthant in $\mathbb{R}^\ell$ for functions and all of their derivatives.

2   Roughly, the problem is that there are both a continuum of commodity bundles and a continuum of price values on which to condition expected utility. If the utility of each commodity bundle is viewed as a separate random variable, then – since the conditional expected utility of each bundle is arbitrary on a set of price values having probability measure 0 – for each price some bundle can be given an arbitrarily high conditional expected utility, making nonsense of conditional expected utility maximization. Kreps (1977) suggests defining conditional expected utility as an integral with respect to a fixed regular conditional probability distribution in order to avoid this problem, but viewing the utility function as a single random variable works just as well. For further details, see the appendix on measurability of demand in Allen (1981a).

In the conventional definition of rational expectations equilibrium, traders augment their private signals with the information revealed by market prices. Formally, a *rational expectations equilibrium* (REE) is a Borel-measurable function $(\tilde{p}(\cdot), (\tilde{y}^i(\cdot))_i): S \to M$ satisfying, for each i,

$$\tilde{y}^i(s) \text{ maximizes } E\{v^i \mid s^i, \tilde{p}(s)\}(e^i + y^i)$$

subject to $\tilde{p}(s)y^i = 0$ for a.e. s. $\qquad$ (3)

3   Existence and Nonexistence of REE

The earliest simple example of the nonexistence of REE was given by Kreps (1977). In this example, there are only two possible states. Since there are only two states, if prices differ between the states then an REE must be an FCE, whereas if prices are the same in the two states then an REE must be a PIE. Nonexistence of REE is proved by showing that in the unique FCE, the prices are the same in the two states, and in the unique PIE, the prices differ between the two states.

Formally, consider a variant of the counterexample that appears in Allen (1984). Suppose there are two traders and two commodities, and suppose that the support of the probability measure π on traders' signals consists of the two-point set $\{(s_a^1, s^2), (s_b^1, s^2)\}$, where $s_a^1 \neq s_b^1$, and that the two states have equal probability. Thus trader 1 is privately fully informed of the state, while the private signal of trader 2 does not reveal the state. Let $s_a = (s_a^1, s^2)$ and $s_b = (s_b^1, s^2)$, and define v^1 and v^2 on these states as follows:

$$v^1(s_a)(x) = 2\ln x_1 + \ln x_2,$$
$$v^1(s_b)(x) = \ln x_1 + 2\ln x_2,$$
$$v^2(s_a)(x) = \ln x_1 + 2\ln x_2,$$
$$v^2(s_b)(x) = 2\ln x_1 + \ln x_2.$$

The state-independent endowments are $e^1 = e^2 = (3,3)$. Then the unique FCE satisfies $\tilde{p}(s_a) = \tilde{p}(s_b) = (1/2, 1/2)$ while $\tilde{y}^1(s_a) = (1, -1)$, $\tilde{y}^1(s_b) = (-1, 1)$, and $\tilde{y}^2(\cdot) = -\tilde{y}^1(\cdot)$. Since $\tilde{p}(s_a) = \tilde{p}(s_b)$, the FCE cannot be an REE. In a PIE, trader 2 is uninformed of the state and so, for any given price, trader 2 will have the same demand in both states. It is also clear (from the definition of v^1 and the fact that trader 1 is privately informed of the state) that, for any given price, trader 1 will demand more of commodity 1 in state s_a than in state s_b. Thus no PIE can have the same prices in both states; in fact, the unique PIE has $\tilde{p}(s_a) = (7/12, 5/12)$ and $\tilde{p}(s_b) =$

(5/12, 7/12). Hence there is no rational expectations equilibrium for this economy.

Radner (1979) also developed an example with log-linear utility functions. However, in his framework, the information signals concern traders' conditional probabilities of various events, while the relationships between states of the world and agents' preferences are considered fixed. We find it simpler to identify signals and states of the world, thereby replacing Radner's conditional probabilities with 0s and 1s. As in Allen (1981a, 1984), we consider a space of economies that is defined by state-dependent preferences. By contrast, Radner's (1979) model fixes the state-dependent preferences and then specifies various economies by their collections of conditional probabilities.

Radner (1979) showed that the property that prevents an FCE from being an REE in such examples is nongeneric in the space of arrays of conditional probabilities of states of the world, given agents' signals. Radner's result was stated in the context of financial asset markets, but the essential idea is easily expressed in the present model. For each state of information s, the economy $(e^i, v^i(s)(\cdot))_{i=1}^n$ is a *smooth economy* as defined by Debreu (1972). Suppose that the support of π is a finite set $S^o = \{s_k\}_{k=1}^K$. Then an FCE consists simply of a Walrasian equilibrium $(\tilde{p}(s_k), (\tilde{y}^i(s_k))_i)$ for the economy $(e^i, v^i(s_k)(\cdot))_i$, for each k. If $\tilde{p}(\cdot)$ is one-to-one then the FCE is an REE as well. The contrary condition that $\tilde{p}(s_k) = \tilde{p}(s_{k'})$ for some k and k' is a "knife-edge" property that Radner showed is nongeneric in the smooth economies $\{(e^i, v^i(s_k)(\cdot))_i\}_{k=1}^K$ parameterized as described here. A formal statement and proof of the analog of this result for the present model is given by Allen (1984).

Allen (1981a and 1982b) showed that the generic existence of fully revealing rational expectations equilibria extends well beyond the class of economies considered by Radner (1979). Whereas Radner's analysis relied heavily on the finiteness of the set of possible states of information, Allen showed that the essential condition is merely that the price have a higher dimension than the state. Allen (1981a) established that if dim $S < (1/2)$ dim Δ, then an FCE price function $\tilde{p}(\cdot)$ is generically one-to-one. Moreover, Allen (1982b) showed that if dim $S <$ dim Δ, then an FCE price function is generically one-to-one on the complement of a subset of S having Lebesgue measure 0. In particular, if π is absolutely continuous with respect to Lebesgue measure, then an FCE price function is generically one-to-one on a set having probability 1 and is thus generically an REE. The first result relied on the Whitney embedding theorem from differential topology while the second used the related ideas of self-intersections of immersed manifolds (based on multijet transversality).

Stimulated by Allen's results, Jordan and Radner (1979, 1982) considered the equal-dimension case, that is, dim S = dim Δ. They showed via an example that in this case neither the existence nor the nonexistence of an REE is a generic property. This left the higher-dimensional case, dim S > dim Δ. In this case, an FCE generically cannot be an REE, since an FCE price function $\tilde{p}$ generically is smooth enough that it cannot map S to a lower-dimensional space and still be one-to-one on a subset of S with full Lebesgue measure. However, Jordan (1982b) demonstrated the generic existence of REE price functions $\tilde{p}$ that are two-to-one. Moreover, the price functions $\tilde{p}$ can be made arbitrarily close to one-to-one in the sense that the pairs of states mapped to the same price can be made uniformly arbitrarily close to one another. In particular, there are many such equilibria. However, the constructed price functions are discontinuous on a dense subset of S, so one would hesitate to interpret such equilibria as the natural outcome of a market mechanism. Thus, in the higher-dimensional case, the generic existence of economically plausible rational expectations equilibria remains an open question.

4   Generalized Rational Expectations Equilibrium

In the conventional definition of rational expectations equilibrium, prices are the only market variables that traders use to augment their private information. This accords with the usual interpretation of prices as the coordinating signals that enable the competitive market to achieve Pareto optimal allocations. Indeed, Grossman (1981) argues that the existence of a fully revealing REE is the appropriate formalization of Hayek's famous assertion that the market mechanism is informationally efficient (Hayek 1945). This interpretation suggests that the informational discontinuity discovered by Radner constitutes a serious flaw in the market mechanism that may preclude the possibility of informationally efficient price systems. However, there is a prior line of research on Hayek's conjecture that suggests that the sole reliance on price constitutes a misunderstanding of the market mechanism.

Hurwicz (1977) and Mount and Reiter (1974) have constructed an explicit model of competitive equilibrium as an informationally decentralized allocation mechanism. In their model, the market signal, which these authors call the "competitive message," is the entire list of market variables, $(p, (y^i)_i)$. Moreover, they show that it is not possible for a decentralized allocation mechanism to use a message of smaller dimension, such as the price vector alone, and still achieve Pareto optimal allocations for all classical pure exchange environments. The Hurwicz (1977) and Mount and Reiter (1974) model is nonstochastic, but the reasoning behind the result can be illustrated using the two-person, two-commodity example of the previous section. Let $\overline{M}$ be an arbitrary set of *equilibrium messages*, let $Y = \{(y^1, y^2) \in \mathbb{R}^2 \times \mathbb{R}^2 : y^1 + y^2 = 0\}$, and let $h: \overline{M} \to Y$ be an arbitrary *outcome function*. Fix the endowments at $e^1 = e^2 = (3,3)$ as before. A (nonstochastic) *exchange environment* is then specified by a pair of utility functions $(u^1, u^2) \in U^2$. An *allocation mechanism* consists of a correspondence $\mu: U^2 \to\to \overline{M}$, called the *equilibrium message correspondence*, together with the outcome function $h: \overline{M} \to Y$. The correspondence μ associates with each (u^1, u^2) a set $\mu(u^1, u^2)$ of equilibrium messages, and the function h associates with each $m \in \mu(u^1, u^2)$ a net trade outcome $(y^1, y^2) = h(m)$. In order to represent the competitive mechanism in this way, we require $h(\mu(u^1, u^2))$ to be the set of competitive equilibrium trades for each (u^1, u^2). Obviously, each equilibrium message $m \in \mu(u^1, u^2)$ must contain enough information about (u^1, u^2) to determine the competitive equilibrium net trade. In fact, decentralization requires that messages contain still more information.

At this level of abstraction, decentralization means simply that the concept of equilibrium can be decomposed into separate equilibrium conditions for each trader. Formally, the allocation mechanism $(\mu, \overline{M}, h)$ is *informationally decentralized* if there are individual equilibrium message correspondences $\mu^1, \mu^2 : U \to\to \overline{M}$ such that, for every (u^1, u^2),

$$\mu\left(u^1, u^2\right) = \mu^1\left(u^1\right) \cap \mu^2\left(u^2\right). \tag{D}$$

For example, to define the *competitive mechanism* $(\mu_c, \overline{M}_c, h_c)$, let $\overline{M}_c = M$, let h_c be the projection $h_c: (p, y^1, y^2) \to (y^1, y^2)$, and define $\mu_c^i(u^i)$ to be the set of market signals $(p; y^1, y^2)$ such that y^i maximizes $u^i(e^i + z)$ subject to $pz = 0$. Then use (D) to define μ_c by setting $\mu_c(u^1, u^2) = \mu_c^1(u^1) \cap \mu_c^2(u^2)$. In effect, $\mu_c^i(u^i)$ is trader i's offer curve, and the set of competitive equilibrium messages is defined as the intersection of the offer curves.

The decentralization condition (D), as a property of μ, is existential, since it requires the existence of suitable correspondences μ^i. However, it is easily seen that the following property is necessary and sufficient for the existence of correspondences μ^1 and μ^2 satisfying (D):

$$\mu\left(u_a^1, u_a^2\right) \cap \mu\left(u_b^1, u_b^2\right) = \mu\left(u_a^1, u_b^2\right) \cap \mu\left(u_b^1, u_a^2\right) \tag{D'}$$

for every pair of environments (u_a^1, u_a^2), (u_b^1, u_b^2) (Mount and Reiter 1974, Lemma 5).

To see why decentralization requires the equilibrium messages to contain more information than just the equilibrium trades, consider the utility functions used in Section 3:

$$u_a^1(x) = 2\ln x_1 + \ln x_2,$$

$$u_b^1(x) = \ln x_1 + 2\ln x_2,$$

$$u_a^2(x) = \ln x_1 + 2\ln x_2,$$

$$u_b^2(x) = 2\ln x_1 + \ln x_2.$$

Note that in the environments (u_a^1, u_b^2) and (u_b^1, u_a^2) there is no trade in equilibrium. Therefore, if the equilibrium messages were just the equilibrium trades, we would have $\mu(u_a^1, u_b^2) \cap \mu(u_a^1, u_b^2) = \{(0,0)\}$, which contradicts (D′) because the environments (u_a^1, u_a^2) and (u_b^1, u_b^2) have nonzero equilibrium trades.

The reason for this digression into informational decentralization theory is the rather surprising result that a version of (D′) is necessary for the existence of rational expectations equilibrium. Consider the stochastic exchange environment described in Section 3, but suppose now that the expectations of the uninformed trader are conditioned on the equilibrium message of some allocation mechanism $(\mu, \overline{M}, h)$. To ensure that conditional expectations are well-defined, suppose that the equilibrium message correspondence μ is a single-valued function. Then a fully revealing equilibrium exists if $\mu(u_a^1, u_a^2) \neq \mu(u_b^1, u_b^2)$ (recall that $v^1(s_a) = u_a^1$, $v^2(s_a) = u_a^2$, etc.), because in that case the equilibrium message reveals the state to trader 2. However, if, as is the case with the equilibrium price, $\mu(u_a^1, u_a^2) = \mu(u_b^1, u_b^2)$, then only a nonrevealing equilibrium is possible, the existence of which requires that $\mu(u_a^1, \pi_a u_a^2 + (1 - \pi_a)u_b^2) = \mu(u_b^1, \pi_a u_a^2 + (1 - \pi_a)u_b^2)$, where π_a denotes the probability of the state s_a. Hence the existence of a "message-conditional expectations equilibrium" requires that

$$\mu(u_a^1, u_a^2) = \mu(u_b^1, u_b^2)$$

$$\Rightarrow \mu(u_a^1, \pi_a u_a^2 + (1 - \pi_a)u_b^2) = \mu(u_b^1, \pi_a u_a^2 + (1 - \pi_a)u_b^2).$$

Suppose we further require that equilibrium exist for all values of π_a. If we assume that the function μ is continuous with respect to π_a and let $\pi_a \to 1$, we obtain the implication

$$\mu(u_a^1, u_a^2) = \mu(u_b^1, u_b^2) \Rightarrow \mu(u_a^1, u_a^2) = \mu(u_b^1, u_a^2).$$

Letting $\pi_a \to 0$ strengthens the implication to

$$\mu(u_a^1, u_a^2) = \mu(u_b^1, u_b^2) \Rightarrow \mu(u_a^1, u_a^2) = \mu(u_b^1, u_a^2) = \mu(u_a^1, u_b^2).$$

If we further require that equilibrium exist for the stochastic environments obtained by permuting the state-dependent utilities to $v^2(s_a) = u_b^2$ and $v^2(s_b) = u_a^2$, then we add the reverse implication to obtain

$$\mu\left(u_a^1, u_a^2\right) = \mu\left(u_b^1, u_b^2\right) \Leftrightarrow \mu\left(u_a^1, u_a^2\right) = \mu\left(u_b^1, u_a^2\right) = \mu\left(u_a^1, u_b^2\right),$$

which is simply (D′) for single-valued μ. Thus the decentralization condition (D′) is necessary for the existence of a message-conditional expectations equilibrium for every two-state stochastic environment, provided that μ is single-valued and continuous in π_a.

The assumption that μ is single-valued throughout its domain U^2 is much too restrictive. For the purpose of establishing necessary conditions for the existence of equilibrium, however, we can confine the domain of μ to the set of log-linear utility pairs. On this domain, the competitive mechanism μ_c: $(u^1, u^2) \to (p, (y^i)_i)$ is single-valued and also has the required continuity with respect to the utility coefficients. Moreover, any μ obtained as a continuous function of the competitive message also inherits these properties. That is, if the market variables $(p, (y^i)_i)$ are condensed via any continuous function $f: \overline{M}_c \to \overline{M}$, the resulting $\mu(\cdot) = f(\mu_c(\cdot))$ must satisfy (D′) on log-linear utility pairs as a necessary condition for the general existence of equilibrium with expectations conditioned on the condensed market data. In particular, an REE fails to exist in the example of Section 3 because condensing the competitive message $(p, (y^i)_i)$ to the price alone violates (D′). It is natural to ask whether other condensations might be consistent with (D′). Unfortunately, Jordan (1977, Thm. 5.4) shows that there is no other continuous condensation, except for the trivial case of the constant function, that satisfies (D′). However, as will be shown in what follows, the force of this negative result can be lessened by permitting different traders to condition their expectations on different condensations.

Fortunately, the contribution of informational decentralization theory to rational expectations equilibrium is not limited to nonexistence results. It also suggests that, in order to obtain general existence theorems, we should extend the concept of rational expectations equilibrium to allow traders to condition their expectations on additional market variables. More formally, suppose that each trader i has a set of market signals M^i that are generated by a function $f^i: M \to M^i$. Define a *generalized rational expectations equilibrium* (GREE) as a Borel measurable function $(\tilde{p}(\cdot), (\tilde{y}^i(\cdot))_i): S \to M$ satisfying, for each i,

$$\tilde{y}^i(s) \text{ maximizes } E\left\{v^i \,\middle|\, s^i, f^i\left(\left(\tilde{p}(s), \left(\tilde{y}^i(s)\right)_i\right)\right)\right\}(e^i + y^i)$$

$$\text{subject to } \tilde{p}(s)y^i = 0 \quad \text{for a.e. } s. \tag{4}$$

Taking each f^i to be the projection $(p, (y^i)_i) \to p$ reduces (4) to (3). Alternatively, suppose that each f^i is the identity, so that each trader observes the entire competitive message. Then one can show that an FCE is always a GREE. In fact, the same is true if each f^i is taken to be the projection $(p, (y^j)_j) \rightarrow (p, y^i)$. The proof of this is nearly immediate. Suppose that $(\tilde{p}(\cdot), (\tilde{y}^i(\cdot))_i)$ is an FCE. We need to show that, for each i,

$$\tilde{y}^i(s) \text{ maximizes } E\left\{v^i \middle| s^i, \tilde{p}(s), \tilde{y}^i(s)\right\}(e^i + y^i)$$

subject to $\tilde{p}(s)y^i = 0$ for a.e. s.   (5)

In other words, we need to show that when trader i's information is reduced from s to $(s^i, \tilde{p}(s), \tilde{y}^i(s))$, the trade $\tilde{y}^i(s)$ remains expected utility maximizing. Given any $(\bar{s}, \bar{p}, \bar{y}^i)$, let $\bar{S} = \{s \mid s^i = \bar{s}^i, \tilde{p}(s) = \bar{p}, \text{ and } \tilde{y}^i(s) = \bar{y}^i\}$. Thus $\bar{S}$ is the set of states that trader i cannot distinguish from one another. The FCE condition (1) states that, for almost every $s \in \bar{S}$, $\bar{y}^i$ maximizes $v^i(s)(e^i + y^i)$ subject to $\bar{p}y^i = 0$. It follows immediately that $\bar{y}^i$ maximizes any convex combination of the functions $\{y^i \rightarrow v^i(s)(e^i + y^i) : s \in \bar{S}\}$ subject to $\bar{p}y^i = 0$. The conditional expectation in (5) is simply one such convex combination. Thus the market data (p, y^i) are informationally sufficient to support an FCE as a GREE. It may be interesting to note that this proof is very similar to the usual demonstration that a correlated equilibrium of a game can be supported by using the players' actions as the correlating messages (Aumann 1987).

The proof indicates that the conditional expectation in (5) can be conditioned on the market data $(\tilde{p}(s), \tilde{y}^i(s))$ alone, so that the private signal s^i is unnecessary. However, it is *not* possible to reduce the data to $\tilde{y}^i(s)$ alone, since a trade that is optimal in different states at different prices may fail to maximize the trade-conditional expected utility at any of the respective prices. It is essential to the foregoing proof that the budget constraint $\bar{p}y^i = 0$ be the same for all $s \in \bar{S}$. In fact, Jordan (1982a, Thm. 2.5) shows that the data (p, y^i) cannot be further condensed, except to a constant, without losing the general existence of equilibrium.

The interpretation of (5) seems troublesome. How can a trader choose a trade to maximize expected utility conditional on the trade itself? This question can be blunted somewhat by adopting $-\Sigma_{j \neq i} y^j$ as a euphemism for y^i or by recalling that, in auction theory, bidders are assumed to avoid the "winner's curse" by choosing a bid that maximizes their expected payoff conditional on the bid being accepted. However, Beja (1976) has shown that when one attempts to formalize an REE as a Bayesian Nash equilibrium, as in auction theory, in which traders choose excess demand functions, the existence problem is severe. Thus, although the equilibrium concept defined by (5) completely neutralizes the informational discontinuity, it is not persuasive as a self-contained description of the process by which markets aggregate and communicate information.

One approach to interpreting (5) is to model more explicitly the dynamics of information transmission. A particularly simple model, first suggested by Reiter (1976), is the following. Suppose that traders initially use only their private information, so that the market initially moves to a PIE. However, before the PIE trades are executed, traders add to their private information the information revealed by the PIE prices. This will typically change traders' expectations, requiring a new round of trade, and so on. In the example described in Section 2, the PIE prices $\bar{p}(s_a) = (7/12, 5/12)$ and $\bar{p}(s_b) = (5/12, 7/12)$ reveal the state to the uninformed trader, so the second and final iteration is the FCE. When there are more than two possible states, more than two iterations will typically be required to reach a price function $\bar{p}(\cdot)$ that reveals no further information. In general, the final iteration need not be an FCE.

The two-state example of Section 2 has the interesting property that the final price function, in this case the FCE $\bar{p}(s_a) = \bar{p}(s_b) = (1/2, 1/2)$, does not itself reveal the information revealed by earlier prices. Instead, the information is revealed by the trade function $\bar{y}^2(\cdot)$. Jordan (1982c, Thm. 5.7.C) shows that, in general, the information revealed by earlier prices that is decision-relevant to trader i is revealed by the pair $(\bar{p}(\cdot), \bar{y}^i(\cdot))$ at the final iteration. Thus one can interpret (5) by viewing the pair $(\bar{p}, \bar{y}^i(\cdot))$ as a representation of the decision-relevant information revealed to trader i during the trading process.

A very similar trading process was formulated independently by Kobayashi (1977) in a financial asset market model under the assumptions that (i) traders have constant absolute risk aversion and (ii) the joint distribution of future asset values and traders' private information is normal. These assumptions guarantee the existence of an REE (Grossman 1976 and 1978), and Kobayashi proved that the trading process reaches the REE in a number of iterations equal to the number of traders. In Kobayashi's model, the trades at each iteration are actually executed, but the assumption of constant absolute risk aversion prevents the resulting capital gains or losses from having any effect on the process. In both models, it is critical that traders behave myopically and choose their demand as though each iteration were the last.

If traders attempt to anticipate future prices, the informational discontinuity reappears, albeit in a more subtle form (see, e.g., Border and Jordan 1979, Dubey, Geanakoplos, and Shubik 1987, and Futia 1981). For example, consider a finite-period stochastic exchange environment, with only spot markets in each period, in which traders' preferences are not

intertemporally separable. Because future consumption affects preferences for current consumption, a trader will attempt to anticipate future
prices when choosing current demand. Suppose that traders condition
their expectations on private information and past prices. Then current
prices influence future information, and thus influence future prices.
Traders' rational expectations of future prices, conditional on current
information, influence current demands, which determine current prices.
Because of this feedback, the discontinuous relation between prices and
information can again prevent the existence of equilibrium.

5   Efficiency Properties of REE

One reason for dissatisfaction with fully revealing rational expectations
equilibria and the microeconomic models that generate them is that,
realistically, such equilibria are too good to be true. The situation
described in Sections 2 and 3 contradicts our economic intuition in a
significant way. We do not believe that prices can transmit all information of interest to economic agents because information may be
extremely complicated, with different types of information being most
relevant for different trades. No finite number of (even continuously
variable) prices for commodities that are transacted in markets can
completely capture this complex information.

If all useful information were to be carried by equilibrium prices,
the equilibrium would be at least informationally efficient and, in the
absence of other potential market distortions, one could perhaps expect
the resulting allocation to be optimal in a wider sense. However, full
Pareto optimality cannot be expected if traders wish to share their risks
– insurance markets may be desirable yet precluded by information.
Hence, we must restrict efficiency properties by stressing that we only
consider efficiency relative to existing markets as well as with respect to
the given information structure. With these two important qualifications,
fully revealing rational expectations equilibrium allocations are necessarily ex ante Pareto optimal, as observed by Radner (1967).

The situation is rendered more complicated by an important point elu-
cidated, by means of an example, in Green (1981). In a general equilibrium model, more information may be undesirable unless complete
information is achieved; additional partial information can give rise to
Pareto inferior equilibrium allocations because the new information
can destroy some previously feasible opportunities for risk sharing.
Essentially, the presence of information can destroy insurance markets,
thereby producing inefficiency unless all agents can freely obtain complete information.

A further examination of the optimality of rational expectations equilibrium allocations appears in Laffont (1985). This article considers the issue of whether partially revealing rational expectations equilibrium allocations satisfy constrained efficiency. Unfortunately, the answer is generally negative. In partially revealing cases, competitive markets do not lead to the transmission of those parts of consumers' information that matter most for achieving Pareto improving trades. Even if equilibrium prices transmit the maximal amount – in a dimensional sense – of information that can be communicated given the number of commodities present in the economy, the information that is carried by prices could be such that it doesn't affect traders' utilities very much. In short, one cannot expect the most important information to be conveyed by prices if prices cannot transmit all information.

The "efficient markets hypothesis" article of Jordan (1983) makes a similar point. Only for three special parametric classes of utility functions – linear, logarithmic, and exponential – do we find informationally efficient rational expectations equilibria. Moreover, these economies obviously constitute "knife-edge" examples; they are not generic in any reasonable sense.

6   Partially Revealing REE

In addition to the objection discussed in the previous section – that informationally efficient rational expectations equilibria cannot be expected to arise in most economic situations – fully revealing REE are inconsistent in a more inclusive economic model in which the information is endogenous. Specifically, Beja (1976) argues that strategic players in a REE market game would not gather information and, as a result, information cannot be conveyed by prices. A similar point was made by Grossman and Stiglitz (1976) in a parametric model of a market for a financial asset. They observe that if information can be freely communicated by prices then no trader would ever pay to gain information, and so REE models with endogenous costly acquisition of information are therefore not consistent.

The standard model of partially revealing equilibrium in financial asset markets is that of Hellwig (1980), which generalizes and extends the model of Grossman and Stiglitz (1976, 1980). Traders are assumed to have constant absolute risk aversion, and the joint distribution of private information and future asset values is assumed to be normal. The full revelation of private information is prevented by the device of adding a random noise term to the aggregate supply, so that price movements can be caused by either private information or supply shocks. Unfortunately, the existence of the partially revealing REE appears to depend on the special assumptions of this model. The fact that the original nonexistence example of Green (1977) was created by adding noise to traders' endowments suggests that there is little hope that endowment noise could serve as the basis for a general theory of partially revealing REE.

Progress in analyzing the possibilities for genuinely partially revealing rational expectations equilibria has been disappointing in general. An explicit example of partially revealing rational expectations equilibrium prices was provided in Allen (1981b), but that class of economies suffers from the observation that the combination of price information and any agent's initial private information corresponds to full information. Thus, the rational expectations equilibrium allocations exactly equal the full communication demands evaluated at the resulting market prices. More recently, Ausubel (1990) has studied partially revealing rational expectations equilibrium, albeit for a somewhat special economic model.

More generally, results for the partially revealing case all feature some form of approximation, either to exact market clearing or to complete rationality in agents' use of information. To see that slight deviations from precise market clearing greatly simplify the situation, consider our basic model when there are many more (in a dimensional sense) parameters than prices and when (for simplicity) all agents are either fully informed or completely uninformed. Divide the compact parameter set into sets of small diameter and choose a single distinct price for each set in the partition so as to make demand arbitrarily close to zero when the uninformed agents condition on the partition. This forms a rational expectations approximate equilibrium which, by definition, is not fully revealing. A similar trick can be used to construct rational expectations approximate equilibria based on those in Allen (1981a, 1982b) rather than the finite-state case of Radner (1979) or Allen (1984). See Allen (1982a) for details.

A more complicated approach based on the general idea of "noise" or dispersion was pursued in simultaneous and independent work by Allen (1981c, published as 1985a,b) and by Anderson and Sonnenschein (1981, published in the 1982 *Journal of Economic Theory* symposium issue). One interpretation of this research is that it illustrates the tradeoff between exact rationality and exact market clearing in the partially revealing context with noise. These papers take a different approach to the addition of noise than Hellwig (1980), who adds noise to supplies whereas Allen (1981c, 1985a,b) and Anderson and Sonnenschein (1981, 1982) use the concept of noise to alter the definitions of rational expectations equilibria in various ways – that is, noisy rationality or noisy market clearing. Unfortunately, this literature provides only approximations to rational expectations equilibrium.

The big question of formulating a satisfactory and consistent concept of partially revealing rational expectations equilibrium has remained open. An additional desideratum is that these equilibria display the usual properties of the equilibrium price correspondence and, ideally, the same decentralization or implementation features as in the standard model of an exchange economy without asymmetric information.

7   Conclusion

Radner's influence on the general equilibrium theory of rational expectations was seminal. Radner (1967, 1968, 1972) provided the first models of trade among agents with differing private information, the first analysis of the revelation of private information by equilibrium prices, and the first discovery of the informational discontinuity that creates the equilibrium existence problem. Radner (1979) established the first result on the generic existence of equilibrium.

Now that subsequent researchers on the existence problem appear to have followed Radner's example of moving on to other topics, it is appropriate to take stock of the results (see Allen 1986 and Radner 1982). The existence, if not the economic interpretation, of fully revealing equilibrium is well established. In the case of complete markets, Grossman (1981, Thm. 2) shows the general existence of fully revealing equilibrium. In the usual incomplete markets model, other results mentioned here establish the generic existence of fully revealing equilibrium in the lower-dimensional case and of nearly fully revealing equilibrium in the higher-dimensional case. More generally, expanding the market signal to include net trades, as in (5), will always produce a fully revealing equilibrium whenever a full communication equilibrium exists, which requires only the classical assumptions.

The existence of partially revealing equilibrium, in contrast, remains precarious. Results mentioned in Section 6 show that, in various senses of approximation, there exist approximate equilibria with intuitively reasonable revelation properties. With respect to exact equilibria, however, the authors are aware of no existence results that do not rely on very special assumptions on preferences (e.g., constant absolute risk aversion) or the stochastic structure of information (e.g., joint normality). When one reflects on the pervasive use of partially revealing equilibrium in the theory of financial asset markets (see, e.g., Black 1986), the absence of a firm foundation for partially revealing equilibrium is especially disquieting.

References

Allen, Beth, 1981a, Generic existence of completely revealing equilibria for economies with uncertainty when prices convey information, *Econometrica* 49, 1173–99.

1981b, A class of monotone economies in which rational expectations equilibria exist but prices do not reveal all information, *Economics Letters* 7, 227–32.

1981c, The existence of expectations equilibria in a large economy with noisy price observations, Working Paper no. 81-01, Center for Analytic Research in Economics and the Social Sciences, Department of Economics, University of Pennsylvania, Philadelphia.

1982a, Approximate equilibria in microeconomic rational expectations models, *Journal of Economic Theory* 26, 244–60.

1982b, Strict rational expectations equilibria with diffuseness, *Journal of Economic Theory* 27, 20–46.

1984, Equilibria in which prices convey information: The finite case, M. Boyer and R. Kihlstrom (eds.), *Bayesian Models in Economic Theory*. Amsterdam: North Holland, pp. 63–92.

1985a, The existence of rational expectations equilibria in a large economy with noisy price observations, *Journal of Mathematical Economics* 14, 67–103.

1985b, The existence of fully rational expectations approximate equilibria with noisy price observations, *Journal of Economic Theory* 37, 213–53.

1986, General equilibrium with rational expectations, W. Hildenbrand and A. Mas-Colell (eds.), *Contributions to Mathematical Economics in Honor of Gerard Debreu*. Amsterdam: North-Holland, pp. 1–23.

Anderson, Robert M., and Hugo Sonnenschein, 1981, On the existence of rational expectations equilibria, Mimeo, Department of Economics, Princeton University, Princeton, NJ.

1982, On the existence of rational expectations equilibrium, *Journal of Economic Theory* 26, 261–78.

Aumann, Robert, 1987, Correlated equilibrium as an extension of Bayesian rationality, *Econometrica* 55, 1–18.

Ausubel, Lawrence M., 1990, Partially-revealing rational expectations equilibrium in a competitive economy, *Journal of Economic Theory* 50, 93–126.

Beja, Abram, 1976, The limited information efficiency of market processes, Working Paper no. 43, Research Program in Finance, University of California, Berkeley.

Black, Fisher, 1986, Noise, *Journal of Finance* 41, 529–43.

Border, Kim, and J. S. Jordan, 1979, Expectations equilibrium with expectations conditioned on past data, *Journal of Economic Theory* 22, 395–406.

Debreu, Gerard, 1972, Smooth preferences, *Econometrica* 40, 603–15.

Dubey, Pradeep, John Geanakoplos, and Martin Shubik, 1987, The revelation of information in strategic market games: A critique of rational expectations, *Journal of Mathematical Economics* 16, 105–37.

Futia, Carl A., 1981, Rational expectations in stationary linear models, *Econometrica* 49, 171–92.

Green, Jerry R., 1973, Information, efficiency and equilibrium, Discussion Paper no. 284, Harvard Institute of Economic Research, Harvard University, Cambridge, MA.

1975, The non-existence of informational equilibria, Discussion Paper no. 410, Harvard Institute of Economic Research, Harvard University, Cambridge, MA.

1977, The non-existence of informational equilibria, *Review of Economic Studies* 44, 451–63.

1981, Value of information with sequential futures markets, *Econometrica* 49, 335–58.

Grossman, Sanford J., 1976, On the efficiency of competitive stock markets where trades have diverse information, *Journal of Finance* 31, 573–85.

1978, Further results on the informational efficiency of competitive stock markets, *Journal of Economic Theory* 18, 81–101.

1981, An introduction to the theory of rational expectations under asymmetric information, *Review of Economic Studies* 48, 541–59.

Grossman, Sanford J., and Joseph E. Stiglitz, 1976, Information and competitive price systems, *American Economic Review Papers and Proceedings* 66, 246–53.

1980, On the impossibility of informationally efficient markets, *American Economic Review* 70, 393–408.

Grunberg, E., and F. Modigliani, 1954, The predictability of social events, *Journal of Political Economy* 62, 465–78.

Handel, Christopher J., 1980, Allocational efficiency in a competitive capital market, Ph.D. Dissertation, Stanford University.

Hayek, F., 1945, The use of knowledge in society, *American Economic Review* 35, 519–30.

Hellwig, Martin F., 1980, On the aggregation of information in competitive markets, *Journal of Economic Theory* 22, 477–98.

Hurwicz, L., 1977, On the dimensional requirements of informationally decentralized Pareto-satisfactory processes, K. J. Arrow and L. Hurwicz (eds.), *Studies in Resource Allocation Process*. Cambridge University Press.

Jordan, J. S., 1977, Expectations equilibrium and informational efficiency in stochastic environments, *Journal of Economic Theory* 16, 354–72.

1982a, Admissible market data structures: A complete characterization, *Journal of Economic Theory* 28, 19–31.

1982b, The generic existence of rational expectations equilibrium in the higher dimensional case, *Journal of Economic Theory* 26, 224–43.

1982c, A dynamic model of expectations equilibrium, *Journal of Economic Theory* 28, 235–54.

1983, On the efficient markets hypothesis, *Econometrica* 51, 1325–44.

Jordan, J., and R. Radner, 1979, The nonexistence of rational expectations equilibrium: A robust example, Mimeo, Department of Economics, University of Minnesota, Minneapolis.

60   **Beth Allen and James S. Jordan**

1982, Rational expectations in microeconomic models: An overview, *Journal of Economic Theory* 26, 201–23.

Kobayashi, T., 1977, A convergence theorem on rational expectations equilibrium with price information, Working Paper no. 79, The Economic Series, Institute for Mathematical Studies in the Social Sciences, Stanford University.

Kreps, David M., 1977, A note on "fulfilled expectations" equilibria, *Journal of Economic Theory* 14, 32–43.

Laffont, J. J, 1985, On the welfare analysis of rational expectations equilibrium with asymmetric information, *Econometrica* 53, 1–29.

Mount, K., and S. Reiter, 1974, The informational size of message spaces, *Journal of Economic Theory* 8, 161–92.

Muth, John F., 1961, Rational expectations and the theory of price movements, *Econometrica* 29, 315–35.

Radner, Roy, 1967, Équilibre des marchés à terme et au comptant en cas d'incertitude, *Cahiers d'Econométrie* (C.N.R.S., Paris) 4, 35–42. [Translated as: Equilibrium of spot and futures markets under uncertainty, Technical Report no. 24, Center for Research in Management Science, University of California, Berkeley.]

1968, Competitive equilibrium under uncertainty, *Econometrica* 36, 31–58.

1972, Existence of equilibrium of plans, prices, and price expectations in a sequence of markets, *Econometrica* 40, 289–303.

1979, Rational expectations equilibrium: Generic existence and the information revealed by prices, *Econometrica* 47, 665–78.

1982, Equilibrium under uncertainty, K. J. Arrow and M. D. Intriligator (eds.), *The Handbook of Mathematical Economics*, vol. II. Amsterdam: North-Holland, pp. 923–1006.

Reiter, Stanley, 1976, On expectations equilibrium, Mimeo, Northwestern University, Evanston, IL.

CHAPTER 3

Rational Expectations and Rational Learning

Lawrence E. Blume and David Easley

1   Introduction

The issue of expectation formation arises naturally in economies with a sequence of spot and incomplete futures markets. In such economies, individuals use forecasts of future prices in order to make decisions about current consumption and investment. Equilibria in the markets for current consumption and currently available futures contracts may exist even if individuals have differing and incorrect expectations. Such equilibria are called *temporary* equilibria, and other than the usual conditions on preferences and endowments, their existence requires only weak conditions on expectations about future prices. However, absent any structure on price expectations, there is little more to be said about equilibria at any date.

One attempt to tie down expectations is the rational expectations hypothesis: that individuals hold common, correct price expectations in economies with incomplete markets. The existence of rational expectations equilibria was first addressed by Roy Radner in his seminal 1972 paper on plans, prices, and price expectations. Radner fixed expectations by requiring that agents hold common price expectations and that their plans be consistent with market clearing at all future dates at prices equal to their expected prices. The term "self-fulfilling" has been used to describe these "rational" expectations. It is particularly apt because it emphasizes that the actual sequence of prices is determined by the expectations agents use.

In the 1972 model, payoff-relevant information was distributed

We thank participants at the June 1992 Economic Theory Workshop in honor of Roy Radner, Cornell University, and two anonymous referees for their helpful comments. We also want to thank seminar participants at CORE, Erasmus University, Tel Aviv University, and The Technion for helpful discussions. Finally, we thank Mukul Majumdar for organizing the Radner workshop and for his help in constructing this article. Financial support from NSF Grant SES-8921415 is gratefully acknowledged.

"symmetrically"; that is, all traders had the same information. Consequently there is nothing to be learned from other traders, and so in equilibrium there is nothing to be inferred from current prices about prices in the future. In 1979, Radner demonstrated the existence of a rational expectations equilibrium when payoff-relevant information is "asymmetrically" distributed – that is, when not all players have the same information. In these equilibria, traders infer the information of others by observing current-period prices.

It is inconceivable that individuals should be born with the complete understanding of the economy required by rational expectations equilibria in either model. Thus it is natural to ask if traders can *learn* to hold rational expectations. Outside of a rational expectations equilibrium, traders entertain different models of the relationship between present prices and private information. They use equilibrium prices to help identify the correct models. Blume and Easley (1982) was the first paper to address this learning problem in a general equilibrium setting. The answer offered to the learning question in that paper is "no" for a large class of learning models. Rational expectations equilibria are locally but not globally stable, under reasonable learning dynamics, and other non–self-fulfilling equilibria may also be locally stable. Convergence fails because the likelihood functions used to assess the relative worth of various models are correctly specified at equilibria but are not correctly specified far away from equilibrium. On the other hand, Blume and Easley (1984) show that, when the likelihood function is correctly specified away from equilibria as well as near, Bayesian estimation of the true models is consistent; that is, Bayesian traders learn rational expectations and prices converge to those of a rational expectations equilibrium.

The origin of the likelihood function raises an important problem that has been ignored until recently. In order to carry out the Bayesian analysis in Blume and Easley (1984), the likelihood function for each trader must describe the correct likelihood of various paths for the evolution of prices. This likelihood depends upon a number of parameters, including the prior beliefs and likelihood functions of the other traders. Thus the mutual consistency of correctly specified likelihood functions and prior beliefs is a kind of equilibrium existence problem. In Section 4 we define appropriate equilibrium stochastic processes and call them *Bayesian equilibrium processes* (BEPs). (A similar construct arises in noncooperative game theory: in Section 3, we define and discuss Bayesian strategy revision processes.) The existence question is easy to solve. Rational expectations equilibria are BEPs, but these are trivial equilibria in which no learning about models takes place. The important question to ask, which we duck in this paper, is how rich is the set of prior beliefs that lead to BEPs. Although we do not have an answer, recent work of Nachbar (1997) on learning in games suggests that the set of prior beliefs for which learning is possible is quite small.

A natural question for the reader to ask at this point (if not earlier) is why we focus on Bayesian learning. It is conceptually incredibly demanding, and it seems that – because of the need to tie priors together – this approach could never answer the learning question completely. We do not dispute this, and in fact we will argue that the Bayesian approach has already been pushed too far. Nonetheless, the Bayesian approach is surely the natural place to start. If a market participant is an expected utility maximizer then, as a consequence of this assumption, beliefs must be revised in light of new information according to Bayes's rule. Because Bayesian learning is a consequence of assumptions about preferences, it is frequently referred to as *rational learning*. We will follow this practice, but the reader should keep in mind that there is nothing necessarily irrational about ad hoc learning. To label non-Bayesian learning as irrational is to invest the Savage axioms that are at the foundation of expected utility maximization with normative content, which we (and we believe most economists) would reject.

Game theory presents learning issues similar to the issues of expectation formation in economies with a sequence of incomplete markets and markets with differentially informed traders. In games with incomplete information, a (Bayes–Nash) equilibrium implies that, throughout the course of play, players will be learning. But many different structures of beliefs will be consistent with many, distinctly different, equilibria. Jordan (1991, 1995) investigates the equilibrium behavior of infinitely repeated games. He demonstrates how the effects of learning force a relationship between limit beliefs in such a game and the equilibria of complete information versions of the game. Kalai and Lehrer (1993a) and Nyarko (1991, 1994b) ask whether players can learn their way to a Nash equilibrium when they do not necessarily start in a Bayes–Nash equilibrium. In different, but related, models they both provide positive answers. The issues that arise in this literature are essentially the same as those that arise in the microeconomic rational expectations literature.

In this paper, our goal is not to survey the work on equilibrium under uncertainty or on the existence of rational expectations equilibrium, nor even to survey all the recent work on rational learning.[1] Instead, our goal

---

[1] Blume, Bray, and Easley (1982) provide a survey of learning in economies with differential information; Blume and Easley (1993) provide a partial survey of the recent work on learning in games; and Jordan (1992) provides an exposition of recent results on Bayesian learning in games and a non-Bayesian interpretation of some of these results.

is to provide an overview of the methods of analysis and results obtained and, most important, an assessment of the success of rational learning dynamics in tying down limit beliefs and limit behavior in game-theoretic and economic equilibrium models. We illustrate the features common to rational or Bayesian learning in single-agent, game-theoretic, and equilibrium frameworks. We show that rational learning is possible in each of these environments. The issue is not whether rational learning can occur, but rather what results it produces.

The key to the success or failure of rational learning lies in identifying the proper parameter set. If we assume a natural complex parameterization of the choice environment, then all we know is the rational learner believes that his posteriors will converge somewhere with prior probability 1. Alternatively, if we as modelers assume the simple parameterization of the choice environment that is necessary to obtain positive results, then we are closing our models in the ad hoc fashion that rational learning was introduced to avoid. We do not believe that any further resolution of this issue is possible. Rational learning can indeed produce convergence of beliefs to rational expectations equilibria in competitive economies or to Nash equilibria in games. But in naturally complex environments, it can only do so if the modeler first imposes an equilibrium condition on the learning process. This equilibrium condition is weaker than rational expectations equilibrium or Bayes–Nash equilibrium, but it is nonetheless an equilibrium condition.

We believe that a partial resolution of this conundrum is to pay more attention to how learning interacts with other dynamic forces. In the penultimate section of this paper we show that, in a simple economy, the forces of market selection can yield convergence to rational expectations equilibria even without every agent behaving as a rational learner. Similar evolutionary forces have been shown to be successful in producing Nash equilibrium or even refinements of Nash in repeated games. How successful such forces are in general, and how they interact with rational or nonrational learning, needs more study. We believe that this is a promising direction for future research.

In the next section we discuss learning in the context of a single-agent decision problem. Along the way we introduce some of the tools that have proven useful in the analysis of learning dynamics. Section 3 discusses the role of learning in the analysis of repeated games, and Section 4 discusses learning in general equilibrium models. In Section 5 we discuss the robustness of learning in equilibrium models. Our conclusions about what we have learned from the learning literature are contained in Section 6.

2   Learning Dynamics

The rational learning literature takes off from the analysis of Bayesian decision problems. Here we establish the basic results for the single-agent learning problem. The problem fundamental to the statistical literature is *consistency*. That is, will a decision maker ultimately learn the truth? We will introduce another problem which is important for equilibrium dynamics: the *prediction problem*. That is, does the prediction of the future path of the process, given its history through date t, converge to the correct conditional distribution as t grows? We will see that the relationship between consistency and the prediction problem is not as straightforward as it might seem. In this section we discuss the dynamics of Bayesian posterior belief revision and the problems of consistency and predication. We then describe a canonical decision problem, and discuss the problem of incomplete learning in some examples.

2.1   The Dynamics of Posterior Revision

Bayesian posterior revision works on a set of sample histories $H = \Pi_{t=1}^{\infty} H_t$ (where H_t is the set of possible observations at time t), a set of parameters Θ, and for each $\theta \in \Theta$ a probability measure μ_θ on H. We assume that Θ and each H_t are Polish (complete, separable metric) spaces. We let $\boldsymbol{S}$ denote the product σ-field of subsets of H derived from the Borel σ-fields on each H_t, and we assume that, for each event $S \in \boldsymbol{S}$, the map $\theta \to \mu_\theta(S)$ is Borel measurable.

The Bayesian "learner" begins with a prior distribution ν on Θ. Corresponding to each prior ν is the (unique) joint distribution ϕ_ν on $\Theta \times H$ such that, for any set $A \times B$ with A a measurable subset of Θ and $B \in \boldsymbol{S}$,

$$\phi_\nu(A \times B) = \int_A \mu_\theta(B) \, d\nu(\theta).$$

Just as ν is the marginal distribution of ϕ_ν on Θ, let μ_ν denote the marginal distribution of ϕ_ν on H.

Posterior beliefs are just conditional distributions derived from ϕ_ν. Let $H^T = H_1 \times \ldots \times H_T$ denote the set of possible observations through time T, and let $\sigma(h_1, \ldots, h_T)$ be the σ-field generated by the observation of $h^T \in H^T$. The date $T+1$ posterior distribution $\nu_{T+1}(\cdot \,|\, h_1, \ldots, h_T)$ is a regular version of ϕ_ν conditional on $\sigma(h_1, \ldots, h_T)$.

There are two key results on the consistency of Bayes learning, both essentially due to Doob (1949).

Theorem 2.1.   *Given any prior belief* v *on* Θ, *posterior beliefs converge* v-*almost surely.*

This is to say, for v-almost all θ, the posterior beliefs $v_{T+1}(\cdot \mid h_1, \ldots, h_T)$ converge in the weak convergence topology with μ_θ-probability 1. In other words, for most parameter values θ conceivable from the ex ante point of view of the learner, for almost all possible realizations of the data, posterior beliefs will converge somewhere. This result is an immediate consequence of the Martingale convergence theorem.

Theorem 2.1 does not imply learning; limit posterior beliefs may not be correct. It may not be the case that for v-almost all θ, posterior beliefs converge μ_θ-almost surely to δ_θ, point mass at θ. The second result is as follows.

Theorem 2.2.   *If for* v-*almost all* θ, *the measures* μ_θ *on* H *are mutually singular, then for* v-*almost all* θ, *posterior beliefs will* μ_θ-*almost always converge to* δ_θ.

In this case, Bayes learning is said to be *consistent.*

The condition that the measures μ_θ be mutually singular seems very strong but in fact is true in many conventional statistics problems. Consider, for example, learning the mean θ of a normal random variate from independent draws. Let x_t denote the outcome of the tth draw. According to the strong law of large numbers, the support of each μ_θ (the induced measure on the infinite product space) is almost surely contained in the set of all sample paths whose sample means converge to θ:

$$\lim_{T \to \infty} \frac{1}{T} \sum_{t=1}^{T} x_t = \theta.$$

Thus the intersection of the supports of any two distinct parameters θ and θ′ has measure 0 according to both μ_θ and $\mu_{\theta'}$.

A slightly more useful result for our purposes will account for the fact that the measures μ_θ may not all be mutually singular. Let A be a Borel subset of Θ, and let H_A denote the subset of paths $h \in H$ such that h is not in supp μ_θ for any $\theta \in A$. It is easy to see that H_A is a Borel set. The following result follows immediately from the definition of v_{T+1} and the Martingale convergence theorem.

Theorem 2.3.   *For* μ_v-*almost all* $h \in H_A$, *the posterior probability* $v_{T+1}(A \mid h_1, \ldots, h_T)$ *converges to 0.*

There is one important issue here that we have avoided. The notion of "almost sure" for parameters is from the point of view of the individual, and not necessarily from the point of view of the modeler. Non-pathological examples are known in which the exceptional sets are very large from some other, (say) topological, point of view. Thus, one would like to show that Bayes learning is "uniformly consistent" if posterior beliefs converge uniformly across $\theta \in \Theta$ to δ_θ with probability 1. One approach to this problem is introduced in Schwartz (1965) and extended in Barron (1989).

These results are concerned with whether individuals will almost surely learn parameters, and it is with this topic that much of the learning literature is concerned. Consistency is an important issue, but – for the questions of learning to play Nash equilibrium, learning rational expectations, or even learning to make the optimal choice in a single-agent dynamic programming problem – it is not the correct issue to focus on. What really matters is whether individuals learn to make correct conditional predictions about the future. More formally, do individuals' predictions, their conditional beliefs about the future given the past, converge to correct conditional beliefs? This prediction problem is at the heart of the foregoing questions. In simple environments, consistency is sufficient for prediction. In complex environments it is not. Before we illustrate this point in a game-theoretic context, we examine it in some simple estimation examples.

Example 2.1. Let each $H_t = \{0, 1\}$, so that H is the set of all possible sequences of 0s and 1s. Let $\Theta = \{\mathbf{p}, \mathbf{q}\}$. The elements of Θ are sequences of probabilities: $\mathbf{p} = (p_1, p_2, \ldots)$ and $\mathbf{q} = (q_1, q_2, \ldots)$. The draws of 0s and 1s are independent over time, and either the draw at each time t gives 1 with probability p_t, or at each time t the probability of 1 is q_t. Suppose that all the p_t and q_t are uniformly bounded away from 0 and 1. Let us also suppose that $\mathbf{p}$ is the "true" distribution of the process. Suppose the decision maker's job is to estimate θ. A necessary and sufficient condition for Bayes estimates of θ to be consistent is that the sum

$$\sum_{t=1}^{\infty} \left(p_t \log\left(\frac{p_t}{q_t}\right) + (1 - p_t)\log\left(\frac{1 - p_t}{1 - q_t}\right) \right)$$

diverge. On the other hand, suppose the decision maker's job is to predict, at each time t, the probability that $h_{t+1} = 1$. The optimal prediction is p_{t+1} or q_{t+1}, depending on whether θ is $\mathbf{p}$ or $\mathbf{q}$. If the condition for consistency is satisfied, then posterior beliefs will converge to point mass on $\mathbf{p}$ (resp. $\mathbf{q}$) $\mathbf{p}$-almost surely ($\mathbf{q}$-almost surely), and so the prediction at time t will almost surely converge to p_{t+1} (q_{t+1}). If the consistency condition fails, then $p_{t+1} - q_{t+1}$ is converging to 0, so again the prediction will almost surely converge to the correct conditional distribution, even though the decision maker never learns θ.

In Example 2.1 it was possible to forecast without learning the parameter. In the next two examples, parameter estimation is consistent but forecasting becomes hard. The first is similar to an example found in Kalai and Lehrer (1993a).

Example 2.2. Let each $H_t = \{0, 1\}$, so that H is the set of all sequences of 0s and 1s. Let Θ index the set of all point masses on the elements of H. In other words, $\Theta = H$, and μ_θ is a point mass on the sequence θ. Let p be a number between 0 and 1. Let the prior distribution ν_p be the distribution on H that is derived from independent and identically distributed draws from each H_t that assign probability p to 0 at each date t.

Obviously, the distributions μ_θ on H are all singular with respect to each other. We conclude from Theorem 2.2 that, for almost all μ in the support of ν_p, posterior beliefs converge almost surely to δ_θ. But the conditional distribution of $(x_{T+1}, x_{T+2}, \ldots)$ given $(h_1, \ldots, h_T)$ never changes with respect to T; it is always the distribution derived from i.i.d. draws of 0s and 1s that assign probability p to 0.

In this example, learning about θ does take place, but after time T all the observer has learned about θ is its first T components. And given her beliefs, the observer can infer nothing about the behavior of subsequent components of θ from those she already knows. As contrived as this example may seem, this is exactly the root of the problem of convergence to Nash-like play in infinitely repeated games.

Here is another example, which we will later (in Section 3) put in a game-theoretic setting. Here learning occurs, but forecasting becomes increasingly difficult over time because the sensitivity of the forecast to the parameter grows at a rate faster than that at which learning occurs.

Example 2.3. A deterministic system on the unit interval I evolves according to the "tent map" dynamic:

$$f(x) = \begin{cases} 2x & \text{if } 0 \le x \le 1/2; \\ 2 - 2x & \text{if } 1/2 \le x \le 1. \end{cases}$$

The initial position x_0 of the process is unknown. A Bayesian decision maker will estimate the location of x_{T+1} given information on the sequence $x_0, \ldots, x_T$. He will be told at the beginning of stage $T + 1$ in which half of the unit interval x_T is to be found: the upper interval $U = [1/2, 1]$ or the lower interval $D = [0, 1/2]$. Thus, each $H_t = \{D, U\}$. His information begins at stage 0. At the beginning of stage $T+1$, before x_{T+1} is realized, the decision marker is asked to guess its coming location. In other words, after observing h^T he must forecast h_{T+1}.

The observations available at the beginning of date $T+1$ describe an interval of width 2^{-T}, and so Bayes estimates of x_0 are consistent. Let prior beliefs have density with respect to Lebesgue measure given by $\phi_0(x)$, with c.d.f. $\Phi_0(x)$. For Φ_0-almost all initial positions x_0, the posterior predicted distribution of x_{T+1} (given the observations available at the beginning of date $T+1$) converges to the uniform distribution on the unit interval, and the probability that $h_{T+1} = D$ given previous history converges almost surely to 1/2 (see Blume and Easley 1993 for a proof). The decision maker has ever-increasing knowledge of x_0, but the residual uncertainty is so magnified by the chaotic dynamics that predicting the location of the forthcoming state becomes increasingly difficult.

When is prediction possible? Given the prior predicted probability distribution μ_ν on sample paths, let $\mu^T(\cdot \,|\, h_T)$ denote the conditional probability of the future given the past – a probability distribution on $\Pi_{t=T+1}^\infty H_t$.

Theorem 2.4. *Let* $C_\nu = \{\theta : \mu_\theta \ll \mu_\nu\}$. *For all* $\theta \in C_\nu$, μ_θ^T *and* μ_ν^T *converge together in variation norm for* μ_θ-*almost all sample paths.*

The requirement of absolute continuity is very strong, since it is on the entire space of paths and not on any finite partial histories. Theorem 2.4 excludes, for instance, the case of i.i.d. coin flips where the prior ν on the parameter is absolutely continuous with respect to Lebesgue measure. An important case where Theorem 2.4 does apply is the case where ν has finite support. We emphasize that this absolute continuity condition is a *sufficient* condition. It is easy to construct examples where the convergence of posterior predictive distributions is assured yet the condition of Theorem 2.4 is violated. This theorem is an immediate consequence of the main theorem in Blackwell and Dubins (1962), which itself is a consequence of the Radon–Nikodym and Martingale convergence theorems.

2.2 Bayesian Decision Problems

Now that we have the basic results on learning from an exogenous data process, we consider environments where the data process is partially under the control of a decision maker. To illustrate the common elements in the literature we build a general decision model with learning and then specialize it to various problems.

At each date t, the decision maker chooses an action $x_t \in X$. After choosing x_t he observes $y_t \in Y$, which has a distribution conditional on the history prior to date t, his current action x_t, and parameter θ. This distribution is described by $\eta_\theta(\cdot \mid x_t, h_1, \ldots, h_{t-1})$, where $h_\tau = (x_\tau, y_\tau)$. Finally, he receives a reward $r_t \in \mathbf{R}$, which is a function of history, the observation, and the action: $r_t = u(x_t, y_t, h_1, \ldots, h_{t-1})$.

In this framework, the set of observations possible at time t is $H_t = X \times Y$. As before, the set of sample histories is $H = \Pi_{t=1}^{\infty} H_t$ and the set of partial histories to date t is $H^t = H_1 \times \cdots \times H_t$. The decision maker's history-dependent plan of action is described by a policy $\pi = (\pi_1, \pi_2, \ldots)$, that is, a sequence of Borel-measurable functions $\pi_t : H^{t-1} \to P(X)$ mapping partial histories into probability distributions on actions.

For each policy π and parameter θ, the probability $\mu_{\theta,\pi}$ on histories describing the data process is given by the composition of the decision maker's policy and the distribution η_θ of observations. The decision maker is assumed to have sufficient prior knowledge to calculate $\mu_{\theta,\pi}$ for each (θ, π). In particular, he knows the map $\theta \to \eta_\theta$. Formally, this is an innocuous assumption, but for results it is not. Anything that the decision maker is uncertain about goes in Θ, and he holds beliefs in the form of a prior probability distribution on Θ. Then, of course, the decision maker knows how the system will evolve given any θ and policy π. But there is a potential problem with this assumption. Suppose the decision maker knows everything up to the specification of a finite (or at most countable) number of parameters; that is, suppose Θ is not just a finite-dimensional set, but a set with a countable number of elements. Then we can apply the theorems in Section 2.1 to obtain convergence and predictions results. Frequently, however, we do not want to assume that the decision maker has so much prior knowledge about the environment. In many problems it is more natural to assume that the decision maker knows the environment up to the specification of a parameter from a finite-dimensional set. In this case, beliefs about parameters converge, but convergence of conditional beliefs to correct conditional beliefs is problematic. The absolute continuity condition of Theorem 2.3 will not be satisfied, and Example 2.3 shows how badly behaved predictions can be even in a one-dimensional world. In other problems we may want to allow Θ to be an infinite-dimensional space (say, all probability measures on a finite-dimensional set). This case is even more problematic since the exceptional sets (those of prior measure 0) that we have ignored can be large. Feldman (1991) has built on Freedman's (1965) analysis of the consistency of Bayes estimates to construct an example of a so-called bandit problem in which, for "most" prior beliefs (the complement of a first-category set), Bayes estimates are not consistent.

The decision maker's objective is to choose a policy π to maximize his expected discounted reward

$$E_v \left\{ E_{\mu_\theta, \pi} \left\{ \sum_{t=1}^\infty \beta^{t-1} r_t \right\} \right\},$$

where $0 \le \beta < 1$ is the discount factor. This is now a conventional nonstationary dynamic programming problem. Ignoring, for the moment, the question of existence of an optimal policy, let us suppose that the decision maker has selected policy π^* (on existence, see Hinderer 1970). To address the question of rational learning in the single-agent problem, we can now apply the results on Bayesian learning to see that beliefs converge almost surely (with respect to the prior) and to check conditions for consistency. Alternatively, in an equilibrium setting we need to solve the decision problem for each individual, find equilibria, and then apply the learning theorem. In the remainder of this section, we briefly discuss the single-agent problem in order to illustrate the known results and some issues. Learning in games and market economies will be discussed in the following sections.

2.3   *The Single-Agent Problem*

The large literature on single-agent problems with learning includes such diverse problems as the classical multi-armed bandit problems, the behavior of monopolists and perfectly competitive firms in stochastic environments, and optimal stochastic growth. We will not attempt to survey this literature. Instead, we present one problem that illustrates the basic results and points to the issues raised in Section 1 about the sensitivity of the results to the presence of intertemporal links other than belief revision. We build a simple capital accumulation model using the results of Easley and Kiefer (1988), Feldman and McLennan (1989), and McLennan (1987). El-Gamal and Sundaram (1993) observed in a similar model that including capital as an intertemporal link would simplify the analysis of asymptotic behavior of the system. Nyarko (1994a) makes a similar observation in an optimal control problem.

To fix ideas, consider a single-agent, two-good economy. The agent derives utility from her consumption of the produced good, corn, and leisure. In each period the amount of corn produced is a random function of corn saved from last period and current labor. From the individual's point of view, the randomness arises from two sources. There are identically and independently distributed shocks affecting the output and the agent is uncertain about a parameter of the production process.

The agent maximizes expected discounted utility. From her observations of inputs and output she will learn about the production process. The questions are: Does she learn the parameter and does she learn to correctly predict the distribution of output?

Let $Y \subset \mathbf{R}_+$ denote the set of potential outputs. In each period the decision maker observes the previous output $y \in Y$, then chooses the fraction $\alpha \in [0, 1]$ of output to be consumed and a labor input $\ell \in L$, a compact subset of $\mathbf{R}$. The reward is then the utility from consumption and leisure,

$$U(\alpha, y, \ell) = u(\alpha y) + v(\ell),$$

which is increasing in consumption, αy, and decreasing in ℓ. We assume that $u(\cdot)$ and $v(\cdot)$ are continuous and bounded.

That output not consumed, $(1 - \alpha)y$, and labor, ℓ, are used to produce new output through a stochastic and partially unknown technology. The density of new output $\tilde{y}$ given investment $(1 - \alpha)y$, labor ℓ, and an unknown parameter $\theta \in \Theta$ is $f(\tilde{y} \mid (1 - \alpha)y, \ell, \theta)$. We assume that $\Theta = \{\theta_1, \theta_2\}$, that f is continuous in all other variables, and that the support of f is all of Y for any $(1 - \alpha)y$, ℓ, and θ.

The decision maker does not know the value of θ. Instead, she begins with prior beliefs ν_0 on Θ and learns over time. We exclude the degenerate cases where all prior mass is concentrated on one parameter value.

This model is richer than the usual "learning model" in that two dynamical forces are at work: belief revision and capital accumulation. As a technical device to help us understand the general problem, we consider the special case in which labor is the only productive input:

$$f(\cdot \mid y, \ell, \theta) \equiv f(\cdot \mid y', \ell, \theta) \quad \text{for all } y, y' \in Y.$$

We will simply write $f(\cdot \mid \ell, \theta)$ for the production function. This is no longer a capital accumulation problem; instead, we can focus on the learning problem in isolation. In this case, the agent should consume all output in each period, and so the optimal consumption rate is $\alpha = 1$. Despite its triviality, think of this problem as an example of a Bayesian decision problem like that described in the previous section, with parameter space Θ, action space $X = L$, observation space Y, and nonrandom reward $u(y) + v(\ell)$. Now the only connection across periods is through the decision maker's beliefs, ν_T. She thus solves a dynamic programming problem with state space $P(\Theta)$, the set of probability distributions on Θ.

Although the interpretation is different, this problem is analogous to the monopolist example studied in Easley and Kiefer (1988). With the standard assumptions made there, we know that there is an optimal (stationary and deterministic) policy $\pi^*(\nu)$ describing the labor choice for any prior, as well as a *convex* value function $V(\nu)$ describing the value of the problem for any prior.

Theorem 2.5. *(1) For any initial output y_0, there is a unique, continuous, and convex solution $V^* : P(\theta) \to \mathbf{R}$ to the equation*

$$V(\nu) = \sup_{\pi} E_\nu \left\{ E_{\mu_{\pi,\theta}} \left\{ \sum_{t=1}^{\infty} \delta^t \left(u(y_{t-1}) + v(\ell_t) \right) \right\} \right\},$$

and the optimal policies are all characterized as those policies π that attain the supremum.

(2) There is a stationary and deterministic policy $\pi^* : P(\Theta) \to L$ that is optimal.

The optimal policy correspondence is upper hemicontinuous in beliefs. At any date, the optimal action is selected to maximize the sum of reward and discounted expected value. When this sum is concave in actions, the optimal action correspondence is convex-valued. Normally, in dynamic programming problems, one would make sufficient concavity assumptions to ensure that the expectation of the value function is concave in the action. However, in learning problems the value function is convex in the state.[2] Thus, in general, there is no way to generate a convex-valued action correspondence.

An application of the Bayes learning results in Section 2.1 shows that beliefs converge almost surely. The question is: Are limit beliefs consistent? The answer to this question depends upon whether "confounding policies" exist. *Confounding policies* are policies that are (a) optimal for the discount rate $\delta = 0$ and (b) such that, for some $\bar{\nu}$ in the domain, the parameter θ is not identified:

$$\pi(\bar{\nu}) = \bar{\ell}, \qquad f(\cdot | \bar{\ell}, \theta_1) = f(\cdot | \bar{\ell}, \theta_2).$$

The existence of confounding policies is important for consistency because potential limit beliefs ν_∞ and limit actions ℓ_∞ must satisfy two conditions. First, given limit beliefs, limit actions ℓ_∞ maximize one-period expected reward:

[2] Convexity is a consequence of Blackwell's (1951) theorem on the value of information.

$$r\big(\ell,v_\infty\big)=\delta\sum_\theta v_\infty\big(\theta\big)\int u\big(\tilde{y}\big)f\big(\tilde{y}\big|\ell,\theta\big)\ d\tilde{y}+v\big(\ell\big);$$

$$V^1\big(v_\infty\big)=\sup_\ell r\big(\ell,v_\infty\big)$$

$$=r\big(\ell_\infty,v_\infty\big).$$

Second, limit beliefs must put mass only on parameter values that are consistent with the data generated by the limit actions.

In any Bayes decision problem with no confounding policies, Bayes learning is necessarily consistent. If confounding policies do exist, the consistency of Bayesian learning depends upon the discount factor. If the discount factor is 0, corresponding to a completely myopic decision maker, and if prior beliefs are $v_0=\bar{v}$, then the confounding policy will choose an action at time 1 such that θ is not identified, posterior beliefs will equal prior beliefs, and so forth for all time. Easley and Kiefer (1988) prove such a theorem in a slightly different context. McLennan (1987) and Feldman and McLennan (1989) have shown that if all this is true at discount factor 0 then it will remain true for small positive discount factors. Alternatively, when the discount factor is sufficiently near 1 and information is strictly valuable, the gain from learning is large enough to compensate for a deviation from the short-run optimal quantity. Thus (according to Easley and Kiefer 1988), Bayes learning will be consistent. In summary, we have the following collection of results.

Theorem 2.6. *Suppose that* θ_1 *is the true parameter value, and suppose that* V^1 *is strictly convex. Then there is a* $\delta^*<1$ *such that, for* $1>\delta>\delta^*$, $v_\infty=\delta_{\theta_I}$ *a.s. If the policy* π *is confounding for nondegenerate beliefs* $\bar{v}$ *then there is a* $\bar{\delta}>0$ *such that, for all* $0<\delta<\bar{\delta}$ *and* $v_0=\bar{v}$, $v_t=\bar{v}$ *for all t and Bayes learning is not consistent.*

These results show that it need not be optimal for an individual to learn to form statistically correct beliefs (from the point of view of the modeler who knows θ) even when learning is feasible. If "rational expectations" is interpreted to mean that decision makers know θ, then it may be optimal *not* to learn to be rational. Alternatively, if "rational expectations" is interpreted to mean that decision makers optimally use all available information, then any Bayesian decision maker is, by hypothesis, rational. It should also be noted that, even when the individual's learning is not consistent, conditional predictions of output do converge to correct conditional predictions. This follows immediately from the definition of a confounding policy; given the individual's choice of labor input, the distribution of output is the same for all parameters in the support of his beliefs. So the individual is rational in the sense that his beliefs about the distribution of output are not contradicted by the data that he generates.

Theorem 2.6 also has implications for continuity of the optimal policy. Suppose that, as in Easley and Kiefer's monopolist example, the optimal actions given $v(\theta_1) = 0$ and $v(\theta_1) = 1$ bracket a confounding action $\bar{l}$. Then, for high discount factors, the optimal policy cannot be continuous. If it were, there would be some prior $\bar{v}$ such that $\pi(\bar{v}) = \bar{l}$. This prior would be invariant under Bayesian revision, and the monopolist would never learn. However, for high discount rates we know he must learn with probability 1, starting from any nondegenerate prior.

The potential for incomplete learning is greatly reduced if we reintroduce capital as a productive input – in other words, if we add another intertemporal link to our model. Now we must track both the labor choice and a savings choice, so the action space for the dynamic program is $X = L \times [0, 1]$. As before, an optimal stationary, deterministic policy will exist; now it takes the form $\pi: Y \times P(\theta) \to X$. In this case, confounding policies are unlikely to exist. Now, assuming that θ_1 is the true parameter value, the requirement for π to be confounding is that the set

$$A = \left\{ y: f\left(\cdot \left| \left(1 - a(y, \bar{v})\right) \right| y, \ell(y, \bar{v}), \theta_1 \right) = f\left(\cdot \left| \left(1 - a(y, \bar{v})\right) \right| y, \ell(y, \bar{v}), \theta_2 \right) \right\}$$

have full measure with respect to the density

$$f\left(\cdot \left| \left(1 - a(y, \bar{v})\right) \right| y, \ell(y, \bar{v}), \theta_1 \right)$$

for all $y \in A$. In other words, for any y in A, optimal production must land back within A with probability 1. Otherwise, at each step there would be some probability of landing outside of A and learning something about the parameter. This information would move beliefs away from $\bar{v}$. This condition is very restrictive, and is unlikely to be met in any economic problem with intertemporal connections in addition to those through beliefs. This observation is summarized in the following theorem.[3]

---

[3] A related theorem can be found in El-Gamal and Sundaram (1993), which weakens our main hypothesis yet also requires continuity of the optimal policy function. But assuming continuity is problematic, because continuity is intimately tied up with learning. In the Easley and Kiefer (1988) analysis, continuity is established only for those discount rates low enough that one could fail to learn. When Bayes learning is consistent regardless of the prior, it is easy to see in the Easley–Kiefer problem that the optimal policy *must* be discontinuous at that point in the domain of the policy function where the confounding policy fails to identify the two models.

Theorem 2.7. *Let θ_1 denote the true parameter value. Suppose that, for any nondegenerate prior belief* v, *there is a set* $A \subset Y \times L$ *of actions such that:*

(1) *there is an* $\varepsilon > 0$ *such that, for all* $y \in Y$ *and* $v \in P(\Theta)$, $((1 - \alpha(y, v))y, l(y, v)) \in A$ *with* θ_1-*probability at least* ε; *and*

(2) *there is a* $\delta > 0$ *such that, for all* $(z, l) \in A$, *the relative entropy of model* θ_1 *with respect to* θ_2 *exceeds* δ,

$$\int f\left(\tilde{y} \big| z, \ell, \theta_1\right) \log \frac{f\left(\tilde{y} \big| z, \ell, \theta_1\right)}{f\left(\tilde{y} \big| z, \ell, \theta_2\right)} d\tilde{y} > \delta.$$

Then Bayes learning is consistent.

Theorem 2.7 can be proven using the methods of Blume and Easley (1992). The idea of the theorem is that the decision maker infinitely often chooses actions that make the two models uniformly different. The condition looks unusual, but is not that hard to check. We have constructed examples of the capital accumulation problem where the condition of the theorem can be verified without knowing anything about the optimal policies at all, just by relying on features of the stochastic production technology.

We conclude that incomplete learning is possible, but delicate. The other dynamic forces working on the decision maker break her out of the learning "sink" caused by the confounding policy. In Section 5 we shall argue that, in equilibrium models with heterogeneous agents, it is even easier for other dynamical forces to overwhelm the effects of learning dynamics.

Our analysis of the single-agent decision problem has not touched on predictability. This is a consequence of the stationarity of the stochastic environment. In stationary environments, consistency makes prediction possible. In the decision problems arising from game theory, the stochastic environment may be nonstationary, and predictability emerges as a distinct separate issue. We discuss these problems in the next section.

3   Learning in Games

Learning issues are central to the interpretation of Nash equilibrium as a multi-person statistical decision theory. In this interpretation, each player solves a decision problem, and equilibrium expresses a consistency relationship between the actions of each player and the beliefs of his opponents; specifically, the support of other players' beliefs about any one player is contained in the set of best responses of that player to his own beliefs. Suppose however, that beliefs and actions are not initially configured in this fashion. Will the collection of players "learn" their way to a Nash equilibrium? Will the dynamics of posterior revision so adjust beliefs that this coordination property emerges in the course of play? This question is naturally posed in the context of repeated play when players know their own payoffs but not necessarily those of their opponents. Jordan (1991, 1995), Kalai and Lehrer (1993a, 1993b), and Nyarko (1991, 1994b) study the convergence problem in repeated games. Kalai and Lehrer provide sufficient conditions for the emergence of a kind of equilibrium play in continuation games. In this section we formulate the learning problem in games and identify some assumptions that guarantee convergence to Nash equilibrium play or beliefs. We will see that Bayes rationality by itself implies very little about asymptotic play of repeated games. In order to derive powerful conclusions from Bayes rationality, such as convergence to Nash outcomes or convergence of beliefs to Nash-like beliefs, it is necessary to make further assumptions about the joint configuration of players' prior beliefs. These assumptions must guarantee the predictability of the future play of other players, in the sense discussed in the previous section. Not surprisingly, the further belief restrictions will involve some kind of joint absolute continuity of prior beliefs. It will be obvious that these conditions are difficult to meet. Even though they are only sufficient, and not necessary, for asymptotic convergence, they leave us very skeptical about the possibility for robust convergence to Nash-like behavior.

In focusing explicitly on rational learning we rule out a large number of papers. We neglect the ad hoc learning papers, such as Fudenberg and Kreps (1988) or Marimon, McGrattan, and Sargent (1990), which either search for learning procedures that will guarantee convergence to Nash equilibrium or investigate the learning implications of some given rule whose motivation originates elsewhere. We also overlook papers that consider the role of learning as an adaptive process at work on a population of players, such as Fudenberg and Levine (1993a, 1993b). This mesh of epistemic and evolutionary reasoning we believe to be more promising than either the raw application of biological ideas to social processes or the Savage–Bayesian analysis that we now survey.

3.1   Bayesian Strategy Revision Processes

As in any sequential Bayesian decision problem, we need to identify a set of parameters, the parameter-conditional observation processes, actions, and rewards. We consider N-player strategic form games where player n has a finite set S_n of possible actions. After actions are selected, each player observes the joint action vector $s \in S = S_1 \times \cdots \times S_N$ and receives the reward $u_n(s)$. The stage game described by $(S_n, u_n)_{n=1}^N$ will be repeated infinitely many times, and player n discounts future rewards with discount factor $\beta_n \in [0, 1)$.

Most of the learning literature has focused on games with perfect monitoring and simultaneous move stage games, and we will do so here. After each stage, each player observes the choices of his opponents. At the beginning of round t, each player will have observed the sequence of play through all the preceding stages of the game. Thus, the set of sample histories for player n is $H = \Pi_{t=1}^\infty S$. The set of partial histories up to round t is $H_t = \Pi_1^{t-1} S$ for $t > 1$, and H_1 is the set containing the null history. Finally, define $H^t = \Pi_t^\infty S$ to be the "future history" beginning at date t, and let S_n^t denote the set of plays by player n at date t.

Now we will build a parameter space for the players' decision problem. Each player is completely defined by his *type*. A player's type is a specification of his utility function, discount parameter, and beliefs about the other players' types. This notion seems to have some circularity to it, since player 1's type contains his beliefs about 2's type, which in turn contains 2's beliefs about 1's type, and so forth. Mertens and Zamir (1985) have nonetheless shown that the type space can be defined in a self-consistent manner. The set of possible types for player n is denoted by T_n, with generic element τ_n. The important thing to know about the types space T_n is that we can think of a type as a vector (θ, γ), where $\theta \in \Theta$ describes the utility and discount parameters, and $\gamma \in \Gamma$ describes the "belief hierarchy." (We will assume that Θ is a Polish space; throughout the remainder of the paper we will neglect to mention necessary measurability assumptions.) Thus $T_n = \Theta_n \times \Gamma_n$, where Θ_n is the set of potential utility functions and discount parameters for player n. Let $T = T_1 \times \cdots \times T_N$ denote the space of joint types.

Nyarko (following Jordan) has found it useful to distinguish several levels of prior beliefs. For Nyarko, a prior belief is a probability distribution μ_n on $T \times H$. An "interim prior" is the probability distribution $\mu_n(\cdot \mid \gamma_n)$. The "prior" is constructed before players know who they are. The "interim prior" contains the beliefs held by player n when he knows who he is but before any play has occurred. We say "contains" and not "is" because $\mu_n(\cdot \mid \gamma_n)$ is a distribution over the future actions of all players, including player n. At stage 0, the marginal of this distribution on the actions of players other than n at stage 1 represents n's beliefs about how others will behave in the first round of play.

Although we are accustomed in game theory to thinking of the interim prior as the initial set of beliefs for each player's decision problem, it is useful for the learning problem to distinguish beliefs ex ante and ex post the arrival of information about type. The key to proving learning results is to tie players' decision problems together. We will see some learning results that do this through the interim prior beliefs, and others that place hypotheses on the (unconditional) priors.

Every player in the strategic situation we have just described is solving a sequential decision problem. These problems are coupled together, because the solution to player 1's problem determines what player 2 sees. The simultaneous solutions to the decision problem are described by a *Bayesian strategy revision process*, a concept first introduced by Jordan. Our formulation differs slightly from his. If μ and v are measures on spaces A and B, respectively, then $\mu \otimes v$ denotes the product measure on the product space $A \times B$.

Definition 3.1. A *Bayesian strategy revision process* (BSRP) is a collection of probability distributions $\{\mu_n\}_{n=0}^{N}$ on $T \times H$ such that:

(1) for $n \geq 1$ and μ_n-almost all types (θ, γ), $\text{Proj}_\Theta \mu_n(\cdot \mid \gamma) = \delta_\theta$;
(2) for $n \geq 1$, μ_n-a.s., $(\gamma_n, h_t, s_{nt}) \in \Gamma_n \times H_t \times S_n^t$,

$$s_n \in \underset{s_n^{t+1}}{\arg\max}\, E_{\mu_n}\left\{u_n\left(\cdot, \tilde{s}_{-n}^{t+1}, \tilde{\theta}_n\right)\middle|\gamma_n, h_t\right\};$$

(3) for $n \geq 1$, $\text{Proj}_{S_{-n}^t}\mu_n\{\cdot \mid \gamma_n, h_t\}$ is almost surely a product;
(4) for $n \geq 1$, $\text{Proj}_{T_n}\mu_0 = \text{Proj}_{T_n}\mu_n$; and, for all t,

$$\text{Proj}_{S^t}\mu_0\left(\cdot\middle| \gamma, h_t\right) = \underset{n>0}{\otimes} \text{Proj}_{S_n^t} \mu_n\left(\cdot\middle|\gamma_n, h_t\right).$$

The probability distribution μ_0 is the actual joint distribution of types and actions. Condition 1 states that each player knows her own payoff function. Condition 2 states that each player chooses actions to maximize her expected utility given her beliefs. Condition 3 states that each player believes the actions of her opponents to be chosen independently conditional upon history and her type. Condition 3 without conditioning on γ_n would be a much stronger statement – close to saying that types are independent across players. Notice that all a BSRP requires is that players maximize with respect to their beliefs; nothing has yet been said about the correctness of those beliefs.

3.2   The Content of Bayesian Learning

In general, requiring decision makers to be good Bayesians imposes few constraints on strategy selection, as the following theorem shows. Let D denote the set of all distributions on $T \times H$ such that, if $\mu \in D$, then almost all conditional distributions $\text{Proj}_H\mu(\cdot \mid \gamma_n)$ are processes of players' choices that are independent across players and dates, and such that $\text{Proj}_{S_n}\mu(\cdot\,|\,\gamma_n)$ is almost surely an undominated mixed strategy in the stage game for player n of type τ_n.

Theorem 3.1. *If* $v \in D$, *then there is a BSRP* $(\mu_0, \mu_1, \cdots, \mu_N)$ *with* $\mu_0 = v$.

Proof. Constructing such a BSRP is just a matter of constructing beliefs for each player n so as to make the policy $\text{Proj}_{S_n} v(\cdot\,|\,\theta)$ optimal. If p_n^t is the distribution of n's play at stage t (from v), then since it is undominated there is a distribution q_n^t on the choices of the other players for which p_n^t is a best response. Let $\mu_n(\cdot\,|\,\theta_n)$ be the product of $p_n^t \otimes q_n^t$ over all t. This is the basic idea, but the actual construction is a bit more complicated due to the fact that one must make everything measurable with respect to θ_n. This can be done with the aid of a measurable selection theorem from the correspondence whose image is the set of beliefs that make p_n^t a best response for θ_n. So $\mu_n(\cdot\,|\,\theta_n)$ defines a transition probability. Integrating with respect to the marginal distribution of v on Θ_n gives v_n. $\square$

If we replace D with the set of all un-weakly dominated strategies, the converse is true for sufficiently low discount rates.

Theorem 3.1 demonstrates that the hypothesis of Bayesian learning in games has, by itself, little content. Whatever power the Bayesian hypothesis possesses will only emerge when restrictions are placed on the nature of the Bayesian's beliefs. This power will only appear asymptotically, since the Bayesian hypothesis puts few restrictions on beliefs arising from small numbers of observations.

It is evident from Section 2 that posterior beliefs on opponents' types, and posterior beliefs on sequences of play, will converge to some limit beliefs. In fact, under some mild assumptions, posterior beliefs on play histories will converge almost surely to point mass at the true history. But this has no implications for play, as the following example shows.

Example 3.1. Consider a two-person repeated game for which, in the stage game, player 2 has two strategies A and B. Suppose player 1 correctly believes that player 2's strategy (not just actions) is a fixed sequence independent of history. Suppose the probability distribution representing prior beliefs is product measure with parameter p. In this case, Bayes learning is consistent. Player 1 will ultimately assign probability 1 to the actual strategy employed by player 2. But at each stage he will always predict A with probability p and B with probability $1 - p$.

Example 3.1 simply places Example 2.2 in a game-theoretic context. It shows that convergence of beliefs about strategies does not imply convergence in beliefs about strategies in continuation games.

3.3   *The Conditional Harsanyi Hypothesis*

Learning about strategies in a continuation game is a prediction problem rather than a consistency problem. To achieve consistency of predictions of future play by Bayesian learners, restrictions on prior beliefs must be assumed. Kalai and Lehrer's (1993a) approach to this issue uses the Blackwell–Dubins Theorem presented in Section 2. We will present the Kalai–Lehrer analysis within the framework of BSRPs in order to understand the nature of the restrictions on prior beliefs required by this approach.

The appropriate absolute continuity condition requires that, for almost all types, the actual distribution of play be absolutely continuous with respect to each player's beliefs. If this is so, then the Blackwell–Dubins theorem states that the conditional distributions on future play (given histories and types) must converge. This approach requires belief restrictions on interim prior beliefs. We call these restrictions the *conditional Harsanyi hypothesis*.

Conditional Harsanyi Hypothesis.   *For all* n, $Proj_H \mu_0(\cdot \mid \gamma_n) \ll Proj_H \mu_n(\cdot \mid \gamma_n)$ μ_0 *almost surely.*

The conditional Harsanyi hypothesis has two important consequences for beliefs. First, fix the type of player 1. The actual distribution of play for all types of player 2 must be absolutely continuous with respect to player 1's beliefs. Thus, the actual play of player 2 cannot change too much with respect to 2's type. In particular, this will require that 2's play cannot vary too much with respect to his type. For instance, suppose that player 1 believes, given his type, that the frequency with which player 2 is going to play "left" converges almost surely to 1/2. Then actual play will also require this *for almost all possible values of player 2's type*. The second observation is that the connection between player 1's beliefs and player 2's actions requires that player 2's beliefs be configured in certain ways. Suppose this configuration requires that the limit frequency of "up" for player 1 is 3/4. Then this requirement must be satisfied by the actual play of player 1. In other words, beliefs must initially satisfy a kind of consistency condition not too different from the consistency required by Nash equilibrium.

3.4   Belief Convergence for Myopic Players

The Kalai–Lehrer result is easiest to see in those BSRPs where the discount factor for each player is almost surely zero. The Kalai–Lehrer results state a conclusion about how the actual path of play far out in the game is almost like that of an approximate Nash equilibrium. This is complicated to state, but there are some clean conclusions to be had about the limit behavior of beliefs about future play: They converge to Nash equilibrium beliefs.[4] Let $M_n(\theta_n) = \{\sigma_1 \otimes \cdots \otimes \sigma_N \in P(S) : \sigma_n$ is a best response to $\sigma_{-n}\}$. The Nash equilibria for the single-stage game are $N(\theta) = \cap_n M_n(\theta_n)$. Let $\| \cdot \|$ denote the variation norm on the appropriate space of measures.

Theorem 3.2. *Suppose that the BSRP $(\mu_n)_{n=0}^N$ satisfies the conditional Harsanyi hypothesis. Then*

$$\mu_0\left\{(\gamma, h_\infty): \left\| Proj_{S^t}\mu_n\left(\cdot \mid \gamma_n, h_t\right) - Proj_{S^t}\mu_0\left(\cdot \mid \gamma, h_t\right) \right\| \to 0 \right\} = 1$$

and

$$\mu_0\left\{(\gamma, h_\infty): \left\| Proj_{S^t}\mu_n\left(\cdot \mid \gamma_n, h_t\right) - N(\theta) \right\| \to 0 \quad for\ all\ t \right\} = 1.$$

Proof. The second statement follows from the first and part (2) of the BSRP definition, which states that

$$\mu_0\left\{(\gamma, h_\infty): Proj_{S^{t+1}}\mu_n\left(\cdot \mid \gamma_n, h_t\right) \in M_n(\theta_n) \quad for\ all\ t \right\} = 1.$$

The first statement is a consequence of the conditional Harsanyi hypothesis and the Blackwell–Dubins theorem.   □

Requirement (1) of the definition of a BSRP is unnecessary. Theorem 3.2 can be extended to include games with incomplete information about one's own type. We have reported an example of this in Blume and Easley (1993).

3.5   Subjective Equilibrium

When the discount factor is positive, matters are more complicated because at any decision node the entire future course of play, and not just the current play, is payoff-relevant. Again the Blackwell–Dubins theorem will imply that limit predictions are correct. But this does not

---

[4] It may be the case, however, that the distribution of play does not converge to a mixed strategy Nash equilibrium profile. See Jordan (1991, 1995) for a discussion of this point.

mean that each player eventually knows the other players' strategies, since information about "off-path play" may never be observed. It does imply that limit beliefs are stable in the sense that subsequent information gives no cause to revise them. Kalai and Lehrer (1993b) have introduced the concept of *subjective equilibrium* to summarize the notion of best responding to beliefs that correctly predict the course of play.[5] Here is the definition for a finite game.

Definition 3.2. A *subjective equilibrium* (SE) is a strategy profile–prediction profile 2N-tuple $(\sigma_n, \pi^n)_{n=1}^N$, where $\sigma_n \in P(S_n)$ is player n's strategy and $\pi^n \in P(S_{-n})$ is player n's (product) beliefs about the play of players $m \neq n$, such that:

(1) each σ_n is a best response to π^n; and
(2) for all n, $\sigma_1 \otimes \cdots \otimes \sigma_N = \sigma_n \times \pi^n$.

For repeated games, the definition is essentially the same, but more notation is required. Let $F_n = \{(f^1, \ldots) : f^t : H_t \to P(S_n)\}$ denote strategies for player n. Let $F = F_1 \times \cdots \times F_N$. If v is a probability distribution on F, let $\sigma(v)$ denote its (Kuhn-equivalent) strategy in F. Let $v(f) \in P(H)$ denote the distribution on play induced by strategy profile f. Finally, define

$$u_n(\theta_n, h_\infty) = \sum_{t=1}^{\infty} \delta_n(\theta_n)^{t-1} u_n(\theta_n, s_t),$$

$$v_n(\theta_n, f) = E_{v(f)}\{u_n(\theta_n, \tilde{h}_\infty)\}.$$

Definition 3.3. A subjective equilibrium for a repeated game is a strategy profile–prediction profile 2N-tuple $(f_n, g^n)_{n=1}^N$, where $f_n \in F_n$ is player n's strategy and $g^n = (f^{nm})_{m \neq n}$ $(f^{nm} \in F_m)$ is the Kuhn representation of player n's beliefs about the play of players $m \neq n$, such that:

(1) for all n, each f_n is a best response to g^n: $v_n(\theta_n, f^n, g^n) \geq v_n(\theta_n, f'^n, g^n)$ for all $f'^n \in F_n$; and
(2) for all n, $v(f^n, g^n) = v(f)$.

Notice that the conditional distributions $\text{Proj}_{S_n^t} \mu_n\{\cdot \mid \gamma_n, h_t\}$ are a *plan* for player n. They do not define a *strategy* for player n in the traditional sense because the conditional expectations given unreached nodes are not well-defined. These conditional distributions can be extended to all of $T_n \times H_t$, and a collection of these extensions is a strategy. However, these extensions are somewhat arbitrary, and this is why convergence will be to a subjective equilibrium and not to a Nash equilibrium.

---

[5] Kalai and Lehrer originally called this concept "private beliefs equilibrium."

In two-person repeated normal-form games with perfect monitoring (this excludes the multi-armed bandit problem), the set of subjective equilibrium outcomes and the set of Nash equilibrium outcomes coincide. This is a consequence of Kuhn's theorem, which states that beliefs over strategies are themselves equivalent to strategies. We will state and prove this theorem for the trivial case of finite games; it can be extended to repeated games with perfect monitoring.

Theorem 3.3. *Consider a two-person game, and let $(\pi_1, \pi_2, \pi^1, \pi^2)$ be a subjective equilibrium. Then the prediction profile pair (π^1, π^2) is a Nash equilibrium, and $v(\pi_1, \pi_2) = v(\pi^1, \pi^2)$.*

Proof. Let R_n denote the collection of information sets belonging to player n that are reached in the equilibrium (π_1, π_2). Notice first that the π^n can be represented by strategies (Kuhn's theorem), and $\pi^n | R_n = \pi_n |$ R_n. Since the two strategy pairs agree on all reached information sets, $v(\pi_1, \pi_2) = v(\pi^1, \pi^2)$. Let $V(\pi, \pi^2, \theta_1)$ denote the expected return to player 1 from playing $\pi \in \Pi_1$ conditional upon his type against strategy π^2. Then $V(\pi^1, \pi^2, \theta_1) = V(\pi_1, \pi^2, \theta_1)$ since π^1 and π_1 coincide on R_1. Since π_1 is a best response to π^2, so is π^1. $\square$

The conclusion of Theorem 3.3 remains true for general N-player normal-form games and, more generally, multi-stage games with observable actions, when the beliefs are symmetric in the sense that any two players i and j share common beliefs about what k will play, and when each player's beliefs about the strategic choice of the other players are independent. Even when the symmetry condition fails, the independence hypothesis guarantees a related conclusion: There is a Nash equilibrium strategy profile $(\pi'_n)_{n=1}^N$ such that

$$\mu\big(\pi'_1, \dots, \pi'_n\big) = \mu\big(\pi_1, \dots, \pi_n\big) = \mu\Big(\pi_n, \big(\pi^k\big)_{k \neq n}\Big).$$

In general N-player games there may be subjective equilibria whose outcomes are not Nash equilibrium outcomes. See Blume and Easley (1993) for an example.

3.6   *Convergence to Subjective Equilibria*

The notion of BSRPs defined in Section 3.1 is inadequate for discussing dynamic games, because conditional distributions from μ_n of future play of player n's opponents, given a potential deviation by player n, may not be well-defined. This does not matter for myopic players because future play is payoff-irrelevant, but it does matter when discount rates factors are positive. We will use the same term (BSRP) to refer to the equilibrium concept with and without inclusion of repeated game strategies. The relevant definition should be clear from the context.

Definition 3.4. A *Bayesian strategy revision process* (BSRP) is a collection of probability distributions $\{\mu_n\}_{n=0}^N$ on $T \times F \times H$ such that:

(0) for $n \geq 1$ and μ_n-almost all, $\mathrm{Proj}_H \mu_n(\cdot \mid f) = \nu(f)$;

(1) for $n \geq 1$ and μ_n-almost all types (θ, γ), $\mathrm{Proj}_\Theta \mu_n(\cdot \mid \gamma) = \delta_\theta$;

(2) for $n \geq 1$, μ_n-a.s., $(\gamma_n, h_t, f_n) \in \Gamma_n \times H_t \times F_n$,

$$f_n \in \underset{F_n}{\mathrm{argmax}}\, E_{\mu_n}\left\{ E_{\nu(f_n, f_{-n})}\left\{ \sum_{r=t+1}^{\infty} \delta_n\left(\tilde{\theta}_n\right)^r u_n\left(\theta_n, s_r\right) \right\} \middle| \gamma_n, h_t \right\}$$

(3) for $n \geq 1$, $\mathrm{Proj}_{F_{-n}} \mu_n\{\cdot \mid \gamma_n, h_t\}$ is almost surely a product;

(4) for $n \geq 1$, $\mathrm{Proj}_{T_n} \mu_0 = \mathrm{Proj}_{T_n} \mu_n$; and, for all t,

$$\mathrm{Proj}_{S^t} \mu_0\left(\cdot \middle| \gamma, h_t\right) = \underset{n>0}{\otimes} \mathrm{Proj}_{S_n^t} \mu_n\left(\cdot \middle| \gamma_n, h_t\right).$$

The interpretation of these conditions is exactly as before; they have just been rewritten to accommodate the present payoff-relevance of future play.

Bayesian strategy revision processes and SEs are very different kinds of objects. We will ultimately show that, under some conditions, BSRPs asymptotically "look like" subjective equilibria. We mean this in the sense that the beliefs about the future and the play in the BSRP satisfy the SE conditions. The following lemma is an immediate consequence of the definitions.

Lemma 3.1. *Suppose $(\mu_n)_{n=0}^N$ is a Bayesian strategy revision process such that μ_0-almost surely,*

$$\mathrm{Proj}_{S^t} \mu_n\left(\cdot \middle| \gamma_n, h_t\right) = \mathrm{Proj}_{S^t} \mu_0\left(\cdot \middle| \gamma, h_t\right). \tag{3.1}$$

Then $(\sigma(\mathrm{Proj}_F \mu_n(\cdot \mid \sigma_n)))_{n=1}^N$ is a subjective equilibrium.

Bayesian strategy revision processes have players maximizing given their beliefs and information, and the hypothesis of Lemma 3.1 states that each player correctly predicts the actual distribution of play.

Our version of the Kalai–Lehrer theorem states that expectations over strategies of weak subsequential limits of BSRPs satisfying the conditional Harsanyi hypothesis are SEs.

Theorem 3.4.   *Suppose that the Bayesian strategy revision process* $(\mu_n)_{n=0}^N$
satisfies the conditional Harsanyi hypothesis. Then

$$\mu_0\left(\left(\tau, h_\infty, f\right): \left\|\mathrm{Proj}_{H^t}\mu_n\!\left(\cdot\,\middle|\,\gamma_n, h_t\right) - \mathrm{Proj}_{H^t}\mu_0\!\left(\cdot\,\middle|\,\gamma, h_t\right)\right\| \to 0\right) = 1.$$

Let $(\mu_n^*)_{n=0}^N$ *denote a collection of measures such that: (1)* $(\mu_n^*)_{n=1}^N$ *is a weak
subsequential limit of the sequence*

$$\left\{\left(\mu_n\!\left(\cdot\,\middle|\,\gamma_n, h_t\right)\right)_{n=1}^N\right\}_{t=0}^\infty ;$$

(2) $\mathrm{Proj}_T\,\mu_n^* = \mathrm{Proj}_T\,\mu_0$; *and (3) for all* t, $\mathrm{Proj}_{S^t}\,\mu_n^*(\cdot\,|\,\gamma)$ *are constructed
from the* μ_n^* *as in condition (4) of the definition of a Bayesian strategy
revision process. Then* μ_0-*almost surely,* $\sigma(\mathrm{Proj}_F\,\mu_n^*(\cdot\,|\,\gamma_n))_{n=1}^N$ *is a subjective
equilibrium.*

Proof. The first statement follows from the Blackwell–Dubins theorem.
To prove the second statement we observe that, as a consequence of the
first statement, any subsequential limit satisfies equation (3.1). Thus the
claim will follow from Lemma 3.1 once it is shown that the limit is a
BSRP. Conditions (1), (3), and (4) of the definition are clearly preserved
under weak limits. We need to show that Condition (2) is preserved as
well.

Lemma 3.2.   *Let* $\{\mu_n^0\}_{n=0}^\infty$ *be a BSRP, and let* $\{(\mu_n^t)_{n=0}^N\}_{t=1}^\infty$ *be a sequence of
BSRPs. Let* $K \subset T$ *denote the set of types for which*

$$\lim_{t\to\infty}\left(\mathrm{Proj}_{H_\infty}\,\mu_n^t\!\left(\cdot\,\middle|\,\gamma_n\right)\right)_{n=1}^N = \left(\mathrm{Proj}_{H_\infty}\,\mu_n^0\!\left(\cdot\,\middle|\,\gamma_n\right)\right)_{n=1}^N.$$

Then, for all $\gamma \in K$ *and* n, $\mathrm{Proj}_{H_\infty}\,\mu_n^0(\cdot\,|\,\gamma_n)$ *satisfies condition (2).*

Proof. Condition (2) states that each player is solving a discounted
dynamic programming problem: that the conditional distributions Proj_{S_n}
$\mu_n(\cdot\,|\,\gamma_n, h_t)$ are an optimal solution to a dynamic programming problem
specified in condition (2). A characterization of optimal plans is that for
all $\varepsilon > 0$ there is an R such that, for all $r > R$, the optimal plan gives an
ε-optimal solution to the dynamic programming problem with horizon r.
The horizon length R can be chosen with reference only to the discount
factor and utility function, and independent of the state transition rule.
Thus R can be chosen for each ε uniformly in the μ_n^t. We will show that
this condition is preserved in the limit.

  The sets H_n are finite, and so weak convergence of the marginal dis-
tributions $\mathrm{Proj}_{H_r}\mu_n^t(\cdot\,|\,\gamma_n)$ implies norm convergence. Thus, for all $s < t$, the

conditional probabilities $\text{Proj}_{S_{-n}^{s+1}} \mu_n^t(\cdot \mid \gamma_n, h_s)$ converge. Let $v_n^t(r)$ denote the optimal value for the r horizon problem for player n whose transition rule is given by the conditional distributions from μ_n^t. As a consequence of norm continuity, $\lim_{t \to \infty} v_n^t(r) = v_n^0(r)$ for all r. Then, given $\varepsilon > 0$, choose $r > R$. The value of the plan $\{\text{Proj}_{S_n} \mu_n(\cdot \mid \gamma_n, h_s)_{s < r}\}$ for the r-horizon problem is at least $v_n^t(r) - \varepsilon$. Since the value of the plan is clearly continuous in $\text{Proj}_{H,t} \mu_n^t(\cdot \mid \gamma_n)$, and since the value of the problem is continuous in t, it follows that the plan $\{\text{Proj}_{S_n} \mu_n^0(\cdot \mid \gamma_n, h_s)_{s < r}\}$ is ε-optimal for the r-horizon problem with transitions $\text{Proj}_{S_{-n}^{s+1}} \mu_n^0(\cdot \mid \gamma_n, h_s)$ for $s < r$. For all $\varepsilon > 0$ there is an R such that for all $r > R$ this plan is ε-optimal for the r-horizon problem, so this plan is optimal and hence condition (2) is satisfied. This proves the lemma and the theorem. $\quad\square$

3.7 Other Learning Results

Much of what is known about rational learning as a device for achieving equilibrium comes from Kalai and Lehrer. Another important body of work on the equilibrium dynamics of repeated games played by Bayesian players comes from Jordan (1991, 1995). Jordan addresses the question of whether the sequence of Bayes equilibria converges to a Nash equilibrium for the underlying game. Jordan's framework has been used by Nyarko (1991, 1994b) in an analysis that is conceptually more closely related to Kalai and Lehrer's work. Nyarko replaces the conditional Harsanyi hypothesis with a weaker assumption, the Harsanyi hypothesis, that requires absolute continuity only of players' prior beliefs rather than almost-sure absolute continuity of type-conditional beliefs.

Harsanyi Hypothesis. *For all* n, $\text{Proj}_H \mu_0(\cdot) \ll \text{Proj}_H \mu_n(\cdot)\mu_0$ *almost surely.*

Again the goal is to characterize the asymptotic behavior of BSRPs. We will summarize these results for the zero–discount factor case. A sensible version of part (2) of the following theorem is not yet known for positive discount factors.

Suppose that players' types are independently distributed. The main result is that, for almost all type profiles $\gamma = (\gamma_1, \ldots, \gamma_N)$, the conditional distribution of beliefs on future play *given history, but not types*, converges weakly to a Nash equilibrium of the repeated game with type profile γ. If the type distribution is not a product, then the limit of the conditional distribution of beliefs on future play given history is a correlated equilibrium. Let $C(\theta)$ denote the set of all probability distributions on H_∞ that are distributions of play arising from the correlated equilibria of the game with characteristic parameters $\theta = (\theta_1, \ldots, \theta_N)$. Let

$$G = \left\{ (\tau, h_\infty) : \text{Proj}_{s^{t+1}}\, \mu_n\left(\cdot\,|h_t\right) \to C(\theta) \text{ for all } n \right\},$$

where limit means weak-convergence limit. Let $\alpha(\cdot\,|h_t)$ denote the empirical distribution of play through date t. Let

$$F = \left\{ (\tau, h_\infty) \in G : \mu_n\left(\cdot\,|h_t\right) - \alpha\left(\cdot\,|h_t\right) \to 0 \right\},$$

again with weak convergence. The following theorem is proven in Nyarko (1994b).

Theorem 3.5. *Suppose that the Bayesian strategy revision process* $(\mu_n)_{n=0}^N$ *satisfies the Harsanyi hypothesis. Then*:

(1) $\mu_0(G) = 1$; *and*
(2) $\mu_0(F) = 1$.

If players' types are independent, then correlated equilibrium can be replaced with Nash equilibrium. It is hard to interpret these results as statements about limits of players' beliefs, because players' beliefs are formed by conditioning on their type as well as the history of play. The one case where such an interpretation is possible is when types are independently distributed. In the language of BSRPs, this is the requirement that the projection onto T of the distribution μ_0 is a product. In this case the conditional distribution of future play given history and type is type-independent, and so the limiting distributions measured by the Jordan and Nyarko theorems are the belief distributions of the players.

Nonetheless, because of Theorem 3.5 (2), these results provide an important nonepistemic foundation for Nash and correlated equilibrium that is distinct from the epistemic hypothesis explored by Kalai and Lehrer. Nyarko (1994b) has proven that, in a BSRP satisfying the Harsanyi condition, the *empirical distribution of play* converges to the limit-correlated or Nash equilibrium. Thus these equilibrium concepts are justified as descriptions of the average behavior of play emerging from the process of active learning. This does not justify Nash or correlated equilibrium as the stable limit of players' actions as they jointly learn about the play of each other. Instead, it justifies these equilibrium concepts as an observable feature of play even though player choices never settle down in the stronger sense described by Kalai and Lehrer.

The Harsanyi hypothesis required by Jordan and Nyarko is significantly weaker than the conditional Harsanyi hypothesis required for Kalai–Lehrer style results. It is not hard to build examples of BSRPs similar to Example 3.1 for which the conditional Harsanyi hypothesis fails and yet the Harsanyi hypothesis holds. Nonetheless, it seems intuitive that the set of BSRPs satisfying the Harsanyi hypothesis is small.

Hypotheses such as the Harsanyi hypothesis and the conditional Harsanyi hypothesis should be viewed as equilibrium conditions. They are requirements on the consistency of beliefs with play of the game. The existence issue is already settled: a repeated-game Nash equilibrium can be described as a BSRP satisfying the conditional Harsanyi hypothesis. But if the only environments in which learning is possible are those in which all the necessary learning about equilibria (as opposed to inferring within an equilibrium) has already taken place, then the Bayesian approach has nothing to offer as an epistemic foundation for Nash equilibrium.

The important question to ask is then how rich, or how large, is the set of prior beliefs that generate asymptotically consistent predictions. This question has been addressed directly by Nachbar (1997). Space does not permit rewriting his results in the framework of BSRPs, but this can be done. He considers beliefs in a class of repeated two-by-two games (including hawk–dove, chicken, and battle of the sexes) where the strategic interaction is not trivial. He requires that beliefs permit optimization: a best response to player 1's beliefs about player 2 is in the support of player 2's beliefs, and vice versa. He also requires that beliefs assure prediction: if repeated game strategy σ_1 is in the support of player 2's beliefs about player 1 and σ_2 is in the support of player 1's beliefs about player 2, then both players learn to predict the continuation path of play. These two properties are satisfied by any Nash equilibrium, where beliefs are certain knowledge of one's opponents' strategies. But are there richer beliefs, with larger supports, where prediction is assured and optimization is permitted? If the support of each player's beliefs is all possible strategies of her opponents, then either prediction or optimality (or both) will fail.

Nachbar gives a more restricted diversity condition, which again is inconsistent with the simultaneous satisfaction of predictability and optimality. In chicken, for example, the diversity condition requires that, for each player's beliefs, along with every mixed strategy in the support of the belief distribution is a pure strategy in the support of the mixed strategy; and that the supports of the beliefs (although not the beliefs themselves) are identical for the two players. In many games it is possible to have beliefs with countable support that satisfy the diversity condition. Suppose optimization were permitted; then the absolute continuity condition must hold and thus prediction would be possible. This contradicts the theorem, so we can conclude that optimization could not be permitted by such beliefs. Although a sharp characterization of BSRPs is not yet at hand, Nachbar's results conclusively demonstrate that the set of BSRPs satisfying the conditional Harsanyi hypothesis is not very rich.

4   Learning in Competitive Economies

The learning problem in competitive economies shares many features with the problem of learning in games. In this section we formulate the problem and provide a positive, but limited, result. As in the previous section, our analysis draws heavily on the work by Jordan (1991, 1995) and Nyarko (1991, 1994b). Arrow and Green (1973), Townsend (1978), Blume and Easley (1984), Bray and Kreps (1987), and Feldman (1987) all pose the same question that we pose here. All of these authors use equilibrium models with rational learning and so examine the long-run implications of learning within a "grand rational expectations equilibrium" (Bray and Kreps 1987). Kalai and Lehrer (1990) provide an analysis of learning in competitive economies which does not use conditioning on contemporaneous data and which focuses on learning about an equilibrium rather than learning within an equilibrium. Other than not conditioning on contemporaneous data, Kalai and Lehrer's analysis is, at a formal level, virtually identical to the analysis presented here. The primary difference lies in interpretation.

We consider a simple version of the dynamic economy analyzed by Radner (1972). Our economy has a sequence of incomplete markets; at each date there will be a spot market for the single physical good and a market for one-period–forward delivery of the good. To keep things simple, we do not consider uncertainty or differential information about asset payoffs. The market structure and endowments are fixed and known, but various preference profiles are possible. Given Radner's assumptions, our economy would have an equilibrium of plans, prices, and price expectations for each specification of preferences. Each of these equilibria specifies (ignoring issues of multiplicity) a sequence of prices that Radner's consumers are assumed to perfectly forecast. Suppose, however, that consumers do not initially know the price sequence. They would then learn about future prices by watching the evolution of past prices. This learning problem could be modeled with individuals learning directly about price sequences as in Kalai and Lehrer. We take an alternative approach and assume that consumers do not know preferences but instead learn about them over time. (If they knew each other's preferences as well as the map from preferences to prices then they could, in principle, compute the price sequence.)

Upon observing a price in any period, each individual revises his beliefs about other's preferences and about future prices. As we allow individuals to condition on contemporaneous prices, we immediately encounter the problem addressed by Radner in his 1979 paper on rational expectations equilibria (REE). Current prices may reveal to individuals information about the preferences of others, about others' beliefs about the preference profile, and so on; that is, current prices may reveal information about types. To infer this information, and to use it in forecasting future prices, each consumer needs a model of the relationship between types and prices. If individual's models are correct, and markets clear at each date, we have a sequence of REEs. We will not assume that individuals have correct models, but in order to learn they will need to put positive probability on the correct price system given knowledge of the type vector.

We consider an economy with I consumers. At each of an infinite sequence of dates indexed by t, consumer i receives a positive endowment e^i of the single physical good. The amount of the good consumed by i at date t is denoted c_t^i and her forward purchase for delivery of the good at date $t + 1$ is denoted f_t^i. We assume that individuals at date 1 have no endowment of forward contracts, that is, $f_0^i = 0$. Finally, we let $p_t \in P = \mathbf{R}_+^1$ be the price of the forward contract at t in terms of the numeraire consumption good.

We suppose that each consumer knows the functional form of everyone's utility function $U^i(c^i, \theta^i)$, where c^i is a consumption sequence for i and $\theta^i \in \Theta^i$ is a utility parameter for i. Each consumer knows her own parameter, but does not know other consumers' parameters. Consumer i's type, τ^i, specifies her parameter θ^i and hierarchy of beliefs about the joint parameter vector $\theta = (\theta^1, \ldots, \theta^I)$, just as in the previous section. Let T^i be the set of possible types for i and $T = \Pi_{i=1}^I T^i$.

At date t, consumer i will know the prices $p^t = (p_1, \ldots, p_t)$ through date t, the amount f_{t-1}^i of the good that she has contracted for, and her own type τ^i. Given this data, i must decide how much to consume and how many forward contracts to purchase or sell. Let i's date-t demand correspondence be $(C_t^i(p^t, f_{t-1}^i, \tau^i), F_t^i(p^t, f_{t-1}^i, \tau^i))$. A plan $(C^i, F^i) = (C_t^i, F_t^i)_{t=1}^\infty$ for i specifies her demands at each date. Given a price system $p^\infty = (p_1, p_2, \ldots) \in P^\infty$, the set of feasible plans for consumer i is

$$\Gamma\left(p^{\infty}\right) = \left\{\left(C^i, F^i\right) : c_t^i + p_t f_t^i = e^i + f_{t-1}^i, c_t^i \geq 0,\right.$$

$$\left.\text{for each } \left(c_t^i, f_t^i\right) \in \left(F_t^i, C_t^i\right), \forall t\right\}.$$

Consumer i will choose a plan to maximize her expected utility. The maximization hypothesis is included in the following definition of an equilibrium process.

Let $f_t = (f_t^1, \ldots, f_t^l)$ and $c_t = (c_t^1, \ldots, c_t^l)$. The data that an outside observer could see at date t is $h_t = (p_t, f_t, c_t) \in H = P \times \mathfrak{R}^l \times \mathfrak{R}_+^l$. Let the history of the process to date t be $h^t = (h_1, \ldots, h_t) \in H^t$, and let H^{∞} be the set of histories.

Definition 4.1. A *Bayesian equilibrium process* is a collection of probabilities $(\mu^i)_{i=0}^I$ on $T \times H^{\infty}$ such that the following conditions hold.

(1) For each i, $\tau^i = \text{Proj}_T \mu^i(\cdot \mid \tau^i)$.

(2) For each i, μ^i almost surely, $(c_t^i, f_t^i) \in (C_t^i(p^t, f_{t-1}^i, \tau^i), F_t^i(p^t, f_{t-1}^i, \tau^i))$, where

$$\left(C^i, F^i\right) \in \text{argmax } E\left(U\left(c^i, \theta^i\right) \mid \tau^i\right), \quad \left(C^i, F^i\right) \in \Gamma\left(p^{\infty}\right).$$

(3) Prices evolve according to the price system p^{∞} where, for all t:
(a) $\text{Proj}_{P^{\infty}} \mu^0(p^{\infty} \mid \tau) = 1$, where $\tau = (\tau^1, \ldots, \tau^I)$; and
(b) markets clear at each date,

$$\sum_i c_t^i - e^i = 0, \quad \sum_i f_t^i = 0.$$

There are several elements of this definition that need comment. First, μ^i represents i's beliefs on types cross histories. Part (1) simply restates the definition that i's type gives her beliefs on the type space. Part (2) of the definition requires each consumer to maximize her expected utility using her beliefs. Finally, part (3) specifies a true equilibrium price process. The artificial agent 0 has beliefs μ^0 that place probability 1 on the price system that is selected given the consumer's types. Thus, we have assumed that a sequence of equilibria exist for each possible draw of types. For standard utility functions, proving that a Bayesian equilibrium process exists is straightforward. Just let each μ^i place probability 1 on the same price system and apply the analysis from Radner (1972). Proving that an equilibrium exists for nontrivial beliefs would be difficult.

To demonstrate that our definition of an equilibrium process permits nontrivial beliefs, and to show how learning occurs, we provide an example of an equilibrium process. Consider an economy in which, for each consumer i,

$$U^i(c^i, \theta^i) = \sum_{t=1}^{\infty} (\theta^i)^{t-1} \log(c_{t-1}^i),$$

where $0 < \theta^i < 1$. Define the mean of the discount factor distribution with respect to the endowment distribution to be $m = \Sigma_{i=1}^{I}(\theta^i e^i/e)$, where $e = \Sigma_{i=1}^{I} e^i$. Define the variance of the discount factor distribution with respect to the endowment distribution to be $v = \Sigma_{i=1}^{I}((\theta^i)^2 e^i/e) - m^2$. We assume that the joint parameter vector is drawn from a distribution on

$$\left\{ \theta \in (0,1)^I : \sum_{i=1}^{I} \frac{(\theta^i)^2 e^i}{e} - m^2 = v, m < \frac{1}{2}, v < \frac{1}{4} \right\},$$

where the value of v and the distribution are common knowledge.

We construct a Bayesian equilibrium process for this economy by first finding an equilibrium of plans, prices, and price expectations. Let $z_t = 1 + p_{t+1} + p_{t+1}p_{t+2} + p_{t+1}p_{t+2}p_{t+3} + \cdots$. Calculation shows that

$$f_t^i = \frac{\theta^i(e^i + f_{t-1}^i) - (1 - \theta^i)e^i p_t z_t}{p_t}.$$

In an equilibrium, these forward demands must sum to zero in each period. So, for each t we have

$$p_t z_t = \frac{\sum_i \theta^i(e^i + f_{t-1}^i)}{\sum_i (1 - \theta^i)e^i}.$$

This equation system, along with the initial condition $f_0 \equiv 0$, determines the equilibrium price sequence. To be specific, in period 1,

$$p_1 = m - \frac{v}{(1 - m)} \quad \text{and} \quad z_1 = \frac{m}{(m - (v + m^2))}.$$

These prices were calculated under the assumption that each consumer knew all future prices, but as consumers do not know θ they cannot calculate these prices prior to first-period trade. Notice, however, that first-period futures demands depend on future prices only through z_1. Given knowledge of v and of the equation system determining equilibrium prices, p_1 reveals m. So each consumer can calculate z_1. In each period beyond the first, z_t can be inferred from p_t and knowledge of z_{t-1}. Thus, the foregoing equilibrium of plans, prices, and price expectations is also a sequence of rational expectations equilibria for this economy.

The common priors in the description of this economy and its equilibrium define a Bayesian equilibrium process for the economy. This equilibrium is, even in the first period, an equilibrium of plans, prices and price expectations. More interesting would be an equilibrium in which consumers eventually – but not instantly – learn all payoff-relevant information. Bray and Kreps (1987) provide, in a slightly different model, an example of this sort. They focus on an economy with no intertemporal links other than learning and show that agents' beliefs eventually converge to "correct beliefs." Yet results of Jordan (1982) suggest that, in the typical economy, revelation (or near revelation) in the first period may be possible. Jordan shows (in a model that is different from the model here) that in the generic economy, with the dimension of the space of private information greater than the number of relative prices, approximately full revelation occurs in an REE. This remarkable result uses a map from private information to prices that is pathological. The approach to learning taken in this section assumes that individuals know this map, or at least put positive prior probability on it, and use their prior knowledge to learn the private information of others. This can at best produce partial answers to the learning question.

At this point it is important to be careful about what is meant by the "learning question." At one level the question is: Do individuals learn each other's type? The more important question is: Does the sequence of equilibria converge to an equilibrium with common, correct expectations for the underlying true economy? A positive answer to the first question does not ensure a positive answer to the second. In both Bray and Kreps (1987) and Blume and Easley (1984), a positive answer to the first question is used to produce a positive answer to the second. However, both papers are about stationary economies with no intertemporal connections other than learning. Further, Bray and Kreps exploit the continuity that their example produces, and Blume and Easley look at an economy with only a finite number of types.

We first examine the question of learning types. Convergence of beliefs about types follows immediately from Theorem 2.1.

Corollary 4.1. *Posterior beliefs on types* $Proj_T \mu^i(\cdot \mid p^t, \tau^i)$ *converge* τ^i-*almost surely.*

This result does not say that individuals learn τ. If the price system does not reveal τ then it could not be learned, but then – as the preceding example shows – learning types only up to the equivalence classes induced by the price system is sufficient. An application of Corollary 2.3 produces the desired result.

Corollary 4.2. *Let* A *be a Borel subset of* T, *and let* P_A *denote the subset of paths* $p^\infty \in P^\infty$ *such that* p^∞ *is not in supp* $Proj_{P_\infty} \mu^i(\cdot \mid \tau)$ *for any* $\tau \in A$. *For*

$Proj_{P_\infty} \mu^i$ -almost all $p^\infty \in P_A$, the posterior probability $Proj_T \mu^i(A \mid p^t)$ converges to 0.

Hence, from i's point of view, she will learn the type vector up to the equivalence classes induced by prices.

The examples in Section 2 show that learning the parameter is not necessarily enough to ensure that individuals' conditional forecasts about the future given the past converge to correct conditional beliefs. We have not translated these examples into an equilibrium setting because constructing equilibria that do not reveal types in the first period is difficult. But we believe that the points made in Section 2 about the difference between learning types and learning to forecast are valid in an equilibrium setting.

In order to prove that consumers' conditional beliefs about future prices converge to the true conditional distribution of future prices, we need some structure on initial beliefs. The following is a translation of the conditional Harsanyi hypothesis to our competitive framework.

Axiom 1. $Proj_{T \times P_I} \mu^0$ almost surely $Proj_{P^\infty} \mu^i(\cdot \mid p_1, \tau^i) \gg Proj_{P^\infty} \mu^0(\cdot \mid p_1, \tau^i)$, for all i.

This absolute continuity assumption is placed on individuals' beliefs about price systems at the time decisions are made. This is after they have seen their own type and the first-period price. In any economy in which the first-period price reveals types up to the equivalence classes induced by price systems, this assumption is easy to satisfy. But in this case the assumption is almost the result. Consumers are not assumed to know what prices will occur or to perfectly forecast future prices given the first-period price, but they are assumed to place strictly positive probability on the prices that will occur given the first-period price.

The following result is an immediate consequence of the Blackwell and Dubins (1962) theorem on the merging of opinions. It implies that, outside of a set of μ^0 measure zero, consumers' beliefs converge to the true conditional distribution $Proj_{P^\infty} \mu^0(\cdot \mid \tau)$. Thus, the economy will eventually be approximately in an equilibrium of plans, prices, and price expectations.

Corollary 4.3. *Suppose that Axiom 1 holds. Let $\mu^i(\cdot \mid p^t, \tau^i)$ be consumer i's date-t conditional probability given his observation of prices up to date t and his own type. Then*

$$Proj_P \mu^i\left(p_{t+1} \mid p^t, \tau^i\right) \to 1 \quad almost \ surely \ \mu^0.$$

Corollary 4.3 would be true with Axiom 1 replaced by an absolute continuity assumption on beliefs conditioned only on types and not on first-period prices. But such a revised axiom would be very restrictive; it would require each $\text{Proj}_{P^\infty} \mu^i(\cdot \mid \tau^i)$ to have an atom. This effectively restricts the type space to a finite or countably infinite set. Unlike the axiom that we use, this assumption is not met in the preceding example.

Kalai and Lehrer's (1990) paper on learning in equilibrium begins with beliefs directly over price systems. They show that, under an absolute continuity assumption on beliefs (not conditioned on first-period prices), learning leads to an equilibrium of plans, prices, and price expectations. Although we begin with beliefs over parameters, these beliefs induce beliefs over price systems. Further, the stronger absolute continuity assumption just referred to, when translated to beliefs over price systems, is essentially the same as Kalai and Lehrer's assumption.

5   Robustness of Equilibrium Learning

In Section 4 we examined the implications of incredibly sophisticated Bayesian learning. Individuals were assumed to place positive prior probability on the correct model and to behave exactly as Bayes's rule requires in updating their beliefs. We believe that both of these assumptions are unrealistic. In this section we consider, in a simpler model than was used in Section 4, what happens if we drop either of these assumptions. We perturb Bayes learning in two ways – by misspecifying the model and by employing different updating rules – and show in each case how the asymptotic posterior distributions change. Our results suggest that the ability to learn is not a robust property of learning rules.

Even if the belief adjustment dynamic fails, there may be other forces at work in the economy that cause the sequence of temporary equilibria to converge to a rational expectations equilibrium. For some economies it is sufficient to have only some Bayesian traders, as the non-Bayesians will be driven out of the market by the Bayesians. In other economies, however, the market may select for traders who do not even asymptotically have rational expectations. To analyze the market selection force, we use a simple general equilibrium model with uncertainty but without differential information.

5.1   A Prototype Economy

In this section we introduce a prototype economy in which our points are easily illustrated. Our economy contains one good, which can be either invested or consumed. At the end of period $t - 1$, investors choose a portfolio of investments that pay out one period hence contingent upon the occurrence of some event. At the beginning of date t, the state of nature is realized and the assets pay out. Investors then decide how much to consume as well as how to invest that which is not consumed in assets, which pay out at the beginning of date $t + 1$.

Investment payouts are state-contingent, but investors do not know which state will be realized at the time of their investment. To present the learning model in its simplest form, we also suppose that no investor has inside information about the state to be realized. The most that any investor can hope to know is the stochastic process generating the states. Investors do not even know this, but they can learn it. Here "rational expectations" means that investors know the true distribution of future states.

Now we turn to formalities. Time is discrete and is indexed by t. There are two states of the world, indexed by $s \in \{0, 1\}$, one of which will occur at each date. States follow an i.i.d. process with probability $1 > q > 0$ of state 0 being realized at any date. Let X_t denote the random variable whose value is the realization of the process at date t. Let $(X, \mathcal{F}, \mu)$ denote the measurable space of values of the process ($X = \prod_{t=1}^{\infty} X_t$, $\mathcal{F}$ is the product σ-field, and μ is the product measure induced by q), and let $\mathcal{F}_t$ denote the σ-field of events measurable through time t.

At each date there is one unit each of the two available assets. If state s occurs at date t, then asset s pays off \$1 and all other assets have a zero payoff. Total wealth in the economy at date t will thus be \$1 regardless of which state occurs. This wealth will be distributed among the traders proportionately according to the share of the successful asset each trader owns.

Let w_{t-1}^i denote trader i's wealth net of date $t - 1$ consumption, and let α_{st}^i denote the fraction of that wealth he invests in asset s that pays off at the beginning of date t. We assume that all wealth is invested either in asset 0 or in asset 1. (Any money not invested disappears.) The price of asset st (which pays out in state s at date t) is denoted by ϱ_{st}. So trader i owns $\alpha_{st}^i w_{t-1}^i / \varrho_{st}$ shares of asset st at the end of date $t - 1$. Thus, his investment income at date t is $(\alpha_{st}^i w_{t-1}^i / \varrho_{st})$ if state s occurs.

After realizing his investment income, trader i consumes fraction $1 - \delta_{st}^i$ and saves fraction δ_{st}^i to invest in assets paying out at date $t + 1$. So, if state s occurs at date t, trader i's wealth at the end of date t will be $\delta_{st}^i (\alpha_{st}^i w_{t-1}^i / \varrho_{st})$. We refer to $\{\alpha_{0t}^i\}_{t=1}^{\infty}$ as trader i's *portfolio rule* and the pair $\{\alpha_{0t}^i, \delta_t^i\}_{t=1}^{\infty}$ as trader i's *investment rule*.

Given the trader's wealth and portfolio rules, the asset prices must satisfy:

$$\sum_{i=1}^{I} \frac{\alpha_{0t}^i w_{t-1}^i}{\varrho_{0t}} = 1, \qquad \sum_{i=1}^{I} \frac{\alpha_{1t}^i w_{t-1}^i}{\varrho_{1t}} = 1.$$

Let $p_{st} = \varrho_{st}/\omega_{t-1}$ be a normalized asset price, where w_{t-1} is the market wealth at the beginning of date t. Let $r_{t-1}^i = w_{t-1}^i/w_{t-1}$ be trader i's wealth share. Then, in equilibrium,

$$p_{st} = \sum_{i=1}^{I} \alpha_{st}^i r_{t-1}^i \tag{5.1}$$

and

$$p_{0t} + p_{1t} = 1.$$

The variables α_{st}^i and δ_{st}^i describe the demand for assets and for the consumption good at each date–event pair. Typically they would depend on current market prices and wealth levels, and perhaps on previously observed information as well. We will derive them from particular preferences.

We suppose that our investors are dynamic programmers. The reward function for current-period consumption is $u(c) = \log c$, and investor i has discount factor δ^i. Investors are learners. Each investor believes that the true probability of state 0 is either θ_a^i or θ_b^i. Her prior belief that model a holds is v_0^i. After each trading date, the trader observes the state realized at the beginning of that day. Her posterior beliefs after t such observations is v_t^i. The predicted probability of state 0 is then $q_t^i = v_t^i \theta_a^i + (1 - v_t^i)\theta_b^i$. Solving the dynamic program as in Section 2.2, we find that

$$\alpha_{0t}^i = q_t^i, \quad \delta_{st}^i = \delta^i. \tag{5.2}$$

The "problem" of rational expectations takes a very simple form here. There is no information asymmetry that can lead to market failure if expectations fail to be rational. There are no information flows from informed to uninformed traders. Nonetheless, with respect to the dynamics of expectation formation, there is no difference between this example and the learning dynamics in the previous section.

We use this example to study three aspects of equilibrium behavior with learning dynamics: the effects of misspecified models, the robustness of convergence with respect to the updating rule, and the interaction between learning dynamics and the dynamics of wealth distribution.

5.2   Misspecified Models

The first question we take up is the workings of learning dynamics when every model considered by the traders is misspecified. This issue does not appear to be very interesting in the example economy just described. It is of greater concern when there exist information asymmetries, and when traders are learning some structural features of the economy as necessary to extrapolate from prices to contemporaneous information. The importance of model misspecification in this context arises because the structural model of the economy depends upon, among other things, traders' beliefs about the unknown structural parameter. If traders recognize this dependence and their structural model of the economy takes this into account, Bayesian learning can lead to rational expectations. This is the point of Blume and Easley (1984), Bray and Kreps (1987), and Feldman (1987). If, on the other hand, traders do not recognize this dependence, then models that are correct when traders fully believe them are incorrectly specified when traders give some weight to other hypotheses. Blume and Easley (1982) show that as a consequence of this incorrect specification, beliefs may not converge to rational expectations, and the dynamics of temporary equilibrium driven by learning lead to arbitrary outcomes, including convergence to incorrect beliefs and nonconvergence.

Model misspecification in our prototype example is easy to describe. Suppose that for no i is it the case that θ_a^i or θ_b^i equals q. How does the economy behave in the long run? The first question is: What are limit beliefs? It seems to be well known (and easy to prove in the i.i.d. case) that limit posterior beliefs will put mass 1 on the model that is closest to the "true" model in the sense of relative entropy. For two probability measures q and θ on $\{0, 1\}$, the relative entropy of q with respect to θ is

$$I_q(\theta) = q \log \frac{q}{\theta} + (1 - q) \log \frac{1 - q}{1 - \theta}.$$

The expression $I_q(\theta)$ is nonnegative, and equals 0 only when $\theta = q$. However, relative entropy is not symmetric and fails to satisfy the triangle inequality, so it is not even a pseudometric on its domain. If $I_q(\theta_a^i) < I_q(\theta_b^i)$, then trader i's posterior distributions converge to point mass on θ_a^i. If $I_q(\theta_a^i) > I_q(\theta_b^i)$, then posteriors converge to point mass at θ_b^i. Finally, if $I_q(\theta_a^i) = I_q(\theta_b^i)$, the log of posterior odds is a random walk.

Now we can describe the limit behavior of equilibrium prices. Suppose that there is one trader, say trader 1, who puts some prior weight on a model, say θ_a^1, that is closer to q (in terms of relative entropy) than any other model receiving positive weight from any other trader. Then trader 1's posterior beliefs will converge to point mass at θ_a^1, and q_t^1 converges to θ_a^1. In this case one can show (using the techniques in Blume and Easley 1992) that the wealth share of trader 1 converges to 1 and that market prices p_t converge to θ_a^1. In no sense are the assets correctly priced, but assets are priced according to the best beliefs in the market.

Theorem 5.1. *If* $I_q(\theta_a^1) < I_q(\theta_b^1)$ *and* $I_q(\theta_a^1) < I_q(\theta_z^i)$ *for* z = a, b *and all* i > 1, *then* $p_t \rightarrow \theta_a^1$ *almost surely.*

Next suppose that $I_q(\theta_a^2) = I_q(\theta_a^1)$, and that these two models are closer to q than all other models. Then the wealth share of all traders except traders 1 and 2 fall to 0. The wealth shares of traders 1 and 2 oscillate between 0 and 1 (with limsups and liminfs of 1 and 0, respectively), and market prices have two accumulation points, θ_a^1 and θ_a^2.

Theorem 5.2. *If* $I_q(\theta_a^1) = I_q(\theta_a^2) < I_q(\theta_z^i)$ *for* z = a, b *and all* i > 2, *and* z = b *and* i = 1, 2, *then the almost sure limit points of the price sequence* p_t *are precisely* θ_a^1 *and* θ_a^2.

This result also follows from the analysis in Blume and Easley (1992), and shows again that assets can be no better priced than by the best beliefs in the market.

These results are straightforward because the notion of "best model" – meaning closest in relative entropy to the true model – is exogenously fixed. In the economies of Blume and Easley (1982), this is no longer (necessarily) the case. In these economies, traders are trying to learn about the equilibrium price correspondence, and the misspecification results from the fact that traders do not take account of the effects of their own (and others') beliefs on the correspondence. Now one can imagine more complicated dynamics. A trader may start off with a "best model" but, as she becomes wealthier and as her beliefs put more and more weight on the best model, the equilibrium price correspondence may shift in such a way that the original "best model" is no longer best.

5.3   Robustness of Bayesian Updating

Bayesian updating is a very delicate matter. The manner in which current observations and prior beliefs are combined is balanced so that, on the one hand, beliefs converge, and, on the other hand, limit beliefs are correct whenever it is possible to distinguish the truth in the data. If decision makers put too much weight on their prior beliefs or too much weight on the data, then one or the other of these properties is lost. We will demonstrate this for the case of learning q, and explore its implications for the long-run behavior of prices in the prototype economy.

Consider a Bayesian decision maker who is undecided between two models, θ_a and θ_b. Now we suppose that $\theta_a = q$, so a Bayesian decision maker's posterior beliefs would converge almost surely to point mass at $\theta_a = q$. But now we are going to suppose that our decision maker is not a true Bayesian. The log of the likelihood ratio for the two models is

$$L\left(X_t\right) = \left(1 - X_t\right)\log\left(\frac{\theta_a}{\theta_b}\right) + X_t \log\left(\frac{1 - \theta_a}{1 - \theta_b}\right).$$

A Bayesian decision maker would update posterior beliefs according to the rule

$$\log\frac{P_t\left(\theta_a\right)}{P_t\left(\theta_b\right)} = L\left(X_t\right) + \log\frac{P_{t-1}\left(\theta_a\right)}{P_{t-1}\left(\theta_b\right)},$$

where P_t is the posterior belief distribution after t observations.

We suppose instead that the decision maker updates beliefs according to the following rule:

$$\log\frac{P_t\left(\theta_a\right)}{P_t\left(\theta_b\right)} = \left(1 + \lambda\right)L\left(X_t\right) + \left(1 - \lambda\right)\log\frac{P_{t-1}\left(\theta_a\right)}{P_{t-1}\left(\theta_b\right)}$$

$$= \left(1 + \lambda\right)\sum_{s=0}^{t-1}\left(1 - \lambda\right)^s L\left(X_{t-s}\right) + \left(1 - \lambda\right)^t \log\frac{P_0\left(\theta_a\right)}{P_0\left(\theta_b\right)}.$$

The case of $\lambda = 0$ corresponds to Bayesian updating. If $\lambda > 0$ then the decision maker puts too much weight on the data, while if $\lambda < 0$, the decision maker puts too much emphasis on her beliefs. A negative value for λ is not really sensible, but we include it for completeness.[6]

If $\lambda > 0$ then the effect of the prior beliefs vanishes, as it does in the case of Bayesian revision. Let $Z_t = \sum_{s=0}^{t-1}(1 - \lambda)^s L(X_{t-s})$. The process Z_t satisfies the difference equation $Z_{t+1} = (1 - \lambda)Z_t + L(X_{t+1})$. It should be clear that the random variables Z_t are uniformly bounded by $\lambda^{-1}\log(\theta_a/\theta_b)$ and $\lambda^{-1}\log((1 - \theta_a)/(1 - \theta_b))$, and that they do not converge. Thus $\log(P_t(\theta_a)/P_t(\theta_b))$ does not converge and is uniformly bounded away from $-\infty$ and $+\infty$.

If $\lambda < 0$, take $a = 1 - \lambda$ and consider

---

[6] Suppose, for example, that the models are equally likely, given the data. In that case, if $\lambda < 0$ then the posterior beliefs on θ_a go to 1 if $P_0(\theta_a) > P_0(\theta_b)$ and to 0 in the opposite case.

$$\frac{1}{\sum_{s=0}^{t} a^s} \log \frac{P_t(\theta_a)}{P_t(\theta_b)} = (1 + \lambda) \frac{\sum_{s=0}^{t-1} a^s L(X_{t-s})}{\sum_{s=0}^{t-1} a^s}$$

$$+ \left(\frac{a^t}{\sum_{s=0}^{t-1} a^s} \right) \log \frac{P_0(\theta_a)}{P_0(\theta_b)}.$$

The last term on the right converges to $-\lambda \log P_0(\theta_a)/P_0(\theta_b)$. The first term converges to

$$-\frac{(1+\lambda)\lambda}{(1-\lambda)} \sum_{t=0}^{\infty} \left(\frac{1}{1-\lambda} \right)^t L(X_{1+t}).$$

It follows from the Martingale convergence theorem that this "discounted sum" converges, and so the right-hand side (RHS) converges to some limit random variable. Clearly, for "most" prior beliefs, the right-hand limit will almost surely not be 0, so posterior beliefs must converge to 0 or 1 (since the denominator on the left-hand side is diverging). But in this case the limit beliefs need not be correct. For instance, suppose that prior beliefs assign equal probability to θ_a and θ_b, so that the log of the prior odds ratio is 0. It is easy to see that the limit RHS random variable exceeds 0 with positive probability, and that with positive probability the limit RHS random variable is exceeded by 0. Thus, under θ_b, the probability that posterior beliefs on θ_b go to 1 and the probability that posterior beliefs on θ_b go to 0 are both positive. Alternatively, if prior beliefs on θ_a are sufficiently large (resp. small), then limit posterior beliefs assign probability 1 (0) to θ_a regardless of the data.

In summary, we have the following theorem.

Theorem 5.3. *If decision makers put too much weight on the data ($\lambda > 0$), then posterior beliefs do not converge and predicted distributions are convex combinations of the form $\alpha\theta_a + (1 - \alpha_a)\theta_b$, where α is uniformly bounded away from 0 and 1.*

If decision makers put too much weight on their prior beliefs ($\lambda < 0$), then almost surely posterior beliefs converge to point mass at $\theta_a = q$ or θ_b. If the prior odds ratio is sufficiently near 1, then the limit probability of each point mass is positive. If the prior odds ratio is sufficiently different than 1, then limit posterior beliefs will put probability 1 on the model that was initially regarded as more likely.

We conclude that, when beliefs and data are incorrectly balanced in the updating formula for posterior odds, the posterior revision process will be inconsistent – correct beliefs will fail to almost-surely emerge.

Now we turn to the question of long-run prices. Let us assume that, for all traders, $\theta_a^i = q$ and $\theta_b^i = \theta_b > q$. Thus, all traders consider the same models. Suppose first that traders put too much weight on the data ($\lambda > 0$). Then each trader's predicted distribution q_t^i will not converge, but will bounce around on some closed interval contained in (q, θ_b). Because prices are a wealth share–weighted average of beliefs, we can conclude that, in the limit, prices move in that same interval. Notice that prices do not converge, and that prices are biased: the market odds ratio is always higher than the true odds ratio.

Theorem 5.4. *If traders put too much weight on the data, then market prices do not converge. If q is an extreme point of the set of models considered by the traders, then the market price will be systematically biased (too high or too low, depending on the position of q).*

When traders put too much weight on their prior beliefs, a variety of things can happen. Suppose that trader 1 assigns sufficiently high prior probability to the correct model. Then her posterior beliefs will converge to point mass on the correct model, and her predicted distribution q_t^1 converges to q. The aggregate wealth share of all traders with beliefs like hers converges to 1, and the equilibrium price converges to q. Suppose, on the other hand, that all traders place too much prior weight on the false model. Then all beliefs converge to the false model, and the market price converges to θ_b. Finally, if the prior odds of all traders are sufficiently near 1, then the updating dynamics is (with positive probability) driven by the data (with earliest observations getting the most weight). In this case, posterior beliefs converge either to point mass at q or at θ_b, predicted distributions converge either to q or to θ_b, and each happens with positive probability. However, all traders see the same information, and so all posterior beliefs move together. It is not the case that some traders will ultimately predict q and others will simultaneously predict θ_b. Thus market prices will converge either to q or to θ_b, each with positive probability.

Theorem 5.5. *If traders put too much weight on their prior beliefs, then – depending upon what the prior beliefs are – market prices will converge either to q with probability 1, to θ_b with probability 1, or to each with positive probability.*

When traders put too much weight on their prior beliefs, convergence to "correct" prices in the limit, when it occurs, is an accident of prior specification or fortuitous data gathering.

5.4   Learning Dynamics and Wealth Accumulation

Throughout most of the literature on learning in general equilibrium models, the dynamics of expectations adjustment provides the only link between temporary equilibria at different dates. In this section we provide examples to demonstrate the variety of ways in which learning can interact with other intertemporal connections to determine the long-run behavior of equilibrium prices. In our prototype economy, the additional intertemporal connection comes from the dynamics of wealth share adjustment. Over time, some traders prosper and others suffer. The prosperous traders come to dominate the market, and the equilibrium price reflects their beliefs. This much is evident from equation (5.1). One can imagine two possible scenarios: First, learning is reinforced by wealth dynamics. Those traders with more accurate beliefs are rewarded by the market and come to dominate it. If some traders are true Bayesians, then in the long run their beliefs are accurate, they will dominate the market, and the asset will be priced correctly. Another possible scenario is that differences in decision rules more than compensate for differences in learning rules, and so rational learners may be driven from the market. In Blume and Easley (1992) we give examples of both phenomena, and we briefly summarize these examples here.

First we describe a situation where the dynamics of Bayesian learning and the dynamics of wealth adjustment complement one another. Suppose that all traders have log reward functions and identical discount factors, and suppose that some subset of traders consists of Bayesian learners who put positive prior probability to the model q. Then those traders' predicted distributions will almost surely converge to q, their collective wealth share will converge to 1, and market prices will converge to q. (This result is proven in Blume and Easley 1992.)

Theorem 5.6.   *If all traders employ identical decision rules derived from logarithmic preferences (with identical discount factors), and if some traders are Bayesian learners who put positive probability on the correct model, then assets are correctly priced in the long run.*

Theorem 5.6 is surprisingly delicate. If traders use different decision rules, or if traders are heterogeneous in an asymmetric way, then the conclusion no longer holds.

Theorem 5.7.   *Suppose some traders have logarithmic preferences with discount rate δ and believe with probability 1 that the correct model is q. The remaining traders have logarithmic preferences, are certain that the true model is r, and have discount rate γ. If*

$$I_q(r) - \log \gamma < -\log \delta,$$

then the market price process will converge almost surely to r.

This theorem, which is a consequence of results in Blume and Easley (1992), shows that the higher savings rates of the incorrectly informed traders overwhelms the better information of the correctly informed traders. Consequently, in order to ensure that market prices converge to q, we would have to assume that information is uncorrelated with rates of time preferences. This certainly would not be true if information gathering were costly.

If traders' reward functions are not logarithmic, then it is possible again that the market would favor traders with incorrect beliefs over those with correct beliefs. We have shown that the market selects over decisions, not beliefs, and that the market will select for those traders whose decisions α_{0t}^i are (on average) nearest to q in the sense of relative entropy. Thus the market will tend to price assets correctly, but may do so by selecting for people with incorrect beliefs because those beliefs, when operated on by the decision rule, give better decisions according to the relative entropy criterion than do those beliefs that are more accurate. In this case the market prices assets correctly, but for reasons having nothing to do with rational expectations.

6   Conclusion

In both single-agent and multi-agent sequential decision problems, the outcome of the analysis is driven by agents' expectations about the internal decision environment and exogenous payoff-relevant events. "Learning" is a device that delimits, at least asymptotically, the set of possible or realizable expectations. In single-agent decision problems, the possibilities are delimited by the choice of a prior distribution representing initial beliefs of the agent. In a single-agent decision problem, the requirements for "rational learning" amount to saying that the true parameter value is in the support of the agent's prior beliefs and that, for every parameter value, the agent knows the likelihood function that would obtain if that parameter value were controlling the evolution of the observations. Even with these assumptions, the asymptotic outcome of the learning process may be incomplete learning, but consistency often occurs.

In multi-agent decision problems, the situation is more complicated. "Rational expectations" represents an attempt to pin down expectations by assuming that they are consistent with the true structure of the decision environment. In some economic equilibrium models this is insufficiently restrictive – many rational expectations equilibria exist. Even when the equilibrium set is small, rational expectations still pose a problem. The knowledge requirements are so great that it is implausible to assume that decision makers just happen to be endowed with correct expectations. Hence one naturally asks if decision makers can learn correct expectations.

In noncooperative, incomplete information, repeated game models, the Bayes–Nash equilibrium concept has embedded in it the idea that players learn over the course of play. Here Jordan (1991, 1995) asks if the result of this learning activity pins down beliefs as the game is repeated. As is the case in economic equilibrium models, the rationality requirements of Bayes–Nash equilibrium are heavy. Responding to this, the focus of Nyarko's and Kalai and Lehrer's research has been to ask if the rationality requirement that players *know* each other's strategic choice can be relaxed so that players can *learn* to play equilibrium strategies.

The crucial issue in rational learning in multi-agent settings concerns identifying the proper parameter set. Consider an equilibrium model in which a payoff-relevant signal is observed only by some traders. Suppose that the uninformed traders do not know the signal–price relationship, and will try to learn it by looking at market prices and the signal at the end of each market period. Rational learning requires that traders place positive prior probability on the true model for the *entire stochastic process*, and not just for what would happen after beliefs converged. Suppose traders know the distribution of endowments, utilities, and priors on the signal process. Then the likelihood functions are, in principle, knowable. Suppose, however, that no agent knows other agents' priors. Since the evolution of the economy depends both on the original parameter value and the prior beliefs, prior beliefs on the signal process must be added to the parameter space. Now agents must have priors on this expanded parameter space – priors on parameters cross signal-process priors, and so forth. The natural parameter space is very large. Nyarko (1991) has carried out this construction for some simple game problems. But with a large parameter space, Bayesian learning will typically fail to yield correct conditional beliefs or even to be consistent.[7] If we, the modelers, assume a simple parameterization of the choice environment, we are closing our models in the ad hoc fashion that rational learning was introduced to avoid. If we assume the natural complex parameterization, all we know is that the Bayesian believes

---

[7] See Diaconis and Freedman (1986) for a discussion of the consistency problem; see Feldman (1991) for an application to a decision problem.

that his beliefs will converge somewhere with probability 1. Nachbar's (1997) work suggests that this criticism is significant. At least in games, diverse beliefs which are rich enough to describe play in games and which allow for the possibility of prediction of future play do not exist.

Throughout this chapter we have argued that too much is being asked of learning dynamics. In economic equilibrium analysis, learning is usually studied in models where the dynamics of belief revision provide the only intertemporal link. But the results of Section 5 suggest that, when other intertemporal connections are present, learning will interact with these other forces in a complicated way and may even be irrelevant to the asymptotic behavior of the model. Similarly, in the single-agent decision problem, the results of Nyarko (1994a) and the example discussed in Section 2 suggest that the failure of learning a parameter of the state transition equation (or conditional probability) due to (asymptotic) underidentification of the parameter, such as in Easley and Kiefer (1988) or Feldman and McLennan (1989), is largely a feature of models in which learning is the only intertemporal connection.

References

Arrow, K., and J. Green (1973), "Notes on Expectations Equilibria in Bayesian Settings," Unpublished manuscript, Department of Economics, Stanford University.

Barron, Andrew (1989), "The Consistency of Bayes Estimators of Probability Density Functions," Unpublished manuscript, Department of Economics, University of Illinois, Urbana.

Blackwell, D. (1951), "The Comparison of Experiments," in *Proceedings of the Second Berkeley Symposium on Mathematical Statistics and Probability*. Berkeley: University of California Press.

Blackwell, D., and L. Dubins (1962), "Merging of Opinions with Increasing Information," *Annals of Mathematical Statistics*, 33, 882–6.

Blume, L., M. Bray, and D. Easley (1982), "Introduction to the Stability of Rational Expectations Equilibrium," *Journal of Economic Theory*, 26, 313–17.

Blume, L., and D. Easley (1982), "Learning to Be Rational," *Journal of Economic Theory*, 26, 340–51.

  (1984), "Rational Expectations Equilibrium: An Alternative Approach," *Journal of Economic Theory*, 34, 116–29.

  (1992), "Evolution and Market Behavior," *Journal of Economic Theory*, 58, 9–40.

  (1993), "What Has the Rational Learning Literature Taught Us," in A. Kirman and M. Salmon (eds.), *Essays in Learning and Rationality in Economics*. Oxford: Blackwell.

Bray, M., and D. Kreps (1987), "Rational Learning and Rational Expectations," in George Feiwel (ed.), *Arrow and the Ascent of Modern Economic Theory*. New York University Press.

Diaconis, P., and D. Freedman (1986), "On the Consistency of Bayes Estimates," *Annals of Statistics*, 14, 1–26.

Doob, J. L. (1949), "Application of the Theory of Martingales," *Colloq. Internat. CNRS*, 22–8.

Easley, D., and N. Kiefer (1988), "Controlling a Stochastic Process with Unknown Parameters," *Econometrica*, 56, 1045–64.

El-Gamal, M., and R. Sundaram (1993), "Bayesian Economists . . . Bayesian Agents I: An Alternative Approach to Optimal Learning," *Journal of Economic Dynamics and Control*, 17, 355–83.

Feldman, M. (1987), "An Example of Convergence to Rational Expectations with Heterogeneous Beliefs," *International Economic Review*, 28, 635–50.

  (1991), "On the Generic Non-Convergence of Bayesian Actions and Beliefs," *Economic Theory*, 14, 301–21.

Feldman, M., and A. McLennan (1989), "Learning in a Repeated Statistical Problem with Normal Disturbances," Unpublished manuscript, Department of Economics, University of Minnesota, Minneapolis.

Freedman, D. (1965), "On the Asymptotic Properties of Bayes Estimates in the Discrete Case II," *Annals of Mathematical Statistics*, 36, 454–6.

Fudenberg, D., and D. Kreps (1988), "A Theory of Learning, Experimentation and Equilibrium in Games," Unpublished manuscript, Graduate School of Business, Stanford University.

Fudenberg, D., and D. Levine (1993a), "Steady State Learning and Nash Equilibrium," *Econometrica*, 61, 547–73.

  (1993b), "Self Confirming Equilibrium," *Econometrica*, 61, 523–45.

Hinderer, K. (1970), *Foundations of Non-Stationary Dynamic Programming with Discrete Time Parameter*. Berlin: Springer.

Jordan, J. (1982), "The Generic Existence of Rational Expectations Equilibria in the Higher Dimensional Case," *Journal of Economic Theory*, 26, 224–43.

  (1991), "Bayesian Learning in Normal Form Games," *Games and Economic Behavior*, 3, 60–81.

  (1992), "Bayesian Learning in Games: A NonBayesian Perspective," Unpublished manuscript, University of Minnesota, Department of Economics, Minneapolis.

  (1995), "Bayesian Learning in Repeated Games," *Games and Economic Behavior*, 9, 8.

Jordan, J., and R. Radner (1982), "Rational Expectations in Microeconomic Models: An Overview," *Journal of Economic Theory*, 26, 201–23.

Kalai, E., and E. Lehrer (1990), "Merging Economic Forecasts," Unpublished manuscript, Managerial Economics and Decision Sciences, Northwestern University, Evanstor, IL.

  (1993a), "Rational Learning Leads to Nash Equilibrium," *Econometrica*, 61, 1019–45.

(1993b), "Subjective Equilibrium in Repeated Games," *Econometrica*, 61, 1231–40.

Marimon, R., E. McGrattan, and T. Sargent (1990), "Money as a Medium of Exchange in an Economy with Artificially Intelligent Agents," *Journal of Economic Dynamics and Control*, 14, 329.

McLennan, A. (1987), "Incomplete Learning in a Repeated Statistical Decision Problem," Unpublished manuscript, University of Minnesota, Department of Economics, Minneapolis.

Mertens, J.-F., and S. Zamir (1985), "Formalization of Bayesian Analysis for Games with Incomplete Information," *International Journal of Game Theory*, 14, 1–22.

Nachbar, J. (1997), "Prediction, Optimization, and Rational Learning in Games," *Econometrica*, 65, 275–310.

Nyarko, Y. (1991), "Bayesian Learning Without Common Priors and Convergence to Nash Equilibrium," Unpublished manuscript, Department of Economics, New York University.

(1994a), "The Number of Equations Versus the Number of Unknowns: The Convergence of Bayesian Posterior Processes," *Journal of Economic Dynamics and Control*, 15, 687–713.

(1994b), "Bayesian Learning in Repeated Games Leads to Correlated Equilibria," *Economic Theory*, 4, 821–41.

Radner, R. (1972), "Existence of Equilibrium of Plans, Prices and Price Expectations in a Sequence of Markets," *Econometrica*, 40, 289–303.

(1979), "Rational Expectations Equilibrium: Generic Existence and the Information Revealed by Prices," *Econometrica*, 47, 655–78.

Schwartz, L. (1965), "On Bayes Procedures," *Zeitschrift für Wahrscheinlichkeitstheorie*, 4, 10–26.

Townsend, R. (1978), "Market Anticipations, Rational Expectations and Bayesian Analysis," *International Economic Review*, 19, 481–94.

CHAPTER 4

Dynamic Games in Organization Theory

Roy Radner

1   Introduction

In any but the smallest human organizations, no one person has all of the information relevant to the organization's activities, nor can he directly control all of those activities. This is so even in organizations that are described as highly "centralized." It follows that individual members of the organization – I shall call them *agents* – have some freedom to choose their own actions. If, in addition, there is some divergence among the agents' goals or objectives, then one can expect some inefficiencies to arise in the organization's operations. The analysis of these inefficiencies, and the possible remedies by means of organizational design, is the subject of this chapter.

If the behavior of the agents is rational in the sense typically used by economists and decision theorists, then the appropriate formal model would appear to be the theory of games, especially games of incomplete information, as developed in the past two decades.[1] This is the methodology that I shall use here, although some aspects of "bounded rationality" will be touched on during the course of my exposition. Furthermore, the relationships among members of an economic organization are typically long-lived, calling for an analysis of *dynamic games*.

Two special paradigmatic models have arisen in the game-theoretic analysis of organization. In the first, which I have elsewhere called a *partnership*, the agents act together to produce a joint outcome (output,

The views expressed here are those of the author, and not necessarily those of AT&T Bell Laboratories or New York University. This is a revised version of a paper with the same title that was originally published in the *Journal of Economic Behavior and Organization* 16 (1991), 217–60. In particular, the references have been updated, and Section 7 has been substantially revised. I thank Elsevier Science Publishers for permission to reproduce this material.
[1] See Harsanyi (1967/1968) and Myerson (1985).

profit). This outcome can be observed by the agents, but they cannot directly observe each other's actions, nor do they completely share each other's information. In the most general – and realistic – case of this model, the outcome is also influenced by random variables that are only partially observed, if at all. The incompleteness of observation leads to what the statisticians call a "confounding" of the sources of variation of the outcomes, making it difficult to assign responsibility to the individual agents for the occurrence of unsatisfactory outcomes. It is this confounding that leads to organizational inefficiency, if the goals of the agents are not identical (and not identical with the goal of the organization).

The second special model is suggested by the hierarchical structure of many organizations. In this model, there is a particular agent, called the "principal," who performs no immediately useful actions himself but rather supervises the activities of the other agents, rewarding them according to their individual outcomes (and other information) and retaining the residual (output or profit) for himself. This is the so-called *principal–agent* model, the word "agent" here denoting a member of the organization who is not the principal.

In fact, most organizations combine aspects of both the partnership and the principal–agent models. A hierarchy can be thought of as a cascade of principal–agent relationships, each supervisor acting as a principal in relation to the persons she supervises, and as an agent in relation to her own supervisor. On the other hand, in most cases the valued outcomes of organizational activity depend on the joint actions of several agents, as in the partnership model, so that the attribution of special outcome variables to specific individuals (as required by the principal–agent model) may not be strictly justified. Unfortunately, I am not aware of significant progress on more comprehensive models of organization that combine these two submodels in a systematic way. This is one of the main challenges that organization theorists face today. (See Radner 1992 for further discussion.)

In the present exposition, I shall start with the partnership model. In fact, I shall start with the special case in which there is complete information and no uncertainty (Section 2). As in most of the models I shall discuss, the behavior of the agents is assumed to be a (Nash) equilibrium of the corresponding game – that is, a combination of actions (or strategies), one for each agent, such that no agent can increase his own utility by *unilaterally* changing his own action. Even in this special case, it is typically true that in the static or one-period game the equilibria are inefficient. Efficiency here is defined in the Pareto sense; a combination of actions is *efficient* if there is no other combination that yields each agent at least as much utility, and yields at least one agent strictly more. On the other hand, if the partnership situation is repeated, leading to a dynamic game, then there will typically be many equilibria. Many of these dynamic equilibria may be inefficient; for example, the repetition of the one-period equilibrium will be a dynamic equilibrium. On the other hand, if the agents do not discount the future too heavily (are not too impatient), then there will typically be equilibria of the infinitely repeated game that *are* efficient.

In Section 4, I introduce uncertainty and incomplete information into the partnership model.[2] Equilibria of the one-period game are again typically inefficient, but in contrast with the certainty case, in the repeated game one cannot guarantee the existence of efficient equilibria when the agents' discount rates are sufficiently small. Indeed, equilibrium outcomes may be *uniformly* bounded away from efficiency as the agents' discount rates approach zero.

I should point out here that the game played by the agents is not well-defined unless one specifies a particular rule for sharing the outcome among the agents (partners) as a function of the observed outcome. The specification of the sharing rule is thus one of the design problems for the organization – or the organizer. From this perspective, the "uniform inefficiency" result alluded to previously is quite strong, since it holds uniformly in the choice of sharing rule as well as in the agents' discount rate.

A special case of interest is the one in which the agents are neutral toward risk (Section 4.3). Here, with uncertainty, if the agents are suitably different then it is possible to design sharing rules such that an equilibrium of the corresponding game is efficient. These efficiency-inducing sharing rules must, however, be tailored to the agents' particular utility functions, which limits the practical implications of this result.

In Section 4.4, I explore the case in which agents can change their actions rapidly. This is done by embedding the problem in a continuous time model. For the risk-neutral case, one can provide explicit calculations of the efficiency-inducing sharing rules and show that the corresponding outcomes converge (in a particular sense) as the time between actions converges to zero. On the other hand, if the sharing rule divides the outcome among the partners in fixed proportions (which is a natural method), then there is an interval of time between actions sufficiently small that, for all smaller intervals, the players cannot attain an efficiency higher than that of the corresponding (inefficient) static equilibrium.

---

[2] Because of limitations of space and time, I shall discuss moral hazard but not adverse selection or strategic misrepresentation of information. For an explanation of this distinction, see Section 4.

In Section 5, I turn to the principal–agent model. The exposition here parallels that of the partnership model, starting with the static case and moving to the repeated game formulation. The latter, however, provides a contrast to the partnership. Here, as the players' discount rate approaches zero, one can find equilibria of the repeated game that approach efficiency in the limit. Such approximately efficient equilibria can be characterized in some detail, depending on the specific model, and have interesting behavioral interpretations. Again, embedding the problem in a continuous time model allows one to obtain sharper characterizations of the equilibrium strategies.

In fact, these equilibria of the principal–agent game lead to optimization problems for the agent that might be called problems of "survival." This prompts me to devote special attention, in Section 7, to the study of such problems, which also have an independent economic interest outside of the field of organization theory.

Finally, it should be recognized that in realistic settings the organizational decision problems are not strictly repeated. Typically, there are one or more state variables that evolve in response to both organizational activities and exogenous random variables; for example, this is characteristic of situations involving investment. Although a comprehensive theory is not yet available, I illustrate this phenomenon in Sections 3 and 6, as well as in the section on economic survival. In Section 3, I discuss a partnership model – with certainty – of the joint exploitation of a productive asset as exemplified by "fishing wars." In Section 6, I sketch a principal–agent model of the regulation of a public utility; in this model, the principal is the regulator and the agent is the firm's manager who is engaging in risky research and development with the goal of reducing costs. In both cases the methods used for the repeated game case can be extended and adapted to construct efficient, or approximately efficient, equilibria.

In this exposition, I shall not attempt any great level of generality. Instead, I shall illustrate the key ideas with a series of elementary mathematical examples, only sketching the directions in which further analysis has been successful. The interested reader may consult the corresponding references for treatments of greater depth and generality.

2　Simple Partnerships with Certainty

2.1　Introduction

In a simple partnership game with certainty, the output of the partners is jointly determined as a function of the individual inputs of the partners. This output is divided among the partners according to some fixed rule. The utility to each partner in any one period is the difference between his compensation (i.e., his share of the output) and the cost (or disutility) of his input.

If the situation is repeated then the resulting game is called a *supergame*. In the supergame, a strategy of a partner is a sequence of functions, one for each period, that determines his input in each period as a function of the history of all inputs and outputs in all previous periods. His utility for the supergame is the sum of his one-period utilities, typically discounted at some fixed (exogenous) rate. (In a variation on this definition, one may prohibit the partners from ever observing the inputs of the other players; this variation will be considered in Section 4.)

In the one-period game, a strategy for a partner is simply an input – a single nonnegative number. The description of the game is completed by specifying the rule according to which the output is shared among the partners. For example, the sharing rule might specify that the output is to be shared equally among the partners. A combination (vector) of inputs is an *equilibrium* (or noncooperative Nash equilibrium) if no individual partner can increase his utility by unilaterally changing his input. A combination of inputs is *efficient* (Pareto optimal) if no other combination of inputs yields each partner at least as much utility, and yields at least one partner strictly greater utility.

With natural assumptions about the output function and the individual cost functions, it is intuitively plausible that an equilibrium cannot be efficient. For example, suppose that the partners share the output equally. At an equilibrium, a small increase in one partner's input will result in an increase in his compensation that is approximately matched by the corresponding increase in his individual cost. On the other hand, the small increase in his input will also increase the compensation of every other partner, without corresponding increases in their own costs. Thus, starting from an equilibrium, a small increase in each partner's input will make all the partners better off.

In economic jargon, each partner's input produces a positive "externality" for the other partners, which he does not take into account in his own (equilibrium) behavior. Another way of putting it is that each partner tries (up to a point) to be a *free rider* on the inputs of the other partners. The result in equilibrium is that each partner's input is smaller than it should be for efficiency.

Example 2.1. Suppose there are two partners, and denote partner i's input by a_i. The corresponding output is

$$y = R\left(a_1 + a_2\right) \tag{2.1}$$

and i's share of the output is $S_i(y)$, where for every y,

$$S_1\left(y\right) + S_2\left(y\right) = y \tag{2.2}$$

Here a_1 and a_2 must be nonnegative, and R is a positive constant. Denote i's individual cost by $Q_i(a_i)$; then i's utility is

$$u_i = S_i\left(y\right) - Q_i\left(a_i\right). \tag{2.3}$$

In particular, suppose that $S_i(y) = y/2$ and

$$Q_i\left(a_i\right) = qa_i^2, \tag{2.4}$$

in which case

$$u_i = R\left(a_1 + a_2\right)/2 - qa_i^2. \tag{2.5}$$

A one-period equilibrium is characterized by the first-order conditions

$$R/2 - 2qa_i = 0, \quad i = 1, 2,$$

so that the equilibrium inputs and utilities are

$$a_i^* = R/4q, \quad u_i^* = 3R^2/16q. \tag{2.6}$$

To characterize the efficient input combinations, first note that if the utility pair (u_1, u_2) is feasible then so is any pair (u_1', u_2') with

$$u_1' = u_1 + s, \quad u_2' = u_2 - s.$$

Hence (a_1, a_2) is efficient if and only if it maximizes

$$\begin{aligned} u_1 + u_2 &= S_1\left(y\right) - Q_1\left(a_1\right) + S_2\left(y\right) - Q_2\left(a_2\right) \\ &= y - Q_1\left(a_1\right) - Q_2\left(a_2\right) \\ &= R\left(a_1 + a_2\right) - qa_1^2 - qa_2^2. \end{aligned}$$

This uniquely determines the efficient inputs $(\hat{a}_1, \hat{a}_2)$,

$$\hat{a}_i = R/2q, \quad i = 1, 2, \tag{2.7}$$

as well as the *sum* of the utilities,

$$\hat{u}_1 + \hat{u}_2 = R^2/2q. \tag{2.8}$$

The various efficient utility pairs $(\hat{u}_1, \hat{u}_2)$ are now determined by varying the sharing rule. In particular, the family of sharing rules

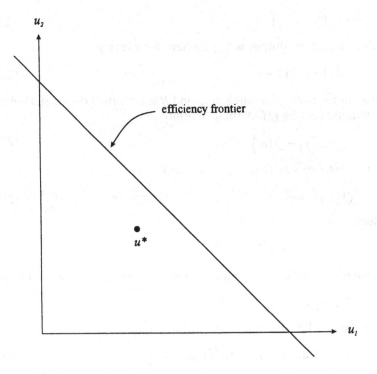

Figure 1

$$S_1(y) = y/2 + s, \qquad S_2(y) = y/2 - s, \tag{2.9}$$

yields all the efficient utility pairs by varying the parameter s, provided the partners use the inputs $\hat{a}_1$ and $\hat{a}_2$.

Comparing (2.6) with (2.7) and (2.8), we see that the efficient inputs are twice as large as the equilibrium inputs, and that the efficient sum of utilities is 4/3 times the equilibrium sum of utilities. Of course not *every* efficient utility pair is Pareto superior to the equilibrium (see Figure 1, where the efficiency frontier is the line with slope -1).

2.2   *The Repeated Game*

Suppose now that the situation of the one-period game is repeated infinitely often. As already described, a partner's strategy determines his inputs in each period as a function of the previous history of inputs and outputs. A partner's utility for the supergame is the sum of his discounted one-period utilities. Extending the notions of equilibrium and efficiency to the supergame in the obvious way, one can show that the supergame typically has many equilibria, some of which may be efficient.

For example, consider a particular equilibrium of the one-period game, and define the *stubborn strategy* of a partner to be the one in which he plays his one-period equilibrium input in every period, no matter what the previous history is. It is easy to see that the strategy is an equilibrium of the supergame; I shall call this the *stubborn equilibrium*. (To each equilibrium of the one-period game, there will correspond a stubborn equilibrium of the supergame.) If the one-period equilibrium is inefficient, then so is the stubborn equilibrium.

To construct efficient equilibria, I shall now consider so-called trigger strategies. Having singled out, as before, some (inefficient) one-period equilibrium, let us also single out some efficient input combination that makes every partner better off; call this the "target input" combination, and call the corresponding output the "target output." A *trigger strategy* for a partner is defined as follows: The partner uses his own target input until the first period (if any) in which some partner does not use his corresponding target input; thereafter, he uses his stubborn strategy.

In order for the combination of trigger strategies to form an equilibrium, it must be the case that, for each partner, the one-period gain derived from deviating (optimally) from the target input combination is less than the subsequent loss due to everyone switching to their respective stubborn strategies. However, as the partner's discount rate approaches zero, the ratio of his one-period gain to his subsequent loss also approaches zero. Thus, for sufficiently low discount rates, the trigger strategy combination will be an equilibrium of the supergame.

Example 2.2. Extending Example 2.1, let a_{it} and u_{it} denote i's input and utility, respectively, in period t ($t = 1, 2, \ldots$, and inf). Then i's supergame utility is

$$U_i = \sum_{i=1}^{\infty} \left(1 - \delta\right)\delta^{t-1} u_{it}, \tag{2.10}$$

where δ, the *discount factor*, is between 0 and 1. (The discount *rate* is defined as $(1 - \delta)/\delta$.) Note that both partners have the same discount factor.

Let $\hat{a}_i$ and a_1^* be defined as in Example 2.1 (efficient and equilibrium inputs). Let the *target utilities* be

$$\hat{u}_i = R^2/4q, \quad i = 1, 2$$

(cf. (2.8)), so that the total efficient utility is divided equally. Define i's trigger strategy by:

(1) $\hat{a}_{i1} = \hat{a}_i$;
(2) if $a_{jt} \neq \hat{a}_j$ for some j and t, then $a_{is} = a_i^*$ for all $s > t$.

Consider partner 1's optimal deviation from the trigger strategy pair; without loss of generality, we can take this to occur in period 1. If 1 deviates in period 1, then 2 will use a_2^* from period 2 on, and so 1 should use a_1^* from period 2 on. Therefore, partner 1's optimal deviation in period 1 is his optimal one-period input given that 2 uses $\hat{a}_2$; it is easy to verify that this is a_1^* and that 1's corresponding one-period utility is

$$u'_{11} = 5R^2/16q > \hat{u}_1.$$

(That a_1^* is optimal against $\hat{a}_2$ is special to this example.) Hence, if partner 1 deviates optimally in period 1 then his supergame utility will be

$$\left(1 - \delta\right)u'_{11} + \sum_{t=2}^{\infty}\left(1 - \delta\right)\delta^{t-1}u_1^* = \left(1 - \delta\right)u'_{11} + \delta u_1^*. \qquad (2.11)$$

On the other hand, if he stays with his target input $\hat{a}_1$ then his supergame utility will be

$$\sum_{t=1}^{\infty}\left(1 - \delta\right)\delta^{t-1}\hat{u}_1 = \hat{u}_1. \qquad (2.12)$$

Because $\hat{u}_1 > u_1^*$, (2.12) will exceed (2.11) when δ is sufficiently close to 1. Hence for δ sufficiently close to 1, it will not be optimal for partner 1 to deviate from the trigger strategy pair, and so the latter is an equilibrium of the supergame.

Note that the foregoing argument is quite general, since it used only the fact that $\hat{u}_1 > u_1^*$. Since the one-period equilibrium is in general inefficient, it will be possible to find an efficient pair of one-period utilities $(\hat{u}_1, \hat{u}_2)$ that is Pareto-superior to the equilibrium $(\hat{u}_i > u_i^*)$, and any such pair can be sustained in a supergame equilibrium for δ sufficiently close to 1.

In fact, using other methods, it can be shown that the set of equilibria of the supergame is quite large. Define the *utility outcome* of a game to be the vector of the players' utilities (one for each player). A utility outcome is *feasible* if it is yielded by some combination of strategies, and it is *individually rational* if it gives each player at least as much utility as she could "guarantee" for herself. One can show that, under fairly general conditions, as the partners' discount factor approaches 1, the set of equilibrium utility outcomes of the supergame approaches the set of feasible and individually rational utility outcomes of the one-period game. (This result is true for a large class of repeated games; see Fudenberg and Maskin 1986 and the references cited there. There is a corresponding result for the limit case in which each player's supergame utility is the long-run average of his one-period utilities; this is sometimes called the "folk theorem" for repeated games.)

3   A Partnership Game with Investment: The "Dynamic Inefficiency" of Capitalism

As noted in Section 1, for most realistic models of long-term relationships the one-period game is not strictly repeated; rather, there are one or more state variables that evolve through time as a function of players' actions and possibly exogenous factors. In this section, I shall illustrate this phenomenon with a model of the joint exploitation of a productive and producible asset.[3]

The phrase "tragedy of the commons" evokes the image of an overgrazed pasture used in common by many husbandmen. By extension, it refers to a situation in which a productive asset is exploited jointly by several economic agents whose noncooperative behavior results in an overexploitation of the asset – that is, an exploitation that is not efficient. Other than grazing, examples of this situation included fishing, forestry, and hunting. A novel example, and the one that first attracted the attention of J. Benhabib and myself, was studied by Lancaster (1973), who viewed the assets of a modern capitalist firm as being jointly exploited by the firm's owners and its unionized workers. For various reasons, the owners and workers cannot or do not bind themselves to long-term cooperative behavior, leading to what Lancaster called "the dynamic inefficiency of capitalism."

Following the direction suggested by the work of Lancaster (1973), Levhari and Mirman (1980), and others, Benhabib and I analyzed a fairly general model of the joint exploitation of a productive asset as a dynamic, noncooperative game. Here the state variable is the stock of the productive asset, which changes through time as a result of its own productivity and the actions of the players. Our goal was to understand the variety of equilibria of this game, and in particular to understand the conditions under which there exist equilibria that are efficient.

In the continuous time model that we study, the (positive) stock at date t, $Y(t)$, evolves according to the differential equation

---

[3] This section is based on Benhabib and Radner (1992).

$$Y'(t) = \eta\big(Y(t)\big) - c_1(t) - c_2(t),$$

where (for the case of two players) $c_1(t)$ and $c_2(t)$ are the rates of consumption of the asset by players 1 and 2, respectively. The "production function" η is assumed to be concave and to take the value zero at both zero and some positive stock level. The strategy of each player determines her consumption rate at each time as a function of the previous history of the process, possibly with some delay. We assume that each player's utility for the game is equal to her total discounted consumption over the duration of the game. The game ends when the stock becomes zero, if ever. The linearity of a player's utility in her consumption is the main special assumption of the model. We also assume that each player's rate of consumption is nonnegative and bounded.

At an efficient equilibrium, the weighted sum of the players' total utility is maximized. Since the instantaneous utilities of the players are linear in consumption, this is equivalent to maximizing the discounted sum of the total consumption of the players. We show that the efficient consumption policy of the two players is to consume nothing until a certain level of the stock is reached. After that, the total consumption of the players is equal to the output of the stock, so that the stock level is stationary. We call a consumption policy of this type a *frugal* policy. By contrast, a player who follows a *prodigal* consumption policy always consumes at the upper bound of consumption rate.

The equilibria of this dynamic game that correspond to the repeated static equilibria are those in which each player uses a strategy in which his action at any date is independent of the current stock of the asset; we might call these "extreme" equilibria. In such equilibria, the players run down the stock of the asset as fast as possible ("prodigal" consumption). By analogy with the terminology of repeated game theory, we define a *trigger strategy equilibrium* to be a Nash equilibrium in which the players threaten to revert to an extreme equilibrium whenever a player is caught deviating from the target efficient path. The effectiveness of such threats depends, of course, on the detection technology – that is, on how much extra utility the deviating player can gain before his deviation is detected by the other players. In the model we study, efficient trigger strategy equilibria may exist from some starting states but not others. More precisely, there is a stock level, say y', such that a trigger strategy equilibrium exists from starting stocks greater than or equal to y' but not from those strictly less than y'. (This statement is meant to include the cases in which y' is zero or infinite.)

Under some circumstances, there may exist a new kind of equilibrium, which we call a *switching equilibrium*. We show that, in our model, if y'

is positive (and finite) then there is an open interval I with upper end-point y' such that, from any starting stock in I, there is an equilibrium of the dynamic game with the following structure: The players follow an inefficient but growing path until the stock reaches the level y', and then follow an efficient trigger strategy after that.

An important feature of our analysis is an explicit modelling of delayed information. In our treatment of trigger strategy and switching equilibria, we assume that each player can observe the state of the system (the stock of the asset) with a fixed delay; that is, at time t each player can observe the *history* of the state variable up through time $(t - \tau)$, where the delay τ is a fixed, positive parameter of the model. The larger the delay, the more a player can benefit from a defection from a pre-scribed path before his defection is detected and the other player can respond. In previous discrete time models, this delay has been implicitly equated to the length of the period between decision times. The use of a continuous time model makes it convenient for us to vary the delay τ as an independent parameter, and we consider this to be an important contribution of our analysis.[4]

Roughly speaking, we show that for any fixed discount rate, (1) efficiency can be sustained by trigger strategy equilibria from any positive initial stock, provided that the delay is sufficiently small, but (2) efficiency cannot be so sustained from any positive initial stock, provided that the delay is sufficiently large. A corresponding result holds for a fixed positive delay as one varies the discount rate.

4   Simple Partnerships with Moral Hazard

4.1   Introduction

In the present section I introduce three new features into the model of a simple partnership that was described in Section 2:

(1)   the joint output is influenced by exogenous random factors (the environment), as well as by the partners' inputs;
(2)   the partners cannot observe the random environmental factors;
(3)   the partners cannot observe each others' inputs.

A consequence of these new features is that, by observing the output alone, the partners cannot infer with certainty the cause of any depar-ture from some target output. This situation is sometimes described as one of *moral hazard*.

---

[4] For an analysis of information processing as a source of delay, see Radner (1992).

In a more realistic model, features (2) and (3) would be relaxed to allow for imperfect observation of the environment and the actions of other partners. In particular, if different partners had different information about the environment, then phenomena such as adverse selection, self-selection, misrepresentation, and so forth might arise. For simplicity, however, I shall restrict my attention to the case of moral hazard.

If one assumes that the objective of each partner is to maximize her own expected utility, then the introduction of the above features does not essentially alter the analysis of the one-period game. On the other hand, the nature of the repeated game is changed in a fundamental way, as we shall see.

Example 4.1. Modify Example 2.1 so that the outcome is a random variable, say Y, whose probability distribution depends on a_1 and a_2. In particular, suppose that Y can take on only two possible values, y_1 and y_0, with

$$\text{Prob}(Y = y_1) = \min\{\alpha(a_1 + a_2), 1\}, \tag{4.1}$$

where a_1 and a_2 are nonnegative. (Think of a_i as i's "effort.") Without loss of generality, we may take $y_1 = 1$, $y_0 = 0$, and $\alpha = 1$.

Let s_{iy} denote partner i's compensation if the outcome is y;

$$s_{11} + s_{21} = 1, \qquad s_{10} + s_{20} = 0. \tag{4.2}$$

Partner i's utility is assumed to be linear in compensation and quadratic in effort:

$$U_i = s_{iy} - qa_i^2.$$

Hence his expected utility is, by (4.1),

$$u_i = s_{i1}(a_1 + a_2) + s_{i0}(1 - a_1 - a_2) - qa_i^2$$
$$= (s_{i1} - s_{i0})(a_1 + a_2) - qa_i^2 - s_{i0} \tag{4.3}$$

(provided that $a_1 + a_2 \le 1$). For example, if $s_{i1} = 1/2$ and $s_{i0} = 0$, then

$$u_i = \frac{1}{2}(a_1 + a_2) - qa_i^2. \tag{4.4}$$

Notice the formal similarity between (4.4) and (2.5) in Example 2.1, the latter with $R = 1$. It follows that the analysis of efficiency and equilibrium in this example is the same as in Example 2.1.

With the introduction of uncertainty, one should take account of the players' attitudes toward risk. In Example 4.1, the partners are represented as neutral towards risk, but of course this is not the general case. The special implications of the assumption of risk neutrality will be explored in Sections 4.3 and 4.4.

4.2 Optimal Sharing Rules with Risk Neutrality

In Section 2.1, I argued heuristically that, in the certainty case, an equilibrium cannot be efficient. That argument was based on the assumption that the partners shared the output equally. In fact, one can show that, under quite general conditions (with certainty), *there is no sharing rule for which a corresponding equilibrium is efficient.*

With the introduction of uncertainty, the situation is changed. Following Williams and Radner (1995), in this section I shall sketch an argument to show that, if the number of possible outputs is at least 3 and if the partners are neutral toward risk, then – generically in the data of the game – there exists a sharing rule for which the corresponding equilibrium of the one-period game is efficient.

Basically, what is required is that the partners be sufficiently different in the effects that their actions have on the distribution of output. On the other hand, if the partnership is symmetric with respect to permutations of the partners, then an efficiency-inducing sharing rule will typically not exist. (Generically, the partnership will not be symmetric.)

I begin by describing the Williams–Radner model, which is a generalization of Example 4.1. There are $m > 1$ partners. The ith partner chooses his input a_i from some closed and bounded subinterval A_i of the real line. His choice is his own private information. Let $a \equiv (a_1, \ldots, a_m)$ denote an input profile, and let a_{-i} denote the $(m - 1)$-tuple $(a_1, \ldots, a_{i-1}, a_{i+1}, \ldots, a_m)$.

Once the partners have chosen their inputs, one of several levels of output results. This output is publicly observable. Let Y denote the range of output levels of the partnership. Except where otherwise noted, the reader should assume that Y is some finite set of real numbers with $n \geq 2$ elements,

$$Y = \left\{ y_1 < y_2 < \cdots < y_n \right\}.$$

The partners' inputs determine a probability distribution over Y. For the input profile a, let $F(\cdot, a)$ denote the cumulative distribution that is determined by a, and let $f(\cdot, a)$ denote the corresponding density function. These functions are common knowledge, and each is a C^1 function of the inputs. For simplicity, let $F_i(y, a) \equiv \partial F(y, a)/\partial a_i$ and $f_i(y, a) \equiv \partial f(y, a)/\partial a_i$.

The ith partner's utility u_i consists of whatever share $s_i(y)$ he receives of the observed output y, minus the disutility $Q_i(a_i)$ of his contribution of the input a_i:

$$u_i \equiv s_i(y) - Q_i(a_i).$$

By assumption, $Q_i(\cdot)$ is a C^1 function of the ith partner's contribution. Let $q_i(\cdot) \equiv \partial Q_i/\partial a_i(\cdot)$. We assume that $q_i(\cdot)$ is strictly positive.

Because utility is transferable, an input profile $\hat{a}$ is Pareto optimal if and only if it maximizes the difference between the expected total output and the total disutility of the input contributions:

$$\hat{a} \in \operatorname*{argmax}_a \left\{ E(y|a) - \sum_{i=1}^m Q_i(a_i) \right\}. \tag{4.5}$$

We assume that there exists a solution to this maximization problem in the interior of $\Pi_{i=1}^m A_i$. Efficiency therefore requires each partner to make a positive input contribution.

Our concern is the existence of a sharing rule $s_1(\cdot), \ldots, s_m(\cdot)$ that satisfies the budget constraint

$$\sum_{i=1}^m s_i(y) = y \quad \text{for all } y \in Y, \tag{4.6}$$

and that also makes the efficient profile $\hat{a}$ into a Nash equilibrium:

$$\hat{a}_i \in \operatorname*{argmax}_{a_i} \left\{ E\big(s_i(y)|(a_i, \hat{a}_{-i})\big) - Q_i(a_i) \right\} \quad \text{for } 1 \le i \le m.$$

The problem of devising a sharing rule with these properties is the *partnership problem*. The following first-order conditions are necessary. If $\hat{a}$ is efficient, then for each partner the marginal expected *total output* must equal the marginal disutility of her contribution at $\hat{a}$,

$$\sum_{j=1}^n y_j f_i(y_j, \hat{a}) = q_i(\hat{a}_i) \quad \text{for all } 1 \le i \le m. \tag{4.7}$$

On the other hand, if $\hat{a}$ is a Nash equilibrium then each partner's marginal expected *compensation* must equal the marginal disutility of her contribution at $\hat{a}$,

$$\sum_{j=1}^n s_i(y_j) f_i(y_j, \hat{a}) = q_i(\hat{a}_i) \quad \text{for all } 1 \le i \le m. \tag{4.8}$$

The problem of devising a sharing rule that satisfies the first-order condition (4.8) and the budget constraint (4.6) is the *first-order problem*.

Our approach is to solve the first-order problem and then to determine whether or not this solution also solves the partnership problem. The main result is that the first-order problem is solvable for a generic choice of $F(\cdot)$ and $Q_1(\cdot), \ldots, Q_m(\cdot)$ when $F(\cdot, a)$ defines a probability distribution over at least three output levels. Efficiency plays a relatively minor role in the proof; we actually prove the stronger result that, in a generic problem with at least three output levels, the budget constraint and the first-order conditions for a Nash equilibrium are solvable at a *generic input profile*. (In other words, for a generic input profile, there will be a sharing rule for which the input profile is an equilibrium.)

To get an idea of the proof, let n be the number of possible output levels y_j. The unknowns in (4.6) and (4.8) are the mn numbers $s_i(y_j)$. Thus we can regard (4.8) and (4.6) as a system of $m + n$ linear equations in the mn variables $(s_i(y_j))_{1 \le i \le m, 1 \le j \le n}$ whose coefficients are determined by the efficient profile $\hat{a}$. The left-hand sides of the first m equations from (4.8) are the marginal expected payments to the partners, and the last n equations from (4.6) are for the budget constraint. Efficiency is used in the analysis of the $n \ge 3$ case only to determine the values of these coefficients; the argument could be carried out using coefficients determined by a generic input profile. The main task of the proof is to show that, generically in the data of the problem, these equations have full rank if $n \ge 3$. On the other hand, it is not difficult to show that, if $n = 2$ or if the equations are symmetric in the partners, then no solution is possible.

It is easy to construct linear examples in which every sharing rule that satisfies both the budget constraint and the first-order conditions for a Nash equilibrium also solves the partnership problem. More generally, Williams and Radner (1995) derive conditions on the output function under which at least one solution to the first-order problem also solves the partnership problem. For simplicity, we derive these conditions only when there are two partners and three levels of output. The conditions are awkward, and at present they have no economic interpretation; however, they are satisfied by "reasonable" examples (see Section 4.4).

We also prove a paradoxical result that concerns the nature of the solutions to the first-order conditions when the output function satisfies stochastic dominance with respect to each partner's input. (For each partner, given the inputs of the other partners, stochastic dominance holds if the observation of a higher level of output allows one to infer, in a probabilistic sense, that the selected partner contributed a greater level of input; see e.g., Whitt 1980.) When stochastic dominance holds, one might expect that a partner's payment should increase with the output; as Alchian and Demsetz (1972, p. 778) suggested in their analysis of the internal structure of firms, a partner may have an incentive to sabotage the organization if his reward and the output are inversely related. In fact, the opposite is true: When stochastic dominance holds, for any sharing rule that satisfies the first-order conditions, some (at least two) of the partners' payments must be nonincreasing over some subsets of the range of output levels. Thus moral hazard can be overcome in some problems in which stochastic dominance holds, but only if some partners do not always benefit when the joint output increases.

This paradox may explain why these results seem surprising, and why they have been overlooked in the literature on partnership. One can show that the Nash equilibria of partnerships are typically inefficient when the budget is balanced, provided that (i) each partner's payment increases with the output; and (ii) for each state of a random environment, the output is an increasing function of each partner's input. This second assumption implies that the output function satisfies stochastic dominance.

Each of these results can be extended to the case where the set of output levels is a subinterval of the real line. Thus, it is possible to solve the partnership problem in our model not because of any special assumption about the range of output levels, but because the joint output is uncertain.

This section focused on the case in which the partners are risk-neutral. It can be shown that, in a generic problem with risk aversion, the partnership problem is unsolvable.

4.3   The Repeated Game

I have alluded to the fact that the introduction of moral hazard into the partnership situation changes the repeated game in a fundamental way. The trigger strategies described in Section 2.2 can no longer be completely effective (even with discount factors close to 1), because departures from the target output can be caused by random variations in the environment as well as by deviations of the partners' inputs from their target values.

However, the partners are not completely powerless to monitor each other's inputs, since they will have *statistical* evidence from the sequence of observed outputs. For example, suppose that, over time, the random environmental factors are independent and identically distributed. It follows that, if each partner uses her target input in each period, then the sequence of outputs will be independent and identically distributed as well; call this the *target distribution* of the outputs. Each partner could now use a statistical procedure to test whether the other partners are adhering to their target inputs, in a manner analogous to the statistical quality control of a production process. A "failure" of the test would trigger a reversion by all of the partners to their respective stubborn strategies.

Notice, however, that a procedure that had any chance of detecting deviations from target inputs would also produce a false alarm from time to time. In other words, even if the partners always used their target input, there would be a positive relative frequency of test failures, so that the reversion to stubborn strategies would, with probability 1, eventually be triggered. The inefficiency caused by this could be mitigated, but not entirely eliminated, by making the reversions to stubborn strategies last only a finite length of time ("relenting" strategies).[5] In this case, there would be an infinite sequence of phases of two types, one in which the partners used their target inputs, and one in which they used their stubborn strategies.

Of course, this does not settle the question of whether, as the players' discount factors approach 1, efficiency can be approached by equilibria of the supergame. The conditions for this to be true are somewhat complicated, and I shall not attempt to describe them precisely here. Roughly speaking, what is required is that, for every pair of partners, the probability distributions of outcomes corresponding to different pairs of deviations from the target inputs should be linearly independent.[6]

4.4 A Continuous Time Model

In this section, I summarize the results of a study by Rustichini and Radner (1996) of a partnership model with uncertainty in a framework that allows the analysis of the effect of varying the reaction time of the partners, including the limiting case of instantaneous adjustment. The one-period outputs are normally distributed random variables, with means and variances depending on the inputs of the partners. The sequence of outputs is a stochastic process of Wiener type, which can be thought of as the discretization of a diffusion process. As the reaction time tends to zero, this process tends to the solution of a stochastic differential equation. The sample paths are (almost surely) continuous. It

---

[5] Note that relenting strategies could also have been used in the case of certainty, but would not have produced any further increase in efficiency.

[6] See Fudenberg, Levine, and Maskin (1989). I should mention here that their analysis makes use of a more general class of supergame strategies than those described in the preceding paragraph. See also Radner (1986a) and Radner, Myerson, and Maskin (1986).

may be objected that in real-world partnerships the reaction time and the flow of information are always, for practical purposes, different from zero; so partners cannot adjust instantaneously all the time. In fact, the same objection may be raised against any model of a dynamic game in continuous time. But since a universal lower bound on the reaction time would certainly be artificial, the following question arises: Do the properties of the set of equilibria and of the strategies approach some limit when the reaction time becomes arbitrarily small? A related nontrivial question is the existence of equilibria. In other words, the analysis of a continuous time model may be considered as a way of testing the robustness of the results for a discrete time (finite reaction) model; the study of the limit situation should clarify which properties of a discrete time model depend critically on the fixed delay in the reaction of the players when that delay is small.

The first question we analyzed is the characterization of *efficient sharing rules* – sharing rules that have the efficient outcome as a (Nash) equilibrium. This question was first examined by Williams and Radner in 1982 (published as Williams and Radner 1995), where the generic existence of efficient sharing rules was demonstrated in a class of partnership models (see Section 4.3). Like Williams and Radner, we assume that the partners are risk-neutral. For our model, we provided a complete characterization of the partnerships for which the design of efficient sharing rules is possible, as well as a characterization of such rules. This characterization has a particularly simple formulation in the case where the outcome is a random variable with a normal distribution. Simply stated, the condition requires that at least two of the partners be sufficiently different, in the sense that the variance and the mean of the outcome vary differently as the efforts of these two partners vary. It is interesting to note that the preferences of the players (in our case, the cost or disutility of the input) plays no role. We then presented a general procedure to design such sharing rules. From this very construction, it will be apparent that the set of possible sharing rules is quite large.

We then examined the problem of the existence of a limit for the optimization problems of each partner. The existence of such a limit is important from the point of view of the robustness of the equilibrium, as the repeated game becomes (in the limit) a continuous time game. In fact the existence of such a limit is a necessary condition for the concept of equilibrium to be well-defined. We proved that it is always possible to construct sharing rules that are both efficient and stable (with respect to this limit process). Indeed, very simple sharing rules can be formed, even with quadratic functions.

Lastly, we discussed the performance of fixed proportion sharing rules as the reaction time tends to zero. We examined the case of two identical partners, with the sharing rule given by equal splitting of the outcome, and examined upper bounds on the efficiency of symmetric equilibria. The main result is that, when the reaction time becomes shorter than a fixed positive quantity, the only equilibrium of the repeated game is the equilibrium of the one-period game. A similar question has been examined, with similar conclusions, in the paper of Abreu, Milgrom, and Pearce (1991) for the not necessarily symmetric case. However, in their model the outcome is a stochastic process of Poisson type (rather than of Wiener type, as in our case), and the action space of the partners consists of two points. Thus the model of the present paper and the one in Abreu et al. together cover all processes in continuous time for which: (1) increments over nonoverlapping time intervals are independent; (2) sample paths have, at most, discontinuities of the first kind; and (3) for any fixed time t, the sample paths are continuous in probability at t. (Such processes are called Lévy processes. See Ito (1985) for an analysis of such processes and a proof that Lévy processes are compositions of constant processes, Wiener processes, and Poisson processes.)

5 Principal–Agent Games

5.1 Introduction

I turn now to the principal–agent model, which is suggested by the hierarchical or supervisory relationships that are common in organizations. From a formal point of view, we may consider the principal–agent model as a special case of the partnership model in which one of the partners, the principal, effectively takes no action (formally, the outcome is independent of his action); the other partners are the agents. In fact, most of the literature deals with the case of only one agent, which is the case I shall discuss here.[7] Also, most analyses assume that it is the principal who chooses the compensation function (sharing rule), subject to some constraints; this choice becomes the strategy of the principal. This is the approach I shall follow in the present section.

To summarize, we shall be considering the following situation. The "enterprise" comprises the principal and the agent. The output of the enterprise depends on the agent's action and on a stochastic environment, but the principal cannot fully monitor the agent's information and

[7] This is clearly a limitation from the point of view of organization theory. See Radner (1987) and Groves (1973) for a more general discussion.

Table 1. *Examples of Principal–Agent Relationships*

Principal	Agent
Board of directors	Chief executive officer
Manager	Subordinate
Foreman	Worker
Client	Lawyer
Customer	Supplier
Regulator	Public utility
Insurer	Insured

action, nor can she fully monitor the environment. The principal can monitor the outcome, however, and in the simplest form of the principal–agent model – the one we shall study here – this is all that she *can* monitor. More generally, the principal could make the agent's compensation depend on anything else that the principal can observe – for example, some incomplete information about the agent's information, action, or environment.

Table 1 lists some principal–agent relationships that can be more or less accurately represented by the general principal–agent model. The insurer–insured relationship is the one that gave rise to the term "moral hazard." The action of the insured (agent) is the care he takes to prevent an accident (say to property), and the outcome is the occurrence or nonoccurrence of the accident. The compensation that the principal (insurer) pays to the agent is negative (the premium) if the accident does not occur, and is typically positive (the claim minus the premium) if the accident does occur. If the preventive care is costly to the agent, then the fact that he has insurance may lead him to lower his level of care, and this is the phenomenon known as moral hazard. In this relationship, the insured party is the agent, since he is the actor whose actions (care) are unobserved, and the insurer is the principal, who compensates the insured according to the outcome.

Although much of the literature on the principal–agent model refers to market or regulatory relationships, my concern here will be primarily with principal–agent relationships within organizations, such as those listed in the first group of Table 1.

In this section I shall use a simple example of a one-period principal–agent model to illustrate how moral hazard can lead to inefficiency. Suppose that the (stochastic) outcome of the enterprise is either "success" or "failure," and that the probability of success depends on the agent's action. In the case of success the principal earns one unit of money (say $1 million), but in the case of failure she earns nothing. The principal will compensate the agent according to the outcome, giving him a compensation of w_1 for a successful outcome and a compensation of w_0 for a failure. (In principle, a compensation may be negative, although institutional constraints might rule that out.) The principal's utility is assumed to equal the difference between the outcome and the compensation she pays the agent; thus the principal is neutral toward risk. The agent's utility is assumed to depend both on his action and on his compensation; he may be neutral toward risk or averse to it.

I shall represent this situation as a two-move game. The principal moves first, announcing a pair of compensations (w_0, w_1) to which she is committed. The agent moves second, choosing his action. The outcome is then observed by both players, and the agent is compensated accordingly. In this game the principal's strategy is the same as her move, namely the compensation pair; but the agent's strategy is a *decision rule* that determines his action corresponding to each alternative compensation pair that the principal could announce.

An *equilibrium*[8] of the game is a pair of strategies, one for the principal and one for the agent, such that:

(1) given the announced compensation pair, the agent chooses his action so as to maximize his own expected utility; and

(2) given the optimizing behavior of the agent described in (1), the principal chooses a compensation pair that maximizes her own expected utility.

In the formulation of a principal–agent model, one typically adds one or both of the following constraints on the compensation pair that the principal may announce:

(1) the compensation pair must enable the agent to attain (ex ante) an "acceptable" expected utility; and

(2) the individual compensations are bounded below by some exogenously given bound.

The first constraint can be interpreted as requiring that the principal must offer the agent an expected utility at least as large as what the agent could obtain in other employment. The second constraint recognizes that the agent's wealth is finite, so the agent cannot pay the principal arbitrarily large amounts of money (negative compensations).

---

[8] The game theorist will recognize that I have added the condition of subgame perfection.

A strategy pair is defined to be *efficient* if no other strategy pair yields one of the players more expected utility and yields the other no less. The main proposition of this section is (with one interesting exception) that, *under realistic conditions, an equilibrium is not efficient.* Precise mathematical statements of the model and the proposition are given at the end of this section. I shall try to make the proposition plausible here with an informal argument.

Suppose that the agent is averse to risk. First, I shall argue that in an efficient strategy pair the agent's compensation must be independent of the outcome, that is, w_0 must equal w_1. Suppose, to the contrary, that the two compensations were different ($w_0 \neq w_1$), and let $\bar{w}$ be the expected compensation corresponding to the agent's action. Since the agent is averse to risk, he would be better off if he used the same action but received a compensation equal to $\bar{w}$ regardless of the outcome. The principal, on the other hand, would be no worse off in this new situation, since she is neutral toward risk. Indeed, if one wanted to make both players strictly better off, the principal could pay the agent a constant compensation that is slightly less than $\bar{w}$.

On the other hand, a strategy pair in which the agent's compensation does not depend on the outcome typically cannot be an equilibrium, unless by coincidence the action that the agent most prefers is in itself also part of an efficient strategy pair. For example, suppose that increasing the probability of success requires more effort by the agent, and that the agent prefers less effort to more. In this case, if the compensation is independent of the outcome then the agent will have no incentive to exert any effort at all! Thus, in an equilibrium, the agent typically must receive a larger compensation for success than for failure. The incentive requirements for equilibrium are therefore incompatible with the conditions for efficiency.

An exception to the proposition occurs if the agent is neutral toward risk and is sufficiently wealthy. In this case, an efficient equilibrium is obtained if the principal sells the agent a "franchise" to the enterprise – that is, the agent pays the principal a fixed fee and then keeps the entire outcome. (It is easy to see that this is equivalent to making the compensation for failure negative, and to making the compensation for success one unit higher than the compensation for failure.)

Are there any remedies for the inefficiency of equilibrium in the principal–agent relationship? One possible remedy is for the principal to expend resources to monitor the agent's action (and, more generally, his information and environment). Whether this will improve net efficiency will depend, of course, on the cost of monitoring. The prevalence of de facto decentralization in large organizations suggests that accurate monitoring of agents' actions is too costly to be efficient or even practicable.

Another remedy for inefficiency of equilibrium may be available if the principal–agent relationship is a long-term one. This topic is discussed in Section 5.2.

Example 5.1. I start with a formal model of the example of the principal–agent game discussed in this section. The notation is chosen, as far as possible, to indicate how this example is related to the model of Section 4. The action of the agent is a nonnegative real number a, and the resulting output is

$$Y = G(a, X),$$

where X is a random variable. In this example, X is distributed uniformly on the unit interval, and

$$G(a, X) = \begin{cases} 1 & \text{if } a \geq X, \\ 0 & \text{if } a < X. \end{cases}$$

We may interpret Y as success or failure, X as the difficulty of the agent's task, and a as his effort. From the specification of G,

$$\text{Prob}(Y = 1) = \min(a, 1).$$

The agent has no information about X (other than its distribution) when he chooses his action. The agent's compensation depends on the output Y according to

$$S(Y) = \begin{cases} w_0 & \text{if } Y = 0, \\ w_1 & \text{if } Y = 1. \end{cases}$$

The agent's resulting utility is

$$U_1 = P(S(Y)) - Q(a),$$

where P and Q are differentiable and strictly increasing functions, P is strictly concave, and Q is strictly convex. Hence, we may assume $a \leq 1$. Notice that I have assumed that the agent is averse to risk. Without loss of generality, I establish the convention that

$$P(0) = Q(0) = 0.$$

The principal receives what is left of the output after compensating the agent. Assume that her utility is equal to what she receives; that is,

$$U_0 = Y - S(Y).$$

(Thus the principal is neutral toward risk.)

In this game, the principal moves first, choosing a compensation function S, and then the agent moves, choosing an action a after learning what S is. Conditional on the agent's action, the resulting expected utility to the principal is

$$v_0 = a(1 - w_1) - (1 - a)w_0, \tag{5.1}$$

and to the agent is

$$v_1 = aP(w_1) + (1 - a)P(w_0) - Q(a). \tag{5.2}$$

The principal's strategy is the compensation function S, and the agent's strategy is a mapping α from compensation functions to actions:

$$a = \alpha(S).$$

An equilibrium of the game is a pair of strategies (S^*, α^*) such that:

(1) S^* maximizes v_0 given α^*; and
(2) $\alpha^*(S^*)$ maximizes v_1 given S^*.

In addition, I shall require that in an equilibrium, for *every* S (not just S^*), $\alpha^*(S)$ maximizes the agent's expected utility given S. (Thus, I require that equilibria be *perfect*; in this two-move game such equilibria are also called Stackelberg.) I shall write $a^* = \alpha^*(S^*)$.

Typically, it is realistic to impose two constraints on the compensations. The first constraint is that the principal may not impose arbitrarily large penalties on the agent; in other words, the compensations are constrained so that the agent's disutility is bounded from below. The second constraint expresses the condition that the agent is free to refuse to enter into the relationship (i.e., to play the game). For this, w_0 and w_1 must be such as to enable the agent to achieve some minimum *expected* utility. For the purposes of this chapter, it is sufficient to impose a constraint of the first type; the addition of the second constraint would slightly complicate the exposition (but would not change the results in any essential way). To express the first constraint, we can assume that the compensations are bounded from below (and that the function P is finite everywhere); without loss of generality, I assume that they are nonnegative:

$$(w_0, w_1) \geq 0.$$

Space limitations do not permit a complete analysis of this game. We can verify easily from (5.2) that if $w_0 = w_1 = w$ then the agent will have no incentive to work, that is, $a^*(w, w) = 0$. In addition, we see from (5.2) that if

$$Q'(0) \geq P(1)$$

then $a^*(w_0, w_1) = 0$ for all w_0 and w_1 between 0 and 1; in this case, the only equilibrium has $S^* = (0,0)$ and $a^* = 0$. On the other hand, if

$$Q'(0) < P(1) \tag{5.3}$$

then the equilibrium is characterized by

$$0 = w_0^* < w_1^* < 1, \tag{5.4}$$
$$a^* > 0;$$

also, $a^*(0, w_1)$ is strictly increasing in w_1 whenever $a^*(0, w_1)$ is strictly between 0 and 1. This is the case I shall discuss from now on.

A pair $(\hat{S}, \hat{a})$ is efficient (Pareto optimal) if no other pair (S, a) yields each player as much expected utility and at least one player strictly more. From the concavity of the function P, it follows that, for the same level of effort, the agent prefers the compensation function $(\bar{w}, \bar{w})$ to the compensation function (w_0, w_1), where

$$\bar{w} = aw_1 + (1 - a)w_0,$$

whereas the principal is indifferent between the two (recall that the agent is risk-averse and the principal is risk-neutral). Hence, if $[(\hat{w}_0, \hat{w}_1), a]$ is efficient then $\hat{w}_0 = \hat{w}_1$. Together with (5.4) this shows that an equilibrium is not efficient.

There are, of course, many efficient pairs $[(\hat{w}, \hat{w}), a]$; one can show that, for $0 < \hat{a} < 1$, they are characterized by the condition $P'(\hat{w}) = Q'(\hat{a})$.

For more thorough treatments of the principal–agent problem and further references, see Grossman and Hart (1983), Myerson (1983), Fudenberg and Tirole (1990), and Dutta and Radner (1995).

5.2   Repeated Games

I now examine some ways that the two players can exploit a long-term principal–agent relationship to escape, at least partially, from the inefficiency of short-term equilibria. The long-term relationship will be modeled as a situation in which the one-period situation is repeated over and over again. These repetitions give the principal an opportunity to observe the results of the agent's actions over a number of periods, and to use some statistical test to infer whether or not the agent was choosing the appropriate action. The repetitions also provide the principal with opportunities to punish the agent for apparent departures from the appropriate action. Finally, the possible dependence of the agent's compensation in any one period on the outcomes in a number of previous periods (e.g., on the average over a number of periods) provides the principal with an indirect means of *insuring* the agent, at least partially, against random fluctuations in the outcomes that are not due to fluctuations in the agent's actions. Thus, the repetitions provide an opportunity to reduce the agent's risk without reducing his incentive to perform well.

The same beneficial results could be obtained, of course, if the agent had some means of self-insurance – for example, through access to a capital market or because his wealth was substantial. However, in many interesting cases (such as the owner–manager relationship), the random fluctuations in outcome are too large compared to the agent's wealth or borrowing power to make such self-insurance practical. With such cases in mind, I shall confine my attention to *nonnegative* compensation functions.

The decision rule that the principal uses to adjust the agent's compensation in any one period in the light of previous observations constitutes the principal's (*many-period*) *strategy*. Likewise, the agent will have a (many-period) strategy for adjusting his actions in the light of the past history of the process. In principle, the player's strategy spaces are very large and contain very complex strategies. For this reason, I shall devote most of my attention to equilibria that are sustained with relatively simple strategies.

It may be helpful to have a stylized example in mind; I shall call this the "owner–manager" story. In this story, the owner is the principal and the manager is the agent. The owner of an enterprise wants to put it in the hands of a manager. In each of a number of successive periods (month, quarter, year), the profit of the enterprise will depend both on the actions of the manager and on the environment in which the enterprise is operating. The owner cannot directly monitor the manager's actions, nor can the owner costlessly observe all of the relevant aspects of the environment. The owner and the manager will have to agree on how the manager is to be compensated, and the owner wants to pick a compensation mechanism that will motivate the manager to provide a good return on the owner's investment, net of the payments to the manager.

I shall consider two kinds of long-term relationships. In the first, the principal "punishes" the agent by replacing him with another agent. I shall call this the *replacement model*. In this model, there may be an infinite sequence of agents, either because an agent has a maximum potential tenure or because the players use strategies that imply that, with probability 1, each agent will eventually be replaced. In the second type of long-term relationship, which I shall call the *nonreplacement model*, a single agent is associated with the principal forever. The players "punish" each other by changing their actions in response to the publicly available information, just as the partners do in equilibria of Section 4.2. I shall discuss the replacement model first.

It is perhaps intuitively plausible that it makes a great difference whether or not the principal can commit herself in advance to a particular compensation strategy.[9] I shall first discuss the case in which, in the context of the replacement model, the principal can so commit herself. One can show that, with simple strategies, the principal can induce the agent to behave in a way that yields both players discounted expected utilities that are close to one-period efficiency, provided that the players' discount factors are close to 1 and the agent's potential tenure is long. An important step in the analysis is the derivation of a lower bound on the expected tenure of the agent as a function of the agent's discount factor, his maximum potential tenure, and minimal information about his one-period utility function.

Here is an informal description of one class of such simple strategies for the principal, which I call "bankruptcy strategies." In this description (as in the remainder of Section 5.2), I shall use the language of the owner–manager story. The owner pays the manager a fixed compensation (wage) w per period until the end of the first period T in which the total of the gross returns in periods 1 through T fall below $T(r + w)$ by an amount at least s (where w, r, and s are parameters of the owner's strategy). At the end of such a period T, the manager is replaced and the owner engages another one under the same regime. This can be interpreted as requiring the manger to produce a "paper" gross return of $(r + w)$ each period (a net return of r), and also allowing any surplus to be added to a (paper) cash reserve and requiring any deficit to be subtracted. The manager starts with a positive cash reserve equal to s and is replaced by a new manager the first time this cash reserve falls to zero. Since the cash reserve is only an accounting fiction, the bankruptcy strategy is really only a scoring formula for evaluating the manager's long-term performance, together with a criterion (based on the manager's score) for ending his tenure. The difference between the gross return in a period and $(r + w)$ is sometimes called *economic value added* (EVA) or *residual income*.

---

[9] Since the agent's actions cannot be observed by anyone else, there is no credible way in which the agent can commit himself in advance to a particular strategy.

One can show that, if the player's discount rate is sufficiently close to 1 and if the manager's potential tenure is sufficiently long, then the parameters of the bankruptcy strategy can be chosen so that the manager's correspondingly optimal strategy yields a stochastic process of outcomes for which the pair of expected discounted utilities is close to one-period efficiency. (See Radner 1986b for an analysis and the statement of appropriate assumptions.)

I turn now to a brief discussion of another class of simple strategies for the owner that will also play a role in the noncommitment, non-replacement case. I call these *review strategies*; in these strategies, the owner periodically reviews the manager's performance, and replaces the manager if his cumulative performance since the last review is unsatisfactory in a sense to be defined.

A review strategy for the owner has three parameters ℓ, r, and s, where:

(1) ℓ is the number of periods covered by each review; and
(2)   the manager is replaced immediately after any review for which the total return during the ℓ periods preceding the review does not exceed $\ell r - s$.

Thus the first review occurs at the end of period ℓ, and the manager is replaced if

$$S_\ell = R_1 + \cdots + R_\ell \le \ell r - s;$$

otherwise, the manager continues in office until the end of period 2ℓ, at which time he is replaced if

$$S_{2\ell} - S_\ell = R_{\ell+1} + \cdots + R_{2\ell} \le \ell r - s,$$

and so on. The manager's total tenure, say T, will be some random multiple of ℓ, that is, $T = N\ell$. I shall call the periods from $[(n-1)\ell + 1]$ to $n\ell$ the nth *review phase*; thus ℓ is the length of each review phase and N is the number of review phases in the manager's tenure.

Assume that, during his tenure, the manager receives from the owner a fixed payment per period. Consider a period t that is in the nth review phase, and take the "state of the system" at the end of period t to be the pair $(t - n\ell, S_t - S_{(n-1)\ell})$; then, with this state space, the manager faces a standard finite-state dynamic programming problem. Without loss of generality, we may therefore suppose that the manager uses a strategy that is "stationary" in the sense that:

(1)   in each period, action depends only on the state of the system at the end of the previous period;

(2)   in periods $1, \ell + 1, 2\ell + 1, \ldots$, action is the same and independent of the history of the process.

In other words, the beginning of each review phase is a point of renewal of the process. (One can prove results for review strategies that are similar to those for bankruptcy strategies; see Radner 1986b.)

Up to this point, I have assumed that the owner (principal) could precommit to a particular strategy, even though the manager (agent) could not. In fact, such precommitments are the exception rather than the rule in owner–manager relations, although precommitment, in the form of contracts, can be found in other principal–agent relationships (e.g., customer–supplier and client–broker).

For the strategies considered in previous sections, there are many situations in which the owner might be tempted to change strategy in midcourse. For example, in the case of the bankruptcy strategy, if the manager has accumulated an unusually large cash reserve then he can be expected to "coast" for many periods while the reserve falls to a lower level (but one that is still "safe" from the manager's point of view). If the manager is near the end of the maximum potential tenure and has a relatively safe cash reserve, he will likewise have an incentive to coast. In both of these situations, the owner would be tempted to replace the manager immediately with a new one. Analogous situations arise under the review strategies. The manager would be expected to move away from the actions that produce the highest returns if his score were sufficiently high or sufficiently low. In both cases, the probability of passing review would be very little affected by the manager's choice of actions during the remainder of the review period, and so the manager would have an incentive to choose actions that gave him higher one-period utility.

On the other side of the balance, there may be costs to the owner of replacing a manager, costs that have not been taken into account in the previous discussion. First, the owner may find it more difficult to find replacements for the manager's position if it is known that the owner has departed in midcourse from a previously announced strategy, or in other words has "reneged" on a promise or understanding. Second, there may be replacement costs that are incurred whether or not the replacement conforms to the announced strategy, owing to a breaking-in period for the new manager, replacements of subordinates, interruptions of established routines, and so on. These costs would give the owner an incentive to avoid replacement as a deterrent even in the announced strategy and to find some other means of inducing good behavior by the manager.

These considerations lead one to consider a model in which the manager is *never* replaced, but the consequence of poor performance is a temporary reversion to a "noncooperative" or "adversarial" phase in which the manager receives a less satisfactory compensation than under the normal, "cooperative" phase. To the extent that the noncooperative phases are also less favorable for the owner, the owner will be deterred from ending the cooperative phases prematurely. One can show that the review strategies described here can be transformed into self-enforcing agreements by prescribing the noncooperative phases to be equilibria of the one-period game that are inferior to the cooperative phases (in expected value) for both the owner and the manager. Furthermore, one can do this in such a way as to sustain supergame equilibria that are approximately efficient, as in the case of the replacement model. (For the details of this construction under various conditions, see Radner 1981, 1985, 1986b.)

In the nonreplacement model, the owner and the manager are bound to each other "forever." A more general model would incorporate explicitly the costs to the owner and manager of the owner replacing the manager and of the manager quitting. The analysis would show how the structure of self-enforcing agreements (supergame equilibria) would depend on those costs and on the other parameters of the model. I am not aware of any such general formal analysis.

5.3   *A Continuous Time Model*

In more specialized models of repeated principal–agent games, one can obtain sharper characterizations of supergame equilibria. This is the case in a particular continuous time version of the replacement model of Section 5.2. In this model (see Dutta and Radner 1994):

(1)   The cumulative gross return is a controlled diffusion process, as in the continuous time version of the repeated partnership game of Section 4.4.

(2)   At each instant of time, the manager's action (control) can take on one of finitely many values. To each action is associated a drift and variability of the diffusion process.[10] The manager's strategy must satisfy certain measurability conditions as a function of the previous histories.

---

[10] The continuous time diffusion process corresponds, roughly speaking, to the limit case of the model of Section 4.4 in which the time between successive actions is infinitesimal. However, in the present model, only the manager controls the drift and the variability of the diffusion.

(3) The owner uses a continuous time analog of a bankruptcy strategy, corresponding in an obvious way to the discrete time analog of a bankruptcy strategy described in Section 5.2. During his tenure, the manager receives a wage rate that is constant. This wage rate (per unit time) is a parameter of the owner's bankruptcy strategy. As before, the other parameters are the initial stock and the (constant) target rate of return.

(4) The manager's supergame utility is the expected integral of his discounted instantaneous utility over his tenure (the latter is a random variable). His instantaneous utility is a function of his wage rate and his current action. Of the several actions, some have a higher instantaneous utility for him, but also have a smaller drift. It is this feature that creates the conflict between him and the owner.

(5) The owner's expected utility is the expected discounted integral of her net return, that is, her "instantaneous" gross return minus the wage rate.[11]

(6) The two players have the same discount rate.

The first result of this analysis is that the manager's optimal policy is of the switch-point type. For example, if there are two actions then there is a critical stock, called the *switch-point*, such that the manager uses the higher-drift action when current stock is below the switch-point but uses the lower-drift action (preferred by him) when the current stock is above the switch-point. The switch-point can be calculated explicitly as the solution of a transcendental equation. In certain extreme cases, the switch-point may be zero or infinite.

As the manager's discount rate approaches zero, his (optimal) switch-point increases without bound, but in the limit there is no optimal policy (i.e., under the expected long-run average objective). One can also characterize the dependence of the switch-point on the other parameters of the bankruptcy policy. With this information, one can characterize in some detail the bankruptcy policy that is optimal for the owner, given the manager's reservation utility – that is, the lowest expected utility that will induce him to take the job.

Finally, one can calculate how fast the players' respective (equilibrium) expected utilities approach efficiency as their discount rate approaches zero. See Section 7 for details of a related model.

---

[11] Strictly speaking, since the time-derivative of a diffusion process is almost everywhere nonexistent, the "instantaneous" gross return is not well-defined. Nevertheless, the theory of stochastic integration provides a basis for defining the cumulated gross return, with or without discounting (see Harrison 1985).

6   A Regulated Firm with Investment in Research and Development

A study by Linhart, Sinden, and Radner (1991) provides an application of the ideas of principal–agent theory to the development of regulatory policy. The policy in question is the "price-cap" method of regulation, which has recently been adopted in the United Kingdom and in the United States, to replace the rate-of-return method in the regulation of telecommunications.[12] From a formal point of view, this study extends the analysis of bankruptcy strategies (Section 5.2) to a nonstationary principal–agent model.

We consider the problem faced by the regulator of a monopoly firm who wants to provide incentives for the firm to effect cost reductions – and hence price reductions – through technological change and other means. For reasons explained elsewhere, we seek an alternative to conventional rate-of-return regulation. We model the manager of the firm as facing constraints imposed by the shareholders and other providers of capital, by the customers, and by the regulator. The regulator's ultimate objective is a secular real decrease in the firm's prices. However, the manager's private utility may not be maximized by activities that are maximally cost-reducing. Moreover, the regulator cannot directly observe all of the manager's actions, the outcomes of which are also influenced by random exogenous events. Hence a problem of moral hazard arises.

We propose a regulatory policy in which the regulator directly requires the firm to lower its real prices at (or faster than) some prescribed target annual rate. We suppose that the manager is replaced when he can no longer simultaneously repay the cost of capital, lower the prices at the rate prescribed by the regulator, and satisfy the market demand at those prices. Whenever a manager is replaced, the regulator reverts to conventional rate-of-return regulation for a period sufficient to enable the firm to build up a new cash reserve.

The resulting situation leads naturally to a model of a sequential principal–agent relationship in which the regulator is the principal and the manager is the agent. This is not a repeated game, however, because both the firm's prices and its productivity are changing through time, endogenously and stochastically. Using new techniques for the analysis of this nonstationary process, we (1) derive a lower bound on the expected length of tenure of a manager, and (2) show that, if the manager

---

[12] This study is reported in more detail in Linhart et al. (1991), which was itself based upon research done at AT&T Bell Laboratories several years earlier as part of the process of developing the price-cap method. See also Linhart and Radner (1983).

does not discount future utility very much, then the realized long-run rate of price decrease will be correspondingly close to the target rate.

The model takes account of the following fundamental characteristics, among others, of the regulatory situation.

(1) The regulator and the firm's manager have different information. In particular, the manager has more information about the possibilities for productivity improvement than regulators. In fact one of the manager's options is to invest in research in order to obtain more of this information. In principle, the regulator could also obtain more information at some cost, but matching the manager's information seldom appears to be part of the regulator's strategy. In the present model the regulator does not even try to elicit information about the firm's costs, so misrepresentation is not a problem.

(2) The regulator and the firm's manager to some extent have different goals. The regulator may strive to provide incentives strong enough to overcome the difference, but in general we would not expect an equilibrium outcome to meet the regulator's goals entirely.

(3) The service is deemed essential, so that its continued availability must be assumed in spite of possible mismanagement and/or bankruptcy.

(4) To be acceptable in the real world, a regulatory mechanism must not differ too radically from those that already exist. The strategies we discuss resemble conventional regulation in that periods of regulatory inaction alternate with periods of action that are intended to be corrective.

The essence of the regulator's problem is that he cannot directly observe the manager's actions, nor can he observe the exogenous random events that also affect productivity. He can, however, observe the consequences of those actions and events, namely the realized profits of the firm and whether or not the demand is met. (He may also, with additional effort, be able to observe productivity changes, but we do not in our model rely on this possibility.)

Suppose that the regulator provisionally fixes a sequence of prices that decline in real terms at a fixed target rate (which must be suitably chosen). If this sequence of prices is beyond the firm's control then it has, essentially, the desirable incentive property of a lump-sum payment. Suppose further that the regulator requires the firm to meet demand at the given prices, as long as it is feasible to do so, and that the shareholders and directors require the manager to pay out the cost of capital at a given rate, again as long as this is feasible. These two requirements can be met as long as the firm's cash reserve is positive. However, through bad luck or bad management, the cash reserve can become negative. This event we call a *crisis*; when a crisis occurs, the manager is fired and replaced. The regulator must now provide some way for the firm to get back on its feet. Thus time is divided into alternating segments: *incentive phases* and *recovery phases*.

In the context of a particular formal model of a single-product firm, we have shown that, under this class of regulatory strategies, the management of the regulated firm will have an incentive to engage in productivity improvement. Furthermore, if the management's behavior is optimal from its *own* point of view, then the incentive phases will be long relative to the recovery phases, and the resulting long-run average rate of actual price decrease will be close to the regulator's target rate of price decrease, provided the management does not discount its own future benefits too strongly. Thus, under suitable conditions, this class of regulatory strategies induces approximately efficient behavior on the part of the manager, without placing a large informational burden on the regulators and their staff, and in particular without requiring the regulators to monitor the firm's rate of return.

Several features of our approach should be emphasized. First, as mentioned previously, we model the firm's manager as the active decision maker in the firm, optimizing his own utility subject to constraints imposed by shareholders, customers, and regulators.

Second, we portray the regulators as seeking a mechanism that is easy to administer and that gives satisfactory results. In this case, "satisfactory" means achieving a target rate of price reduction, perhaps only approximately. Thus, the regulator does not seek an "optimal" mechanism in any precise sense.

Third, we propose a regulatory mechanism that does away with explicit rate-of-return regulation. We are interested in alternatives to rate-of-return regulation because (1) we are concerned about the weakness of its incentive properties, and (2) its informational requirements are heavy. Rate-of-return regulation is also difficult to administer if some of the firm's activities are regulated and others are not, as in the case of telecommunications today; see Linhart and Radner (1983).

Fourth, from a technical point of view, our model requires an analysis that goes substantially beyond currently available results for repeated principal–agent games. The reason for this is that both the firm's productivity and its prices are changing from period to period, and these changes are both endogenous and stochastic. Thus our model leads to a sequential, but not repeated, principal–agent relationship with endogenous state variables – namely, the current prices and productivity.

7   Survival

In the models of Sections 5 and 6, the agent controls the stochastic process so as to maximize his expected total discounted utility up to the (random) time of failure, which may be infinite. In this Section, I shall consider a limiting case in which the agent is solely interested in survival (I shall make this more precise in what follows). I shall call such an agent a *survivalist*. We shall see that the assumption that the agent is a survivalist will have interesting implications for the characteristics of his optimal control policy.

Formally, let $Y(t)$ denote the agent's wealth at time t. The stochastic process $Y(\cdot)$ is a diffusion, with drift $n(t)$ and volatility $w(t)$, at time t. Recall that a diffusion process has the following properties:

(1)   it evolves continuously in time;
(2)   conditional on the agent's choice of controls, the increments in nonoverlapping intervals are statistically independent.

A strong mathematical consequence of these assumptions is that, conditional on the agent's actions, the agent's net earnings in any time interval has a normal (Gaussian) distribution. Roughly speaking, in any very small interval of time dt, the agent's net earnings will be normally distributed with mean $n(t)\,dt$ and variance $w(t)\,dt$. The agent controls the process by choosing that mean and variance at each moment of time – subject, of course, to some restrictions (see Harrison 1985 for details and further references). More specifically, the agent controls $[n(t), w(t)]$ subject to the constraint that it must lie in some specified set B, which may depend on $Y(t)$, and that the agent not be "clairvoyant." The initial wealth $Y(0) = y > 0$ is given, and all probabilities and expectations are conditional on $Y(0) = y$ unless explicitly stated otherwise.

The agent is said to *fail* the first time T, if any, such that $Y(t)$ reaches zero; otherwise, take $T = +\infty$. Given a control $[n(\cdot), w(\cdot)]$, define the corresponding *value* by

$$P_r(y) = Er\int_0^T e^{-rt}\,dt. \tag{7.1a}$$

An interpretation of the integral in (7.1a) is that the agent receives utility 1 per unit time until failure, and then 0 afterwards, with a subjective rate of discount equal to r. Note that

$$P_r(y) = 1 - Ee^{-rT}. \tag{7.1b}$$

Also,

$$P(y) \equiv \lim_{r \to 0} P_r(y) = \text{Prob}\{T = \infty\}. \tag{7.2}$$

(To prove this, observe that if T is finite, then $\lim_{r \to 0}(1 - e^{-rT}) = 0$, whereas if T is infinite then $1 - e^{-rT} = 1$ for all r.)

Thus we can interpret a survivalist as someone who (1) receives a constant (positive) utility per unit time until failure and zero thereafter, and (2) has a discount rate equal to zero (is infinitely patient). (Note that the discounted utility in (7.1a) has been "normalized" by multiplying by the discount rate r. Without this normalization, setting $r = 0$ would give the expected undiscounted total utility up to the failure time T. This would be infinite if the probability of T being infinite were strictly positive, which will typically be the case under the assumptions that will be made here.)

The optimal behavior of the agent will depend on the "technology" that characterizes how the agent can control the wealth process $Y(t)$. This technology is represented by a correspondence $B(\cdot)$; if the current wealth is $Y(t)$ then the current control is constrained by

$$[n(t), w(t)] \in B[Y(t)] \quad \text{for all } t. \tag{7.3}$$

A control strategy is *optimal* if it maximizes $P(y)$, given $Y(t) = y$ and subject to the constraint (7.3).

Example 7.1 (Constant Size Technology). The agent controls a diffusion process of cumulated "gross returns," $X(t)$, by controlling its drift–volatility pair $[m(t), v(t)]$ subject to the constraint that this pair is in some (constant) set A. However, the agent must also pay out of her wealth a constant amount of money per unit time; call this constant rate c. (For example, this payment may be to service a debt, or it may be a payment to a principal, as in Section 5.3). Her resulting net wealth process is therefore given by

$$Y(t) = X(t) - ct, \tag{7.4a}$$

and the drift and volatility of the wealth process are

$$m(t) = n(t) + c \quad \text{and} \quad v(t) = w(t) \tag{7.4b}$$

respectively. The correspondence B is also constant, and is the set of pairs (n, w) such that $(n + c, w)$ is in A.

Example 7.2 (Constant Returns to Scale). The constant-returns-to-scale model is the one most commonly used for an investor in the securities market. Again, I shall suppose that the investor has a payout obligation that is constant per unit time. However, to begin the exposition, suppose that this obligation is zero.

With constant-returns-to-scale technology, if the agent had no payment obligation (e.g., debt service) then his wealth at time t would be

$$G(t) = e^{X(t)},$$

where $X(t)$ is a diffusion with drift $m(t)$ and volatility $v(t)$. By Ito's formula (see e.g. Harrison 1985, p. 64, Prop. 4),

$$G(t) \text{ has drift } \left[m(t) + v(t)/2 \right] \text{ and volatility } v(t)\left[G(t) \right]^2. \tag{7.6}$$

Now suppose that the agent must pay out at a constant rate $c > 0$ per unit time, and let $Y(t)$ denote the corresponding (net) wealth process; then

$$Y(t) \text{ has drift } n(t) = \left[m(t) + v(t)/2 \right] Y(t) - c$$
$$\text{and volatility } w(t) = v(t)\left[Y(t) \right]^2. \tag{7.6}$$

As before, the agent starts with an initial wealth $Y(0) = y > 0$ and *fails* the first time, if any, at which his wealth reaches 0. The agent *survives* if he never fails. The agent wishes to control $m(t)$ and $v(t)$ so as to maximize the probability of survival. Here $[m(t), v(t)]$ is constrained to lie in some (constant) set A, which means that $[n(t), w(t)]$ must lie in some set $B[Y(t)]$. The relation between A and $B(\cdot)$ is, of course, defined by (7.6).

Returning to the general case, I shall start by making the following assumptions about the correspondence $B(\cdot)$:

$$\text{For every } y, \quad B(y) \text{ is compact;} \tag{7.7}$$

there exists $w' > 0$ such that,
$$\text{for every } y \text{ and every } (n, w) \text{ in } B(y), w \geq w'. \tag{7.8}$$

For every y, let $[N(y), W(y)]$ maximize (n/w) for (n, w) in $B(y)$. I assume further that

$$\left[N(\cdot), W(\cdot) \right] \text{ is bounded and measurable.} \tag{7.9}$$

Define the (stationary) control policy (N, W) by

$$n(t) = N[Y(t)], \qquad w(t) = W[Y(t)]. \tag{7.10}$$

I shall show that, subject to a further regularity condition, *the policy* (N, W) *is optimal.* I shall then apply this result to obtain the optimal policies for Examples 7.1 and 7.2. I shall also derive a closed-form expression for the optimal probability of survival.

Let $P(y)$ denote the probability of survival, given that $Y(0) = y$, when the investor uses the policy (N, W). I shall first derive an explicit formula for the function P. Let T denote the failure time; if the investor never fails then T equals infinity. Let $I = 1$ or 0 according as T is infinite or finite, respectively; then

$$P(y) = E\{I|Y(0) = y\}. \tag{7.11}$$

For each t, define

$$T(t) = \min(T, t), \qquad Y^*(t) = Y[T(t)]. \tag{7.12}$$

Here $Y^*(t)$ is known as the "stopped" process corresponding to the original process $Y(t)$. Let $H(t)$ denote the history of all variables[13] up to time t. By the elementary properties of conditional expectation,

$$E\Big[E\{I|H(t)\}\Big] = E(I). \tag{7.13}$$

On the other hand, since the policy (N, W) is stationary,

$$E\{I|H(t)\} = P[Y^*(t)]. \tag{7.14}$$

Combining (7.11)–(7.14), we have

$$E\{P[Y^*(t)]\} = P(y); \tag{7.15}$$

in other words, $P[Y^*(t)]$ is a martingale and hence has drift equal to 0. By Ito's formula, this drift is equal to

$$N[Y^*(t)]P'[Y^*(t)] + \frac{1}{2}W[Y^*(t)]P''[Y^*(t)],$$

---

[13] More formally, $\{H(t)\}$ is a filtration of σ-fields of the underlying probability space, and every relevant stochastic process is adapted to this filtration. For example, the random variable $Y(t)$ is measurable with respect to $H(t)$, etc. In particular, for every control policy, $n(t)$ and $w(t)$ are required to be measurable with respect to $H(t)$; this is the formal representation of the requirement that the policy be "nonclairvoyant."

provided P is twice differentiable. Hence, for every $y > 0$,

$$N(y)P'(y) + \frac{1}{2}W(y)P''(y) = 0. \tag{7.16a}$$

With an additional regularity condition to be stated shortly, this differential equation has a unique solution – subject to the relevant boundary conditions, which are

$$P \geq 0, \quad P(0) = 0, \quad P(\infty) = 1. \tag{7.16b}$$

To exhibit the solution, let

$$h(y) = -\frac{2N(y)}{W(y)},$$

$$H(y) = \int_0^y h(x)dx,$$

$$u(y) = \exp\left[-H(y)\right]. \tag{7.17}$$

Assume that

$$C \equiv \int_0^\infty u(x)dx < \infty, \tag{7.18}$$

and define the function P by

$$P(y) = \frac{1}{C}\int_0^y u(x)dx. \tag{7.19}$$

Then it is easily verified that P is the unique solution to (7.16ab); hence P is the value function for the policy (N, W).

I shall now sketch a proof that the policy (N, W) is optimal, and thus that P gives the maximum probability of survival. In fact, the optimality of (N, W) follows by a limiting argument from a theory of Pestien and Sudderth (1985), but the proof that I shall sketch here is more direct and also (I hope) more accessible.

Theorem. *Under assumptions (7.7)–(7.9) and (7.18), the policy (N, W) is optimal.*

Proof. Let q be any policy, let Q be its value, let $\{Y(t)\}$ denote the corresponding wealth process, let T be its failure time, and define

$$T(t) = \min(T, ty), \quad Y^*(t) = Y\left[T(t)\right].$$

Note that T now denotes the failure time for the policy q, rather than the policy (N, W), and that $Y^*(t)$ is defined as in (7.12) but corresponding to the policy q. For each nonnegative time s, define

$$U(s) = P[Y^*(s)],$$
(7.20)

where, as before, P is the value function for the policy (N, W). We can interpret $U(s)$ as follows. Suppose that the agent uses the policy q up to (but not including) the time s, and then uses the policy (N, W) thereafter; then $U(s)$ is his conditional probability of survival, given his stopped wealth process at time s. By Ito's formula, the drift of $U(s)$ is

$$n(s)P'[Y^*(s)] + \frac{1}{2}w(s)P''[Y^*(s)],$$
(7.21)

where $n(s)$ and $w(s)$ are the drift and volatility, respectively, determined by the policy q at time s. By the definition of N and W, and since $w(s) > 0$ (see (7.8)),

$$n(s) \le w(s)N[Y^*(s)]/W[Y^*(s)].$$
(7.22)

Because P' is strictly positive, (7.22) and (7.16a) together imply that the drift (7.21) of $U(s)$ is nonpositive. *Hence $U(s)$ is a supermartingale and, in particular, $EU(s)$ is nonincreasing.*

Now note that $U(0) = P(y)$. Hence the proof will be completed if we can show that

$$\lim_{s \to \infty} EU(s) = Q$$

(recall that Q is the value of the policy q). Since $U(s)$ is a uniformly bounded supermartingale, it converges to some random variable, say U^*. Recall that P is strictly increasing and hence invertible, so that $Y^*(s)$ must either converge to a finite limit, say Y^*, or diverge to $+\infty$, in which case we shall set $Y^* = +\infty$.

Lemma. Y^* *finite implies that* T *is finite, a.s.*

In other words, the random variable Y^* can take on either (1) the value 0, in which case T is finite, or (2) the value $+\infty$, in which case T is infinite (the investor survives). If $Y^* = 0$ then $U^* = 0$, whereas if $Y^* = +\infty$ then $U^* = 1$. Hence

$$\lim_{s \to \infty} EU(s) = \text{prob}\{T = \infty\} = Q,$$
(7.23)

so that $Q \le P(y)$, which was to be proved. $\square$

Proof of Lemma. As before, fix the policy q, let $\{Y(t)\}$ be the corresponding wealth process, and let b be any positive real number. I shall show that either (1) $Y(t)$ reaches 0 in finite time, or (2) $Y(t)$ eventually remains strictly greater than b. For any time s, define the following events:

$$F(s) = \{Y(t) \text{ reaches } 0 \text{ at some } t > s, \text{ before reaching } 2b\};$$

$$G(s) = \{Y(t) \text{ reaches } 2b \text{ at some } t > s, \text{ before reaching } 0\};$$

$$H(s) = \{Y(t) \text{ reaches } b \text{ at some } t > s\};$$

$$I(s) = \{Y(t) > b \text{ for all } t > s\}.$$

Recall that the volatility of $Y(t)$ is bounded away from zero. For any initial wealth $Y(0) = y$, suppose first that y is different from 0 or b. If $0 < y < b$, then $Y(t)$ will eventually reach 0 or b. If $y > b$, then one of the two events $H(0)$ or $I(0)$ will occur. Hence, without loss of generality, we can suppose that at some (random) time S, $Y(S) = b$. Although we have not assumed that the policy q is stationary, the fact that $w(t)$ is bounded away from 0 implies that the process $Y(t)$ will subsequently reach either 0 or $2b$ in finite time – for example, events $F(S)$ or $G(S)$ will occur in finite time – and the conditional probability of each of these events is bounded away from 0, say at least $h > 0$. Similarly, conditional on reaching $2b$ before 0, say at time $S' > S$, the probability of event $H(S')$ is bounded away from zero, say at least $k > 0$. Thus the process will continue to visit b and $2b$ alternately in finite times, until at some finite (random) time S'' either event $F(S'')$ or event $I(S'')$ occurs, which is the desired conclusion. Since this conclusion holds for every $b > 0$, it follows that either (1) $Y(t)$ reaches 0 in finite time or (2) $Y(t)$ diverges to plus infinity. $\square$

I now apply the theorem to the preceding examples.

Example 7.1 (Constant Size Technology) (*cont.*). The set A is constant, and hence so is the set B and so is the optimal control, say (N, W). In fact, let (M, V) *maximize the ratio* $(m - c)/v$ for (m, v) in the set A; then $N = M - c$ and $W = V$. It is easily verified from equations (7.18)–(7.19) that the maximum probability of survival is

$$P(y) = \begin{cases} 1 - \exp\left[2(M - c)/V\right] & \text{if } M > c, \\ 0 & \text{otherwise.} \end{cases}$$

Example 7.2 (Constant Returns to Scale) (*cont.*). To apply the Theorem, it is convenient to take as the state variable the logarithm of the agent's wealth, rather than the wealth itself. Accordingly, define

$$Z(t) = \ln Y(t) \quad \text{for } Y(t) > 0. \tag{7.24}$$

I shall call $Z(t)$ the investor's *logfortune*. By Ito's formula and (7.6),

$$Z(t) \text{ has drift } m(t) - ce^{-Z(t)} \text{ and volatility } v(t). \tag{7.25}$$

Because $Z(t)$ tends to $-\infty$ as $Y(t)$ tends to 0, and to $+\infty$ as $Y(t)$ tends to $+\infty$, we start the analysis by stopping the Z process at the first time T that $Z(T)$ reaches a, where $a < 0$; later we shall let a tend to $-\infty$. Accordingly, for the given value of a, let $P(z)$ denote the optimal probability of survival given that $Z(0) = z$.

At this point, in order to simplify the exposition, I introduce an additional assumption about the set A. (At the end of this section, I shall indicate how one can dispense with this additional assumption.) Define

$$v' = \min\{v : (m, v) \in A\}, \quad v'' = \max\{v : (m, v) \in A\},$$

and define the function f by

$$f(v) = \max\{m : (m, v) \in A\}, \quad v' \le v \le v''. \tag{7.26}$$

Assume that f is twice differentiable and strictly concave, that $f(v) > 0$ for some v, and that

$$f'(v') = +\infty, \quad f'(v'') = -\infty.$$

The investor controls the drift and volatility of $Z(t)$ by controlling (m, v) in A. From the Theorem and (7.25), for any z we want to choose (m, v) in A to maximize the ratio

$$\left[m - ce^{-z}\right]/v. \tag{7.27}$$

First, for any v, one must take $m = f(v)$. Hence, for any z we must choose v to maximize the ratio

$$\left[f(v) - ce^{-z}\right]/v. \tag{7.28}$$

Define the function g by

$$g(v) \equiv f(v) - vf'(v). \tag{7.29}$$

The strict concavity of f implies that g is strictly increasing, and that

$$g(v') = -\infty, \quad g(v'') = +\infty. \tag{7.30}$$

It is an exercise in calculus to show that the optimal value of v, say $V(z)$, is determined by the equation

$$g\big[V(z)\big] = ce^{-z}. \tag{7.31a}$$

The foregoing properties of the function g ensure that this equation has a unique solution for every z. Correspondingly, the optimal value of m, say $M(z)$, is given by:

$$M(z) = f\big[V(z)\big]. \tag{7.31b}$$

Recall that $M(z)$ and $V(z)$ are the optimal drift and volatility, respectively, of the cumulative gross rate of return, $X(t)$.

From the characterization (7.31ab) we can deduce some interesting properties of the optimal control policy. First, note that *the optimal policy is independent of the constant a.* Hence, as we let a tend to $-\infty$, the optimal control policy remains unchanged. From now on, I shall consider this limiting case.

Second, it is easy to verify from (7.31a) that the optimal volatility, $V(z)$, is strictly decreasing in z. Thus, the smaller the investor's fortune, the greater the "risk" he takes. In fact, as the investor's fortune approaches 0 (z tends to $-\infty$), $V(z)$ tends in the limit to V_0, where (m_0, v_0) maximizes the ratio (m/v) in the set A. On the other hand, as the investor's fortune tends to $+\infty$, $V(z)$ approaches its maximum possible value, η''. Third, as the investor's fortune increases, $M(z)$ first increases to its maximum possible value in the set A and then decreases towards m_0. These last two properties of the optimal control policy are illustrated in Figure 2.

Fourth, from (7.29) and (7.31ab) we have

$$\big[M(z) - ce^{-z}\big]\big/V(z) = f'\big[V(z)\big]. \tag{7.32}$$

The left-hand side of (7.32) is, of course, the drift–volatility ratio of the logfortune. Let m^* denote the maximum value of m for (m, v) in A, let v^* denote the corresponding value of v, and let z^* be the value of the logfortune such that $V(z^*) = v^*$. I shall call z^* the *critical logfortune*. In other words: at the critical logfortune, the optimal control maximizes the drift of the cumulative rate of return. But even more important, we see from (7.25) and (7.32) that for logfortunes less than z^*, the drift of the logfortune is negative, whereas for logfortunes greater than z^*, the drift of the logfortune is positive.

Furthermore, for fortunes less than z^*, *the optimal volatility is the maximum possible, given the drift.* This would appear to contradict the "efficiency hypothesis" of capital markets – according to which the

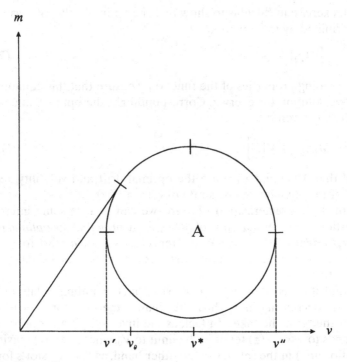

m

v′ v₀   v*   v″

v

Figure 2

optimal risk is the minimum consistent with the given yield – at least for investors who are averse to risk. Indeed, for logfortunes less than the critical value z^*, our survivalist investor appears to behave as if she were a "risk lover."

These last two properties of the optimal control are related. If $Z(t) < z^*$ then the drift of $Z(t)$ is negative, and the only way to escape this trap is to use increasingly risky controls. Thus, the apparent risk-loving behavior of the investor is a consequence of her technology and the fact that she has a fixed payout obligation, independent of her fortune.

Further light is shed on this matter by the formula for the maximum probability of survival, $P(z)$, which can be derived in a manner analogous to the derivation of (7.16)–(7.19) in the general case. (Recall that the state variable is now the logfortune z, rather than the fortune y.) From (7.32) we have

$$N(z)/W(z) = -f'[V(z)].$$
(7.33)

Now, parallel to (7.17)–(7.18), define:

$$h(z) = -2f'(z),$$

$$H(z) = \int_{z^*}^{z} h(x)\,dx,$$

$$u(z) = \exp\left[-H(z)\right],$$

$$C = \int_{-\infty}^{+\infty} u(x)\,dx. \tag{7.34}$$

It is left as an exercise to show that C is finite (use the properties of the function f). Hence, the maximum probability of survival, conditional on $Z(0) = z$, is

$$P(z) = \frac{1}{C}\int_{-\infty}^{z} u(x)\,dx. \tag{7.35}$$

From (7.34) it follows that $C > 0$, and one verifies from (7.34) and (7.35) that

$$CP'(z) = u(z) > 0,$$

$$CP''(z) = 2f'(z)e^{-H(z)}. \tag{7.36}$$

Hence the function P is (1) strictly increasing, as well as (2) strictly convex for $z < z^*$ and strictly concave for $z > z^*$. (Recall that z^* is the critical logfortune.)

Claim (2) has an interesting interpretation. Analogous to (7.15), we have

$$P(z) = E\left\{P\left[Z^*(t)\right]\right\}. \tag{7.37}$$

Thus $P[Z^*(t)]$ is a kind of "virtual utility" for ending up in the state $Z^*(t)$ at time t. For t small and z finite, $Z^*(t)$ is very likely to be close to z. If $z > z^*$ then, roughly speaking, the investor will be acting during the small interval $[0, t]$ to maximize a concave function of $Z(t)$, and hence will appear to be averse to risk. This is the region in which the investor chooses a drift–volatility pair in the northwest, or "efficient," part of the boundary of the set A. On the other hand, if $z < z^*$ then the investor will be acting to maximize a convex function of $Z(t)$, and hence *will appear to be a risk-lover*! This is in fact the region in which the optimal volatility is the maximum possible for the optimal drift.

I close this discussion of Example 7.2 with some remarks on the case in which the regularity assumptions about the function f do not hold.

Indeed, let A be any compact set such that $v > 0$ for all (m, v) in A, and such that there is an (m, v) in A for which $m > 0$. Let A^* be the convex hull of A, and let E be the upper extreme points of A^*. The optimal control policy will be confined to E and will be qualitatively similar to the one previously described in the more regular case, except that it need not be continuous. Furthermore, the optimal value function P will again be twice differentiable, increasing, and S-shaped as before.

Note: The analysis of Example 7.2 is based on Section V of Majumdar and Radner (1991). However, the proof has been simplified, and a characterization of the optimal value function has been added. A discrete time analog of this model has been analyzed by Roy (1995). In his model it can happen that survival is impossible for sufficiently small initial fortunes, and can be guaranteed for sufficiently large initial fortunes; in an intermediate range of initial fortunes, the optimal policy is similar to that described in Example 7.2. For further material on economic survival, see Majumdar and Radner (1992) and Radner (1996).

8   Concluding Remarks

The models of dynamic games sketched here hardly constitute a theory of economic organizations. For such a theory, the partnership and principal–agent models will have to be merged and subsumed in a richer and more comprehensive model capable of depicting the interactions among many persons. This is particularly true if one's ambition is to develop a theory of the internal workings of today's large industrial enterprises, many of which have tens – even hundreds – of thousands of employees. In addition, it will probably be necessary to take account of the cost of communication and information processing, as well as other aspects of "bounded rationality."[14] Nevertheless, the insights revealed by these relatively primitive analyses of moral hazard and free riding in long-term relationships will probably prove to be durable.

References

Abreu, D., P. Milgrom, and D. Pearce, 1991, Information and timing in repeated partnerships, *Econometrica* 59, 1713–33.

Alchian, A. A., and H. Demsetz, 1972, Production, information costs, and economic organization, *American Economic Review* 62, 777–95.

---

[14] See Radner (1992) for further reflections on these problems.

Benhabib, J., and R. Radner, 1992, Joint exploitation of a productive asset, *Economic Theory* 2, 155–90.

Dutta, P. K., and R. Radner, 1994, Optimal principal–agent contracts for a class of incentive schemes, *Economic Theory* 2, 483–504.

1995, Moral hazard, in: R. Aumann and S. Hart (eds.), *Handbook of Game Theory*, vol. 2 (North-Holland, Amsterdam), 869–903.

Fudenberg, D., D. K. Levine, and E. Maskin, 1989, The folk theorem with imperfect public information, Unpublished manuscript, Department of Economics, Massachusetts Institute of Technology, Cambridge.

Fudenberg, D., and E. Maskin, 1986, Folk theorems for repeated games with discounting and incomplete information, *Econometrica* 54, 533–54.

Fudenberg, D., and J. Tirole, 1990, Moral hazard and renegotiation in agency contracts, *Econometrica* 58, 1279–1319.

Grossman, S. J., and O. D. Hart, 1983, An analysis of the principal–agent problem, *Econometrica* 51, 7–45.

Groves, T., 1973, Incentives in teams, *Econometrica* 41, 617–31.

Harrison, J. M., 1985, *Brownian Motion and Stochastic Flow Systems* (Wiley, New York).

Harsanyi, J., 1967/1968, Games with incomplete information played by Bayesian players, Parts I, II, and III, *Management Science* 14, 159–82, 320–34, 486–502.

Ito, K., 1985, *Lectures on Stochastic Processes* (Springer, Berlin).

Lancaster, K., 1973, The dynamic inefficiency of capitalism, *Journal of Political Economy* 81, 1098–109.

Levhari, D., and L. J. Mirman, 1980, The great fish-war: An example using the Cournot–Nash solution, *Bell Journal of Economics* 11, 322–34.

Linhart, P. B., and R. Radner, 1983, Deregulation of long-distance telecommunications, in: V. Mosco (ed.), *Policy Research in Telecommunications* (ABLEX, Norwood, NJ).

Linhart, P. B., F. W. Sinden, and R. Radner, 1991, A sequential mechanism for direct price regulation, in: M. E. Einhorn (ed.), *Price Caps and Incentive Regulation in Telecommunications* (Kluwer, Norwell, MA), 127–53.

Majumdar, M., and R. Radner, 1991, Linear models of economic survival under production uncertainty, *Economic Theory* 1, 13–30.

1992, Survival under production uncertainty, in: M. Majumdar (ed.), *Equilibrium and Dynamics* (Macmillan, London), 179–200.

Myerson, R. B., 1983, Mechanism design by an informed principal, *Econometrica* 51, 1767–98.

1985, Bayesian equilibrium and incentive compatibility: An introduction, in: L. Hurwicz, D. Schmeidler, and H. Sonnenschein (eds.), *Social Goals and Social Organization: Essays in Memory of Elisha Pazner* (Cambridge University Press), 229–59.

Pestien, V. C., and W. D. Sudderth, 1985, Continuous-time red and black: How to control a diffusion to a goal, *Mathematics of Operations Research* 10, 599–61.

Radner, R., 1981, Monitoring cooperative relationships in a repeated principal–agent relationship, *Econometrica* 49, 1127–48.

158   Roy Radner

1985, Repeated principal–agent games with discounting, *Econometrica* 53, 1173–97.

1986a, Repeated partnership games with imperfect monitoring and no discounting, *Review of Economic Studies* 53, 43–57.

1986b, Repeated moral hazard with low discount rates, in: W. P. Heller, R. M. Starr, and D. Starrett (eds.), *Uncertainty, Information, and Communication, Essays in Honor of Kenneth J. Arrow*, vol. 3 (Cambridge University Press), 25–64.

1987, Decentralization and incentives, in: T. Groves, S. Reiter, and R. Radner (eds.), *Information, Incentives, and Economic Mechanisms* (Blackwell, Oxford), 3–47.

1992, Hierarchy: The economics of managing, *Journal of Economic Literature* 30, 1382–1415.

1996, *Economic survival*, Schwartz Memorial Lecture, Northwestern University, Evanston, IL.

Radner, R., R. B. Myerson, and E. Maskin, 1986, An example of a repeated partnership game with discounting and with uniformly inefficient equilibria, *Review of Economic Studies* 53, 59–69.

Roy, S., 1995, Theory of dynamic portfolio choice for survival under uncertainty, *Mathematical Social Sciences* 30, 171–94.

Rustichini, A., and R. Radner, 1996, The design and performance of sharing rules for a partnership in continuous time, *Games and Economic Behavior* 12, 245–65.

Whitt, W., 1980, Uniform conditional stochastic order, *Journal of Applied Probabilities* 17, 112–23.

Williams, S. R., and R. Radner, 1995, Efficiency in partnerships when the joint output is uncertain, in: J. Ledyard (ed.), *The Economics of Informational Decentralization* (Kluwer, Boston), 79–99.

CHAPTER 5

The Equilibrium Existence Problem in General Markovian Games

Prajit K. Dutta and Rangarajan K. Sundaram

1 Introduction

The framework of *Markovian* (or *stochastic*) *games* has, in recent years, become a popular one for the analysis of strategic interaction in a dynamic economic context. In a precise sense, this framework is obtained by merging two of the most widely used paradigms of modern economic analysis: stationary dynamic programming problems (Blackwell 1965, Maitra 1967) and repeated games (Fudenberg and Maskin 1986, Abreu 1988). As in stationary dynamic programming problems, Markovian games posit the existence of a "state" variable that is designed to capture the environment of the game at each point in time, but that moves through time in response to the actions taken in the game. However, as in the repeated games framework, Markovian games permit the existence of multiple decision makers ("players") in the model.

This merger permits a rich variety of possibilities in a Markovian game; for instance, a player's current actions could affect his future reward prospects in two ways:

(1) through the effect they have on the physical environment in which future decisions must be made;

(2) Through their impact on the behavior of other agents in the model.

Of course, stationary dynamic programming problems permit only the first effect, since they are one-person problems; repeated games permit only the second, since the stage game itself must be unchanging.

As a consequence of these features, the Markovian game framework is ideally suited for the analysis of economic models in which it is necessary to allow for both a changing decision-making environment *and* imperfect competition. One instance of such a situation is the "tragedy of the commons" analyzed initially in an example in Levhari and Mirman (1980) and later in a general model by Benhabib and Radner (1992) and

159

Dutta and Sundaram (1993a,b). The "tragedy" here refers to the problem that arises when several firms have access to a common-property resource (say, a fishery). Increased current exploitation of the fishery by any one firm has an impact on every firm's future profitability, since it reduces the quantity of fish available in the future. This intertemporal externality makes the repeated games framework inappropriate, since the physical environment of the game is changing over time. On the other hand, the presence of multiple agents obviously makes the one-person stationary dynamic programming framework inappropriate also.

The Markovian game framework has also seen several other applications in recent years. Among these are:

(1) strategic investment under oligopoly (Spence 1979, Fudenberg and Tirole 1983, McLean and Sklivas 1988);

(2) research and development under imperfect competition (Fudenberg et al. 1983, Reinganum 1985);

(3) dynamic oligopoly models (Dana and Montrucchio 1986, Maskin and Tirole 1988);

(4) economic growth as a consequence of bequest motives (Kohlberg 1976, Bernheim and Ray 1983, Leininger 1986);

(5) partnership games (Radner, Myerson, and Maskin 1986) and principal–agent problems (Radner 1985).

In addition, and of equal significance, the dynamic programming–Markovian game approach has played a central role in recent breakthroughs concerning repeated games under both complete information (Abreu 1988) and incomplete information (Abreu, Pearce, and Stacchetti 1986, 1990).

Despite these successes, it must be admitted that the use of Markovian games in the economics literature has been disproportionately small when considered in relation to the generality of the framework. The reason for this is not far to seek: Markovian games are significantly more complex from a technical standpoint than either repeated games or stationary dynamic programming. Indeed, as the examples in Dutta and Sundaram (1993b) demonstrate, equilibrium behavior in very simple Markovian games can take on very complex and unintuitive forms.

Nowhere is the increased technical complexity of Markovian games more apparent than in the fundamental issue of the *existence* of a solution in a general formulation of the model. For each of the constituent frameworks this is a nonissue: very general conditions are known under which stationary dynamic programming problems admit an optimal policy (see, e.g., Maitra 1967), while the existence of a subgame-perfect equilibrium in a repeated game requires only that the underlying stage game admit a Nash equilibrium. In contrast, the existence of a subgame-perfect equilibrium in general Markovian games has only been established under some restrictions. The available results are unsatisfactory on at least two grounds:

(1) all of the general results on existence place technical requirements on the transition mechanism for the state variable that preclude the transition from being *deterministic*;

(2) even though a *stationary* Markovian environment is studied, there is no result that demonstrates the existence of equilibrium in stationary Markovian strategies, even with the restrictions on the transition mechanism just mentioned.

The absence of a result permitting deterministic transitions is obviously a serious indictment of the literature, since such mechanisms are employed in a large majority of economic applications. Concerning the second point, the best available result is one by Mertens and Parthasarathy (1991) on the existence of a subgame-perfect equilibrium in possibly non-Markovian strategies under very general conditions. Other results include the existence of "quasi-equilibria" such as the ε-equilibrium existence results of Rieder (1979) and Whitt (1980) and the p-equilibrium existence result in Himmelberg et al. (1976).

The objective of this chapter is to study the existence problem in Markovian games in some detail, focusing on the precise technical and conceptual problems that stand in the way of obtaining a satisfactory and general existence theorem. As an essential part of this exercise, we examine the analysis in several papers in the literature in some detail, with particular reference to the special assumptions that each paper uses to overcome the hurdles that arise.[1]

Section 2 begins our analysis with a detailed description of general Markovian games. Several important topics are introduced here, such as the concepts of a strategy and a subgame-perfect equilibrium. We round off this section with a discussion on the generality of the formulation we have adopted; in particular, we describe the precise manner in which several other widely used paradigms may be obtained as special cases of our framework.

Section 3 provides a first analysis of the existence of subgame-perfect equilibrium. Our focus here is on a class of strategies called *Markovian*

---

[1] It is important to emphasize that our focus is on the existence problem and not on providing a summary of the literature. We make no claims to being comprehensive or complete in our survey. For example, a rich and varied literature has examined the question of solutions to *zero-sum* stochastic games, a class of games we ignore altogether.

strategies. Equilibria in such stratgies, also known as Markov-perfect equilibria (or MPE) have occupied a prominent place in the many applications of the Markovian game paradigm. They offer, in an otherwise Markovian environment, a "natural" starting point for examining the existence issue.

In *finite* Markovian games (i.e., where all state and action spaces are finite sets), the existence of MPE may be verified through a simple argument combining stationary dynamic programming techniques with Kakutani's fixed-point theorem. This result is presented in Section 3.1. When the state (and possibly also action) spaces are of arbitrary cardinality, however, problems of surprising complexity arise in generalizing these arguments. Some are technical issues such as the choice of an appropriate topology on strategy spaces; others go deeper. Our discussion of these issues in Section 3.2 is central to the rest of the paper.

In Section 4, we continue our study of MPE by examining the many (often partial) results that have been obtained in the literature in this context. Sections 4.1 and 4.2 examine the existence of "approximate" equilibria to the game. A number of authors (Rieder 1979, Whitt 1980, Nowak 1985, Amir 1991, and Chakrabarti 1993) have shown the existence of conditions under which, for any $\varepsilon > 0$, there are MPE in which each player obtains a payoff that is within ε of her best response to the strategies of the other players. These "ε-equilibrium" results are typically proved using truncations of the given game. For instance, Rieder (1979) establishes his result by approximating the infinite horizon model with models with a long (but finite) horizon. In contrast, Whitt (1980) and Nowak (1985) use an approximation of the given game by a sequence of "countable state" games. These results are described in Section 4.1.

In Section 4.2 we examine a second kind of approximate equilibrium notion, this time in strategies that are best responses to each other from almost every initial state, where "almost every" is with respect to some fixed measure p on the state space. (Following standard dynamic programming terminology, these are called "p-equilibria.") We present in this section a result from Himmelberg et al. (1976) which shows that, under some strong separability assumptions, the problems outlined in Section 3.2 may be overcome and the existence of p-equilibrium Markovian strategies ascertained.

Section 4.3 describes a result due to Parthasarathy (1982) that gives sufficient conditions under which any model that admits p-equilibrium Markovian strategies also admits an MPE. In particular, this result shows, under a further strengthening of the hypothesis, that full MPE exist in the Himmelberg et al. model.

The results of Sections 3 and 4 use what one may call a "dynamic programming" approach to the existence issue, in the sense that the underlying techniques of proof draw on the literature on Markovian decision processes and stationary dynamic programming (Blackwell 1965 or Maitra 1967). None of these results are satisfactory, since they are either approximate equilibrium results (Rieder, Nowak, etc.) or place severe restrictions on the forms of the reward functions and transition probabilities (Himmelberg et al.). In Section 5, we turn to an examination of results obtained by Mertens and Parthsarathy (1987, 1991) on the existence of subgame-perfect equilibrium strategies in general Markovian games.

Mertens and Parthasarathy employ what we label a "game-theoretic" approach to the existence question.[2] Rather than solve for the equilibrium using a fixed-point mapping (as in the dynamic programming approach), Mertens and Parthasarathy construct a series of "auxiliary" one-shot games parameterized by the state s. Using the equilibria of the games so defined, they describe an iterative procedure through whose limit a subgame-perfect equilibrium may be defined.

The Mertens–Parthasarathy results represent the "state of the art" in Markovian game theory; they are the most general conditions under which subgame-perfect equilibria are known to exist in Markovian games. However, several important open questions remain.

(1) The assumptions made by Mertens and Parthasarathy preclude the transition functions in the game from being deterministic. Can an existence theorem be proved that weakens the assumptions on the transition mechanism to allow for deterministic transitions?

(2) Mertens and Parthasarathy are not able to show that the subgame-perfect equilibria they construct will also be Markovian, although the primitive environment of the game they consider is Markovian. Can Markovian equilibria be shown to exist under their conditions?

The first of these is, perhaps, the most important open question left in this area; an affirmative answer would significantly enhance the economic applicability of Markovian games. It is, of course, likely that the

---

[2] The same approach is also present in the work of Parthasarathy and Sinha (1991), who prove the existence of MPE in games in which transition probabilities do not depend on the current state, under some additional technical hypotheses.

weakened assumptions on the transition mechanism may have to be accompanied by strengthening of some other assumptions. Fortunately, economic theory provides us with a number of conditions, motivated by economic criteria, that could safely be imposed without reducing the framework's applicability. For instance, it is routine in economics to assume *convexity* of the environment; it is also common to make substitutability assumptions such as *supermodularity* on the reward functions. It remains to be seen whether such conditions could substitute for the strong assumptions on the transition mechanism in providing a more user-friendly existence result.[3]

2   Markovian Games: A Description

This section is divided into three parts. Section 2.1 describes a general Markovian game; the notation presented here is maintained throughout the chapter. A verbal interpretation of the formal structure is also provided. Building on this, Section 2.2 formalizes the notion of a strategy as a contingent plan of action and describes an equilibrium of the Markovian game. The important concepts of a Markovian strategy and a Markov-perfect equilibrium are introduced here. Finally, Section 2.3 provides an extensive comment on the generality of the described structure.

2.1   Notation and Definitions

The Formal Description. A *Markovian game* is described by a tuple $\{N, S, (A_i, \Phi_i, r_i, \delta_i)_{i \in N}, q, T\}$, where:

(1) $N = \{1, \ldots, n\}$ is the finite set of *players*. A generic player is indexed by i.

(2) S, a Borel subset of some Polish (i.e., complete, separable, metric) space, is the *state space* of the game, with typical element s.

(3)   Each player $i \in N$ is characterized by four objects $(A_i, \Phi_i, r_i, \delta_i)$, where:

(a) A_i, a Borel subset of some Polish space, is the *action space* of player i. We let $A = \Pi_{i \in N} A_i$, and denote by a a typical element of A.

---

[3] It should be noted that, in some applications, very general existence results have been proved (that admit deterministic transitions) precisely by using assumptions such as convexity and supermodularity. For instance, see Sundaram (1989) and Dutta and Sundaram (1992) in the context of common-property games, or Bernheim and Ray (1983) and Leininger (1986) in the context of bequest games.

- (b) Φ_i, a correspondence from S to A_i, describes for each $s \in S$ the set $\Phi_i(s)$ of *feasible actions* for player i at s.
- (c) r_i, a bounded function from $S \times A$ to $\mathbb{R}$, specifies (for each state s and actions $a \in A$ taken by the players at s) a *reward* $r_i(s, a)$ for player i.
- (d) $\delta_i \in [0, 1)$ is player i's *discount factor*.
- (4) q specifies the *law of motion* (or *transition probabilities*) for the game by associating with each $(s, a) \in S \times A$ a probability $q(\cdot \mid s, a)$ over the Borel sets of S.
- (5) $T \in \{1, 2, \ldots\} \cup +\infty$ is the *horizon* of the game.

A more detailed interpretation of these components, and the role they perform in the play of the game, is given in the following sections. Some additional notation is, unfortunately, required in order to complete the description of the game.

Let $M_i(s)$ denote the set of *mixed* actions available to player i at s. That is, letting $\Delta(X)$ denote the set of all probability measures on a Borel set X, we have

$$M_i(s) = \Delta[\Phi_i(s)].$$

Define also

$$M(s) = M_1(s) \times \cdots \times M_n(s).$$

Generic elements of $M_i(\cdot)$ and $M(\cdot)$ will be denoted μ_i and μ, respectively.

With a slight abuse of notation, we now let $r_i(s, \mu)$ be the expected payoff to i from the vector of mixed actions μ at the state s:

$$r_i(s, \mu) = \int_A r(s, a) \, d\mu_1(a_1) \cdots d\mu_n(a_n).$$

Finally, denote by $q(\cdot \mid s, \mu)$ the corresponding expected transition probabilities:

$$q(\cdot \mid s, \mu) = \int_A q(\cdot \mid s, a) \, d\mu_1(a_1) \cdots d\mu_n(a_n).$$

This completes the description of the components of the Markovian game.

A Verbal Interpretation. Informally speaking, the Markovian game is played as follows. At the beginning of each period $t \in \{0, 1, \ldots, T - 1\}$,[4] each player $i \in N$ observes the state s_t at the beginning of period t, and chooses an action $\mu_{it} \in M_i(s_t)$. This choice is made with full knowledge of

---

[4] Observe the notational convention that the first period is period 0; thus, the last period of a T-period model is period $(T - 1)$. If $T = +\infty$ then this has the obvious interpretation.

the history of the game up to t and of the strategies of the other players. Subsequent to the action choices, two things happen. First, player i receives the reward r_i (s_t, μ_t), where $\mu_t = (\mu_{it})_{i \in N}$ is the chosen vector of actions. Second, the state transits to its period-$(t + 1)$ value s_{t+1} according to the distribution $q(\cdot \mid s_t, \mu_t)$. The situation now repeats itself until the terminal date $(T - 1)$ is reached.[5]

The objective of each player is to select a strategy (i.e., a contingent plan of action) that maximizes the player's expected total discounted reward over the model's horizon. Since the game is noncooperative, the strategy choices of the other players are taken as given in this exercise. An equilibrium results when no player has a profitable unilateral deviation from a suggested vector of strategies.

A formal description of this procedure follows in Section 2.2, after a brief detour.

Maintained Assumptions. It is evident that some structure will have to be imposed on the problem if the Markovian game framework is to be analytically tractable. The following regularity assumptions will be maintained throughout the paper, and will be strengthened wherever necessary.

A1   For all i, A_i is compact and $\Phi_i : S \to A_i$ is a continuous, compact-valued correspondence on S.

A2   For all i, r_i is bounded and jointly measurable in (s, a) and is continuous on A for each fixed $s \in S$.

A3   For each Borel subset B of S, $q(B \mid \cdot, \cdot)$ is measurable jointly in (s, a), and is weakly continuous on A for each fixed s; that is, if $a_n \to a$ then the sequence of measures $q(\cdot \mid s, a_n)$ converges weakly to $q(\cdot \mid s, a)$.[6]

None of these assumptions require any comment, except perhaps the second part of A3 on the weak continuity of q in the actions a. As explained in Appendix A, there are (at least) three different notions of continuity we can impose on the transition probabilities: that they be weakly continuous, setwise continuous, or strongly continuous. These are nested concepts of continuity: if q is strongly continuous then it is also setwise continuous, and if it is setwise continuous then it is also weakly continuous. The containments are strict; for example, it is not true in general that weakly continuous transition probabilities are also setwise continuous. Thus, weak continuity is the mildest continuity requirement

---

[5] If $T = +\infty$ then the situation repeats indefinitely.
[6] Weak convergence of probability measures is formally defined in Appendix A.

that can be imposed on the transition mechanism and so constitutes a natural starting point for analysis.

There is a second – and equally important – reason for requiring only weak continuity and not setwise or strong continuity. Suppose we wish to consider a game with a deterministic transition mechanism; that is, suppose there is a function $h: S \times A \to S$ with the property that, if the action vector a is taken at the state s, then the next-period state is realized as $h(s, a)$ with probability 1. The transition probabilities q implied by h are

$$q\big(B \,\big|\, s, a\big) = \begin{cases} 1 & \text{if } h\big(s, a\big) \in B, \\ 0 & \text{otherwise,} \end{cases}$$

where B is any Borel subset of S. If $h(s, \cdot)$ is a continuous function of a for each $s \in S$, then the transition probabilities q will be weakly continuous in a as required by A3. However, they will not, except in pathological cases, be setwise or strongly continuous.[7] Thus, the assumption of weak continuity enables us to encompass deterministic and continuous transition mechanisms as a special case, but this will be precluded if we were to impose the stronger requirements of either setwise or strong continuity.

2.2 Histories, Strategies, and Equilibrium

For expositional ease, we will assume here and elsewhere in the sequel (except where stated to the contrary) that the game has an infinite horizon. With simple modifications, all the definitions provided here may be extended to include finite horizon problems; the details are left to the reader.

Histories. A *t-history* of the game is a complete description of the evolution of the game up to the beginning of period t. Thus, a t-history specifies the state s_τ that occurred in each previous period $\tau \in \{0, \ldots, t - 1\}$, the actions $a_\tau = (a_{i\tau})_{i \in N}$ taken by the players in those periods, and the state s_t at the beginning of period t.

Let H_t denote the set of all possible t-histories, with h_t denoting a typical element of H_t. Of course, h_t is a vector of the form

$$h_t = \big(s_0, a_0, s_1, \ldots, s_{t-1}, a_{t-1}, s_t\big).$$

Given any t and any t-history h_t, we will denote by $s[h_t]$ the period-t state s_t that results under the t-history h_t.

---

[7] It is easy to see all this from the definitions.

Strategies. Intuitively, a strategy for a player is simply a contingency plan: at each point, the strategy takes into account the past conduct of the game and recommends a continuation action for the player. Formally, a *strategy* σ_i for player i is a sequence $\{\sigma_{it}\}$ where, for each t and for each t-history h_t up to t, σ_{it} specifies the action $\sigma_{it}(h_t) \in M_i(s[h_t])$ to be taken by player i in period t as a measurable function of the history h_t up to t.

Let Σ_i denote the set of all strategies for player i, and let $\Sigma = X_{i \in N} \Sigma_i$. A generic element of Σ is denoted by σ. As is usual in this literature, the vector $(\bar{\sigma}_i, \sigma_{-i})$ will signify the profile σ with player i's strategy σ_i replaced by $\bar{\sigma}_i$.

Equilibrium. Each profile of strategies σ defines, in the obvious manner, a period-t expected reward $r_{it}(\sigma)(s)$ for player i from the initial state s. Thus, each profile σ defines from each s, a total discounted expected reward

$$W_i(\sigma)(s) = \sum_{t=0}^{\infty} \delta_i^t r_{it}(\sigma)(s). \tag{2.1}$$

A *Nash equilibrium* (or, simply, "equilibrium") of the game is a strategy profile σ^* such that no player can benefit by unilateral deviation from the profile – in other words, such that

$$W_i(\sigma^*)(s) \geq W_i(\bar{\sigma}_i, \sigma^*_{-i})(s) \quad \text{for all } s \in S, \bar{\sigma}_i \in \Sigma_i, i \in N. \tag{2.2}$$

Subgame-Perfect Equilibrium. Let σ^* be an equilibrium strategy profile. Each t-history h_t (not necessarily consistent with σ^*) induces through σ^* a strategy profile for the players for the remainder of the game. Denote this profile by $\sigma^*[h_t]$. The equilibrium σ^* is then said to be a *subgame-perfect equilibrium* if, for all t and for any t-history h_t, the strategies $\sigma^*[h_t]$ constitute an equilibrium of the remainder of the game from h_t.

It is well known that subgame perfection is a minimal rationality criterion to place on equilibrium strategy profiles. An equilibrium that is not perfect must necessarily involve an "incredible threat," that is, it must prescribe continuation behavior for some agent that is inconsistent with rational, profit-maximizing behavior. In the sequel, therefore, the word "equilibrium" will be used to refer to "subgame-perfect equilibrium" without further comment.

Markovian Strategies. Observe that, at any given time t, the past history of the game influences continuation reward possibilities for the players only through its effect on the value of the period-t state s_t. Of special interest in this context is a class of strategies known as *Markovian strategies*, which exhibit similar conditioning.

A Markovian strategy for player i is a strategy σ_i such that, for each t and for each history h_t up to t, σ_{it} depends on h_t only through the period–t state $s[h_t]$. Such a strategy can evidently be represented by a sequence of measurable functions $\{\pi_i^t\}$ where, for each t, π_i^t is a function from S to $\Delta(A_i)$ satisfying $\pi_i^t(s) \in M_i(s)$ for each t and for each $s \in S$.

If a Markovian strategy also satisfies the condition that

$$\pi_i^t = \pi_i^\tau \left(= \pi_i, \text{say}\right) \quad \text{for all } t \text{ and } \tau,$$

then the strategy is called a *stationary Markovian strategy* or simply a stationary strategy. Abusing notation, we denote such a strategy simply by π_i. Finally, we will denote by Π_i^M(resp. Π_i) the set of all Markovian (resp. stationary) strategies available to player i.

A caveat is important before proceeding. Although the general notion of a Markovian strategy applies to all Markovian games, the notion of a stationary strategy applies only to Markovian games with an infinite horizon. A finite horizon game is inherently nonstationary, so it does not make sense to talk of stationary strategies in such a setting. Therefore, it is implicit in all references to stationary strategies in the sequel that an underlying *infinite horizon* game is presumed.

Markov-Perfect Equilibrium. In keeping with the literature in this area, a subgame-perfect equilibrium in which all players use only Markovian strategies will be called a *Markov-perfect equilibrium*, abbreviated MPE.

A moment's reflection reveals that any equilibrium in *stationary* Markovian strategies is necessarily also subgame-perfect. (Indeed, this is an immediate consequence of the definitions.) It is important to note, however, that this is not necessarily true of equilibria in nonstationary Markovian strategies; that is, such equilibria need not be subgame-perfect. Thus, the requirement of subgame perfection in the definition of a MPE is not vacuous except in the context of stationary strategies.

2.3   Remarks on the Framework

In this section we point out that the framework of Markovian games we have just described is sufficiently general to encompass as special cases many of the popular models of economics and game theory, such as the frameworks of stationary dynamic programming and repeated games. There may not always be a conceptual gain from adopting this point of view (e.g., in viewing dynamic programming models as one-person

Markovian games), yet the recent work of Abreu (1988) and Abreu et al. (1986, 1990) shows that sharper analyses can sometimes emerge.

Stationary Dynamic Programming. Stationary dynamic programming models constitute what is, perhaps, the single most popular mathematical framework in dynamic economic theory. Among the great variety of issues that have been examined using this framework are economic growth, dynamic general equilibrium, firm investment, capital taxation, the theory of search and matching, and the optimal acquisition of information. The Markovian game structure we have outlined here constitutes a minimal and natural generalization of this framework from a one-person to an *n*-person setting, and permits us to move from "representative agent" models to models permitting a richer notion of interaction between agents.

For instance, one-person optimal learning models, as those in Easley and Kiefer (1988) or El-Gamal and Sundaram (1993), have highlighted the critical nature of the trade-off economic agents face between current reward maximization and the acquisition of information that might better future reward prospects. In a multi-agent setting, one would also be able to capture the "free-rider" problem that arises if all agents are able to learn something of value from any particular agent's experimentation. This is an issue of special importance when information is not a public good but instead becomes less valuable to the holder when other agents also possess it.

Repeated Games. Although there have been a number of investigations of oligopolistic models in more general settings, it would be fair to say that the framework of repeated games has remained the preeminent model for the study of dynamic strategic interaction. As with stationary dynamic programming, Markovian games also constitute a simple and natural generalization of repeated games. To wit, one can think of the Markovian game as specifying, for each state s, a normal form game $G(s)$ in which the payoffs to player i from the action profile $a \in \Phi_1(s) \times \cdots \times \Phi_n(s) \subset A$ are given by $r_i(s, a)$. In particular, when S is a one-point set $\{s\}$ – or, more generally, when for some s the probability $q(\cdot \mid s, a)$ is degenerate at s for all a – the stochastic game from the state s reduces to an indefinite repetition of the n-player simultaneous-move normal-form game $G(s)$.

Thus, traditional repeated games with observable actions (see e.g. Fudenberg and Maskin 1986 or Abreu 1988) form a special case of the framework we have described. However, the incorporation of a state variable into a repeated game also enables consideration of more general situations, as discussed in the opening remarks of this chapter. For instance, in the strategic investment model of Fudenberg and Tirole (1983), firms in an oligopoly industry are presumed to be constrained at each point in time by their capital levels, but these capital levels, in turn, move through time in response to the profits generated by the firms each period.

Repeated Games with Imperfect Monitoring. Perhaps less obviously, the models of Green and Porter (1984) and of Abreu et al. (1986, 1990) can also be accomodated by our framework. These papers study repeated games in which monitoring of players is imperfect in the sense that no player can observe the actions taken by other agents in any period. Instead, each agent observes (in addition to her own action) the realization of a public random variable whose distribution in any period is determined partially by the vector of actions taken by the players that period. A question of primary interest in these papers is the kind of equilibrium paths that can be sustained by using the observations of the public random variable to "trigger" punishment phases.

This class of games may be derived as a special case of Markovian games if we generalize our assumptions on the primitives of the Markovian game just a little. Specifically, suppose that, in the description of a general Markovian game, we allow for the reward functions r_i to depend upon not only the current state s and the current action vector a but also upon the state s' that is realized next period under (s, a).[8] (That is, a typical reward is denoted $r_i(s, a, s')$.)

In order to obtain the class of repeated games with imperfect monitoring as a special case, we simply impose the following restrictions on the model and require additionally that each player's strategy depend on history only through the previous states and the player's own previous actions. The state variable s then plays the role of the public random variable.

C1 $q(\cdot \mid s, a)$ is independent of s.
C2 $\Phi_i(s) \equiv A_i$ for all $s \in S$ and all i.
C3 $r_i(s, a, s')$ depends only on a_i and s' and *not* on s or a_{-i}.

Assumptions C1 and C2 essentially make the game a repeated one: the only connection between periods is the memory of past outcomes. Assumption C3 implies that all information apart from A_i that is observed by agent i is "public information" and is encoded in s.

---

[8] Of course, at the time the action is taken, the *expected* reward will still depend only on (s, a), so this "general" framework actually fits into the model we have already described!

For a situation in which these assumptions make sense, it might help to consider the oligopoly model of Green and Porter (1984). In the Green–Porter model, the action choices a_i refer to the quantity choice of firm i, and the state variable s' denotes the price that results from the action choices $(a_1, \ldots, a_n)$. In this context, therefore, assumption C1 simply states that the distribution of prices depends only on the vector of quantities produced and not on the price that was realized *last* period. Assumption C3 similarly states that firm i's profits can be computed with knowledge only of firm i's quantity choice a_i and the output price s'.

Nonstationary Markovian Games. Our description of the Markovian game has concentrated on a stationary infinite horizon model, but it is important to note that nonstationary (in particular, finite horizon) models are also covered. This is true because such games can always be converted into stationary infinite horizon games without any accompanying loss in continuity or compactness of the underlying structure.

To see this, suppose we are given such a game. Let

(1) S denote its state space;
(2) T (possibly equal to $+\infty$) be its horizon;
(3) A_i be the action space of the ith player;
(4) $\Phi_i^t(s) \subset A_i$ be the set of feasible actions for player i at the state s in period t;
(5) $r_i^t(s, a)$ be the reward received by player i if the actions a are taken at the state s in period t;
(6) $\delta_i \in [0, 1)$ be the discount factor of player i;[9] and, finally, let
(7) $q^t(\cdot | s, a)$ be the distribution of the period-$(t + 1)$ state if the actions a are taken at the state s in period t.

To convert this game into a stationary, infinite horizon game, we simply expand the state space to include time as one of the coordinates. Specifically, the state space of this new game, denoted Z, is defined by

$$Z = S \times \{1, \ldots, T + 1\}.$$

For $z = (s, t) \in Z$ and $a \in A$, let

$$r_i(z, a) = \begin{cases} r_i^t(s, a) & \text{if } t \neq T + 1, \\ 0 & \text{otherwise,} \end{cases}$$

and let

---

[9] $\delta_i = 1$ is permissible if T is finite.

$$\Phi_i(z) = \Phi_i^t(s).$$

Finally, define the new transition probabilities by the following. First, consider $(s,t) \in Z$, where $t \in \{1,\dots,T\}$. For B a Borel subset of S and $\tau \in \{1,\dots,T+1\}$, let

$$q\big(B \times \{\tau\} \big| (s,t), a\big) = \begin{cases} q^t(B|s,a) & \text{if } \tau = t+1, \\ 0 & \tau \neq t+1. \end{cases}$$

For $t = T+1$, let

$$q\big(B \times \{T+1\} \big| (s,t), a\big) = p(B),$$

where $p(\cdot)$ is any probability measure on S.

It is straightforward to check now that this newly defined game faithfully represents the old game. It is also immediate from construction that the new game is a stationary infinite horizon Markovian game, and that no continuity properties of the original game have been lost in the conversion.

Perfect Information Games. A number of investigations in economics have involved games with a Markovian flavor, where players move in a prespecified order (that could, in principle, depend on the play of the game). Included in this category are the papers of Dana and Montrucchio (1986) or Maskin and Tirole (1988) on dynamic models of oligopoly, in which firms move alternately; and Bernheim and Ray (1983, 1987) and Leininger (1986) on models of economic growth driven by bequest motives, where there are a countable infinity of players ($N = \{1, 2, \dots\}$) and player $i \in N$ moves only in period i. It is quite easy to show that such models – and, indeed, any Markovian version of the general perfect information games studied in Harris (1985) – can be accomodated within the Markovian game framework by simply expanding the state space and redefining the other functions appropriately. The arguments are similar to those we have used in the foregoing, but the details are a little messier.

Suppose we are given such a game. Let

(1) S denote its state space;
(2) N be the set of players;
(3) $N(s,t)$ be the players who may move in period t if the state s is reached;[10]
(4) A_j be the action space of player $j \in N$;

---

[10] When $N(s,t)$ is a singleton for all s and t, we obtain a perfect information game.

(5) $M_i^t(s)$ be the set of (mixed) actions available to player i at the state s;[11]

(6) $r_j^t(s, (\mu_i)_{i \in N(s,t)})$ be the reward to player $j \in N$ if the state s is reached in period t and player $i \in N(s,t)$ takes the action $\mu_i \in M_i(s)$; and, finally, let

(7) $q(\cdot \mid s, (\mu_i)_{i \in N(s,t)})$ be the transition probabilities in period t at the state s if the actions $(\mu_i)_{i \in N(s,t)}$ are taken.

Define $Z = S \times T$. Let φ_j be "dummy actions" for player $j \in N$. For $(s, t) \in Z$, define

$$M_j(s,t) = \begin{cases} M_j(s) & \text{if } j \in N(s,t), \\ \varphi_j & \text{otherwise.} \end{cases}$$

Also define, for $(s,t) \in Z$ and $\mu = (\mu_k)_{k \in N}$,

$$r_j\big((s,t), \mu\big) = r_j^t\Big(s, (\mu_i)_{i \in N(s,t)}\Big).$$

Finally, let

$$q\big(\cdot \mid (s,t), \mu\big) = q^t\Big(\cdot \Big| s, (\mu_i)_{i \in N(s,t)}\Big).$$

It is now readily verified that the Markovian game $\{N, Z, (A_j, M_j, r_j, \delta_j), q\}$ is a complete representation of the original game.

A Note on Deterministic Transitions. Our assumptions require only weak-continuity of the transition probabilities q. Thus, deterministic transitions are also covered as a special case, as we have already pointed out. However, as we will see in the sequel, most of the results available in the literature on the existence of equilibrium require us to strengthen this assumption to setwise, or even strong, continuity. Except in pathological situations, this rules out the possibility that transitions may be deterministic.

3 The Existence of Markov-Perfect Equilibria

It appears natural, in an otherwise stationary Markovian environment, to begin the search for equilibria in the class of stationary Markovian strategies. Indeed, the following five-step heuristic argument appears to suggest that stationary MPE may not be too hard to find.

(1) Let $\pi \in \Pi$ be a vector of stationary strategies for the players. In seeking a best-response to π (i.e., to π_{-i}), a generic player i faces

---

[11] This set is, of course, empty if i is not in $N(s,t)$.

a stationary dynamic programming problem with: state space S; action space $\Delta(A_i)$; feasible action correspondence $M_i(s) = \Delta(\Phi_i(s))$; reward function $r_i(\pi)(s,\mu_i) := r_i(s,(\pi_{-i}(s),\mu_i))$; and transition probabilities $q_i(\pi)\,(\cdot\mid s,\mu_i) := q(\cdot\mid s,(\pi_{-i}(s),\mu_i))$.

(2) An appeal to a well-known result in the theory of dynamic programming (Blackwell 1965, Thm. 6) establishes that this problem possesses a solution if and only if it admits a stationary Markovian solution.

(3) Therefore, in seeking a best response to $\pi \in \Pi$, player i loses no strategic flexibility in restricting his search to Π_i.

(4) Under suitable restrictions on π, the set $BR_i(\pi)$ of stationary best responses of player i to π, can also be guaranteed to be nonempty.

(5) Thus, we "should" be able to obtain a stationary MPE of the Markovian game as a fixed-point of a map from (some subset of) Π into itself.

Unfortunately, this intuition turns out to be only partly useful. In fact, when all spaces are finite, one can obtain an equilibrium in Markovian strategies using a fixed-point argument in the manner just outlined; the details are presented in Section 3.1. When spaces of arbitrary cardinality are admitted, however, problems of surprising complexity arise; these are discussed in Section 3.2. The arguments we present here appear to imply that existence of MPE in the general case may be provable only by imposing some additional structure on the problem's primitives. Indeed, as we explain in Section 4, all the available results in the literature have involved a considerable strengthening of Assumptions A1–A3.

3.1   Finite Markovian Games

The following result (proved by Rogers 1969 and Sobel 1971) provides an affirmative answer to the existence question for finite Markovian games.

Theorem 3.1. *Suppose* S *is finite and* A_i *is finite for each* i. *Then the Markovian game has an equilibrium in stationary strategies.*

Remark. Parthasarathy (1973) shows that Theorem 3.1 may be extended to the case of countable S without too much difficulty.

Proof of Theorem 3.1. We proceed via a routine application of Kakutani's theorem. We sketch the details here, dividing the argument into three steps for expositional convenience.

Step 1: The Space Π. Because A_i is a finite set, the set $\Delta(A_i)$ of all possible mixed actions for player i is simply the positive unit simplex of dimension $|A_i| - 1$. Since S is also a finite set, the $|S|$-fold Cartesian product of this simplex (denoted, say, $\mathcal{A}_i$) is just a compact subset of a finite-dimensional Euclidean space. Now, every stationary strategy for player i can be associated in the obvious way with a unique element of $\mathcal{A}_i$; it follows easily from this observation that the space Π_i of all stationary strategies for player i is just a closed, convex subset of $\mathcal{A}_i$ in the Euclidean topology. Thus, Π_i is compact and convex. So, therefore, is $\Pi = \Pi_1 \times \cdots \times \Pi_n$.

Step 2: Best Responses. Given $\pi \in \Pi$, the best-response problem faced by player i is a stationary dynamic programming problem $\{S, \Delta(A_i), M_i, r_i(\pi), q_i(\pi)\}$, whose components we have described in the sketch of our heuristic argument. It is a simple matter to see from the finiteness of S that, for any $\pi \in \Pi$, $r_i(\pi)$ is continuous on $S \times \Delta(A_i)$ and $q_i(\pi)$ is weakly continuous on $S \times A_i$. An appeal to Maitra (1967) establishes that the set $\mathrm{BR}_i(\pi)$ of player i's stationary best responses to π is nonempty. It is also easy to see from the definitions that $r_i(\pi)(s, \cdot)$ and $q_i(\pi)(\cdot \mid s, \cdot)$ are linear in μ_i. Therefore, $\mathrm{BR}_i(\pi)$ is convex-valued.

Step 3: Continuity of the Best-Response Map. Define the correspondence $\mathrm{BR}:\Pi \to \Pi$ by $\mathrm{BR}(\pi) = (\mathrm{BR}_i(\pi))_{i \in N}$. Since each BR_i is nonempty-valued and convex-valued, so is BR. To apply Kakutani's theorem, we must also show that BR is an upper-semicontinuous (usc) correspondence on Π. This will be established if we can show that BR_i is a usc correspondence for each i. So fix i. Let

$$\pi^n \to \pi, \quad \alpha_i^n \in \mathrm{BR}_i(\pi^n), \quad \alpha_i^n \to \alpha_i \in \Pi_i.$$

We are to show that $\alpha_i \in BR_i(\pi)$.

Let V^n denote player i's value function in a best response to π^n. Since $\delta < 1$, the sequence V^n is uniformly bounded by

$$(1 - \delta)^{-1} \max\{r_i(s, a) \mid (s, a) \in S \times A\}.$$

We may thus assume, without loss of generality, that V^n converges pointwise to a limit V. Now let r^n denote $r_i(\pi^n)$ and q^n denote $q_i(\pi^n)$. It is trivial that

$$r^n \to r \equiv r_i(\pi) \quad \text{and} \quad q^n \to q \equiv q(\pi).$$

Because V^n satisfies the Bellman equation for each n, for any s and any $\mu_i \in M_i(s)$ we have

$$V^n(s) = r^n(s, \alpha_i^n(s)) + \delta_i \int V^n(s') \, dq^n(s' \mid s, \alpha_i^n(s)), \tag{3.3}$$

$$V^n(s) \geq r^n(s, \mu_i) + \delta_i \int V^n(s') \, dq^n(s' \mid s, \mu_i).$$ (3.4)

Now observe that the integrals on the right-hand side (RHS) are just finite sums; that is,

$$\int V^n(s') \, dq^n(s' \mid s, \alpha_i^n(s)) = \sum_{s' \in S} \left[V^n(s') \times \mathrm{Prob}(s' \mid s, \pi_{-i}^n(s), \alpha_i^n(s)) \right]$$

and

$$\int V^n(s') \, dq^n(s' \mid s, \mu_i) = \sum_{s' \in S} \left[V^n(s') \times \mathrm{Prob}(s' \mid s, \pi_{-i}^n(s), \mu_i) \right].$$

Therefore, taking limits as $n \to \infty$, we obtain

$$\int V^n(s') \, dq^n(s' \mid s, \alpha_i^n(s)) \to \int V(s') \, dq(s' \mid s, \alpha_i(s))$$

and

$$\int V^n(s') \, dq^n(s' \mid s, \mu_i) \to \int V(s') \, dq(s' \mid s, \mu_i).$$

It follows that, letting $n \to \infty$ in (3.3) and (3.4), we obtain the expressions

$$V(s) = r(s, \alpha_i(s)) + \delta_i \int V(s') \, dq(s' \mid s, \alpha_i(s)),$$ (3.5)

$$V(s) \geq r(s, \mu_i) + \delta_i \int V(s') \, dq(s' \mid s, \mu_i).$$ (3.6)

These expressions establish precisely that $V(\cdot)$ is the value function in a best response of i to π_{-i}, and that $\alpha_i(\cdot)$ is a stationary best-response – that is, $\alpha_i \in \mathrm{BR}_i(\pi)$. Thus, BR_i is a usc correspondence for each i, establishing upper semicontinuity of BR.

An appeal to Kakutani's fixed-point theorem now implies the existence of $\pi^* \in \mathrm{BR}(\pi^*)$, completing the proof. $\square$

3.2   *MPE in General Markovian Games: Some Observations*

A number of attempts have been made in the literature to extend Theorem 3.1 to the case where S and A_i have arbitrary cardinality, but thus far only partial success has been witnessed. In this section we discuss the problems of obtaining a general existence theorem. As with the rest of the paper, our focus is primarily on the infinite horizon problem (at the end of Section 3 we briefly examine finite-horizon Markovian games). The discussion here will especially underscore the need to strengthen the hypotheses placed on the primitives of the problem, in particular on the transition probabilities.

We will suppose throughout Section 3.2 that the state space S and the action spaces A_i are arbitrary Borel sets. However, to keep the arguments transparent, we shall strengthen assumptions A2 and A3 to requiring full joint continuity in (s, a).

A2*   For each i, the reward function r_i is a continuous function on $S \times A_1 \times \ldots \times A_n$.

A3*   The transition probability q is weakly continuous on $S \times A_1 \times \cdots \times A_n$.

Two distinct problems arise in obtaining an analog of Theorem 3.1 for the general case. First, there is what we shall call the "self-referential problem" concerning best responses. Briefly put, the problem is that restrictions on the space of admissible strategies π must be strong enough to ensure that best responses to these strategies always exist and yet weak enough to allow for at least one best response that itself satisfies these restrictions. Second, there is the problem of suitably topologizing strategy sets in order to ensure that fixed-point theorems can be applied. We shall now examine these two problems in turn.

The Self-Referential Problem in Best Responses. The environment of each player's best-response problem is determined jointly by the problem's primitives and the strategy vector chosen by the other players. Thus, in order to ensure that each player i has a well-defined best response, some conditions must be imposed on the (Markovian) strategies π_{-i} of the other players. However, for a fixed-point argument to be applicable, these conditions must also be met by at least one of i's best responses. We will argue that this requirement is very difficult to satisfy under assumptions A1, A2*, and A3*.

At an intuitive level, the problem that arises is simply that, in any optimization environment, the continuity and curvature properties of the optimal strategy will not be as strong as the continuity and curvature properties of the primitive problem. For example, as the theorem of the maximum (see e.g. Berge 1963) shows, the correspondence of maximizers in a continuous optimization environment can be guaranteed only to be upper-semicontinuous, and will not always admit a continuous selection. For such a continuous selection to exist, the optimization environment must also be convex, but this is sufficient only to guarantee a continuous selection, and not also a convex one.

Since the continuity and curvature properties of a player's best-response environment in the Markovian game are determined by the continuity and curvature properties of the other players' strategies, this effectively means the properties of a player's best response can never be as strong as the properties of her opponents' strategies; in particular, they may not meet the minimal restrictions on the opponents' strategies that will guarantee the existence of at least one best response. In a nutshell, this is the self-referential problem.

To formalize these arguments in the context of the Markovian game, let a vector of Markovian strategies $\pi \in \Pi$ be given. Consider the best-response problem of player i, namely, the stationary dynamic programming problem $\{S, A_i M_i, r_i(\pi), q_i(\pi)\}$. From standard arguments, the value function $V_i(\pi)$ of this problem can be shown to satisfy the Bellman "principle of optimality" equation at each $s \in S$:

$$V_i(\pi)(s) = \sup_{\mu_i \in M_i(s)} \left\{ r_i(\pi)(s, \mu_i) + \delta_i \int V_i(\pi)(\cdot) \, dq_i(\pi)(\cdot \,|\, s, \mu_i) \right\}. \quad (3.7)$$

For the best-response problem itself to have a solution, it is *necessary* that we be able to replace the "sup" in (3.7) with a "max" at each s; this is possible, in general, only if the expression in braces on the RHS of (3.7) is upper-semicontinuous in μ_i.

The results of Maitra (1967) show that sufficient conditions for such upper semicontinuity to obtain – and, therefore, for $BR_i(\pi)$ to be nonempty – are that:[12]

(1) $r_i(\pi)$ be upper-semicontinuous on $S \times A_i$; and
(2) $q_i(\pi)$ be weakly continuous on $S \times A_i$.

For $r_i(\pi)$ and $q_i(\pi)$ to satisfy these continuity conditions (even under A2* and A3*), we would need π_j to be *continuous* on S for each $j \neq i$. Although it ensures that $BR_i(\pi)$ is nonempty, the continuity of π_j for $j \neq i$ *is not sufficient to ensure that $BR_i(\pi)$ contains a continuous element.*

Indeed, dynamic programming problems in general admit continuous solutions only under restrictive *convexity* conditions. Of course, we could ensure that the appropriate convexity conditions are met by further restricting the class of admissible strategies π_j (and by placing restrictions on the problem's parameters). However, this would suffice to ensure the existence of only a continuous best response and not a convex one also; thus, the problem remains of ensuring that at least one best response exists that meets all the required restrictions.

An Extended Remark on Setwise Continuity.   One possible solution to the self-referential problem is to strengthen the requirement on the transition probabilities q to *strong* or, at least, *setwise* continuity on A. That is, we replace the weak continuity condition in A3 with the following condition:

---

[12] These conditions are also minimally sufficient in that, were either condition to fail, a counterexample to existence of optimal solutions could be constructed.

If a^k is a sequence in A converging to a, then $q(B\,|\,s,a^k) \to q(B\,|\, s,a)$ for each $s \in S$ and each Borel set $B \subset S$.[13]

An important implication of assuming setwise (rather than weak) continuity may be described as follows. Let $f\colon S \to \mathbb{R}$ be a measurable function, and define

$$I_f(s, a) = \int f(s')\, dq(s'\,|\,s, a).$$

Under weak continuity, $I_f(s, \cdot)$ is a continuous function of a only if f is itself a continuous function on S; whereas, under setwise continuity, $I_f(s, \cdot)$ is a continuous function of a for *any* measurable function f.

Replacing weak continuity with setwise continuity eliminates the self-referential problem immediately. To see this, suppose that assumptions A1–A3 are met, and that q is setwise continuous on A for each $s \in S$. Let a vector of measurable stationary strategies $\pi \in \Pi$ be given. Denote by $B(S)$ the space of all bounded measurable functions on S endowed with the sup-norm. Define the map T_i on $B(S)$ as follows: for $w \in B(S)$, let

$$T_i w(s) = \max_{\mu_i \in M_i(s)} \left\{ r_i(\pi)(s, \mu_i) + \delta_i \int w(\cdot)\, dq_i(\pi)(\cdot\,|\,s, \mu_i) \right\}. \tag{3.8}$$

Since q is setwise continuous on A (in particular, on A_i), it is the case that

$$\int w(\cdot)\, dq_i(\pi)(\cdot\,|\,s, \mu_i)$$

is continuous in μ_i. Thus, so is the entire expression in braces on the RHS of (3.8), and the maximum – and $T_i w$ – are well-defined. The usual arguments show that T is a contraction and has a unique fixed point, and that this fixed point is precisely $V_i(\pi)$. A standard selection theorem also shows that $\mathrm{BR}_i(\pi)$ is nonempty.

On the downside, there is a cost to be paid for obtaining the extra flexibility that setwise continuity provides. Most importantly, as we have seen in Section 2.1, transitions that are deterministic (and continuous) are weakly continuous but will not typically be setwise continuous. This point becomes especially significant when one notes that a majority of economic applications of the Markovian game paradigm do not involve any uncertainty in the transitions mechanism.

The Fixed-Point Problem. The application of a fixed-point argument typically requires two conditions: first, that the strategy space be compact

---

[13] Weak continuity also requires the same condition, but only for those Borel sets B whose boundary has $q(\cdot\,|\,s, a)$-measure zero.

(in some chosen topology); and second, that the best-response mapping be continuous (in that topology). This makes the choice of topology critical.

When S and A are finite sets, we have seen that the space Π may be associated with a subset of the unit sphere in some finite-dimensional Euclidean space. Thus, in this case, the product or pointwise convergence topology (i.e., a sequence π^k converges to π if and only if $\pi^k(s) \to \pi(s)$ for each $s \in S$) suggests itself as a natural choice. The space Π will then have all desired compactness (and convexity) properties.

It is less than apparent, however, that the product topology remains an appropriate choice in the general case. The reason is simple: for general S, the pointwise convergence topology is not first-countable, so sequential arguments cannot be used; on the other hand, the limit of a net of measurable functions need not be measurable.

Choosing a topology to ensure compactness is only part of the problem (and not a very difficult one, at least in select situations – see Section 4). The other part lies in ensuring that the best-response map is continuous in the chosen topology, and this involves a difficult "integration to the limit" question. To see the problem, suppose that best responses are well-defined on (some compact subset of) the strategy space. Let π^k be a strategy profile sequence in this space, and suppose $\pi^k \to \pi^*$. Let $\mathrm{BR}_i(\cdot)$ denote player i's best-response map. Let $\pi_i^k \in \mathrm{BR}_i(\pi^k)$, and assume – without loss, since compactness is presumed – that $\pi_i^k \to \pi_i$.

To show continuity of the best-reponse map in this setting is to show that $\pi_i \in \mathrm{BR}_i(\pi^*)$. Equivalently, letting V_i^k (resp. V_i^*) denote player i's value functions in best responses to π^k (resp. π^*), we are given that, for each k and at each s, $\pi_i^k(s)$ solves

$$V_i^k(s) = \max_{\mu_i \in M_i(s)} \left\{ r_i(\pi^k)(s, \mu_i) + \delta_i \int V_i^k(\bar{s}) \, dq_i(\pi^k)(\bar{s} \,|\, s, \mu_i) \right\}; \quad (3.9)$$

our aim is to show that, for each s, $\pi_i(s)$ solves

$$V_i^*(s) = \max_{\mu_i \in M_i(s)} \left\{ r_i(\pi^*)(s, \mu_i) + \delta_i \int V_i^*(\bar{s}) \, dq_i(\pi^*)(s, \mu_i) \right\}. \quad (3.10)$$

To derive (3.10) from (3.9) requires, in particular, that we be able to prove that

$$\int V_i^k(\bar{s}) \, dq_i(\pi^k)(\bar{s} \,|\, s, \mu_i) \to \int V_i^*(\bar{s}) \, dq_i(\pi^*)(\bar{s} \,|\, s, \mu_i). \quad (3.11)$$

In the finite case, the convergence in (3.11) obtained from the fact that the integrals were merely finite sums. In the general case, however, this is a nontrivial exercise. In particular – although even these hypotheses would not be easy to ensure – it is *not* sufficient that V_i^k converge point-wise to V_i^* and that $q_i(\pi^k)$ converge weakly to $q_i(\pi^*)$.

Of course, there do exist conditions under which (3.11) obtains, but these conditions involve severe restrictions on the sense in which V_i^k and q^k can converge to V_i^* and q^*. Moreover, it is in general very difficult to determine if these restrictions will obtain in a given problem. For example, Billingsley (1968) shows that (3.11) will obtain as long as:

(1)   the sequence q^k converges weakly to q^*; and
(2)   the q^*-measure of the following set of points is zero:

$$\left\{ s \middle| \text{there is a sequence } s^k \to s \text{ but } V_i^k\!\left(s^k\right) \nrightarrow V_i^*\!\left(s\right) \right\}.$$

In general, the second condition will be met only if *either* the V_i^k sequence and its limit V_i^* have some strong properties, such as

V_i^k and V_i^* are continuous on S, and V_i^k converges *uniformly* to V_i^*;

or the q and V sequences have some joint properties, such as

The set $\{s \mid \text{there exist } s^k \to s \text{ but } V_i^k(s^k) \nrightarrow V_i^*(s)\}$ has ν-measure zero, where ν is some measure on S and where q^* is absolutely continuous with respect to ν.

Since V is not itself a primitive of the problem, and since the properties of both V and q depend on the chosen vector of strategies π, it should be apparent that, in general, it is extraordinarily difficult to ensure that conditions such as these obtain.[14]

Problems with Backward Induction in Finite Horizon Games. The fore-going discussion indicates that existence of MPE in the infinite horizon model may be difficult to prove without imposing additional structure on the components of the Markovian game. A natural question that arises in this context is whether a similar statement is true of *finite* horizon games also; in particular, are there problems with using the familiar backward induction procedure to obtain an equilibrium? The answer to this question, unfortunately, turns out to be in the affirmative; an analog of the self-referential problem in best response is the reason.

---

[14]   At a superficial level, it appears that the condition of setwise continuity may also be of help here. It is shown in Royden (1968) that (3.10) obtains whenever: (1) q^k converges setwise to q^*; and (2) V_i^k converges pointwise almost surely (under q^*) to V_i^*. The second condition is significantly weaker than the corresponding condition under weak continuity quoted above. However, this only suggests that the problem is *potentially* simpler; ensuring these conditions hold remains non-trivial.

It suffices to consider a two-period horizon to explain the difficulties that arise. In any subgame-perfect equilibrium, the last period actions at any state s must be Nash equilibrium actions at that state. Let $N(s)$ denote the set of Nash action pairs at the state s:

$$N(s) = \left\{(\mu_1, \ldots, \mu_n) \middle| r_i(s, \mu_i, \mu_{-i}) \ge r_i(s, \mu_i^*, \mu_{-i})\right.$$

$$\left. \text{for all } \mu_i^* \in M_i(s), i = 1, \ldots, n \right\};$$

and let $V(s)$ be the set of Nash payoff vectors of the one-period game at the state s:

$$V(s) = \left\{(v_1, \ldots, v_n) \middle| v_i = r_i(s, \mu) \text{ for some } \mu \in N(s)\right\}.$$

In the backward induction procedure, a measurable selection $v(\cdot) = (v_1(\cdot), \ldots, v_n(\cdot))$ from the correspondence $V(\cdot)$ will be used as the continuation payoffs in the two-period game. That is, if the players take the action vector a at a first-period state s, then player i receives the overall reward

$$r_i(s, a) + \delta_i \int v_i(\cdot) \, dq(\cdot \mid s, a). \tag{3.12}$$

The implicit idea is that players receive first-period rewards according to $r_i(s, a)$; if the state s' is reached in the continuation, then the players play the Nash actions that yield the reward vector $v(s')$.

Thus, to find an MPE by backward induction, it suffices to find a selection $v(\cdot)$ from $V(\cdot)$ under which the one-shot game with payoffs described by (3.12) admits a Nash equilibrium vector of actions at each s. In general, the existence of such a Nash equilibrium can be guaranteed only if the payoffs described by (3.12) are continuous in a. Essentially, then, we must ensure the existence of a selection $v(\cdot)$ such that the payoffs described by (3.12) are continuous in a.

The overall payoffs described by (3.12) are continuous in a only when the integral

$$\int v_i(\cdot) \, dq(\cdot \mid s, a) \tag{3.13}$$

is continuous in a. Under weak continuity of q, this integral will be continuous in a only if v_i is itself a continuous function on S. Therefore, for the backward induction procedure to be operative under weak continuity, we need to find a selection $v(\cdot)$ that is continuous on S.

Unfortunately, a well-known result in the theory of normal-form games shows that, under A1, A2*, and A3*, $V(\cdot)$ will be an upper-semicontinuous, compact-valued correspondence on S but it will *not*, in general, be either lower-semicontinuous or convex-valued. In particular, it will not admit a continuous selection in general. Therefore, the payoff functions given by (3.12) may be discontinuous in a, and the corresponding game may not admit a Nash equilibrium. The backward induction procedure breaks down.

As with the self-referential problem, it turns out that the solution to this problem lies in strengthening the requirements on the transition probabilities to setwise continuity on a. This guarantees that continuity of the integral in (3.13) in a, and makes the backward induction procedure feasible. We discuss this point in detail in Section 4.1.

4   MPE in General Markovian Games

This section has a simple objective: to show how an appropriate strengthening of assumptions A1–A3 can help overcome, at least partially, the problems highlighted in Section 3.2. Toward this end, we present a number of results from the literature, breaking them up into three groups for expositional convenience.

In Section 4.1 we examine the many results that have been established on the existence of ε-equilibria in Markovian strategies. An ε-equilibrium is simply a profile of strategies in which each player obtains within ε of his best response to the other players' strategies, where $\varepsilon \geq 0$ is a fixed real number. Such a profile may be regarded as an "approximate equilibrium," with ε measuring the degree of approximation; the smaller ε becomes, the more nearly the given strategy profile is actually an equilibrium. Of course, for $\varepsilon = 0$, an ε-equilibrium strategy profile is simply an equilibrium strategy profile in the sense in which we have already defined it. A byproduct of our proof of the existence of ε-equilibria (indeed, an essential ingredient in this proof) is a result on the existence of MPE in *finite* horizon Markovian games.

In Section 4.2 we present a result on the existence of a p-equilibrium in Markovian strategies. A p-equilibrium is a strategy profile in which each player's strategy is a best-response to those of the other players from p-almost every initial state, where p is a fixed measure on the state space. Like an ε-equilibrium, a p-equilibrium strategy profile represents an "approximate equilibrium"; when the expression "p-almost every" is replaced by "every," we are back at our original notion of an equilibrium.

Finally, in Section 4.3, we present a result due to Parthasarathy (1982). The result describes technical conditions under which any model that admits a p-equilibrium in Markovian strategies will also admit a "full" MPE. Combining these conditions with those in Himmelberg et al.

(1976), we obtain one set of assumptions (restrictive though they are) under which Markovian games may be guaranteed to admit MPE.

4.1   Existence of ε-Equilibria in Markovian Strategies

We begin with a formal definition of an ε-equilibrium. Toward this end, recall that $W_i(\sigma)(s)$ denotes the total discounted expected payoff to player i from the initial state $s \in S$.

Definition.   Let $\varepsilon \geq 0$ be given. A strategy profile σ^*, not necessarily Markovian, is said to be an *ε-equilibrium* of the game if

$$W_i\big(\sigma^*\big)\big(s\big) \geq W_i\big(\sigma^*_{-i}, \sigma_i\big)\big(s\big) - \varepsilon \quad \text{for all } s \in S, \sigma_i \in \Sigma_i, i \in N.$$

$$(4.1)$$

Note that:

(1)   for $\varepsilon = 0$, this is just the equilibrium we defined by (2.2); and
(2)   as ε varies, the set of ε-equilibria is nested in the sense that, if σ^* is an ε_1-equilibrium for some $\varepsilon_1 \geq 0$ and if $\varepsilon_2 > \varepsilon_1$, then σ^* is also an ε_2-equilibrium.

Combining these points, we see that every equilibrium is also an ε-equilibrium for any $\varepsilon > 0$. The converse is, evidently, false.

There are two different approaches in the literature to proving the existence of ε-equilibria; the critical step in each is the approximation of the given game by a family of simpler games. In the first approach (presented originally in Rieder 1979 and subsequently in Amir 1991 and Chakrabarti 1993), the approximation is achieved via finite horizon truncations of the Markovian game; as the horizon becomes larger, the truncated games become closer to the given game. In the second approach (used, e.g., in Nowak 1985), discretizations of the state and action spaces are employed to simplify the original game; as these discretizations get finer, we get closer to the original game.

Both approaches involve strengthening assumption A3 significantly. In the first case, the weak continuity assumption is replaced by one of setwise continuity. In the second, it is assumed that the family of transition probabilities is absolutely continuous with respect to a fixed probability measure p on the state space. We present Rieder's (1979) result in detail first, followed by a discussion of Nowak (1985).

Theorem 4.1.   *Suppose that Assumptions* A1–A3 *hold, and that* q *is setwise continuous on* A *for each fixed* s. *Then, for each fixed integer*

$T \in \{1, 2, \ldots\}$, *the game with horizon* T *admits an equilibrium in (possibly nonstationary) Markovian strategies.*

Proof. The result is an easy consequence of the following lemmata. The first lemma essentially shows that the theorem is true for $T = 1$; the combination of the lemmata, together with a selection theorem, then establishes the result for general T through an induction argument. $\square$

Lemma 4.2. *Consider a* n-*player, simultaneous-move, normal-form game in which* (a) *the players' action spaces are given by metric spaces* $B_1, \ldots, B_n,$ *and* (b) *the reward functions are given by real functions* $h_1, \ldots, h_n$ *defined on* $B = B_1 \times \cdots \times B_n$. *If* B_i *is compact and* h_i *is continuous on* B *for each* i, *then the game admits a Nash equilibrium (in possibly mixed strategies). That is, there exist* $\beta^* = (\beta_1^*, \ldots, \beta_n^*) \in \Delta(B_1) \times \cdots \times \Delta(B_n)$ *such that, for each* i,

$$h_i\left(\beta^*\right) \ge h_i\left(\beta_{-i}^*, \hat{\beta}_i\right) \quad \forall \hat{\beta}_i \in \Delta\left(B_i\right).$$

Proof. For each $\beta = (\beta_1, \ldots, \beta_n)$ and for each $i \in N$, let $\mathrm{BR}_i(\beta)$ denote the set of best responses in $\Delta(B_i)$ to β:

$$\mathrm{BR}_i\left(\beta\right) = \left\{ \hat{\beta}_i \in \Delta\left(B_i\right) \middle| h_i\left(\beta_{-i}, \hat{\beta}_i\right) \ge h_i\left(\beta_{-i}, \bar{\beta}_i\right) \text{ for all } \bar{\beta}_i \in \Delta\left(B_i\right) \right\}.$$

A well-known result (see e.g. Billingsley 1968) establishes that if $\Delta(B_i)$ is given the topology of weak convergence then, like B_i, $\Delta(B_i)$ is also compact metric. Since h_i is also continuous on $\Delta(B_i)$, it follows that $\mathrm{BR}_i(\beta)$ is nonempty for each β. An appeal to the maximum theorem of Berge (1963) shows that $\mathrm{BR}_i(\beta)$ is an upper-semicontinuous correspondence. That $\mathrm{BR}_i(\beta)$ is also convex-valued follows simply from the fact that h_i is linear in β_i.[15]

Therefore, the correspondence $\mathrm{BR}(\cdot)$ defined by $\mathrm{BR}(\beta) = \Pi_{i \in N} \mathrm{BR}_i(\beta)$ is a nonempty-valued, convex-valued, upper-semicontinuous correspondence from Δ^* into itself, where Δ^* is defined by

$$\Delta^* = \Delta\left(B_1\right) \times \cdots \times \Delta\left(B_n\right).$$

The existence of a fixed point of $\mathrm{BR}(\cdot)$ now follows from Glicksberg's fixed-point theorem. Every fixed-point is clearly a Nash equilibrium of the given game. $\square$

Lemma 4.3. *Let a Markovian game be given in which assumptions* A1–A3 *hold and in which* q *is setwise continuous on* A. *Let* $\mathrm{v} \colon S \to \mathbb{R}^n$ *be*

---

[15] This linearity obtains from the definition of expected payoffs under a mixed-strategy: for any β_{-i}, we have $h_i(\beta_{-i}, \beta_i) = \int_{B_i} h_i(\beta_{-i}, b_i) \, d\beta_i(b_i)$.

any bounded measurable function. Given $i \in N$, $s \in S$, $a \in \Phi(s)$, *and* $\mu \in$ *M(s), define*

$$H_i[v](s, a) = r_i(s, a) + \delta_i \int v_i(\hat{s}) \, dq(\hat{s} \mid s, a)$$

and

$$H_i[v](s, \mu) = \int H_i(v)(s, a) \, d\mu_1(a_1) \cdots d\mu_n(a_n).$$

Fix any $s \in S$. *Then the* n-*player, simultaneous-move, normal-form game in which player* i*'s action space is given by* A_i *and player* i*'s reward function is given by* $H_i[v](s, \cdot)$ *has a Nash equilibrium point* $\xi(s)$ = $(\xi_1(s), \ldots, \xi_n(s))$. *Moreover,* $\xi(\cdot)$ *may be chosen to be a measurable function of* s.

Remark. The setwise continuity in a of the transition probabilities q is essential for this result.

Proof of Lemma 4.3. Let v be given, and fix any $s \in S$. Since $q(\cdot \mid s, \cdot)$ is setwise continuous on A, we have

$$\int v_i(\cdot) \, dq(\cdot \mid s, a)$$

is a continuous function of a. Since $r_i(s, a)$ is also continuous on A, it follows that

$$H_i[v](s, a) = r_i(s, a) + \delta_i \int v_i(\cdot) \, dq(\cdot \mid s, a)$$

is itself a continuous function on A for each fixed s. Because each A_i is compact metric, the existence of a Nash equilibrium for fixed s is simply a consequence of Lemma 4.2. Let $\Xi(s)$ denote the set of Nash equilibrium actions at s:

$$\Xi(s) = \left\{ \mu^* \in M(s) \,\Big|\, H_i[v](s, \mu^*) = \max_{\mu_i \in M_i(s)} H_i(v)(s, \mu_{-i}^*, \mu_i) \right\}.$$

It is readily verified that $\Xi(s)$ is a compact-valued correspondence. Since $H_i[v]$ is evidently jointly measurable in (s, a), a standard selection theorem (see e.g. Rieder 1979, Thm. 3.1; or Amir 1991, Lemma 3.3) shows that Ξ admits a measurable selection ξ, completing the proof. $\square$

We now return to the proof of the theorem. Consider $T = 1$. By assumption, $r_i(s, \cdot)$ is continuous on $\Phi(s)$ for each s, and r_i is measurable on $S \times A$. Thus, by Lemma 4.3, there exists a measurable function $\pi_1: S \to \Delta(A)$, with $\pi_{i1}(s) \in M_i(s)$ for each s, such that

$$r_i(s, \pi_1(s)) = \max_{\mu_i \in M_i(s)} r_i(s, \pi_{-i}(s), \mu_i)$$

for all i. Let $v_{i1}(s) = r_i(s, \pi_1(s))$, and let $v_1 = (v_{i1})_{i \in N}$. Then π_1 is a Markovian equilibrium of the one-period game, with v_1 the corresponding equilibrium payoff vector for the players.

We proceed by induction. Suppose the existence of a Markovian equilibrium $(\pi_\tau, \ldots, \pi_1)$ has been established for all games of horizon less than or equal to τ, where $\pi_k(s) = (\pi_{ik}(s))_{i \in N}$ specifies the actions to be taken if there are k periods remaining and the state is s. Let $v(\tau): S \to \mathbb{R}^n$ denote the corresponding vector of payoff functions in this equilibrium; that is, let $v_i(\tau)(s)$ be the discounted equilibrium payoff to player i in the τ-period game if the initial state is s. We will show that the $(\tau + 1)$-period game also has a Markovian equilibrium with measurable payoff functions.

Indeed, this is immediate. By Lemma 4.3, the game with payoffs

$$H_i\big[v(\tau)\big](s, a) = r_i(s, a) + \delta \int v(\tau)(\cdot)\, dq(\cdot\,|\,s, a)$$

has an equilibrium $\xi: S \to \Delta(A)$. It follows that the $(\tau + 1)$-vector $(\xi, \pi_1, \ldots, \pi_\tau)$ specifies an equilibrium of the $(\tau + 1)$-period game, and that the value function vector in this equilibrium of the game is given by $v_i(\tau + 1)(s) = H_i[v(\tau)](s, \xi(s))$ for each $i \in N$. $\quad\square$

It is a simple matter to use Theorem 4.1, in conjunction with the uniform boundedness of the reward functions r_i and the assumption of strict discounting ($\delta_i < 1$ for all i), to show our next theorem.

Theorem 4.4. *Suppose the hypotheses of Theorem 4.1 hold. Then, given any $\varepsilon > 0$, the Markovian game admits an ε-equilibrium in (possibly nonstationary) Markovian strategies.*

Proof. Let $\varepsilon > 0$ be given. Let $\bar{r}$ denote the supremum over $i \in N$ and $(s, a) \in S \times A$ of the bounded functions r_i. Pick $T(\varepsilon)$ large enough that

$$\delta_i^t \bar{r} < \varepsilon(1 - \delta_i) \quad \text{for all } i \in N, t \geq T(\varepsilon).$$

Since $\delta_i < 1$ for each i, this is possible. Now pick any $T \geq T(\varepsilon)$, and let $(\pi_{i\tau}^*)_{i \in N, \tau = 0, 1, \ldots, T}$ be an equilibrium in Markovian strategies of the T-period game.

Consider any Markovian stategy profile $(\pi(1), \ldots, \pi(n))$ for the players, where for each i we set $\pi(i) \equiv (\pi_{it})_{t=0,1,\ldots}$. Suppose that, for each i, $\pi(i)$ coincides with chosen equilibrium Markovian strategies for the first T-periods; that is, we have $\pi_{it} = \pi_{it}^*$ for $t = 1, \ldots, T$. By construction, $(\pi_1, \ldots, \pi_n)$ is an ε-equilibrium of the infinite horizon game. $\quad\square$

As mentioned previously, the literature contains a number of other results on the existence of ε-equilibria in Markovian games. Perhaps most noteworthy amongst these is the paper of Nowak (1985). Nowak's assumptions are somewhat stronger than the ones we have employed in Theorem 4.4. However, through the use of more sophisticated techniques, he also obtains a significantly stronger result – namely, the existence of ε-equilibria in *stationary* strategies in the infinite horizon Markovian game. A brief discussion of his result follows.

Concerning the hypotheses made, the most important assumption in Nowak's paper is that the transition probabilities admit a density $f(\cdot \mid s, a)$ with respect to some fixed measure p on S. It is further assumed that $f(\cdot \mid s, a)$ is continuous in a and satisfies some additional technical conditions.

The second point of departure in Nowak's paper is in the technique of proof. Rather than approximate the given Markovian game by finite horizon games (as we have done in Theorem 4.4), Nowak approximates the original game by a family of countable state games. Specifically, he introduces a partition $\{S_k\}_{k=1}^{\infty}$ of the state space S and considers a new Markovian game whose transition probabilities and reward functions are constant within each element of this partition. By construction, this is a countable state game and admits an equilibrium in stationary strategies (see the remark following our Theorem 3.1).

As the final step in the proof, Nowak shows that, by making the partition suitably fine, it is possible to define reward functions $\tilde{r}_i$ and transition probabilities $\tilde{q}$ on the restricted game that are as close as desired to those of the original game. In turn, this implies that equilibrium strategies of the restricted game are "close" to being best responses in the original game, making them ε-equilibria of the original game.

4.2   Existence of p-*Equilibrium Strategies*

The ε-equilibrium existence results of Section 4.1 all involved a two-step procedure in which we (1) approximated the given Markovian game by a series of games and (2) then used (exact) equilibria of these approximate games to obtain approximate equilibria of the given game. The approximation procedure (coupled with the strengthened assumptions on the transition probabilities) enabled us to sidestep the question of the "appropriate" topology to use for the strategy space.

In this section we describe a result due to Himmelberg, Parthasarathy, Raghavan, and van Vleck (1976) [henceforth HPRV] that focuses directly on the infinite horizon model without using any approximation arguments. While interesting in its own right, the importance of this result for us also arises from the fact that some of the subsequent results we examine use the same topological structure on strategy spaces and payoff functions.

The authors also employ an "approximate equilibrium" concept, this time that of a p-equilibrium. As mentioned in the opening remarks of this section, a p-equilibrium is simply a strategy profile in which each player's strategy is a best-response to the profile from p-almost every initial state $s \in S$, where p is a given probability measure on S. This may be formalized as follows.

Definition. Let p be a probability measure on the state space S. A strategy profile $\sigma = (\sigma, \ldots, \sigma_n)$ is said to be a p-equilibrium if

$$p\left(\left\{s \mid W_i(\sigma)(s) \geq W_i(\sigma_{-i}, \hat{\sigma}_i)(s) \text{ for all } \hat{\sigma}_i \in \Sigma_i, i = 1, \ldots, n\right\}\right) = 1.$$

As with the notion of an ε-equilibrium, the idea of a p-equilibrium is an "approximate equilibrium" idea. In an ε-equilibrium, each player must obtain a reward within ε of her best-response reward from *every* initial state. In a p-equilibrium, each player must receive her *full* best-response reward, but only from p-almost every initial state. Just as every equilibrium is an ε-equilibrium for every $\varepsilon > 0$, so too is every equilibrium a p-equilibrium for any probability p on S. The converse is (obviously) false.

The following theorem is the main result in HPRV.

Theorem 4.5. *Suppose that the following statements hold.*

(1) $S = [0,1]$, $N = \{1,2\}$, *and* A_1 *and* A_2 *are finite sets.*

(2) $\Phi_i(s) = A_i$ *for all* $s \in S$, $i = 1, 2$.

(3) *The reward functions have the form*

$$r_i(s, a) = k_i(s, a_1) + l_i(s, a_2)$$

for each i and for each $(s, a) \in S \times A$, *where* k_i *and* l_i *are bounded measurable functions on* $S \times A_1$ *and* $S \times A_2$, *respectively.*

(4) *The transition probabilities have the form*

$$q(\cdot \mid s, a) = \frac{1}{2}\left[q_1(\cdot \mid s, a_1) + q_2(\cdot \mid s, a_2)\right]$$

for each $(s, a) \in S \times A$, *where* $q_1 (B \mid \cdot, a_1)$ *and* $q_2 (B \mid \cdot, a_2)$ *are measurable in s for each fixed Borel subset B of S and each* (a_1, a_2) *in* A.

Then, for any probability measure p on S such that $q(\cdot \mid s, a) \ll p$ *for all* (s, a), *there exists a p-equilibrium stationary strategy profile* (π_1, π_2).

Remark 1. The separability assumptions on the reward functions and transition probabilities are invoked to show continuity of the best-response mapping, in particular, to overcome the "integration to the limit" problem (see Step 3).

Remark 2. This result generalizes in the obvious manner to n-person games. The details are left to the reader.

Proof of Theorem 4.5. We sketch the essential ingredients of the proof, with particular focus on how this structure enables HPRV to overcome the problems described in Section 3.2. For expositional clarity, we organize the proof in three steps. Recall that Π_i is the space of all stationary strategies for player i (i.e., the space of all measurable functions π_i from S to ΔA_i).

Step 1: Best Responses. Because the action spaces are assumed finite, the self-referential problem in best responses that was highlighted in Section 3.2 is not relevant here. Indeed, simple arguments show that best responses to *any* stationary strategy profile are well-defined. To see this, suppose that π is a given stationary strategy profile. Pick any i, and let $V_i(\pi)$ represent player i's value function (i.e., the supremum over attainable rewards) against π. Then $V_i(\pi)$ satisfies the Bellman optimality equation at all $s \in S$:

$$V_i(\pi)(s) = \sup_{\mu_i \in M_i(s)} \left\{ r_i(\pi)(s, \mu_i) + \delta_i \int V_i(\pi)(\cdot) \, dq_i(\pi)(\cdot \,|\, s, \mu_i) \right\}.$$
(4.2)

Define the correspondence $\Phi_i(\pi)(\cdot)$ from S to $\Delta(A_i)$ by

$$\Phi_i(\pi)(s) = \arg\max_{\mu_i \in M_i(s)} \left\{ r_i(\pi)(s, \mu_i) + \delta_i \int V_i(\pi)(\cdot) \, dq_i(\pi)(\cdot \,|\, s, \mu_i) \right\}.$$
(4.3)

From the definition of expected rewards, it is immediate that a mixed action $\mu_i \in M_i(s)$ will maximize the RHS of expression (4.2) if and only if every pure action in its support does so. Since there are only finitely many pure actions, it follows that the correspondence of maximizers defined by (4.3) is nonempty-valued at each $s \in S$. A selection theorem due to Olech (see HPRV 1976, Lemma 2) shows that this correspondence admits a measurable selection. Any such selection defines a stationary strategy for player i that – by construction – is a best response to π, completing Step 1.

Step 2: Topologizing the Strategy Spaces. It would appear from Step 1 that the "natural" choice of strategy space is $\Pi_1 \times \cdots \times \Pi_n$, with the topology of pointwise convergence. However, we have seen in Section 3 that this is not, technically speaking, a good choice. Therefore, HPRV adopt a different route. The essential idea in their approach is to regard Π as a closed convex subset of the dual space of $\mathbb{R}^{|A_i|}$-valued integrable functions, where $|A_i|$ is the cardinality of A_i. With the weak-* topology, Π_1 and Π_2 are then compact metric spaces.

To elaborate, fix $i \in N$ and define the Banach space $\mathcal{B}(i)$ of real-valued functions φ on $S \times A_i$ as follows: $\varphi \in \mathcal{B}(i)$ if it is measurable in s for each fixed a_i and if there exists a real function ψ on S that is integrable with respect to p such that $|\varphi(s, a_i)| \le \psi(s)$ for all $s \in S$. The norm $|\cdot|_{\mathcal{B}}$ is defined as:

$$|\varphi|_{\mathcal{B}} = \int_S \left(\max_{a_i \in A_i} |\varphi(s, a)| \right) dp(s).$$

Let $\mathcal{B}^*(i)$ denote the dual space of $\mathcal{B}(i)$. Equip $\mathcal{B}^*(i)$ with the weak-* topology; that is, a sequence Λ_k converges to a limit Λ if and only if $\Lambda_n(\varphi)$ $\to \Lambda(\varphi)$ for every $\varphi \in \mathcal{B}(i)$.

Now suppose that a stationary strategy $\pi_i \in \pi_i$ for player i is given. Letting $\pi_i(a_i | s)$ denote the probability of the action a_i in the state s under π_i, we can identify π_i uniquely with a linear functional $\Lambda_{\pi_i} \in \mathcal{B}^*(i)$ by the relationship

$$\Lambda_{\pi_i}(\varphi) = \int_S \left(\sum_{a_i \in A_i} \pi(a_i | s) \varphi(s, a_i) \right) dq(s).$$

Therefore, if we consider strategies that coincide p-almost everywhere to be identical, we can identify the set Π_i itself with a subset of $\mathcal{B}^*(i)$. It is not very difficult to show now that Π_i is a closed subset of the unit ball in $\mathcal{B}^*(i)$ and is thus compact (and metrizable) by Alaoglu's theorem. We omit the details here; the interested reader may consult Parthasarathy (1982).[16] Because Π_i is evidently also convex, one part of the setup for using a fixed-point theorem is complete.

Step 3: Continuity. It remains to show the continuity of the best-response map. Let L^∞ denote the space of all p-essentially bounded, measurable functions on S. For $v \in L^\infty$ and $\pi \in \Pi \equiv \Pi_1 \times \Pi_2$, let $T_i(\pi)(v)$ be defined by

$$T_i(\pi)(v)(s) = \max_{\mu_i \in M_i(s)} \left\{ r_i(\pi)(s, \mu_i) + \int v(\cdot) \, dq_i(\pi)(\cdot \,|\, s, \mu_i) \right\}.$$

Then T is a contraction and has a unique fixed point, denoted by (say) $V_i(\pi)$. Define $BR_i: \Pi \to \Pi_i$ as follows:

$$BR_i(\pi) = \left\{ \hat{\pi}_i \,\middle|\, V_i(\pi)(s) = r_i(\pi)(s, \hat{\pi}_i(s)) + \int V_i(\pi)(\cdot) \, dq_i(\pi)(\cdot \,|\, s, \hat{\pi}(s)), \, p\text{-a.e.} \right\}.$$

Let $BR: \Pi \to \Pi$ be given by $BR(\pi) = (BR_1(\pi), BR_2(\pi))$.

---

[16] That Π_i is contained in the unit sphere of $\mathcal{B}^*(i)$ follows simply from the following observation: for any $\varphi \in \mathcal{B}$, we have

$$\int \left(\sum_a \pi(s, a) \varphi(s, a) \right) p\,(ds) \le \int \max_a |\varphi(s, a)| p\,(ds) = |\varphi|_{\mathcal{B}}.$$

The proof of the following lemma, which establishes continuity of this best-response correspondence, may be found in Appendix B. The argument used to show that integration to the limit is no longer a problem heavily exploits the separability assumptions on the problem's primitives (as also the absolute continuity of the transition probabilities $q(\cdot\,|\,s,a)$ with respect to the fixed measure p).

Lemma 4.6. *Let* π^k *be a sequence in* Π *converging weak-* to* π. *Let* $\hat{\pi}_i^k$ $\in BR_i(\pi^k)$, *and suppose without loss that* $\hat{\pi}_i^k$ *converges weak-* to some* $\hat{\pi}_i$ $\in \Pi_i$. *Then* $\hat{\pi}_i \in BR_i(\pi)$.

An appeal to Glicksberg's theorem shows that BR has a fixed point π^*. By construction, any fixed point of BR is a p-equilibrium, completing the proof. $\square$

4.3 MPE in General Markovian Games

A natural question that now arises is whether the result on the existence of approximate equilibria can be extended to show the existence of full equilibria. The answer turns out to be in the affirmative. Parthasarathy (1982) provides a general result on when the existence of a p-equilibrium may be extended to assert the existence of a full equilibrium; we present his main result here.

Theorem 4.7. *Let* S *and* A$_1, \ldots,$ A$_n$ *be compact subsets of metric spaces. Suppose that*:

(1) r$_i$ *is continuous on* S $\times$ A *for each* i; *and*
(2) q *is setwise continuous on* S $\times$ A.

Let p *be any probability measure on* S *such that* q$(\cdot\,|\,s, a) \ll$ p *for all* $(s, a) \in$ S $\times$ A. *Then, if there exists a* p-equilibrium strategy profile $\pi = (\pi_1, \ldots, \pi_n)$, *there exists an MPE* $\pi^* = (\pi_1^*, \ldots, \pi_n^*)$.

Remark 1. As mentioned previously, it follows from this result that full MPE exist in the HPRV model under a strengthening of the assumptions.

Remark 2. Parthasarathy makes the more restrictive assumption that q be strongly continuous on $S \times A$. This appears to be unnecessary.

Proof of Theorem 4.7. Let V_i represent player i's value function from the strategy profile π. Then, by definition of the profile π, there is a set $Z \subset S$ with $p(Z) = 1$ such that, for each i and for all $s \in Z$, the following equation holds and is solved by $\pi_i(s)$:

$$V_i(s) = \max_{\mu_i \in \Delta(A_i)} \left\{ r_i(\pi)(s, \mu_i) + \delta \int V_i(\cdot) \, dq_i(\pi)(\cdot \mid s, \mu_i) \right\}. \tag{4.4}$$

Now define, for each i and for all $(s, a) \in S \times A_1 \times \cdots \times A_n$,

$$L_i(s, a) = r_i(s, a) + \delta \int V_i(\cdot) \, dq(\cdot \mid s, a).$$

By the setwise continuity of q, the integral on the RHS (and hence L_i) is continuous on $S \times A$. Fix $s \in S$, and consider the one-shot game in which player i's payoff from the action profile $a \in A$ is given by $L_i(s, a)$. We now have the following.

(1) If $s \in Z$ then $(\pi_1(s), \ldots, \pi_n(s))$ is a Nash equilibrium of this one-shot game, since $\pi_i(s)$ solves (4.4) for each i for $s \in Z$. The payoff vector in this Nash equilibrium is, of course, simply $(V_1(s), \ldots, V_n(s))$.

(2) If $s \notin Z$, Glicksberg's fixed-point theorem establishes the existence of some Nash equilibrium to this game at each s. (This follows from Lemma 4.2.)

An appeal to a standard selection theorem shows that, in fact, there are measurable functions h_i from $S - Z$ to $\Delta(A_i)$ such that, at each $s \in S$ and $s \notin Z$, the action profile $h(s) = (h_1(s), \ldots, h_n(s))$ defines a Nash equilibrium of this one-shot game. Let $L_i^*(s) = L_i(s, h(s))$ denote the payoff to player i in this equilibrium.

Now define, for each $s \in S$,

$$\pi_i^*(s) = \begin{cases} \pi_i(s), & s \in Z, \\ h_i(s), & s \notin Z, \end{cases} \qquad V_i^*(s) = \begin{cases} V_i(s), & s \in Z, \\ L_i^*(s), & s \notin Z. \end{cases}$$

Observe that, since $q(\cdot \mid s, a) \ll p$ for all (s, a) and since $p(Z) = 1$, we also have

$$\int V_i^*(\cdot) \, dq(\cdot \mid s, a) = \int V_i(\cdot) \, dq(\cdot \mid s, a).$$

From the definition of L_i we therefore have that, for all i and for all $s \in S$,

$$V_i^*(s) = \max_{\mu_i \in \Delta(A_i)} \left\{ r_i(\pi^*)(s, \mu_i) + \delta \int V_i^*(\cdot) \, dq_i(\pi^*)(\cdot \mid s, \mu_i) \right\} \tag{4.5}$$

and that $\pi_i^*(s)$ solves this maximization problem. Standard dynamic programming arguments show that π_i^* is a best response to π^* for each i completing the proof. □

4.4 A Note on Parthasarathy and Sinha (1991)

All the results we have examined so far have taken an approach to the existence issue that has a strong dynamic programming flavor. The paper by Parthsarathy and Sinha (1991) represents an interesting turning point in this regard. The route they adopt involves contruction of a series of auxiliary one-shot games, which are then used to identify the value functions – and, thereby, the strategies – in an equilibrium. We state (but do not prove) their result here, since the same method of proof is used in Mertens and Parthasarathy (1987, 1991), whose results we discuss in Section 5.

Theorem 4.8. *Let* S *be a compact metric space, and let* A_i *be finite for each* i. *Suppose that* r_i *is continuous on* $S \times A_1 \times \ldots \times A_n$ *for each* i. *Suppose further that there is a fixed probability measure* p *on* S *such that* p *is nonatomic and* $q(\cdot \,|\, s, a) \ll p$ *for all* $(s, a) \in S \times A_1 \times \cdots \times A_n$. *Suppose finally that the transition probabilities are "state-independent" in the sense that* $q(\cdot \,|\, s, a) = q(\cdot \,|\, \hat{s}, a)$ *for all* $s, \hat{s} \in S$. *Then the game admits an equilibrium in Markovian strategies.*

Remark. Among the generalizations of this structure in the work of Mertens and Parthasarathy (1987, 1991) is eliminating the requirement that transitions be state-independent. However, this assumption is crucial for showing that equilibrium exists in *Markovian* strategies in the Parthasarathy–Sinha proof. Without it, Mertens and Parthasarathy (1991) – whose structure is otherwise identical[17] to Parthasarathy and Sinha – are able to show the existence only of equilibria whose equilibrium strategies depend on the current state and immediate past state.

5 Equilibrium in History-Dependent Strategies

We now turn to an examination of the results of Mertens and Parthasarathy (1987, 1991) on the existence of subgame-perfect equilibria in general Markovian games. We state and prove the result found in Mertens and Parthasarathy (1991). The existence theorem in Mertens and Parthasarathy (1987) uses essentially the same line of proof, except that the details are considerably more involved, owing to the extreme generality of the setup in that paper. We will comment on the directions in which Mertens and Parthasarathy (1987) is a more general result than Mertens and Parthasarathy (1991) after proving the 1987 result.

Theorem 5.1. *Let* S *be a Borel subset of a complete metric space, and let the action spaces* $A_1, \ldots, A_n$ *be finite sets. Suppose that the reward*

---

[17] Almost. Mertens and Parthasarathy (1991) allow for the dominating measure p to have atoms, but even if p were atomless, their proof would still not yield the existence of Markovian equilibria.

functions r_i *are bounded measurable functions on* $S \times A$, *and that the transition probabilities* $q(\cdot \mid s, a)$ *are absolutely continuous with respect to some fixed probability measure* p *on* S *for all* $(s, a) \in S \times A$. *Then there exists a subgame-perfect equilibrium strategy profile* σ *in which, at each point in time* t, *each player's action depends on the history* h_t *up to* t *only through the states* (s_{t-1}, s_t) *in periods* t *and* $(t-1)$ *and the index* t.

Before proceeding to the actual proof of the theorem, it will be useful to describe the intuition underlying the proof. The Mertens and Parthasarathy approach generalizes the Bellman-like characterization of the set of subgame-perfect equilibria, first introduced into (repeated) game theory by Abreu et al. (1986, 1990). In a manner similar to the Bellman operator of dynamic programming, this approach provides an operator whose fixed points identify subgame-perfect equilibria of a stochastic game. In order to establish that the operator has any fixed points at all, Mertens and Parthasarathy first apply the operator interactively to generate a sequence of candidate equilibria. To be more precise, what they actually generate is a sequence of *sets* of candidate equilibria. (Because we are dealing with a game rather than a decision problem, and hence there will typically be multiple equilibria, a set-valued concept is the appropriate one.) At a second step these sets of candidate equilibria are shown to converge to a limiting set, say Ψ_∞, and this limiting set is then demonstrated to be a subset of the equilibrium payoff set. This second step again bears a family resemblance to analogous arguments that are used in dynamic programming; for instance, the fact that Ψ_∞ is a fixed point of the equilibrium operator implies that every payoff in Ψ_∞ can be supported by continuation payoffs that are themselves in Ψ_∞. This fact is critically used to show that Ψ_∞ is a subset of the equilibrium payoff set in much the same way that the fixed point of the Bellman operator is shown to be the value function in a dynamic programming problem.

There are also some important differences – and technical subtleties – in the game-theoretic approach that are not present in the Bellman approach of dynamic programming. For instance, the equilibrium operator is not a contraction mapping and hence convergence of the sequence of candidate equilibrium sets cannot be ensured through the contraction mapping theorem. Second, the set of equilibrium payoffs is typically not convex. As will become clear in the sequel, convexity is required of the candidate sequence of sets; hence, what actually needs to be used is a pseudo-equilibrium operator that convexifies the actual equilibrium operator. Finally, candidate equilibria may well be discontinuous in the state variable; this necessitates some care in the selection of a topology for the set of equilibrium selections.

The procedure of the proof is as follows. Start with a "large" set of candidate equilibria payoffs, say Ψ_0. Elements of Ψ_0, in other words, are candidate equilibrium payoff functions $V_0(s)$, $s \in S$. For every state s', consider now an artificial one-shot game in which any action vector $a = (a_1, \ldots a_N)$ yields player i a payoff of $r_i(s', a) + \delta \int V_0(\cdot) \, dq(\cdot \mid s', a)$. Let $V_1(s')$ denote an equilibrium payoff to this one-shot game starting at state s'; by extension, let $V_1(s)$, $s \in S$, denote an equilibrium payoff function – that is, a selection from the equilibrium payoff correspondence for different initial states s. Let Ψ_1 denote the set of all such equilibrium selections. In this fashion, iteratively define Ψ_n, $n = 0, 1, \ldots$. The second step is to show that this sequence has a limit Ψ_∞ and that this limit is a subset of the set of equilibrium payoffs to the stochastic game. The three subtleties referred to previously are relevant at this stage of the proof, but the exact details are withheld until the actual proof of the theorem.

Proof of Theorem 5.1. Let Ψ_0 be the set of p-equivalent measurable functions[18] on S taking values in $[-c, c]$, where $c(1 - \delta)$ is a uniform upper bound for the one-period payoff functions. That is,

$$\sup_{(i, s, a)} \left| r_i(s, a) \right| < c(1 - \delta).$$

Take any (measurable) selection V from Ψ_0 and define a one-shot game from initial state s to be the game with strategy sets A_i and payoff

$$r_i(s, a) + \delta \int V(\cdot) \, dq(\cdot \mid s, a),$$

$i = 1, \ldots, N$. Denote this game $G(s, V)$. Define

$$N(V, s) = \text{Nash equilibrium payoffs of } G(s, V);$$

$$\overline{N}(V, s) = \begin{cases} \text{co } N(V, s) & \text{if } s \text{ is not an atom of } p, \\ N(V, s) & \text{if } s \text{ is an atom of } p. \end{cases}$$

(Here, "co" denotes the convex hull of the relevant set.) In words, $N(V, s)$ is the set of equilibrium payoffs at state s. Now let $N(V)$ denote the set of measurable selections from $N(V, \cdot)$:

$$N(V) = \left\{ V' \mid V' \text{ is measurable and satisfies } V'(s) \in N(V, s) \text{ for all } s \right\}.$$

Analogously, define

---

[18] Recall that p is the measure on S with respect to which all transition probabilities, $q(\cdot \mid s, a)$, are absolutely continuous.

$$\bar{N}(V) = \left\{ V' \middle| V' \text{ is measurable and satisfies } V'(s) \in \bar{N}(V, s) \text{ for all } s \right\}.$$

Observe that $N(V)$ is simply the set of equilibrium payoff functions when Nash equilibria vary measurably as a function of the state. We are finally in a position to define the Mertens–Parthasarathy operator Γ:

$$\Gamma \Psi_0 = \bigcup_{V \in \Psi_0} \bar{N}(V).$$

Let $\Psi_1 = \Gamma \Psi_0$. Now iteratively define $\Gamma \Psi_n = \Psi_{n+1}$, $n = 1, 2, \dots$. The following lemmata are critical intermediate steps in the proof of the theorem.

Lemma 5.2. Ψ_n *is nonempty and weak-* compact, for every n.*

Lemma 5.3.   *Write* $\Psi_\infty \equiv \cap_n \Psi_n$. *Then* Ψ_∞ *is nonempty and is a fixed point of the Mertens–Parthasarathy operator; that is,*

$$\Psi_\infty = \Gamma \Psi_\infty.$$

Proof of Lemma 5.2. We will prove the lemma by induction. The set Ψ_0 is clearly nonempty. Furthermore, by repeating the arguments of Section 4.2, we can also see that it is weak-* compact.[19]

We therefore make the induction hypothesis for Ψ_n. Take any measurable selection V from Ψ_n. Because the action sets are finite, it follows from Nash's theorem that, at every s, the set of Nash equilibrium payoffs $N(s, V)$ is nonempty. It further follows from a standard selection theorem that there is a measurable Nash equilibrium selection as s varies – that is, $N(V)$ is nonempty. In particular, therefore, $\bar{N}(V)$ is nonempty and hence so is Ψ_{n+1}.

We turn now to compactness of Ψ_{n+1}. Note that, by arguments identical to those employed in Section 4.2, it can be easily shown that Ψ_{n+1} is a subset of the closed unit ball[20] (which is compact, by Alaoglu's theorem). Since the unit ball is compact, it suffices to show that Ψ_{n+1} is a closed set. Let W^k be a sequence of (measurable) selections from Ψ_{n+1}, and let W be the weak-* limit of this sequence. By definition, there is an associated sequence V^k with $V^k \in \Psi_n$ and $W^k \in \bar{N}(V^k)$, $k = 1, 2, \dots$. Since

---

[19] Recall that we can identify with every $V \in \Psi_0$ the member $\Lambda(\cdot; V)$ of its dual space, where for every $h \in \Psi_0$ we define $\Lambda(h; V) \equiv \int_s h(s) V(s) \, dp(s)$. We then say that $V_k \to V$ in the weak-* topology if and only if $\Lambda(h; V_k) \to \Lambda(h; V)$ for every $h \in \Psi_0$. It has been shown (see e.g. Parthasarathy 1982) that, equipped with the weak-* topology, Ψ_0 is a closed subset of the unit ball and is thus compact (and metrizable) by Alaoglu's theorem.

[20] Take any $V \in \Psi_{n+1}$. For any integrable function h, $|\Lambda(h; V)| = |\int h(s) V(s) \, dp(s)| \leq \int |h(s)| \, |V(s)| dp(s) \leq c \int |h(s)| \, dp(s)$. Hence, viewed as a subset of the dual space of Ψ_0, Ψ_{n+1} is a subset of the unit ball. Note that, in deriving this inequality, we also used that $r_i(s, a) + \delta \int V'(s) \, dp(s) \leq (1 - \delta)c + \delta c = c$, whenever $|V'| \leq c$.

Ψ_n is weak-* compact, by the induction hypothesis it follows that V^k has a (sub)sequential limit, say V. In order to show that $W \in \Psi_{n+1}$, we will prove that $W \in \bar{N}(V)$.

Step 1: Since W^k converges weak-* to W, it follows that there is a sequence $\widetilde{W}^k$ that converges to W a.e. in which each element of the sequence $\widetilde{W}^k$ is in fact a convex combination of elements from the original sequence. Let S' denote the subset of the state space on which $\widetilde{W}^k$ converges pointwise. Note that, if s is an atom of the measure p, then it must be the case that the original sequence $W^k(s)$ itself converges to $W(s)$. We will show that $W(s) \in \bar{N}(s, V)$ for any $s \in S'$, which will evidently prove the lemma.

Step 2: Fix $s \in S'$. We know that $W(s) = \lim \widetilde{W}^k(s)$. Since $\widetilde{W}^k(s)$ is a convex combination of elements from the original sequence $W^k(s)$, and since, in turn, each of these elements is a convex combination of members of $N(s, V_k)$, it follows (after invoking Caratheodory's theorem) that $\widetilde{W}^k(s) = \Sigma_{i=1}^m \lambda(i, k) W(n(i, k))$, where $W(n(i, k)) \in N(s, V^{n(i,k)})$ and m is a fixed finite number. Since the convexification weights $\lambda(i, k)$ as well as the payoffs $W(n(i, k))$ come from bounded sets, it follows that on a subsequence they must have a limit. The limit of the convexification weights is itself a set of convexification weights, the limit of the payoffs belong, by definition, to $\overline{\lim} \, N(s, V^k)$. Hence what we have actually proved is that $W(s) \in \mathrm{co} \, \overline{\lim} \, N(s, V^k)$.

Step 3: We now show that $\overline{\lim} \, N(s, V^k) \subseteq N(s, V)$. Let w^{n_k} be a subsequence that converges to some limit, say w, where it is known that $w^{n_k} \in N(s, V^{n_k})$. Note that the absolute continuity assumption implies that there is a measurable density function, say $f(\cdot, s, a)$, such that $\int V^{n_k}(\cdot) \, dq(\cdot \mid s, a) = \int V^{n_k}(\cdot) f(\cdot, s, a) \, dp(s)$. Since V^k converges weak-* to V (and hence so does V^{n_k}), it follows that $\int V^{n_k}(\cdot) f(\cdot, s, a) \, dp(s)$ converges to $\int V(\cdot) f(\cdot, s, a) \, dp(s)$ for every a. That implies, however, that $G(s, V^{n_k})$ converges to $G(s, V)$ or, put differently, that $w \in N(s, V)$.

Step 4: It now follows from the previous step that $\mathrm{co} \, \overline{\lim} \, N(s, V^k) \subseteq \mathrm{co} \, N(s, V)$ or, in terms of the notation used so far, $\mathrm{co} \, \overline{\lim} \, N(s, V^k) \subseteq \bar{N}(s, V)$.

This is all that we needed to prove. In particular, we have proved that on the full measure set S' we have $W(s) \in \bar{N}(s, V)$ or, equivalently, $W \in \bar{N}(V)$. This in turn proves that Ψ_{n+1} is a closed set and therefore compact. Lemma 1 is proved. $\square$

Proof of Lemma 5.3. We will first show that Ψ_∞ is nonempty. Note that it has already been proved that Ψ_n is weak-* compact for each n. Note further that the operator Γ is a monotone operator: if $\Psi \subseteq \Psi'$, then $\Gamma\Psi \subseteq \Gamma\Psi'$. Since, by construction, $\Psi_1 \subseteq \Psi_0$, it follows that $\Psi_2 \subseteq \Psi_1$.

Of course the argument repeats; that is, $\Psi_{n+1} \subseteq \Psi_n$ for $n = 0, 1, \ldots$. Hence $\Psi_\infty \equiv \cap_n \Psi_n$ is nonempty as the intersection of a decreasing family of compact sets.

We turn now to the argument that establishes $\Gamma\Psi_\infty = \Psi_\infty$. Because the operator Γ is monotone, it follows that $\Gamma\Psi_\infty \subseteq \Gamma\Psi_n = \Psi_{n+1}$ for all n. In particular, therefore, $\Gamma\Psi_\infty \subseteq \Psi_\infty$. For the other inclusion, let W be an element of Ψ_∞ and hence an element of Ψ_n for all n. By definition, there is an associated sequence V^n with $V^n \in \Psi_n$ and $W \in \bar{N}(V^n)$, $n = 1, 2, \ldots$. Since Ψ_∞ is weak-* compact and since each V^n is an element of Ψ_∞, it follows that V^n has a (sub)sequential limit, say $V \in \Psi_\infty$. In order to show that $W \in \Gamma\Psi_\infty$, we need to prove that $W \in \bar{N}(V)$. The argument that establishes this is simply a repetition of Steps 2–4 in the proof of Lemma 1. Lemma 2 has been proved. $\square$

The last part of the proof will follow from our next lemma.

Lemma 5.4. *There is a sequence of measurable functions* $g_t(\cdot, \cdot)$ *defined on* $S \times S$ *with the property that, for every* (s_{t-1}, s_t), $g_t(s_{t-1}, s_t)$ *is a Nash equilibrium payoff of the game* $G(s_t, g_{t+1}(s_t, \cdot))$.

Proof. Consider any selection $V_0 \in \Psi_\infty (= \Gamma\Psi_\infty)$. By definition, therefore, there is a $V_1 \in \Psi_\infty$ with the property that $V_0 \in \bar{N}(V_1)$. However, since we also have $V_1 \in \Gamma\Psi_\infty$, it follows that there exists a $V_2 \in \Psi_\infty$ with the property that $V_1 \in \bar{N}(V_2)$. As should now be clear, there is, more generally, a sequence $V_0, V_1, \ldots, V_t \in \Psi_\infty$ for all t, with the further property that $V_t \in \bar{N}(V_{t+1})$.

Fix a state $s \in S$. It is straightforward to see that, for every $a \in A$, $\int V_t(s') \, dq(s' \,|\, s, a)$ – which is an element in $\mathbb{R}^N$ – is a member of the set $\{\int h(s') \, dq(s' \,|\, s, a) \,|\, h \in \bar{N}(V_{t-1})\}$. Indeed, one can extend this logic to all action vectors by writing $\int V_t(s') \, dq(s' \,|\, s, \cdot)$ for the element of $\mathbb{R}^{N \times A}$ that comprises the integrals taken successively for all action vectors in $A \, (= \Pi_{i=1}^N A_i)$. To summarize, in this extended notation, $\int V_t(s') \, dq(s' \,|\, s, a)$ – an element in $\mathbb{R}^{N \times A}$ – is a member of the set $\{\int h(s') \, dq(s' \,|\, s, \cdot) \,|\, h \in \bar{N}(V_{t+1})\}$.

By Lyapunov's theorem, the set of integrals is a convex set. Hence it follows that the two sets $\{\int h(s') \, dq(s' \,|\, s, a) \,|\, h \in \bar{N}(V_{t+1})\}$ and $\{\int h(s') \, dq(s' \,|\, h \in N(V_{t+1})\}$ coincide. In particular, therefore, $\int V_t(s') \, dq(s' \,|\, s, a)$ is actually a member of the set $\{\int h(s') \, dq(s' \,|\, s, \cdot) \,|\, h \in N(V_{t+1})\}$. Hence there is a selection from the Nash correspondence $N(V_{t+1})$, call it $g(s, \cdot)$, with the property that $\int V_t(s') \, dq(s' \,|\, s, a) = \int g(s, s') \, dq(s' \,|\, s, a)$ for all $a \in A$.

The preceding argument could be repeated state by state; that is, for every state s we could find an appropriate selection $g(s, \cdot)$ with the property just described. The question of interest is whether one could additionally derive these selections as a measurable function of the state $\dot{s}$. That the answer is in the affirmative is precisely the content of Mertens (1987). Hence, there is a function $g_t(s_{t-1}, \cdot) \in N(V_{t+1})$ with the property that $\int V_t(s_t) \, dq(s_t \mid s_{t-1}, a) = \int g_t(s_{t-1}, s_t) \, dq(s_t \mid s_{t-1}, a)$ for all $(s_{t-1}, a) \in S \times A$ and for all t.

Armed with this result, we can now prove the remainder of Lemma 5.4. Since $g_t(s_{t-1}, \cdot) \in N(V_{t+1})$, it follows by definition that in the game $G(s_t, V_{t+1})$ there is a Nash equilibrium, say $\sigma(s_t, V_{t+1})$, whose equilibrium payoffs equal $g_t(s_{t-1}, s_t)$. Put differently, $g_t(s_{t-1}, s_t) = r(s_t, \sigma(s_t, V_{t+1})) + \delta \int V_{t+1}(s_{t+1}) \, dq(s_{t+1} \mid s_t, \sigma(s_t, V_{t+1}))$ and $\sigma(s_t, V_{t+1})$ is a Nash equilibrium for these payoffs.

However, from these arguments we also know that $\int V_{t+1}(s_{t+1}) \, dq(s_{t+1} \mid s_t, a) = \int g_{t+1}(s_t, s_{t+1}) \, dq(s_{t+1} \mid s_t, a)$ for all a. Hence it follows immediately that $\sigma(s_t, V_{t+1})$ is also a Nash equilibrium of the game $G(s_t, g_{t+1}(s_t, \cdot))$ and that $g_t(s_{t-1}, s_t) = r(s_t, \sigma(s_t, g_{t+1}(s_t, \cdot))) + \sigma \int g_{t+1}(s_t, s_{t+1}) \, dq(s_{t+1} \mid s_t, \sigma(s_t, g_{t+1}(s_t, \cdot))$. Lemma 5.4 has been proved. $\square$

The theorem has essentially been proved: at period t, play $\sigma(s_t, g_{t+1}(s_t, \cdot))$. No one-shot deviation from this strategy is profitable, by construction. Furthermore, the promised payoffs can actually be realized by playing this strategy. A standard argument (see Abreu 1988) establishes that this strategy is a subgame-perfect equilibrium. $\square$

Remark 1. In Mertens and Parthasarathy (1987) the authors show that the foregoing result can be strengthened in several directions. Possibly the most important of these is allowing the action sets to be arbitrary compact action spaces. The action sets can also be allowed to vary measurable with the state. For these and other generalizations – which complicate the proof a great deal – we refer the reader to the original paper.

Remark 2. Letting $\sigma_{it}(s_{t-1}, s_t)$ denote player i's tth-period action in this equilibrium as a function of the previous two states (s_{t-1}, s_t), in general it need not be the case that $\sigma_{it}(\cdot, \cdot) = \sigma_{i\tau}(\cdot, \cdot)$ for $t \neq \tau$. When the dominating measure p is atomless, however, this stronger result can be obtained; see Corollary 5.5.

Remark 3. The proof of Theorem 4.8 is easily derived as a consequence of the proof of Theorem 5.1. See Corollary 5.6.

Corollary 5.5. *When* p *is atomless, there exists an equilibrium* σ *of the form described in Remark 2 in which we also have the property that, for each* i *and for each* t *and* τ, $\sigma_{it}(\bar{s}, s) = \sigma_{i\tau}(\bar{s}, s)$ *for all* $(\bar{s}, s) \in S \times S$.

Proof. See Mertens and Parthasarathy (1991).

Corollary 5.6.   *When* p *is atomless and* q *is state-independent, an MPE exists.*

Appendix A: Topologies on $\Delta(X)$

Let S be a complete, separable metric space, and let $\Delta(S)$ denote the set of all probability measures on S. Three different topologies may be defined on $\Delta(S)$: the weak, setwise convergence, and strong topologies.

The Weak Topology. Let $C(S)$ denote the space of all bounded continuous real-valued functions on S. For $f \in C(S)$ and $\mu \in \Delta(S)$, define

$$I_f(\mu) = \int f \, d\mu.$$

The weak topology on $C(S)$ is defined as follows: A sequence ν_n in $\Delta(S)$ converges to a limit ν if and only if

$$I_f(\nu_n) \to I_f(\nu) \quad \text{for all } f \in C(S).$$

There are several equivalent definitions of the weak topology. For a complete list, see Billingsley (1968). One of these equivalent definitions is: A sequence ν_n in $\Delta(S)$ converges in the weak topology to ν if and only if

$$\nu_n(B) \to \nu(B)$$

for all Borel subsets B of S that satisfy $\nu(\partial B) = 0$, where ∂B is the boundary of the set B.

The Setwise Convergence Topology. In this topology, a sequence ν_n converges to a limit ν if and only if

$$\nu_n(B) \to \nu(B)$$

for *every* Borel subset B of S.

The weak topology requires this convergence only for sets B whose boundaries have ν-measure zero, so setwise convergence is more restrictive than weak convergence. Consequently, it carries stronger implications. Let $B(S)$ denote the set of all bounded measurable real functions on S. For $f \in B(S)$ and $\nu \in \Delta(S)$, define

$$I_f(\nu) = \int f \, d\nu.$$

If v_n converges setwise to v, then it can be shown that $I_f(v_n) \to I_f(v)$ for every $f \in B(S)$ (see Royden 1968). As we have seen, a similar result holds for weak convergence only if f belongs to the smaller set $C(S)$.

The Strong Topology. The most restrictive of the three topologies considered here is the *strong topology*, which is also frequently referred to as the *norm topology*. This is the topology induced by the total variation norm. Under this norm, a sequence v_n in $\Delta(S)$ converges to a limit v if and only if

$$\sup \left| v_n(B) - v(B) \right| \to 0 \text{ as } n \to \infty,$$

where the supremum is taken over Borel subsets B of S.

The relationship between setwise convergence and strong convergence is akin to the difference between pointwise convergence of a sequence of functions and uniform convergence of the sequence. Setwise convergence requires simply that, for each fixed Borel subset B of S, we have

$$\lim_{n \to \infty} \left| v_n(B) - v(B) \right| = 0.$$

Strong convergence requires in addition that the rate of convergence be uniform over all B.

Appendix B: Proof of Lemma 4.6

In order to prove continuity of the best-response map, we first require a preliminary result. Let $\pi_i(a_i \mid s)$ be the probability under π_i that a_i is used at the state s.

Lemma B.1. *Let π^k be a sequence in Π converging in the weak-* sense to π. Then $r_i^k(s) := \sum_{a_1 \in A_1} \sum_{a_2 \in A_2} r_i(s, \pi_1^k(a_1 \mid s), \pi_2^k(a_2 \mid s))$ converges in the weak-* sense to $r_i(s) := \sum_{a_1 \in A_1} \sum_{a_2 \in A_2} r_i(s, \pi_1(a_1 \mid s), \pi_2(a_2 \mid s))$.*

Remark. The proof uses the separability of r_i, and remains valid for any function separable in this manner. We use this fact in what follows.

Proof. We are required to prove that

$$\int r_i^k(s) \varphi(s) p \, (ds) \to \int r_i(s) \varphi(s) p \, (ds)$$

for any integrable function φ on S. We have:

$$\int r_i^k(s)\varphi(s)p\,(ds) = \int \varphi(s)\left(\sum_{a\in A}\left(l(s,a_1)+k(s,a_2)\right)\pi_1^k\left(a_1\mid s\right)\pi_2^k\left(a_2\mid s\right)\right)p\,(ds)$$

$$= \int \varphi(s)\left(\sum_{a\in A}l(s,a_1)\pi_1^k\left(a_1\mid s\right)\pi_2^k\left(a_2\mid s\right)\right)p\,(ds)$$

$$+\int \varphi(s)\left(\sum_{a\in A}k(s,a_2)\pi_1^k\left(a_1\mid s\right)\pi_2^k\left(a_2\mid s\right)\right)p\,(ds)$$

$$= \int \varphi(s)\left(\sum_{a_1\in A_1}l(s,a_1)\pi_1^k\left(a_1\mid s\right)\right)p\,(ds)$$

$$+\int \varphi(s)\left(\sum_{a_2\in A_2}k(s,a_2)\pi_2^k\left(a_2\mid s\right)\right)p\,(ds)$$

$$\to \int \varphi(s)\left(\sum_{a_1\in A_1}l(s,a_1)\hat\pi_1\left(a_1\mid s\right)\right)p\,(ds)$$

$$+\int \varphi(s)\left(\sum_{a_2\in A_2}k(s,a_2)\hat\pi\left(a_2\mid s\right)\right)p\,(ds),$$

where the limits obtain by weak-* convergence of the π^k sequence. $\quad\square$

Now, returning to the proof of Lemma 4.6, let V_i^k denote player i's value function in a best response to π^k. Since V_i^k is uniformly bounded and integrable, it has a convergent subsequence, and we can assume without loss that it has a weak* limit V_i.[21] For each k, V_i^k satisfies

$$V_i^k(s) = r_i\left(s,\pi_{-i}^k(s),\hat\pi_i^k(s)\right)+\delta_i\int V_i^k(\cdot)\,dq\left(\cdot\mid s,\pi_{-i}^k(s),\hat\pi_i^k(s)\right),\ p\text{-a.e.}$$

From Lemma B.1, $r_i(s,\pi_{-i}(s),\hat\pi_i(^ks))$ converges weak-* to $r_i(s,\pi_{-i}(s),\hat\pi_i(s))$. We will show that similar convergence also obtains for the second term on the RHS by using the separability assumptions.

Note first that, for fixed $a \in A$, we have

$$\int V_i^k(\cdot)\,dq\left(\cdot\mid s,a\right)\to \int V_i(\cdot)\,dq\left(\cdot\mid s,a\right),$$

since V_i^k converges weak-* to V_i and $q(\cdot\mid s,a)$ is absolutely continuous with respect to p for each (s,a). For notational simplicity, let $h^k(s,a) = \int V_i^k(\cdot)\,dq(\cdot\mid s,a)$, and $h(s,a) = \int V_i(\cdot)\,dq(\cdot\mid s,a)$. Then, for any integrable function φ on S,

$$\int \varphi(s)\sum_{a\in A}h^k\left(s,a\right)\pi_{-i}^k\left(a_{-i}\mid s\right)\hat\pi_i^k\left(a_i\mid s\right)dq(s)$$

$$-\int \varphi(s)\sum_{a\in A}h(s,a)\pi_{-i}\left(a_{-i}\mid s\right)\hat\pi_i\left(a_i\mid s\right)dp(s)\Bigg|$$

[21] See Problem 6 in Dunford and Schwartz (1957, p. 339).

$$\le \left| \int \varphi(s) \sum_{a \in A} \left[h^k(s, a) - h(s, a) \right] \pi^k_{-i}(a_{-i} \mid s) \hat{\pi}^k_i(a_i \mid s) \, dp(s) \right|$$

$$+ \left| \int \varphi(s) \sum_{a \in A} h(s, a) \left[\pi^k_{-i}(a_{-i} \mid s) \hat{\pi}^k_i(a_i \mid s) - \pi_{-i}(a_{-i} \mid s) \hat{\pi}_i(a_i \mid s) \right] dp(s) \right|$$

$$\le \sum_{a \in A} \int \left| \varphi(s) \right| \left| h^k(s, a) - h(s, a) \right| dp(s)$$

$$+ \left| \int \varphi(s) \sum_{a \in A} h(s, a) \left[\pi^k_{-i}(a_{-i} \mid s) \hat{\pi}^k_i(a_i \mid s) - \pi_{-i}(a_{-i} \mid s) \hat{\pi}_i(a_i \mid s) \right] dp(s) \right|.$$

The first term in the last expression goes to zero by Lebesgue's dominated convergence theorem. For the second term, we use the separability assumption on q to note that h^k and h are themselves separable in (s, a_1) and (s, a_2). An appeal to Lemma B.1 then shows that the second term also goes to zero as $k \to \infty$.

Thus, we now have

$$V_i(s) = r_i\big(s, \pi_{-i}(s), \hat{\pi}_i(s)\big) + \delta_i \int V_i(\cdot) \, dq\big(\cdot \mid s, \pi_i(s), \hat{\pi}_i(s)\big), \quad p\text{-a.e.}$$

Using this expression, it is straightforward to show that V_i is itself the value function in a best response to π, and therefore that $\hat{\pi}_i \in \mathrm{BR}_i(\pi)$. This, in turn, establishes upper semicontinuity of the best-response map, proving the lemma. $\square$

References

Abreu, D. (1988) On the Theory of Infinitely Repeated Games with Discounting, *Econometrica* 56, 383–96.

Abreu, D., D. Pearce, and E. Stacchetti (1986) Optimal Cartel Equilibria with Imperfect Monitoring, *Journal of Economic Theory* 39, 251–69.

——— (1990) Towards a General Theory of Discounted Repeated Games with Imperfect Monitoring, *Econometrica* 58, 1041–65.

Amir, R. (1991) On Stochastic Games with General State and Action Spaces, in *Stochastic Games and Related Topics* (T. E. S. Raghavan, T. S. Ferguson, T. Parthasarathy, and O. Vrieze, eds.), Kluwer, Boston.

Benhabib, J., and R. Radner (1992) Joint Exploitation of a Productive Asset: A Game-Theoretic Approach, *Economic Theory* 2, 165–91.

Berge, C. (1963) *Topological Spaces*, Macmillan, New York.

Bernheim, B. D., and D. Ray (1983) Altruistic Growth Economics, Technical Report no. 419, IMSSS, Stanford University.

——— (1987) Economic Growth with Intergenerational Altruism, *Review of Economic Studies* 54, 227–42.

Billingsley, P. (1968) *Convergence of Probability Measures*, Wiley, New York.

Blackwell, D. (1965) Discounted Dynamic Programming, *Annals of Mathematical Statistics* 36, 226–35.

Chakrabarti, S. (1993) Equilibria in Discounted Stochastic Games with Weak-Star Continuous Transition Probabilities, Mimeo, Department of Economics, Indiana University – Purdue University at Indianapolis.

Dana, R. A., and L. Montrucchio (1986) Dynamic Complexity in Duopoly Games, *Journal of Economic Theory* 40, 40–56.

Dunford, N., and J. Schwartz (1957) *Linear Operators*, vol. 1, Wiley, New York.

Dutta, P. K., and R. K. Sundaram (1992) Markovian Equilibrium in a Class of Stochastic Games: Existence Theorems for Discounted and Undiscounted Models, *Economic Theory* 2, 197–214.

(1993a) The Tragedy of the Commons? *Economic Theory* 3, 413–26.

(1993b) How Different Can Strategic Models Be? *Journal of Economic Theory* 60, 42–62.

Easley, D., and N. Kiefer (1988) Controlling a Stochastic Process with Unknown Parameters, *Econometrica* 56, 1045–64.

El-Gamal, M. A., and R. K. Sundaram (1993) Bayesian Economists, . . . , Bayesian Agents: An Alternative Approach to Optimal Learning, *Journal of Economic Dynamics and Control* 17, 355–83.

Federgruen, A. (1978) *Markovian Control Problems*, Ph.D. Thesis, Mathematisch Zentrum, Amsterdam.

Fudenberg, D., R. Gilbert, J. Stiglitz, and J. Tirole (1983) Preemption, Leapfrogging, and Competition in Patent Races, *European Economic Review* 22, 3–31.

Fudenberg, D., and E. Maskin (1986) The Folk-Theorem in Repeated Games with Discounting and with Incomplete Information, *Econometrica* 54, 533–54.

Fudenberg, D., and J. Tirole (1983) Capital as Commitment: Strategic Investment to Deter Mobility, *Journal of Economic Theory* 31, 227–56.

Green, E., and R. Porter (1984) Noncooperative Collusion under Imperfect Price Information, *Econometrica* 52, 87–100.

Harris, C. (1985) Existence and Characterization of Perfect Equilibrium in Games of Perfect Information, *Econometrica* 53, 613–28.

Himmelberg, C. J., T. Parthasarathy, T. E. S. Raghavan, and F. van Vleck (1976) Existence of p-Equilibrium and Optimal Stationary Strategies in Stochastic Games, *Proceedings of the American Mathematical Society* 60, 245–51.

Kohlberg, E. (1976) A Model of Economic Growth with Altruism between Generations, *Journal of Economic Theory* 13, 1–13.

Leininger, W. (1986) The Existence of Perfect Equilibrium in a Model of Growth with Altruism between Generations, *Review of Economic Studies* 53, 349–67.

Levhari, D., and L. Mirman (1980) The Great Fish War: An Example Using a Dynamic Cournot–Nash Solution, *Bell Journal of Economics* 11, 322–34.

Maitra, A. (1967) Discounted Dynamic Programming on Compact Metric Spaces, *Sankhya A*, 30, 211–21.

Maskin, E., and J. Tirole (1988) A Theory of Dynamic Oligopoly II: Price Competition, Kinked Demand Curves, and Edgeworth Cycles, *Econometrica* 56, 571–600.

McLean, R., and S. Sklivas (1988) Capital Accumulation in an Intertemporal Duopoly, Working Paper no. 145, Department of Economics, Columbia University, New York.

Mertens, J.-F. (1987) A "Measurable" Measurable Selection Theorem, Working Paper no. 8749, CORE, Louvain, Belgium.

Mertens, J.-F., and T. Parthasarathy (1987) Equilibria for Discounted Stochastic Games, Working Paper no. 8750, CORE, Louvain, Belgium.

(1991) Non-Zero Sum Stochastic Games, in *Stochastic Games and Related Topics* (T. E. S. Raghavan, T. S. Ferguson, T. Parthasarathy, and O. Vrieze, eds.), Kluwer, Boston.

Nowak, A. S. (1985) Existence of Equilibrium Stationary Strategies in Discounted Non-Cooperative Stochastic Games with Uncountable State Space, *Journal of Optimization Theory and Applications* 45, 591–602.

Parthasarathy, T. (1973) Discounted, Positive, and Noncooperative Stochastic Games, *International Journal of Game Theory* 2.

(1982) Existence of Equilibrium Stationary Strategies in Discounted Stochastic Games, *Sankhya A* 44, 114–27.

Parthasarathy, T., and S. Sinha (1991) Existence of Equilibrium in Discounted Non-Cooperative Stochastic Games with Uncountable State Space and State-Independent Transitions, *International Journal of Game Theory* 18, 189–94.

Radner, R. (1985) Repeated Principal–Agent Games with Discounting, *Econometrica* 53, 1173–98.

Radner, R., R. Myerson, and E. Maskin (1986) An Example of a Repeated Partnership Game with Discounting, and with Uniformly Inefficient Equilibria, *Review of Economic Studies* 53, 59–69.

Reinganum, J. (1985) Innovation and Industry Evolution, *Quarterly Journal of Economics* 100, 81–99.

Rieder, U. (1979) Equilibrium Plans for Non-Zero Sum Markov Games, in *Seminar on Game Theory and Related Topics* (O. Moeschlin and D. Pallaschke, eds.), Springer, Berlin.

Rogers, P. D. (1969) Non-Zero Sum Stochastic Games, ORC Report no. 69-8, Operations Research Center, University of California, Berkeley.

Royden, H. L. (1968) *Real Analysis*, Macmillan, New York.

Sobel, M. J. (1971) Non-Cooperative Stochastic Games, *Annals of Mathematical Statistics* 42, 1930–5.

Spence, A. M. (1979) Investment Strategy and Growth in a New Market, *Bell Journal of Economics* 10, 1–19.

Sundaram, R. K. (1989) Perfect Equilibrium in a Class of Symmetric Dynamic Games, *Journal of Economic Theory* 47, 153–77.

Whitt, W. (1980) Representation and Approximation of Non-Cooperative Sequential Games, *SIAM Journal of Optimal Control* 18, 33–48.

CHAPTER 6

A Practical Person's Guide to Mechanism Selection: Some Lessons from Experimental Economics

Andrew Schotter

1   Introduction

One of the most interesting developments in economic theory over the past 20 years has been the emergence of the theory of mechanism design. In short, mechanism design theory investigates whether it is possible to design an economic institution (represented formally as a game form) which, when imposed upon a set of individualistic agents, will lead them to take actions consistent with some a priori chosen performance (social welfare) criterion. Starting with the pioneering work of Hurwicz (1972), this theory has become increasingly rich in detail and analysis. (For a wonderful survey of the theory of full information mechanisms see Moore 1993). While this literature has attracted a great deal of interest, it has tended to remain rather abstract and theoretical despite its great potential applicability.

In the real world, however, the mechanisms designed by economists compete for adoption with others whose origins are either historical or are the objects of conscious design by noneconomists. By this I mean that, for any given allocation problem an organization might face, there might be a number of mechanisms available as solutions. The organization's leaders must then choose between these mechanisms based on their characteristics and if, for example, the mechanisms have different distributional consequences for the power groups within the organization, then a political battle may ensue with each power group lobbying for the adoption of their own mechanism. The mechanism that is ultimately chosen will emerge from this bargaining process within the organization. The process of mechanism *design* is therefore different from the

The financial assistance of the C.V. Starr Center for Applied Economics at New York University is gratefully acknowledged, as is the technical assistance of Ken Rogoza. The author would also like to thank an anonymous referee for some extremely helpful comments.

process of mechanism *selection*. Mechanisms that seem natural to a well-trained economist may strike real-world decision makers as bizarre. The reason for this difference is that the criteria by which we economists judge economic institutions are quite different from those used by real-world decision makers. This is the prime reason why so few of our theoretically elegant mechanisms have actually been adopted for use.

In this paper we concern ourselves with the selection criteria that organizations might use to choose between mechanisms. I have called this a "practical person's guide" because the criteria discussed are not the elegant ones used by economic theorists to justify their mechanisms but rather the criteria likely to be used by some no-nonsense corporate CEO or government official.

In the remainder of the chapter I will proceed as follows. In Section 2, I motivate the problem by presenting an example taken from the world of baseball, where an allocation mechanism is needed to allocate free-agent players. In this section I will also outline and discuss relevant criteria for the mechanism selection decision. Some of these criteria I have discovered by speaking to corporate leaders, while others I have simply dreamed up myself. I will let you guess which is which. In Section 3 I will offer some experimental results that demonstrate some of the criteria listed in Section 2. In this section I will rely heavily on my own work, much of which was done jointly with Roy Radner. There are obviously many other works that could be used as well – my egocentric bias is justified only because this is work I am most familiar with and for which I have the necessary raw data. Finally, in Section 4 I offer some comments and conclusions.

2   Selection Criteria

2.1   A Motivating Example

The recent prolonged baseball strike should serve as evidence that the baseball industry is one for which the mechanism selection problem looms large. In stark economic terms, this is a problem of allocating heterogenous indivisible goods (baseball players) among a set of consumers (baseball teams). Although an economist viewing the problem solely through "efficiency" lenses might think this problem straightforward (perhaps involving an algorithm to solve an integer assignment problem), it has led to a great deal of antitrust litigation and has been the source of strikes and bitter disputes over the past 25 years. Because the history of the problem is illustrative of the mechanism selection problem, let us pause and discuss it briefly.

Until the 1970s, professional baseball players did not own the rights to their services; instead, the teams did. Therefore, when a player's contract expired, he did not have the option of shopping around for a team to play with but could only sign the contract offered him, possibly negotiating its terms, or sit out the year. Alternatively, he could hope that his team would sell his rights to another team or trade him. Clearly this mechanism for allocating players was skewed in favor of the teams, since they had exclusive rights to players and in essence played an ultimatum game with each player on their team separately.

This mechanism was challenged in 1972 by the Curt Flood and Andy Messersmith cases. As a result of these cases, baseball players obtained the property rights to their own services, but only after they have played in the major leagues for six years. Now, players who have served six years in "the majors" and whose contracts have expired can declare themselves free agents and negotiate with any team they wish. Clearly, this new mechanism can be expected to have distributional (and perhaps efficiency) properties different from those existing under the old mechanism. As a result, which mechanism is used can be expected to be a matter of intense controversy between the team owners and the players. The first few years under the current free-agent system fulfilled all of the worst nightmares of the team owners. The huge contract signed by Catfish Hunter made headlines, and teams engaged in what appeared to be a bidding war – the very thing the old mechanism was good at avoiding. While player mobility was increased and therefore a more efficient allocation presumably achieved, player salaries were reaching levels that team owners viewed as threatening. The players charged that, in order to prevent a bidding war, the team owners had colluded in an effort to keep salaries low. An arbitrator in the 1986 Kirk Gibson case awarded damages to the players for the teams' refusal to deal. To get around this problem, the team owners then attempted to modify the current free-agent mechanism, in which salary negotiations were conducted in privacy, by publicly reporting the offers made to players. This unilateral modification by the team owners was found to constitute a "facilitating" practice, and hence to be illegal, in a case filed in 1987 and decided in 1992.

This history suggests that both sides of the baseball industry would like a new mechanism to allocate free agents. Teams would like one that prevents the bidding wars that they feel characterize the current system, while players would like one that seems fair to them and perhaps prevents collusion on the part of the teams. The problem, however, is that each side of the market has a veto over which mechanism is to be used. While the court may declare that players have the right to be free agents and let the market decide their salaries, experimental economics has taught us that there are many ways to run such free-agent markets, each of which may have different distributional and efficiency properties. The mechanism finally selected will have to satisfy all of the parties who have a stake in these negotiations – namely, the players, the teams, and the sports lawyers or agents whose livelihoods also are greatly affected by which mechanism is used. Because of the large number of distributional and other criteria that may play an important role in which mechanism is ultimately selected, simply finding a mechanism that determines Pareto optimal outcomes may not be enough.

This paper attempts to list and discuss the properties that such allocating mechanisms should have if they are going to be serious candidates for adoption by the agents whose fates they control. Although it might be useful to keep the baseball example in mind when thinking about these criteria, they are meant to be general in their application. While not all of the criteria listed will be relevant to all mechanism selection problems – that will depend on the specific institutional history of the problem at hand – it is my feeling that the list contains those criteria which are the most important. Let us investigate these criteria one at a time.

2.2   Mechanism Selection Criteria

Understandability. Our first criterion requires of whatever mechanism is suggested that it be understandable to those agents who are going to use it. By "understandable" we can mean one of two things. One is that the participants simply understand the rules of the mechanism and hence physically know what to do when using it. A more demanding criterion would require that the participants understand the theory underlying the mechanism. However, it is rare that the theory underlying a mechanism is included in the user's manual for that mechanism when it is distributed to the general population for use. (The IRS distributes tax tables, yet never distributes journal articles on optimal income taxation to citizens or tips on how to exploit loopholes in the tax law.)

Understandability in the first sense is obviously essential, since confusing mechanisms may be badly misinterpreted by the agents using them and may lead to behavior that is totally unexpected and detrimental to the profitability of the organization. Sometimes a mechanism is perceived as being more understandable if it can be couched in a metaphor that is familiar to the agents. For example, since we (at least in the United States) are inculcated with the jargon of competitive markets, mechanisms wherein people place bids and where goods are allocated by something resembling prices may be easier for agents to comprehend than mechanisms requiring more abstract messages like preference orderings. Hence, they are likely to be taken more seriously as candidates for adoption.

Fairness – Strategic Symmetry. If a mechanism is ever going to be employed it must be perceived as being fair. We call a mechanism "fair" if it is strategically *symmetric*: any strategy available to one side of the market has a comparable strategy available to the other side. In addition, each side has strategies that affect the payoff function in an equivalent manner, given the action of others. Of course, the outcomes that result may be unequal, but that may be an artifact of the types of preferences that agents have. (A double-oral auction mechanism is fair because both sides are treated symmetrically. Prices may be skewed to favor one side of the market simply because the other side has either high willingnesses to pay or low costs.) Our emphasis on the symmetry of the strategy sets of agents is motivated by the fact that economic agents, when presented with a mechanism, judge it to a large extent by the rules; and if one side is offered strategies that the others cannot avail themselves of, a red flag is automatically raised.

There are a number of reasons why perceived equity might be important. First, in many industries a mechanism must be agreed upon by all parties involved in trade. For example, in many labor negotiations if talks are stalemated then some type of arbitration is resorted to. Many different arbitration mechanisms exist, however, including final offer arbitration and tri-offer arbitration (see Ashenfelter et al. 1992), just to mention two. However, not all schemes are equivalent with respect to how they treat the bargaining parties, and if each side has a veto on the matter then no arbitration mechanism that systematically favors one side will likely be chosen.

Efficiency. As we know, efficiency is the ultimate economic criterion. Still, a successful mechanism may have to trade off efficiency for other desirable characteristics. Further, in addition to the overall efficiency of a mechanism, the manner in which that efficiency is determined may be important. For instance, it is possible to have a set of mechanisms all of which are close to being second-best efficient but which achieve this efficiency in different ways. For example, consider a set of different bargaining mechanisms each of whose purpose is to consummate deals between buyers and sellers in an incomplete information environment. In such situations, buyers have only probabilistic information about the costs of sellers, who in turn have only probabilistic information about the values of buyers. However, instead of having one buyer and one seller who could be of different types, let us assume that there are many buyers and many sellers who will be matched pairwise and asked to bargain. At a first-best outcome, all trades that yield positive gains should be made and those buyers and sellers should consummate deals. We know that no mechanism can achieve such first-best outcomes, given the incomplete information just described, but mechanisms achieving or approaching second-best results are sometimes available.

Near-second-best outcomes could be achieved in several ways. One mechanism might make all of the very profitable trades available (i.e., trades between high-value buyers and low-cost sellers) but miss a large number of trades on which the gains are small. Another mechanism might miss a few big and profitable trades but be much more successful on the small-gain trades. If the ex post efficiencies of these two mechanisms are comparable, which one is chosen will depend on exactly how these efficiencies are determined. For example, if there are relatively many more small-gain situations than large gain ones, the cries of small-gain traders may well drown out those of the large-gain traders. Put differently, since high-cost sellers and low-value buyers are most likely to be in situations where the gains from trade are small, they are more likely to prefer the mechanism that makes a majority of the small-gain trades. Again, despite the equality in the overall efficiencies, the composition of these gains may be important.

Strategic Robustness. A successful mechanism should be robust against small or even considerable mistakes or miscalculations on the part of the agents using it. For example, one could not consider a mechanism as satisfactory if, despite its ability to implement Pareto optimal outcomes at a Nash equilibrium, it produces disastrous outcomes for reasonably small mistakes (say, mistakes larger than mere trembles) or deviations. In essence, we are talking here about the shape of the efficiency surface of the mechanism around the Nash equilibrium point and asking that it be flat.

Personality Robustness. In addition to being robust with respect to strategic actions, we might like our mechanism to be robust to the personalities who use it. For example, if the outcomes of a mechanism are greatly influenced by the personalities of those who actually use it, then we can expect a larger-than-usual variance in outcomes and a greater sense of uncertainty about the mechanism's outcomes. For instance, assume a mechanism implements Pareto optimal outcomes but the exact outcome on the Pareto surface that is chosen depends on how the game defined by the mechanism is actually "played" (i.e., different players might select different equilibria). We can think of organizations as infinitely lived entities, so any choice of mechanism commits the players to a game to be played by yet unknown fiduciaries in the future. If the outcomes are sensitive to the play of these yet unknown agents, the choice of a mechanism today may expose future agents of one's type to dismal outcomes. A mechanism that is not "personality robust" would therefore be a risky choice and thus be rejected by a risk-averse agent today.

Agent Profitability. New institutions are never imposed in a historical vacuum. In almost every instance where a new institution is called for, it replaces an old one. When it does so it must make sure to provide a profitable role for all actors who participated in the previous institution, especially if those agents have the ability to veto the use of the new mechanisms. In addition, a new mechanism would have a better chance of being implemented if it were "in the idiom" of the old one. For example, if an industry has historically set its wages by bargaining, a new wage-setting institution might have a better chance of adoption if it likewise provided a role for bargaining. As we saw in the baseball example, the baseball industry contains a number of different economic agents (e.g., team owners, players, the players' association, and sports lawyers). Any new mechanism that does not provide a profitable role for all of these agents is likely to be rejected. For instance, no sports lawyer is likely to endorse a system that eliminates his or her future rents.

No Collusion. If a mechanism is to be acceptable to economic agents, it should be resistant to collusive behavior among the participants using it. Collusion is most easy when participants on one side of the mechanism can cheaply signal their intentions and when defections from an implicit convention of behavior are easily detected.

3   Experimental Evidence

In this section I will review the results of a number of different experimental studies. Each study is presented in an effort to highlight how the mechanisms examined there satisfy the criteria of Section 2.

3.1   *A Comparison of Three Mechanisms in the Baseball Industry*

Because we have motivated the issue of mechanism selection by referring to the free-agent allocation problem, let us look first to that problem for experimental evidence. Such evidence is presented by Nalbantian and Schotter (1995), who investigate three distinctly different mechanisms that might be used in the baseball industry to solve the free-agent allocation problem. One, the current free-agency system (CFA), presents a laboratory version of what they felt were the salient characteristics of the free-agent system now in place in the major leagues. The second mechanism, a complete information English auction (CIEA), incorporates the unilateral information modification of the CFA that the team owners instituted on a voluntary basis in 1987 as a possible solution to what they felt were drawbacks in the current free-agency system. It was this modification that was recently labeled a facilitating practice.

Finally, the authors investigate a simultaneous mechanism (SM), which is a generalization of the Walrasian mechanism of Demange and Gale (1985) and which uses the algorithm of Leonard (1983) to make its calculation. Let us explain these three mechanisms in turn.

Mechanism Types

Free Agency (CFA): The current free-agency system can be described as follows. By a given date, all eligible players declare whether they are free agents or not. After that date any team is free to call any player and vice versa. The content of these negotiations is private information and cannot be verified. At any time a player is free to accept the latest offer made to him by any team; when he does, his participation in the market is over. Negotiations continue until either all players have agreed to a contract, or until time runs out. Payoffs are defined according to the terms of the contracts and whether or not a contract has been made. This system thus constitutes a *partial information sequential* mechanism, since information about the bids made by teams for players is not available while the mechanism is being employed.

Complete Information English Auction (CIEA): The informational asymmetry existing in the current free-agent system can be expected to give an undue advantage to players, and since teams are prevented from finding out what other teams are offering and hence cannot simply bid ε more than the best outstanding offer, one may think of modifying the mechanism so that, at any time, all bids made by any team to any player are available for inspection by everyone. Such a system might be organized as follows. Players and teams sit by computer screens indicating the latest bids by all teams for all players. When a team wishes to bid it enters its bid into its computer terminal. Bids can be changed. When a player wishes to accept a bid, he enters its acceptance and his participation in the market is over. Bidding continues until all players have made a contract or until time runs out. We call such a mechanism a *full information sequential* mechanism, since all bids made are common knowledge to all participants, yet we are aware that all reservation values are privately known.

Simultaneous Mechanisms (SM): A simultaneous mechanism might have the following description.[1] On a given day, all teams and players submit bids to a central computer. The bids submitted by the teams would represent the maximum willingness to pay that any team has for any player. Hence each team enters a vector of bids, one bid for each player. The bids submitted by the players would represent their reservation prices, namely, the minimum price they require in order to play on any given team. Once these bids are submitted the computer would treat them as if they were the truthful values and costs of the teams and players. It would then match players and teams so as to maximize the sum of the surpluses generated by any such matching. In addition to matching the players and the teams, the computer would also indicate a *range* in which the salary of the player must be set. Teams and players would then negotiate their salaries within these ranges. Teams and players who fail to come to a negotiated agreement would be sent to arbitration. Teams and players who fail to make a match would remain unmatched.

The motivation for this type of mechanism comes from the matching literature – especially its earliest concern with the "marriage problem," where the object of analysis is a matching algorithm that permits the matching of people to people like the matching of men and women into monogamous marriages.

Experimental Design. Three sets of experiments were conducted by Nalbantian and Schotter (1995), each aimed at replicating the salient features of a different allocation mechanism and evaluating their performance. For a full description of these experiments see Nalbantian and Schotter (1995).

The objective of the subjects in all three experiments was to try to match themselves with another subject in the experiment and then determine a price for that match. The manner in which this was done changed from experiment to experiment, but the preferences induced on the subjects were identical. This allowed them to impute any differences in behavior and performance to the institutional rule or mechanism used

---

[1] For a full description of the simultaneous mechanism and its laboratory implementation, see Nalbantian and Schotter (1995).

Matrix 1. *U-Type Preferences*

	U_1	U_2	U_3
S_1	4.5	4	5
S_2	5	4.5	4
S_3	4	5	4.5

in the experiment. In all of the main experiments reported,[2] subjects were randomly assigned to be either one of two types, denoted U-types or S-types. The subjects were informed that they could be matched with *at most* one subject of the opposite type and that their payoffs would depend upon whom they were matched with and the price determined for the match. To induce preferences on the subjects, U-types were given a schedule informing them of the amount of money they would be paid if they were matched with any S-type subject, denoted as S_1, S_2, and S_3. These three values were similar in that it was always true that each U-type valued one S-type at $5, one at $4.5, and one at $4. However, no U-type subject knew the preferences of anyone else but himself.

To induce preferences on the subjects, S-types were given a schedule informing them of the amount of money they would have to pay at the end of the experiment if they were matched with any U-type subject, denoted as U_1, U_2, and U_3. These three values were similar in that it was always true that each S-type always valued one U-type at $0.5, one at $1, and one at $2. However, no S-type subject knew the preferences of anyone else but himself. In each round of the experiment we would change these schedules, but these changes merely constituted a permutation of the indices shown in Matrix 1 and Matrix 2. These matrices define all of the information known to the experimenter in each round of the experiment. Looking down each column, we see the value (Matrix 1) or cost (Matrix 2) of each U-type (S-type) for subjects of the opposite type. Each subject knew only the column in the matrix relevant to himself but also knew that U-types had values of either $5, $4.5, and $4 while S-Types had values of either $0.5, $1, or $2. Note that these parameters enabled profitable matches to be formed between any S-type subject and any U-type subject, and that the difference between the

---

[2] Some subsidiary experiments were performed as pilot experiments. We will not refer to them in the main body of this chapter, but some reference to them will be made in footnotes.

Matrix 2. *S-Type Preferences*

	S_1	S_2	S_3
U_1	0.5	2	1
U_2	1	0.5	2
U_3	2	1	0.5

surplus generated by optimal matches and suboptimal matches was not great. This, we expected, would lead to a fair amount of competition between the subjects.

As we see, the optimal (surplus maximizing) set of trades occurs when S-type subjects with a cost of $0.5 were matched with U-type subjects with a cost of $4.5. All of these matches generated a surplus (sum of the consumer's plus producer's surplus) of $4, whereas any other match generated a surplus of only $3. Hence, in every round of the experiment, the set of optimal matches remained unique. (However, because we permuted the indices, it was not always true that U_1 was matched with S_1, U_2 with S_2, and U_3 with S_3.)

Notice that the optimal matching does not allocate U-types their first choice but rather their second. This was done to prevent the first-ranked alternative for the U-types from becoming salient and biasing the process toward an optimal set of matches. In pilot experiments, other preferences were investigated as well. Holding these preferences constant across experiments allows us to impute the differences between experiments to the different sets of rules existing in each one and not to value or cost changes. We cannot here fully describe these mechanisms or the laboratory procedures used to implement them; a full explanation is presented in Nalbantian and Schotter (1995).

Some Preliminary Results. On the basis of the experiments performed, Nalbantian and Schotter (1995) have the following conclusions to offer.

(1) Except for its tendency to yield no matches when extreme bids are entered, the SM mechanism demonstrated good performance character-istics, ones that were on par with the CFA and CIEA mechanisms. For example, while 14 out of a possible 180 potential matching situations (7.7%) led to no matches, for the remaining 166 the mechanism was able to capture 97% of the available gains from trade. It did this by deter-mining optimal matches for 146 of the remaining matches. Although average efficiencies were better under the CFA mechanism, where 94.8% of the potentially available gains from trade were captured as

opposed to 89.4% for SM, the CFA mechanism generated a far greater number of mismatches (31 out of 150) than did SM (which had only 20 out of 180). Further, it appears that the no-match frequency under SM can be accounted for by the "extreme" bids entered by these subjects, misrepresenting their true values and costs by amounts ranging from 56% to over 400%. The CIEA mechanism performed in a manner equivalent to the SM mechanism. It had the greatest fraction of no matches (14 out of 150 potential matches or 9.3%). In addition, when it succeeded in matching subjects it failed to make the optimal match in 14 out of 136 instances. Overall (including the no-match data) it was able to capture 88.3% of the available gains from trade and 97.4% of the gains available when it was successful in matching subjects.

(2) Prices tended to be highest under the CFA mechanism, with the SM mechanism being second and the CIEA mechanism yielding the lowest prices of all. In terms of the actual prices formed, CFA yielded an average price of \$2.65; SM determined an average price of \$2.35 and CIEA an average price of \$2.20. These differences proved to be statistically significant.

(3) Because prices were lower in CIEA than in the SM and CFA experiments (in that order), one would expect that U-type (buyer) payoffs would be ranked in the same order (CIEA, SM, and then CFA), while the S-type (seller) payoffs' ranking would be opposite. This was, in fact, the case. Under CFA, average realized payoffs equalled \$1.87 and \$1.94 per round for U- and S-types respectively, as compared to \$2.00 and \$1.72 for SM and \$2.07 and \$1.45 for CIEA.

In short, by looking at gross summary statistics it would appear that the efficiency properties of all mechanisms were quite good, with the CFA mechanism doing the best (in a statistically insignificant manner). In addition, while CIEA yielded the highest payoffs for U-type subjects, CFA was distinctly more advantageous for S-types.

Evaluating Our Three Mechanisms. If major league baseball were to consider these three mechanisms, it would be relevant to see how they fared when evaluated by our seven criteria. We will do so based on the results of the Nalbantian and Schotter (1995) experiment.

Understandability: Even though our three mechanisms were easily understood by our subjects in the sense that they quickly became comfortable playing the resulting games, the subjects probably had a lesser understanding of the theory underlying the SM mechanism. In fact, only a rudimentary explanation of this theory was even offered to them. Hence they tended to treat it like a "black box" into which they place their bid and get a match and bargaining range as an output. Still, the U-type subjects clearly began to understand, at least statistically, the relationship between their bids and the prices that they might have to pay.

Fairness – Strategic Symmetry: The CFA mechanism clearly meets this criterion and, upon inspection, so does the SM mechanism. The CIEA mechanism, however, does not give the S-type subjects the same strategic capabilities as it does the U-type subjects, since they cannot make counteroffers to the bids made by the other side. This fact was never commented upon by our subjects, a response quite unlike the anger displayed by S-type subjects during a modified version of the SM mechanism that we ran where no bargaining was allowed and where the price of the match was simply the match price p_j.

Efficiency: As mentioned previously, all three of our mechanisms were comparable in terms of efficiencies but achieved these efficiencies in different ways. Although the SM mechanism was relatively successful in making optimal matches when matches were made, it was relatively less successful in making matches than was the CFA mechanism. CIEA seemed to suffer from both afflictions and, while not shown statistically, seemed to perform the worst of the three.

Strategic Robustness: A successful mechanism should be robust against small or even considerable mistakes or miscalculations on the part of the agents using it. For example, in the SM mechanism we see that it takes a considerable amount of misrepresentation on both the parts of the S- and U-types in order to produce a no-match outcome. This fact is encouraging since it means that, except for large deviations (which we can suppose will disappear as time goes on), the SM mechanism might be expected to yield high efficiencies. It is not clear how mistakes or miscalculations can be measured or observed in the CFA or CIEA since the strategies there are so unstructured. Still, mistakes are made in the CFA mechanism when deals are consummated prematurely, and subjects using the CIEA mechanism can miscalculate when they play a game of timing during the last ten seconds of a round and move too late.

Personality Robustness: From our observation of the experiments, we feel that the CIEA and CFA mechanisms exhibit the most severe group effects. What this means is that the CIEA and CFA mechanisms are most susceptible to having the outcome of its deliberations affected by the actual people used in the experiment. We feel that this is true in the CFA experiments because negotiations are voice-to-voice and hence susceptible to personalities, while with the CIEA mechanism U-type subjects had more room to coordinate a collusive buying pattern. Under CIEA, when a group of U-types saw their common interest clearly, they were very successful in securing extremely favorable prices for themselves.

When they did not, prices were as high or higher than observed elsewhere.

Agent Profitability: In the baseball industry there are a set of agents who have historically played an active role in the wage-setting process. These include the team owners, the players' association, the players themselves, and the agents of the players. In addition, salaries have been set by negotiation. Hence any new mechanism might do well to provide a role for all of these actors as well as preserving the negotiation process currently employed. All three of our mechanisms do this, albeit in different ways. Probably the biggest departure from the past is the SM mechanism, because before the bargaining process takes place there is a noncooperative game that must be played whose outcome determines the parameters of the bargaining. To the extent that this prior game helps to structure and focus the bargaining, it may be a valuable addition to the regular bargaining process.

No Collusion: In our opinion, of the mechanisms observed, CIEA was the one most susceptible to collusion. This was true because U-types could easily signal their intentions through the bids they submitted which were common knowledge for all other U-types (and S-types). In a number of instances, a clear "meeting of minds" existed among the U-types, the effect of which was to keep prices low. Evidence of collusion was hard to find in our other experiments.

3.2 *The Sealed-Bid Mechanism versus Face-to-Face Bargaining*

Mechanism Selection. One of the problems that has intrigued economists for quite some time is how to optimally structure bargaining under conditions of incomplete information. While the mechanism design literature long ago revealed that no mechanism exists that can achieve first-best optimal results, a search for second-best optimal mechanisms has come up with just one, the sealed-bid mechanism (or others that are strategically equivalent). Quite briefly, this mechanism works as follows. Assume that a potential buyer B and a potential seller S are bargaining over the terms of a possible trade of a single object. If the object is traded, the value to B is V and the cost to S is C. (The seller incurs no cost if there is no trade.) These values and costs are drawn from the cumulative distribution functions $C = (C/100)^{r_1}$ and $V = (1 - (100 - V/100)^{r_2}$, where $0 \leq r_1, r_2 \leq 1$; B and S simultaneously choose bids v and c, respectively. If $v \geq c$, then the trade takes place and B pays S the price $P = (v + c)/2$, that is, the average of the two bids. If $v < c$, then no trade takes place and B pays S nothing. (The incomplete information in the mechanism occurs because only the buyer is informed about her value V while only the seller is informed about his cost C; both the value and the cost are drawn independently from commonly known prior probability distributions.) In the theory of bargaining under incomplete information, quite a bit of attention has been focused on the sealed-bid mechanism, mostly because of the Myerson and Satterthwaite (1983) result that the linear equilibrium of this mechanism is the only equilibrium of any mechanism capable of achieving second-best welfare results.

In a set of experiments, Radner and Schotter (1989) tested the sealed-bid mechanism and found that, at least in the laboratory, it performed as well or in some cases even better than the theoretical prediction. (This result was replicated by Rapoport and Fuller (1992) in a slightly different design.) More precisely, they found that subjects did, in fact, tend to use linear bidding strategies and as a result were capable of achieving efficiencies that were at least equal to second-best optimal efficiencies.

Because theory tells us that the linear equilibrium of the sealed-bid mechanism is the only one capable of achieving these efficiencies and since laboratory experience supports this contention, it may appear that our search for an optimal way to structure bargaining is over. In fact, quite the opposite is true. Although the sealed-bid mechanism did perform (in the laboratory) at least as well as was expected, simple face-to-face unstructured bargaining did even better. That is, the mechanism in which people simply sit face-to-face and bargain with each other in an unstructured manner appears capable of achieving almost first-best gains from trade. Evidence for this laboratory stylized fact is born out by experiments on Coasian bargaining performed by Hoffman and Spitzer (1982) and others, in a complete information context, and by the face-to-face bargaining experiments of Radner and Schotter (1989) where face-to-face bargaining seemed to be remarkably efficient in attaining first-best gains from trade in incomplete information bargaining situations. Anonymous procedures like those of Roth and Murnighan (1982), where bargainers communicate in a virtually unrestricted manner through computer terminals, were less successful. These results led Radner and Schotter (1989, p. 210) to comment that

The success of the face-to-face mechanism, if replicated, might lead to a halt in the search for better ways to structure bargaining in situations of incomplete information. It would create, however, a need for a theory of such unstructured bargaining in order to enable us to understand why the mechanism is so successful.

From the description of these results it is obvious that we have a *mechanism selection* problem here, since we are faced with a problem (how

Table 1. *Disagreement and Inefficiency Rates*

Experiment type	Number of observations	Disagreement rate (%)			Inefficiency rate (%)		
		1st 7 rounds	Last 8 rounds	Total	1st 7 rounds	Last 8 rounds	Total
Face-to-face	150	6	6	6	1	1	1
Sealed-bid bargaining	150	25	32	30	13	14	13

to structure bargaining within an organization) and two competing mechanisms that can be used to solve it – the sealed-bid mechanism and the face-to-face bargaining mechanism. Which one should we choose?[3] It is at this point that the criteria specified in Section 2 come into play. For many of the criteria there are no real differences between these two mechanisms. For example, both are easily understandable and fair in the sense that the rules treat each agent in a strategically symmetrical manner. As we shall see when we review the paper of Linhart, Radner, and Schotter (1992), the sealed-bid mechanism is strategically robust on both a theoretical and an empirical level in the sense that its efficiencies are relatively high and invariant to considerable deviations of the bidding strategies of subjects away from truth-telling. From the experiment run by Radner and Schotter (1989), face-to-face bargaining seems also to be a robust mechanism in that it almost always leads to efficiencies close to the first-best levels. Of course, it is not possible to say anything theoretical about unstructured face-to-face bargaining since one cannot write down the game form describing it. The big differences between the mechanisms pertains to the efficiency and personality robustness criteria.

Efficiency and Personality Robustness. On efficiency grounds, face-to-face bargaining seems to dominate the sealed-bid mechanism. To illustrate this point, let us look at Table 1. In this table we assess and compare

[3] Roth (1995, p. 297) has suggested that the efficiency of the laboratory face-to-face bargaining mechanism is an artifact of the laboratory environment in which it occurs. He argues that, in the real world, face-to-face bargaining occurs frequently yet often meets with inefficient outcomes (i.e., strikes). See Ashenfelter et al. (1992), Card (1990), and Kennan and Wilson (1990) for some surveys of field data on bargaining breakdowns. Schotter and Zheng (1998), however, point out that face-to-face bargaining in the real world usually takes place through fiduciaries or agents and could therefore break down as a result of the principal–agent relationship between fiduciaries (lawyers) and principals. They also offer experimental evidence for their hypothesis.

the performance of the sealed-bid and face-to-face bargaining mechanisms using various measurements of *inefficiency*, or the failure to realize potential gains from trade when these potential gains are positive.[4] The potential gains from trade for a particular round are the difference between the value V to the buyer and the cost C to the seller. Provided that the value exceeds the cost, any price P such that $C < P < V$ would generate positive profits for both parties. One way of measuring the inefficiency of a bargaining experiment is the *disagreement rate*: the ratio of (a) the number of rounds in which no agreement was reached, despite positive potential gains from trade, to (b) the total number of rounds in which potential gains were positive. An alternative measure, which we call the *inefficiency rate*, is the ratio of the sum of unrealized positive potential gains from trade to total positive potential gains. As we see from Table 1, both in terms of inefficiency and disagreement rates, face-to-face bargaining outperformed the sealed-bid mechanism. Although the sealed-bid mechanism was able to capture 87% of the first-best gains from trade, face-to-face bargaining captured nearly 99%.

Where the face-to-face mechanism failed is in the variance of the payoffs to the players and the prices formed. The face-to-face mechanism determined payoffs that varied greatly across experimental bargaining pairs, as did the prices formed. For example, looking at the percentage of the gains from trade captured by the buyers and sellers when trades took place, we see that while the mean percentage captured by a buyer (resp. seller) in the face-to-face experiment was 51.67 (48.33), the standard deviations around those means were 28.52. For the sealed-bid mechanism the mean payoffs were 50.22 and 49.78, respectively, for buyers and sellers while the standard deviations around these means were 19.63. In short, the variability of payoffs and prices was about 30% smaller in the sealed-bid mechanism when compared to the face-to-face mechanism. The histograms of these payoffs are presented in Figures 1a and 1b.

Note that the distribution of buyer and seller payoffs is far more spread out in the face-to-face bargaining experiment than it is in the sealed-bid mechanism. A similar result can be seen in the price data, as portrayed in Figure 2.

From this data we conclude that, although both mechanisms may be robust in the strategic sense, the face-to-face bargaining mechanism is not robust to the personalities using it. What this means is that, when two people engage in face-to-face bargaining, the outcome is likely to be efficient but the distribution of gains to trade and the prices formed are

---

[4] In both experiments, the prior distribution had coefficients of $r_1 = 0.4$ and $r_2 = 0.4$.

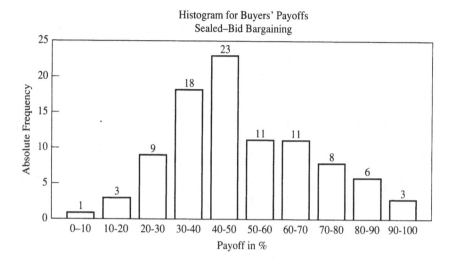

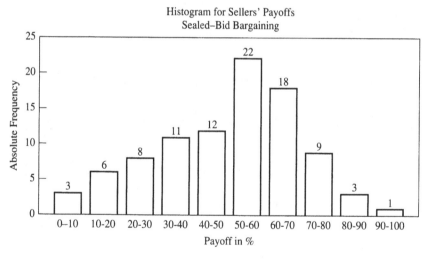

Figure 1a. Payoff histogram for sealed-bid bargaining.

likely to be widely dispersed and dependent on the personalities of the individuals involved. This has a number of consequences. First, it implies that, for reasons of risk aversion, the sealed-bid mechanism may be preferable to the face-to-face mechanism: the former has a lower mean efficiency, but the payoff to any one side has a smaller variability. Second, because future bargaining is likely to be done by agents unknown to today's principals, decision makers may want to opt for the security of a

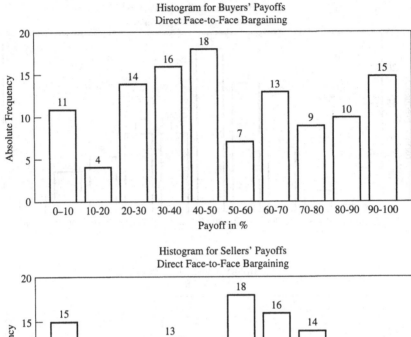

Figure 1b. Payoff histogram for face-to-face bargaining.

mechanism that protects them from the variability introduced by not knowing what agents will use the mechanism in the future. This is the essence of personality robustness.

Which mechanism will ultimately be chosen by an organization forced to consider only these two cannot, of course, be determined without knowing the preferences of the decision makers over efficiency and the variability introduced by personality nonrobustness.

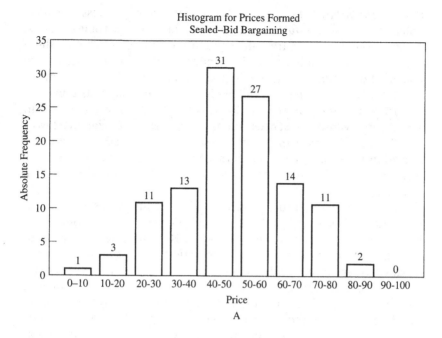

A

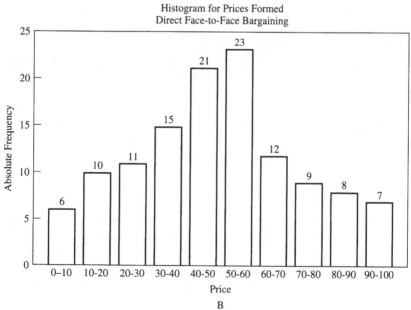

B

Figure 2. Histogram for prices formed.

Strategic Robustness. In addition to personality robustness, we have argued that a successful mechanism should also be robust against strategic deviations away from the equilibrium strategies. Whether these deviations occur by mistake (as in trembles of the hand) or are due to behavioral deviations caused by limited calculating abilities of agents or lack of memory, a mechanism will likely be selected only if its efficiency properties remain sufficiently high when such deviations occur. Mechanisms whose efficiencies plunge when small deviations (away from the equilibrium path) occur are sure to be judged too risky and rejected in favor of some other, perhaps less efficient but more robust, mechanism. The sealed-bid mechanism seems to be a robust mechanism in this respect.

Evidence for this assertion comes from the results of a set of experiments (Linhart, Radner, and Schotter 1992; henceforth LRS) on sealed-bid bargaining with incomplete information. By "robustness" they meant that, although the subjects used a wide variety of bargaining strategies that deviated from the equilibrium bid function in dramatic yet systematic ways, and although the bargainers' strategy pairs were not best responses to each other, still the achieved efficiencies were nevertheless quite high and clustered in a fairly narrow range, about 80–90%. (By "efficiency" we mean total gains from trade captured by the subjects as a fraction of first-best (truth-telling) gains from trade.) Moreover, this robustness was observed for nine different pairs of distributions (priors) of the bargainers' beliefs as to their opponents' true types.

In addition to showing mechanism efficiencies to be robust with respect to strategic deviations, LRS demonstrate that the sealed-bid mechanism is also fairly robust with respect to the buyer's (seller's) profits, but less so than for the total gains from trade. This is important, since risk-averse agents would prefer a mechanism that not only promises them a good payoff but does so with some sense of security.

These results are empirical, yet theoretical support for the robustness of the sealed-bid mechanism has also been supplied by LRS. As stated in Section 2, the strategic robustness of a mechanism is a question of the steepness (or flatness) of the efficiency surface of the mechanism around some salient outcome of the mechanism, such as its Nash equilibrium or the truth-revealing outcome. The efficiency surface of the sealed-bid mechanism has been calculated by LRS; one such surface is presented in Figure 3a. This figure illustrates the efficiency surface for the sealed-bid mechanism when the prior distributions of costs and values are uniform, and when agents deviate from truth-telling linear functions by first choosing piecewise linear functions with a slope of 1 until some critical value V_0 (cost C_0), and then a slope of 0 from that point until the

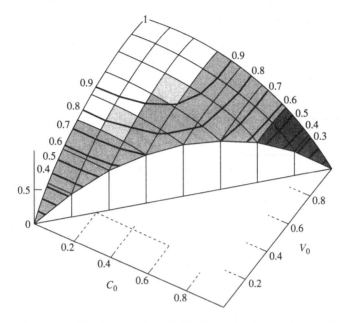

Figure 3a. Efficiency of sealed-bid mechanism using broken-stick strategies, where $r_1 = r_2 = 1.0$.

end of the support of the function (assumed in this diagram to be $[0, 1]$). These deviating strategies are called *broken-stick strategies* because their graphs resemble broken sticks with a break at V_0 and C_0. They were frequently observed in the LRS experiments.

As we can see from this diagram and its associated efficiency contours in Figure 3b, the efficiency of the sealed-bid mechanism is theoretically robust around the truth-telling first-best strategies: for significant deviations of the broken-stick type away from these strategies, the efficiency of the mechanism remains quite high. Similar results are obtained for other, more skewed, prior distributions of types in which high values (low costs) were more likely events for buyers (sellers) than were low values (high costs); this can be seen in Figures 4 and 5.

The robustness of the sealed-bid mechanism, as demonstrated by these diagrams, presents a strong source of support for its use in practical situations. Not only is the sealed-bid mechanism easily understandable and strategically fair (symmetric), but on efficiency grounds it offers hope for achieving second-best optimal outcomes with a great degree of reliability because it is strategically and personality robust. Other mechanisms

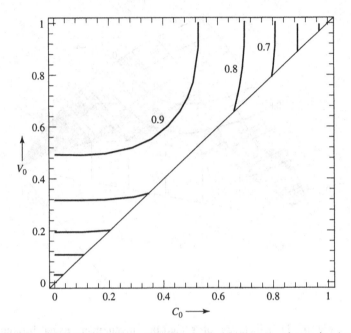

Figure 3b. Efficiency contours for sealed-bid mechanism using broken-stick strategies, where $r_1 = r_2 = 1.0$.

would need to be checked on a case-by-case basis to see if they are as robust as is this mechanism.

3.3   Personality Robustness in an Economic Tournament

One of the areas where mechanisms have been most extensively used is in the field of labor contracting, where the form of the contract between worker and firm is set. Recent years have seen a move away from individual-based incentive formulas and toward group-based formulas (see Nalbantian 1987). Hence, old-style piece rates have yielded way to methods of compensation that rely on variables other than individual performance.

One intensively studied mechanism for compensating individuals at the workplace is a *tournament* mechanism. In a tournament, individuals are rewarded for their performance relative to the performance of others. In other words, the compensation of a worker is not tied to her absolute output (as in a piece rate) but rather to her output relative to the output of others (or perhaps some statistic of the performance of all

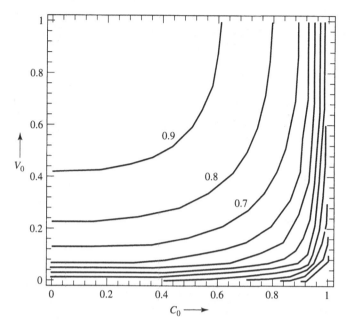

Figure 4. Efficiency contours for sealed-bid mechanism using broken-stick strategies, where $r_1 = r_2 = 0.4$.

workers in a group). For example: car salesman compete for prizes that are given to the salesman who sells the most cars for a given period of time; assistant professors compete for the prize of tenure, which is given to that assistant professor whose work is judged as being best; and corporate vice presidents compete for the big prize in an organization – the presidency. In environments where there are both common and idiosyncratic shocks to output, risk-averse workers may well prefer a tournament to a piece-rate system because, under a tournament, they are immune to the common shock affecting their output – such shocks affect all workers equally and hence do not jeopardize anyone's chances of getting the big prize offered by the organization. As a result, if a piece rate and a tournament both yield equal levels of output from workers, then a tournament would seem to be preferable in an environment with common and idiosyncratic shocks, since risk-neutral firms would be indifferent between the two while risk-averse workers would prefer a tournament. The mechanism selection problem seems easy to solve here since – at least at the theoretical level – tournaments appear to dominate piece rates.

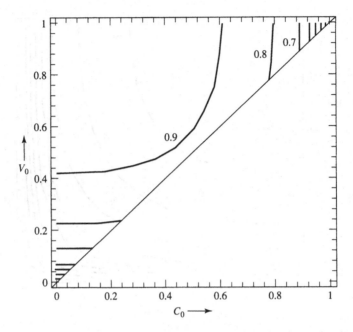

Figure 5. Efficiency contours for sealed-bid mechanism using broken-stick strategies, where $r_1 = r_2 = 0.2$.

At the empirical (experimental) level, things are not so simple. In a series of experiments performed by Bull, Schotter, and Weigelt (1987; hereafter BSW) the authors demonstrate that the laboratory behavior of human subjects is consistent with the predictions of tournament theory as far as the *mean* actions of subjects, but there is great variability around these means. Put differently, let us assume that a corporation has many plants or production units located across the United States. In each plant it uses an identical tournament to compensate its workers and so expects the same level of output. The BSW experiments indicate that although the *mean* output of the corporation (averaged over these plants) may in fact equal the output predicted by the theory, output will vary greatly from plant to plant. Such variability creates uncertainty at the plant level, a risk to which CEOs or plant mangers may be averse. For instance, a manager may be branded as a "bad manager" if his plant output is below the average, even though output under a tournament system has been proven to be a random variable with a known variance. If such variability results because different workers react to the rules of

Table 2. *Experimental Results: Means and Variances*

Experiment	Mean decision number		Mean variance in decision numbers		Mean decision number	Variance in decision numbers
	Rounds 1–6	Rounds 7–12	Rounds 1–6	Rounds 7–12	Round 12	Round 12
Baseline 37	43.62	38.75	508.32	499.67	36.94	577.28
Equilibrium 74	64.92	69.91	867.17	892.05	67.61	1005.37
Piece rate	40.44	38.91	103.61	87.38	37.38	33.66
	Rounds 1–12	Rounds 13–25	Rounds 1–12	Rounds 13–25	Round 25	Round 25
25-round equilibrium 37	50.62	48.00	303.88	362.01	44.63	466.44

the mechanism in different ways and establish different norms of behavior at different plants, such a mechanism would fail the personality robustness criterion described in Section 2. Further, it might be thought that the variability of output might decrease over time as workers learn more about the mechanism. As we will see, such a conjecture has proven not to be the case.

The experiments run by BSW replicated the simple example of a tournament given in the previous section. A comparable piece-rate experiment was also run for purposes of comparison. (See BSW for a full presentation of the experimental design and techniques used.) The broad outlines of the experimental results are given in Table 2 and Figures 6–9.

Table 2 shows summary statistics for the first and last six rounds, as well as the twelfth round, of three tournament experiments and one piece-rate experiment. Of the tournament experiments, two have equilibria in which each subject is supposed to choose a unique pure strategy Nash equilibrium of 37 and one has a unique pure strategy Nash equilibrium at 74. The piece-rate experiment is a one-person optimization problem with a unique maximum at 37. All experiments presented here were run for 12 rounds, except one tournament (with a 37 equilibrium) that was run for 25 rounds to foster learning. For each experiment, Table 2 reports the six-round means and variances of the average (across

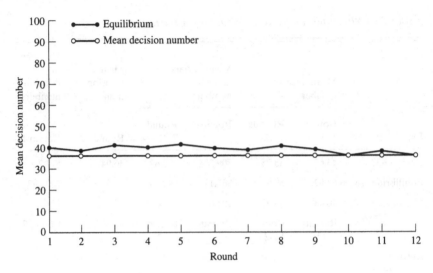

Figure 6. Piece-rate experiment.

pairs) choices made.[5] It also displays the average choice and variance for the last round. Figures 6, 7, 8, and 9 plot the average choices made in each round for each experiment reported in Table 2.

The piece-rate experiment serves as a point of comparison for many of the tournament experiments and so merits our attention first. As can be seen from Figure 6 and Table 2, the piece-rate system did very well. The theoretical mean effort level was 37 (just as in our baseline tournament), and the mean effort level in the twelfth round was 37.38. This mean is not significantly different from 37 at the 95% confidence level using a median test. The variance across subjects was 33.66. This variance is remarkably small when compared with the tournament variances. From observation of Figures 7, 8, and 9 it appears as if tournaments also perform remarkably well in terms of determining behavior; this is, on average, consistent with the predictions of the theory. In all of these figures we see a convergence over time of the mean effort level of subjects toward the theoretical predictions. This is true for experiments where the predicted equilibrium is 37 as well as for tournaments where the parameters were changed so that the equilibrium increased to 74. It was true for experiments where the tournament was repeated 12 times as well as when it was repeated 25 times. What is remarkable, however,

---

[5] Recall that the variance refers to the variance of the average choice of effort within a tournament, across tournaments.

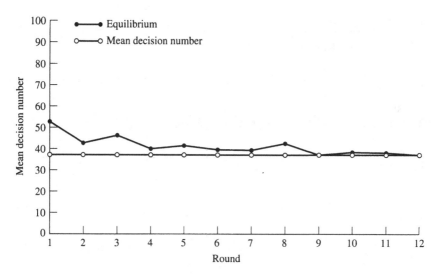

Figure 7. Baseline experiment (37).

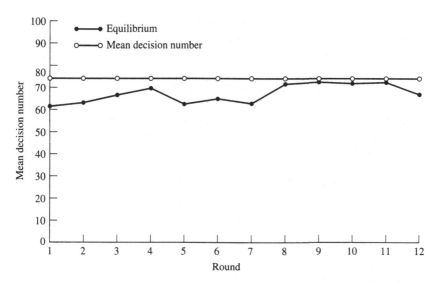

Figure 8. Equilibrium 74 experiment.

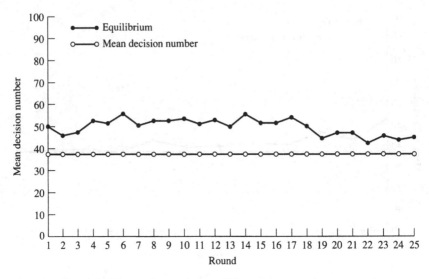

Figure 9. 25-round experiment (37).

is that – despite the convergence of these means – there is a persistence of the variance even in the experiment lasting 25 rounds (where the variance was 466.44 in round 25 as opposed to a variance of 33.66 in the twelfth round of the piece-rate experiment; see Table 2). This large variance is evidence that tournaments may suffer from a personality robustness problem. While they appear to be efficient compensation mechanisms, they also appear to be risky in the sense that their output varies significantly from tournament to tournament. A risk-averse corporate planner might therefore have to think twice before recommending their implementation. Whether this drawback is enough to counter their other benefits is a question left to real-world decision makers. However, I certainly think that this factor should be considered when a mechanism selection problem is present.

4   Conclusions

This chapter has dealt with the problem of mechanism selection. We have tried to emphasize that the criteria used by economists to evaluate the aesthetics of mechanisms they design may not be the same criteria used by real-world decision makers, who must actually decide on which mechanism is the correct one for them to use in their organization. We have outlined seven criteria and have presented a number of experimental studies where mechanisms designed by economic theorists or actually used in industry have been evaluated by these criteria. It is my hope that a better understanding of the mechanism selection problem will lead to the design of more practical mechanisms and their wider adoption in the corporate and governmental world.

References

Ashenfelter, O., Currie, J., Farber, H., and Spiegel, M. (1992), "On Experimental Comparison of Dispute Rates in Alternative Arbitration Systems," *Econometrica* 60, pp. 1387–1407.

Bull, C., Schotter, A., and Weigelt, K. (1987), "Tournaments and Piece Rates: An Experimental Study," *Journal of Political Economy* 95, pp. 1–33.

Card, D. (1990), "Strikes and Bargains: A Survey of Recent Empirical Literature," *American Economic Review, Papers and Proceedings* 80, pp. 405–15.

Demange, G., and Gale, D. (1985), "The Strategy Structure of Two-Sided Matching Markets," *Econometrica* 53, pp. 873–88.

Hoffman, E., and Spitzer, M. (1982), "The Coase Theorem: Some Experimental Tests," *Journal of Law and Economics* 25, pp. 93–8.

Hurwicz, L. (1972), "On Informationally Decentralized Systems," in *Decision and Organization* (R. Radner and C. B. McGuire, eds.). Amsterdam: North-Holland.

Kennan, J., and Wilson, R. (1990), "Can Strategic Bargaining Models Explain Collective Bargaining Data?" *American Economic Review, Papers and Proceedings* 80, pp. 405–9.

Leonard, H. (1983), "Elicitation of Honest Preferences for the Assignment of Individuals to Positions," *Journal of Political Economy* 93, pp. 461–80.

Linhart, P., Radner, R., and Schotter, A. (1992), "Robustness in the Sealed-Bid Mechanism: Theory and Experiment," Mimeo, Department of Economics, New York University.

Moore, J. (1993), "Implementation in Environments with Complete Information," Mimeo, London School of Economics.

Myerson, R., and Satterthwaite, M. (1983), "Efficient Mechanisms for Bilateral Trading," *Journal of Economic Theory* 29, pp. 265–81.

Nalbantian, H. (1987), *Incentives, Cooperation, and Risk Sharing.* Totowa, NJ: Rowman and Littlefield.

Nalbantian, H., and Schotter, A. (1995), "Matching and Efficiency in the Baseball Free-Agent System: An Experimental Examination," *Journal of Labor Economics* 13, pp. 1–31.

Radner, R., and Schotter, A. (1989), "The Sealed-Bid Mechanism: An Experimental Study," *Journal of Economic Theory* 48, pp. 179–221.

Rapoport, A., and Fuller, M. (1992), "Bidding Strategies in a Bilateral Monopoly with Two-Sided Incomplete Information," Mimeo, Department of Psychology, University of Arizona, Tucson.

Roth, A. (1995), "Bargaining Experiments," in *Handbook of Experimental Economics* (J. Kagel and A. Roth, eds.), Princeton, NJ: Princeton University Press.

Roth A., and Murnighan, K. (1982), "The Role of Information in Bargaining," *Econometrica* 50, pp. 1123–42.

Schotter, A. and Zheng, W. (1998), "Bargain through Agents: An Experimental Study of Delegation and Commitment," Mimeo, C.V. Starrr Center for Applied Economics, New York University.

CHAPTER 7

Organizations with an Endogenous Number of Information Processing Agents

Timothy Van Zandt

1 Introduction

1.1 Information Processing Endogenously Many Agents

An organization is a group of people, but not all groups of people are called organizations, nor is the study of every economic interaction classified as the economics of organizations. A defining characteristic of organizations is that the group has some kind of group objective or performance criterion that transcends the objectives of the individuals within the group. We can thus talk about the design of organizations in pursuit of this objective. Sometimes the performance criterion is as weak as Pareto optimality; the design of economic systems can be thought of as the design of organizations on a large scale. More frequently, the performance criterion is a very specific and complete ordering, such as the maximization of a firm's profits.

Models of bounded rationality – defined broadly to mean any models of agent behavior that depart from the paradigm of effortless full rationality – have been appearing in most fields of economics in the last decade. This is because the fields have matured enough that some important open questions require more accurate models of human decision making than full rationality. In contrast, bounded rationality has *always* been an important theme in the economics of organizations. This is because the sharing of information and of information processing tasks is such an important part of the interaction between members of orga-

This research was supported in part by grants SES-9110973 and SBR-9223917 from the National Science Foundation, by a CORE Research Fellowship (1993–1994), and by Grant 26 of the "Pôle d'Attraction Interuniversitaire" program of the Belgian government. The research assistance of Archishman Chakraborty is greatly appreciated. Discussions with Matias Dewatripont and Roy Radner and comments of Mukul Majumdar and an anonymous referee have been very helpful.

239

nizations and because most large organizations contain many agents whose sole duties are to process information.

More recent innovations in the literature on bounded rationality in organizations have been the *explicit modeling of the computation constraints of individual agents* and the *endogenous determination of the number of information processing agents*. This is in contrast to most of team theory and the planning and message-space approaches to communication mechanisms, in which there is information processing by a fixed group of agents. This is also in contrast to research that models organizations with an endogenous number of managers but does not explicitly model the tasks of these managers.[1] The purpose of this chapter is to examine some of this new research.

Models with an endogenous number of information processing agents are particularly well suited for discussing (i) the benefits and costs of decentralized information processing, (ii) organizational structure, and (iii) how information processing constraints affect returns to scale. These themes are outlined in Section 1.3.

This exposition is organized around two subtopics: (i) parallel associative computation and (ii) computation of resource allocations. The associative processing papers include Keren and Levhari (1979, 1983), Radner (1993), Bolton and Dewatripont (1994), Van Zandt (1996f), Meagher (1996a), and Miller (1996). The resource allocation papers include Geanakoplos and Milgrom (1991), Friedman and Oren (1995) and Van Zandt (1996d,e). These two subtopics are outlined in Section 1.2. There are other papers that model organizations with an endogenous number of information processing agents but are given minor or no treatment here because they do not fit into these subtopics. Examples include Malone and Smith (1988), Mount and Reiter (1990, 1998), Reiter (1996), Hong and Page (1995), Jordan (1995), Beggs (1995), and Meagher (1996b).

Besides being narrowly focused, this survey or exposition is detailed and requires some dedication from the reader.[2] Those who choose to explore just one of the two subtopics should also read Section 1.3 and should be aware of the appendix on hierarchies. Furthermore, in order to understand Section 3 (computation of resource allocations), the reader should either be familiar with parallel processing or should review Section 2.2.

---

[1] Examples include Williamson (1967), Beckmann (1983), and Rosen (1982), which take as their starting point a managerial production function.
[2] Van Zandt (1996a) is a broader and less detailed survey of the literature on decentralized information processing in organizations.

1.2   Two Subtopics

1.2.1. Batch Processing (Associative Computation). In order to model organizations with an endogenous number of information processing agents, one must specify the information processing capabilities of individual agents and the means by which multiple agents can jointly process information. One approach is to explicitly specify the data and decision rules of an organization and to decompose the decision rules into elementary operations or steps. Agents are then characterized mainly by their ability to perform these steps and also by their ability to read and send messages. Agents jointly calculate decision rules by performing these steps and sharing partial results. Such a model resembles abstract models of parallel computation in computer science. This is a very flexible approach that is common to nearly all the papers reviewed in this survey.

The simplest way to become familiar with such parallel computation is to study batch processing. In batch processing, the computation problem (function or decision rule to be computed) is fixed, all data for the problem are available at the same moment, and delay is measured by the time between when computation starts and when the answer is processed. Typically, the advantage of decentralization (parallelization) is that it reduces delay because more operations can be performed concurrently.

With this motivation, we study batch parallel processing in Section 2. Like much of the existing economic literature on this topic, we limit our attention to associative computation because it is a very simple but important information processing task. Furthermore, associative computation has a natural hierarchical structure, so it has been easy to relate models of associative computation to the hierarchical structure of firms. For example, Keren and Levhari (1979, 1983, 1989) model hierarchical information processing of an unspecified coordination or planning problem; it turns out that the model in their first two papers can be interpreted as one of associative computation with the Radner (1993) computation model and with an additional restriction that the hierarchies be balanced.

1.2.2. Computation of Decision Rules (Resource Allocation). Implicitly motivating the study of parallel batch processing is that the decision-making process involved in the control of an organization requires the computation of decision rules. However, in the models of parallel associative computation reviewed in Section 2, the underlying decision problem and the endogenous determination of decision rules did not appear explicitly.

The next step toward a full economic model of information processing in organizations is to take a decision problem as the starting point, which we do in Section 3. We limit attention to resource allocation without externalities because it is a fairly simple but very important classical decision problem and one to which we can apply and compare three different models of information processing.

The first of these is a team theory model, by Geanakoplos and Milgrom (1991). In team theory, there are communication constraints but no constraints on the individual computation. Communication constraints that come from the difficulty agents encounter in reading and writing messages reflect bounded rationality, and can also be a proxy for constraints on the ability to use information. In Geanakoplos and Milgrom (1991), these constraints are on the ability to process (acquire) information about the environment. By hiring more agents, it is possible to bring to bear more information on a problem, but the information is always decentralized in that different agents have different information. The paper demonstrates that team theory, as codified in Marschak and Radner (1972), can be used to study information processing with an endogenous number of agents.[3]

The second approach is batch parallel processing, and the third is real-time parallel processing. Real-time parallel processing integrates a parallel processing computation model into a learning problem. Unlike in batch processing, the data become available and decisions are made in multiple epochs.

1.3   Questions Addressed

1.3.1. Benefits and Costs of Decentralization. The most basic and fundamental contributions of this literature, although not always stated in the form of theorems, are about the benefits and costs of decentralized information processing and decision making. Whereas there are other literatures that explain the distribution of decisions among administrators

---

[3] Marschak and Reichelstein (1995, 1996) have recently introduced a model of networked communication mechanisms, demonstrating that the static message-space approach to communication costs can also be used to model information processing in organizations with an endogenous number of agents. Individual communication complexity is measured by the sum of the size of each message that an agent sends or receives, and total communication complexity is the sum of the individual complexity of each agent. These authors use their model to study the structure of firms for a fixed number of agents. However, as with other models with individual communication constraints, the Marschak–Reichelstein paradigm could incorporate an endogenous number of information processing agents.

who are assumed to be present for exogenous reasons, this literature attempts to explain why there are so many administrators in the first place and what these administrators do.

The obvious answer is that these administrators are processing information and making decisions because the task of doing so is too large for a single administrator. However, this answer is not provided by the behavioral model of full rationality that is the foundation of most economic theory. A single, fully rational CEO could instantly process all available information and make optimal decisions conditional on this information.

Information transmission costs could lead such an entrepreneur to decentralize some information processing tasks to agents in an organization if those agents are exogenously assumed to be present and endowed with private information. This is the reason for decentralization in the communication mechanism literatures (which includes the iterative planning and message-space literatures) and most team theory models. However, delegating information processing tasks to administrators who have no private information when hired *increases* rather than decreases transmission costs.

Like communication costs, incentive problems are aggravated by the hiring of information processing intermediaries because such delegation creates problems of private information that did not exist before. Incentive problems may lead the entrepreneur to hire administrators whose sole job is to audit or to watch subordinates so that they do not shirk or lie – as in Calvo and Wellisz (1980), Baron and Besanko (1984), Demski and Sappington (1987), Baiman, Evans, and Noel (1987), and Qian (1994) – but not to delegate other information processing tasks to these agents. Instead, all agents, including auditors or supervisors, should communicate directly with the entrepreneur through a direct revelation mechanism. There is a literature on hierarchical contracting in which a principal delegates certain contracting tasks to some of the agents. However, in nearly all the papers (e.g., McAfee and McMillan 1995, Melumad, Mookherjee, and Reichelstein 1995, and Mookherjee and Reichelstein 1995, 1996), the need to contract hierarchically is imposed exogenously, and the goal is to see whether it is still possible to do as well as without decentralized contracting or whether the intermediaries necessarily earn extra informational rents. In Laffont and Martimort (1996), delegation of contracting to exogenously given and potentially collusive agents can be optimal because the authors assume that delegation redistributes bargaining power and affects the timing of participation constraints. This model also does not explain the existence of purely administrative agents.

Thus, to explain the existence and activities of the administrative apparatus of large organizations, it is necessary to model the bounded information processing capacities of the individual administrators, as do the papers reviewed here.

The *benefits* of decentralization of information processing tasks in the parallel batch processing literature are as follows.

(1) The benefit that has received the most attention is that decentralization *reduces delay* because it allows tasks to be performed concurrently. Hence, it is not that a particular problem is too large for a single agent but rather that agents are bounded in the amount of computation they can perform in a given amount of time.

(2) Another benefit is that, if a fixed organization must process a flow of problems in the same way by the same agents, then decentralizing the computation of each problem *increases the throughput* – that is, the rate at which the organization can process problems.

Although not yet stressed, another benefit is that with heterogeneous tasks, decentralization permits agents to specialize in different types of tasks.[4]

Note that all of these benefits have an analog in the division of labor in production processes. However, the benefit of reducing delay is a decision-theoretic one with no such analog; with decreased delay, decisions can be based on more recent information.

The *costs* of decentralization in the parallel batch processing literature may be listed as follows.

(1) Decentralization of information processing increases communication costs. (Compare this with the reduction in communication costs entailed by decentralization of information processing tasks to agents who are exogenously endowed with private information.)

(2) Decentralization increases administrators' idle time, which is a cost if the administrators must be paid even when idle.

Although not true for associative computation, decentralization can also increase the amount of computation that must be done.

In the parallel batch processing literature, a single answer is produced for each problem that the information processing apparatus must

---

[4] This theme is in Bolton and Dewatripont (1994), but they do not explicitly model heterogeneity of tasks.

compute. Hence, there is no room for decentralized decision making. However, some of the models on computation of resource allocations do attempt to explain decentralized decision making. In Geanakoplos and Milgrom (1991), decentralized decision making is the only form of decentralized information processing; it is a way of bringing more information to bear on a decision problem when individual administrators are bounded in the amount of information they can acquire. Van Zandt (1996d,e) distinguishes between decentralized information processing and decentralized decision making. The advantage of the latter is that it allows lower-level decisions to be based on less aggregate and hence more recent information. The costs are that upper-level decisions are based on slightly older information and that there are additional calculations that must be performed.

1.3.2. Organizational Structure. The endogeneity of information processing resources in the models we study makes them particularly suitable for studying how information processing affects organizational structure. Organizational structure in large organizations is generally thought of as the structure of the information processing of the administrative staff, meaning the patterns of communication between members of this staff and the structure of decision making. Without information processing constraints, one cannot even explain the existence of such a staff, as an unboundedly rational entrepreneur or leader could make all the decisions of the organization perfectly, instantly, and costlessly. The organizational structure inferred from an information processing model is generally the graph representation of the flow of information between individual information processing agents.[5] Exceptions are Van Zandt (1996d,e), in which the nodes of the organizational structure are multi-agent offices and the structure is related to a decomposition of the decision problem.

Hierarchies (trees) appear prominently as organizational structures in the existing models of information processing in organizations. There are three significant reasons for this. One is that firms and other bureaucracies are stereotypically thought of as hierarchical. (Although information flows in organizations do not just follow the hierarchical structure of the organizational charts.) Another is that hierarchies have a simpler structure than general graphs. A third is that the most commonly studied computation problem has been associative computation, which is inherently hierarchical. Appendix A summarizes the notation and definitions for hierarchies that are used in this chapter.

---

[5] See Section 2.1 for caveats about this approach in models of parallel processing.

Besides the generation of hierarchical organizational structures, these papers examine the properties of the hierarchies, such as whether they are balanced (managers in the same tier have the same number of subordinates). Balanced hierarchies have been surprisingly difficult to obtain endogenously, even when the underlying computation or decision problem is very symmetric.

1.3.3. Returns to Scale. Another question that cannot be answered without allowing the number of information processing agents to be endogenous is how information processing constraints affect returns to scale. Economists have long hypothesized that there are organizational limits on returns to scale, due to the problem of coordinating large numbers of activities within a single firm and operating in diverse environments. Such limits are theoretically possible because replication cannot be used to extend the scale of a firm at constant or decreasing unit cost. For a firm truly to mimic the activities of two smaller firms, it must be divided into parts that, like the two smaller firms, communicate only through markets. Such an agglomeration hardly qualifies as a single firm. Understanding the relationship between information integration and the boundaries of firms is an important research agenda, but it is beyond the scope of both this survey and the papers covered by this survey. Instead of providing a general theory of this relationship, each model contains its own definition of informational integrations and scale. Each model's results are directly about the returns to scale of a specific class of computation or decision problems that define an informationally integrated unit. In practice, this unit might correspond to a firm, a subunit of a firm, or even a collection of firms. Nevertheless, for concreteness, we will typically refer to a model's informationally integrated unit as a *firm* (or organization).

If the number of information processing agents were fixed, it would be no surprise that the quality of decision making is degraded in large organizations. However, this conclusion is not automatic when managerial resources can increase with the scale of an organization. All of the results discussed in this survey that show a limit to firm size are based on some kind of difficulty in aggregating information. Geanakoplos and Milgrom (1991) find decreasing returns to scale when there are exogenous restrictions on the availability of aggregate information. In batch processing models, aggregation delay increases with the amount of data that must be aggregated, and in large organizations aggregate data is older. Real-time processing models are better for studying returns to scale because they are based on a decision problem and hence do not rely on ad hoc measures of the cost of delay. In these models the effect of information processing on returns to scale are more complex. Radner and Van Zandt (1992) and Van Zandt and Radner (1996) incorporate statistical assumptions under which delay leads inexorably to decreasing returns to scale, even if managerial wages are zero. However, there are other statistical assumptions where returns to scale can be increasing, because a large firm can do as well as a small firm by processing the same information as a (single) small firm. In Van Zandt (1996e), delay does not lead inexorably to decreasing returns to scale when the managerial wage is zero. However, firm size is bounded when the managerial wage is positive because delay reduces the center's per-subordinate value of information processing, whereas its per-subordinate cost of information processing is approximately constant.

2   Parallel Associative Computation

2.1   Overview

In this section, we study parallel computation of exogenously given problems for which all data become available at the same moment; such computation is called *parallel batch processing*. The mechanics of parallel computation introduced here will also be the basis for the real-time computation of temporal decision problems, which is covered in Section 3.4.

We restrict attention to associative computation for the following reasons.

(1) It is simple, yet allows us to explore a variety of issues in a unified framework.

(2) It is a leading example of computation in organizations, since it includes addition, multiplication, and finding the maximum of two numbers, as well as more interesting and difficult operations such as finding the best project out of a set of projects through binary comparisons. Furthermore, the binary operation $C_A \oplus C_B$ of aggregating cost functions, where $C_A \oplus C_B$ is the function defined by

$$C_A \oplus C_B(x) = \min_{x_A, x_B} C_A(x_A) + C_B(x_B)$$

subject to $x_A + x_B = x$,   (1)

is associative.

(3) It has received the most attention so far in the literature.

(4)   It has a natural hierarchical structure,[6] which makes it easier to relate parallel associative computation to non-computational models of hierarchies.

Section 2.2 outlines some of the available choices when specifying a model of parallel or distributed computation, and we give an example of such a model. Section 2.3 studies efficient computation of a single associative problem, which we refer to as the "one-shot" mode. Here a simple but important theme is already present: Decentralization (parallelization) reduces delay because more operations can be performed concurrently, but it increases communication costs. In Section 2.4, we look at new issues that arise when an organization faces a flow of associative problems that arrive periodically. For example, having to pay managers even when idle creates a scheduling problem and introduces another cost of decentralization. Also, the set of efficient algorithms can change substantially when each problem must be processed in the same way by the same managers.

For both the one-shot and periodic modes, we describe specific results about organizational structure. The organization structure that we infer from a computation procedure is a directed graph in which the nodes are the sources of raw data and the information processing agents. There is an edge from a source to an agent if that agent processes a datum from that source, and there is an edge from one agent to another if the latter processes a message from the former. We call this digraph the *communication graph*. Thus, the organizational structure reflects the micro communication between individual agents.

Such a representation of organizational structure would probably not be of interest if we were not studying associative computation. One reason is that micro communication between individual agents – including each clerk, secretary, manager, and professional in the administrative staff – is not what determines an organizational chart and the decomposition of an organization into divisions and offices. Micro communication in parallel associative computation might be interesting anyway because associative computation is the canonical aggregation of information that occurs in hierarchical structures; even so, a skeptic could argue that the fussing over differences in organizational structure under various assumptions that will be seen in the rest of Section 2 is useful more because it provides practice with parallel computation than because of its specific conclusions about organizational structure.

---

[6] Take $x_1 + x_2 + \cdots + x_n$ and recursively group pairs of objects in parentheses. This defines a binary tree in which the pairs are interior nodes and the children of each node are the two components of the pair.

The second reason concerns tractability. The most common structure seen in this section is a hierarchy (tree), because of the natural hierarchical structure of associative computation. For other classes of problems, the communication is typically much less systematic. It is well known in computer science that a general-purpose parallel computer should not have a hierarchical communication network, because the natural flow of information for most computation problems is not hierarchical and bottlenecks will form at the upper levels if information is forced to flow through a hierarchical network.

2.2 *Parallel and Distributed Computation*

A model of parallel computation has two components:

(1) a model of computation for individual agents; and
(2) a model of how agents communicate and coordinate their computation.

The second item – interaction between agents – is the most interesting aspect of parallel computation. Here are some options the modeler has:

(1) global (shared) versus local (distributed) memory;
(2) broadcast versus networked communication;
(3) synchronous versus asynchronous operation.

In each case, the latter option is more realistic but also more complicated.

When memory is global or shared, all data and partial results are stored in the same memory, to which all the agents have equal access. Communication is then a vacuous concept. When memory is local or distributed, each agent has her own memory, and she can share information in her memory by sending messages to other agents through a communication network.

The difference between networked and broadcast communication is that, in the former, the cost or delay of sending a message may depend on the sender and receivers of the message and these values may depend on the physical topology of the network, whose design may be part of the overall organizational design problem. With broadcast communication, it is still possible to keep track of information flows, but one can do this accounting after designing the algorithms, rather than having to take into account how network costs affect which algorithm is optimal.

Synchronicity of computation means that all agents agree on what time it is, perhaps because their operations are regulated by a single clock. Hence, they can be perfectly coordinated by giving each manager a list of timed instructions.[7] Coordination with asynchronous computation is much more difficult.[8]

Computer scientists often make a distinction between parallel and distributed computation based on the three design issues just described. Parallel processing typically refers to environments in which the processing elements are processors that reside in the same box and for which global memory, broadcast communication, and synchronous computation are reasonable approximations. Distributed computation typically refers to environments in which the processing elements are machines in a network, perhaps spread out over a large distance, and for which local memory, networked communication, and asynchronous computation are important features.

Human computation is even more distributed than computer networks. One aspect of distributed computation that economists have modeled is local memory. This is necessary to capture communication costs and to make the flow of information between agents determinate. Economists have not yet studied models that integrate individual computation and networked communication or that have asynchronous computation.

Consider the following simple model of computation with distributed memory in which the communication costs are the time it takes managers to read and send messages.[9] Each manager has a RAM (random access machine), which is a serial processing model.[10] A RAM has a CPU (central processing unit) and an infinite memory; its capabilities are described by the elementary operations it can perform and the time each operation takes. An elementary operation is some manipulation of its memory, such as reading two numbers, summing them, and storing the answer in another memory register. The RAM represents that manager's brain. Each manager also has another type of memory, called a *buffer*. This represents the manager's in-box or mailbox. A manager communi-

---

[7] This is perfect ex ante coordination. The instruction lists are given before processing starts, and contingencies based on the informational inputs must be written into the instructions.

[8] For example, as shown in Halpern and Moses (1990), synchronicity is roughly equivalent to being able to achieve common knowledge.

[9] The model will not include physical transmission constraints, such as the cost of operating the network and communication latency (time between when a manager sends a message and the message reaches the recipients). Furthermore, the model assumes that sending a message to one person takes the same time as sending a message to many people, that messages do not have to be attended to immediately when they arrive, and that messages have names and can be retrieved from the buffer by their names. See Culler et al. (1993) for a more general model and further discussion of important aspects of parallel computation.

[10] For complexity theory, a RAM is equivalent to a Turing machine.

cates by sending a message from internal memory to the buffer of one or more other managers. The recipients must read these data into their internal memory before operating on them.

For example, suppose manager A knows the qualities of employee 1 and manager B knows the qualities of employee 2, and suppose that manager B will decide which employee should be promoted. Manager A writes a report about the qualities of employee 1 and sends the report to Manager B (*send*). We assume that communication latency is zero, which means that the report immediately arrives in manager B's mailbox. Manager B eventually reads the report (*read*), so that the qualifications of both employees are in her internal memory. She compares the qualifications and determines the name of the employee to promote (*elementary operation*). This name resides in the internal memory of B, who might then write the name on a letter and send the letter to the personnel office (*send*).

The specification of data and elementary operations in this model are at the discretion of the researcher. For example, a datum could be an integer, a real number, or an entire description of an employee or of a project. An operation could be the addition of two integers or real numbers or the ranking of employees. In the case of arithmetic, infinite precision can be a convenient approximation of fixed-precision arithmetic; it allows the researcher to ignore the details of the level of precision, arithmetic overflow, and rounding errors, and it allows the researcher to model computation in standard economics models, which typically are based on functions on the real numbers.[11]

The parameters of this model are:

(1) the elementary internal operations and the time each one takes;
(2) the time it takes to read data from the buffer to the internal memory; and
(3) the time it takes to send a message.

---

[11] One must be careful, however, not to allow operations that neutralize the information processing constraints. For example, to add two pairs of 7-bit integers, one can embed the first pair in the first 8 bits of a two 16-bit integers and the second pair in the second 8 bits of the two 16-bit integers, add the two 16-bit integers, and then extract the sum of the first pair from the first 8 bits of the answer and the sum of the second pair from the second 8 bits of the answer. Hence, if (for simplicity) one ignores limits on the size of integers, it is important not to allow the string concatenation and extraction operations to be done in zero time. Such "computation smuggling" is easily avoided in the models surveyed in this paper, because they involve a limited number of operations. See Mount and Reiter (1990, 1998) for a model of computation on the real numbers that carefully incorporates the continuity restrictions that are required for real computation to approximate discrete computation.

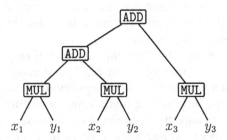

Figure 1. The DAG of a procedure for calculating $(x_1 y_1 + x_2 y_2) + x_3 y_3$ with the elementary operations ADD and MUL.

In applications, one focuses on the constraints that are most relevant to the question at hand. Some models reviewed here consider only computational delay; others consider only communication costs (which include the time it takes to read raw data and simplify the costs of communication between managers).

Without communication delay, the model is equivalent to one with global memory, called a PRAM (parallel random access machine). The PRAM is the simplest model of parallel computation, and it is widely used in theoretical computer science. To compute a problem with a PRAM, the input is written to the shared memory and the managers concurrently perform a sequence of operations on the memory until the memory contains the answer. To describe such computation we need only to state what operations are performed each cycle; the assignment of operations to processors is arbitrary because memory is global.

To fully describe a program or computation procedure, one must specify the list of timed instructions for each agent, including the instructions for reading and sending messages. There is an alternative approach that separates the communication, the exact timing of operations, and the assignment of operations to agents from the sequencing of the elementary operations. The algorithm is represented by a directed acyclic graph (DAG) in which the nodes are elementary operations and sources of data. The immediate predecessors of an elementary operation are its inputs. For example, the DAG of a procedure for calculating $(x_1 y_1 + x_2 y_2) + x_3 y_3$ with the elementary operations ADD and MUL is shown in Figure 1. One obtains a decentralized computation procedure by specifying the agents and the timing of the operations (in computer science this is referred to as *scheduling* or *load balancing*) so that no agent performs two operations concurrently and each operation is executed before its successors in the DAG. This approach is especially simple when communication costs are represented by a weight on each edge that is a cost incurred when the two vertices of the edge are assigned to different agents (or if there are no communication costs at all). This approach is taken in Reiter (1996), in which the elementary operations are referred to as "modules" and in which the DAGs are also a tool for representing the structure of organizations. Related DAGs are also used as a tool in Van Zandt (1996b,e). We will only use DAGs occasionally in this survey in order to illustrate decision procedures.

In serial computation, complexity is measured by space (memory requirements) and, more importantly, run time. The run time measures both how long one has to wait for an answer (delay) and the amount of time the manager or CPU is busy (work). With parallel computation, delay and work are no longer the same and so become two separate measures of complexity. Work is the measure of the managerial costs if the processing agents are paid on an hourly basis and if there are no limits to the number of agents who can be employed at any moment. Otherwise, the number of agents needed for an algorithm (machine size or organization size) is another relevant measure of complexity. Finally, the network costs should also be measured. In summary, rather than the single measure of serial complexity (ignoring memory costs), we have four measures of parallel complexity:

(1) delay;
(2) work (total time agents are busy);
(3) organization size (number of agents); and
(4) network costs.

Our computation model does not have network costs. This leaves three measures of complexity or cost. Organization size we will call the degree of decentralization (parallelization). We will generally not consider it to be costly itself, but instead will focus on how decentralization may reduce delay but increase work.

2.3   One-Shot Associative Computation

We first consider the computation of a single function. One theme is that the decentralization of information processing reduces delay but increases communication costs because the additional managers generate additional messages. Compare this with the models of informational decentralization in the planning and communication mechanism literatures. In the latter, there are agents who are exogenously endowed with private information (e.g., agents who know their own utility, profit, or cost functions). Decentralizing calculations or decisions to these agents can reduce communication costs because the agents no longer have to communicate all their private information to a central office. In contrast, in the batch processing models of this section, agents with no prior private information are hired for the sole purpose of processing information. The tasks of reading the raw data may be distributed among the agents, but the total size of this task does not depend on how many agents are employed. However, the number of messages between the agents does increase with the number of agents who participate in the calculations. The other theme in this section is that efficient procedures are hierarchical but quite irregular.

For associative computation, the relevant parameters in the computation model are the time it takes for an associative operation (d_a), a send (d_s), and a read (d_r). It is easy to show that, if there are communication costs, the communication graph of efficient algorithms are hierarchical and each manager that is not the root sends a single message to her immediate superiors. Therefore, there are $n - 1$ messages, and the managerial time involved in communicating each message is $d_s + d_r$. In addition, there are n reads of raw data, $n - 1$ associative operations, and 1 send of the final result. Hence, the work when there are q managers is

$$(n-1)d_a + nd_r + d_s + (q-1)(d_s + d_r) = (n-1)(d_a + d_r) + q(d_s + d_r).$$

$$(2)$$

As long as $d_s + d_r > 0$, resource costs are an increasing affine function of the degree of parallelization.[12]

However, in the PRAM, only the associative operations involve delay ($d_s = d_r = 0$) and hence the processor time is $n - 1$, whatever the degree of parallelization![13] The efficient algorithms for associative computation with a PRAM are illustrated in Figure 2 for finding a maximum. When computation begins, the data are stored in the memory. Each cycle, the data or previous results are assigned in pairs to processors, and each of these processors computes the maximum of the two assigned numbers. If there is one processor for each pair of data or partial result, the number of partial results can be reduced by half each cycle. Hence, with $[n/2]$ processors, the delay is $[\log_2 n]$.

---

[12] Keren and Levhari (1979) and Radner (1993) measure resources by the degree of parallelization, rather than by the number of operations. The degree of parallelization is a poor measure of resources, but the set of procedures that are efficient with respect to delay and managerial resources is the same for both measures. This is because the number of operations is a constant plus an increasing function of the degree of parallelization. See Meagher and Van Zandt (1998).

[13] This is not true of other classes of problems, where parallelization increases resource costs even with the PRAM. Because of this, and because the parallel computation time is $O(\log n)$, associative computation is considered highly amenable to parallelization.

Cycle   Operations

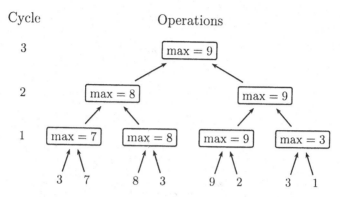

Figure 2. Associative computation by a PRAM via a balanced binary tree (Gibbons and Rytter 1988, Fig. 1.2).

The DAG of the computation is a balanced binary tree, but note that the nodes represent operations rather than processors. Hence, we cannot interpret the tree in Figure 2 as the hierarchical structure of the organization. Furthermore, the flow of information is indeterminate with the PRAM because memory is global. In each cycle, the operations performed can be assigned arbitrarily to the processors. For example, in Figure 2, a processor might perform the leftmost operation (max{3,7}) in cycle 1 and then the right-hand operation (max{9,3}) in cycle 2. On the other hand, this indeterminacy means that it is possible to assign each operation to a different processor, in which case the DAG is also the communication graph and hence the organizational structure is a balanced binary tree.

Suppose instead that reading is the only operation that takes time. That is, $d_a = d_s = 0$ and $d_r = 1$. For parallel batch processing, this is equivalent to a computation model studied by Radner (1993; henceforth Rad93), which is like an adding machine: Internal memory is limited to one register, and in one cycle a manager can read a number and either (i) store it in the register or (ii) add it to the register.[14] The model captures both that the time it takes a single manager to compute increases linearly with problem size and that communication is costly.

[14] Because operations (i) and (ii) take the same time, it may appear that the associative operation takes no time and that reading is the only costly operation. However, this conclusion is deceptive. If we were to use this model to compute multiple comparisons of the same set of projects, it would not be possible for a manager to read in ten projects in ten cycles and then in zero time calculate the best of every subset of the ten projects, because only one project can be stored at a time.

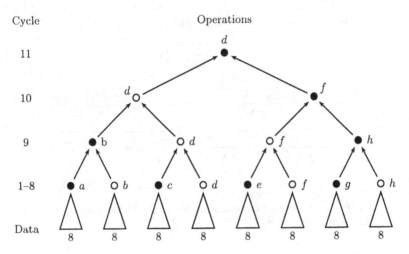

Figure 3. The DAG of a Rad93 associative algorithm. There are 64 reports, 8 managers $\{a, \ldots, h\}$, and a delay of 11. The nodes correspond to operations and are labeled with the manager who performs the operation. Nodes are black if they are the last operation for the manager. For example, at the end of cycle 8, managers a and b each have processed eight raw items. Then manager a passes his result to manager b, who in cycle 9 adds it to her previous result (or performs some other associative operation). Then manager b passes the result to manager d, etc.

Recall that the work depends only on the number of managers. To minimize delay for a fixed number of managers, all the managers should start working at the same time and then finish as close together as possible. If all managers could start and stop processing at the same time, then the delay would just be the total number of operations divided by the number of managers. This is not possible, since as information is aggregated there are fewer and fewer partial results, until only one associative operation remains to be done in the last cycle. However, as shown in Rad93, the raw data should be processed first, by all the managers, and then the partial results should be aggregated as quickly as possible.

Figure 3 shows such an algorithm for 64 reports. The data is divided up evenly among the managers, who process their 8 raw items in 8 cycles. In 3 more cycles, the partial results are aggregated. The total delay is 11, there are 8 managers, and there are 71 operations.

In Figure 3, as in Figure 2 (which shows the efficient associative computation with a PRAM), the nodes in the hierarchy correspond to operations rather than managers. In the PRAM, the assignment of managers to operations is arbitrary (as long as a manager does not have two tasks

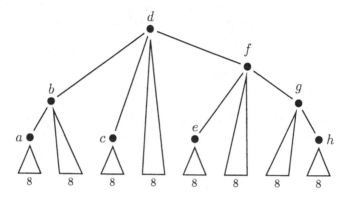

Figure 4. The communication graph of the computation procedure in Figure 3.

at the same time), because all managers have the same access to any data that resides in the global memory. However, when there are communication costs, as in Rad93, the communication graphs are determinate. The communication graph for the Rad93 model is shown in Figure 4.

Although actual organizations are typically not regular, they also do not resemble the Rad93 hierarchies, in which all managers process the same amount of raw data. It is interesting that this irregularity would arise in a model with homogeneous managers and operations. The irregularity may actually be partially attributable to this homogeneity. Most information processing involves a variety of tasks. Specialization can be used to match innate abilities with tasks and to reduce the amount of time managers must spend learning tasks. This point is made in Bolton and Dewatripont (1994), which is discussed in Section 2.4.4.

When the raw items are divided evenly among the q managers, leaving $n \bmod q$ items left over, each manager has $\lfloor n/q \rfloor$ items to process. It then takes $\lfloor \log_2(q + n \bmod q) \rfloor$ cycles to aggregate the leftover items and the q partial results. Therefore, the total delay is

$$\left\lfloor \frac{n}{q} \right\rfloor + \left\lfloor \log_2 \left(q + n \bmod q \right) \right\rfloor.$$

The lowest attainable delay is $\lceil \log_2 n \rceil + 1$, which requires $\lfloor n/2 \rfloor$ managers.

Even though communication is costly in this model, the initial returns to parallelization are striking. The serial processing time when $n = 10,000$ is 10,000. Parallel processing time with two managers is 5,001,[15] which is

---

[15] Each manager computes the best of 5,000 projects in 5,000 cycles, and then one manager sends her result to the other, who compares it with his own.

little more than half the serial processing time, but resource costs increase by only a small fraction, from 10,000 to 10,001. Communication costs are more serious when delay is closer to the lower bound. If the 10,000 items are processed by 250 managers, then delay is 12 and there are 10,249 operations. If they are processed by 500 managers, the delay is 11 and there are 10,499 operations. It is impossible to achieve a lower delay than this.

If we impose the restriction that the hierarchies be balanced, then the general model is equivalent to Keren and Levhari (1979), who study balanced hierarchies that do some kind of information processing. The delay of a manager with span s is equal to $s - 1 + \alpha$, where α is a measure of communication overhead. For associative computation, the delay of a manager with span s is

$$sd_r + (s-1)d_a + d_s = (s-1)(d_r + d_a) + (d_r + d_s),$$

which is equal to $s - 1 + \alpha$ if we normalize $d_r + d_a = 1$ and define $\alpha = d_r + d_s$. For the Rad93 model, $\alpha = 1$.

Here are some properties of efficient hierarchies in Keren and Levhari (1979).[16]

(1) The span of control is weakly increasing moving down the hierarchy.

(2) The span of control is constant in the efficient hierarchy with the lowest delay and is independent of the problem size.

(3) The span of control is strictly increasing in the hierarchies that do not have the lowest delay.

2.4   *Periodic Associative Computation*

2.4.1. Periodic Versus One-Shot Computation. In Section 2.3, we looked at the computation of a single associative problem. In this section, we look at the computation of a series of unrelated associative problems of fixed size that arrive periodically. This is a more realistic representation of computation in long-lived organizations, such as a firm that periodically reallocates resources or updates its production plans. However, we are making two important simplifications.

(1) We assume that the arrival rate is deterministic and that each problem is of the same size, whereas in reality the information

---

[16] Keren and Levhari (1979) derive these results using a formulation with a continuum of tiers that is not always a good approximation, but the results can also be derived using the discrete model. See Van Zandt (1995).

flow may vary with the state of the environment. How the stochastic arrival of problems would affect the results reported in these two sections is an open question.

(2)   We assume that the problems are unrelated, but when a resource allocation or production plan is updated, previous calculations are inputs in the computation of the new allocation or plan (see e.g. Van Zandt and Radner 1996).

The rate at which problems arrive and are computed is called the *throughput*. Higher throughput is another design objective in the periodic model, so that efficiency of computational procedures is with respect to managerial costs, delay, and throughput.

Here is an illustration of why throughput is important. Suppose, for simplicity, that each time the resource allocation or production plan is updated, the data is gathered at the beginning of the computation. The new allocation or plan is based on data that is d cycles old, where d is the computational delay. The allocation or plan is updated $1/\theta$ cycles later, where θ is the throughput. Hence, the age of the data upon which the current allocation or plan is based ranges from d to $d + 1/\theta$. Because the value of information decays, it is advantageous both to increase the throughput and to decrease the delay.

If managers are paid by the hour, then resources in the periodic model are measured by the number of manager-hours per problem, as in the one-shot model. Suppose also that each time a problem arrives, the organization puts together a network of managers to solve it. Then the problems are computationally independent, and the organization will simply use the efficient one-shot algorithm to process each problem. The organization can keep up with any throughput by assembling more networks. Each problem is processed hierarchically, although the organization as a whole is not hierarchical.

Periodic computation becomes interesting under either of the following two assumptions.

(1)   *Managers are salaried*: When idle, such as between problems, they must still be paid. In Section 2.4.2, we will see that this creates a complicated scheduling problem and that idle time increases with parallelization, but the structure of the efficient hierarchies is not much different from those in the one-shot mode.

(2)   *Procedures must be stationary*: Each problem must be processed by the same network of managers following the same algorithm. In Sections 2.4.3 and 2.4.4, we will see that the stationarity assumption can lead to more regular hierarchies for the follow-

ing reason. The manager with the largest workload is the bottleneck that determines the throughput, so if throughput is an important criterion relative to wages and delay then the managers' workload will be more uniform than in the efficient one-shot networks, in which the top manager has the largest workload.

2.4.2. Periodic Model with Salaried Managers. Let's examine whether assuming that managers are salaried leads to stationary or regular hierarchies in the Rad93 model of computation. When managers are salaried, the organization must pay managers even when they are idle between problems. Hence, the organization should schedule the managers (assign managers to problems) with the goal of minimizing idle time. This can affect the way each problem is computed, particularly when throughput is low (when throughput is low, there is more time between the arrival of problems and hence greater possible idle time). This scheduling problem is more difficult when the problems are processed by separate irregular hierarchies such as the efficient one-shot hierarchies in Rad93, because managers work different amounts of time. One might conjecture that the scheduling problem will lead to more regular hierarchies.

For example, a uniform hierarchy, for which the throughput is the inverse of the span, has no idle time. The class of uniform hierarchies is too limited to allow a trade-off between delay and managerial costs for fixed throughput. Rad93 proposes a generalization of uniform hierarchies, called "preprocessing/overhead trees" (PPO), that do allow this trade-off. Imagine that we start with a uniform hierarchy with a span of 4, and then reduce the number of tiers, increasing only the span of the managers in the bottom tier. For example, if we eliminate two tiers, then the span of the bottom tier increases to 64. To maintain the former throughput of 1/4, we replicate the bottom tier 16 times, so that one bottom-tier group finishes every 4 cycles. There is also no idle time in this hierarchy. Fewer managers process each cohort of data, thereby reducing communication costs, but the delay increases by 52 cycles. (The bottom tier in the PPO has a delay of 64 cycles, whereas that tier plus the two that were eliminated have a delay of 12 in the uniform hierarchy.) Processing by the bottom tier is not stationary, but the organization is a balanced hierarchy.

Although these PPO hierarchies do fairly well, Van Zandt (forthcoming) shows that they are not efficient. In the efficient procedures, each network that processes a problem is very similar to the efficient one-shot networks, except that each network has more managers than it needs to achieve the desired delay. Having more managers increases communication costs, but it also creates slack that can be used to adjust the workloads of the managers so that they are multiples of the time between arrivals of cohorts. If a manager's workload is a multiple of the time between arrivals of cohorts then she is never idle; when she finishes with one cohort, she can immediately start the same task with some other cohort. Although each manager's task in the processing of each cohort does not change over time, the composition of the networks does change because tasks have different lengths and managers that finish earlier than other managers in their current network join the network that forms to process the next cohort that arrives, rather than waiting for everybody in their network to finish.

Hence, the conjecture that scheduling problems, by themselves, lead to more regular hierarchies is false. However, perhaps one of the following extensions would increase regularly.

(1) We can take into account the cost of communication channels and the latency of communication between distant senders and receivers. Because of the rotation of managers among networks in Van Zandt (forthcoming), managers may send messages to many other managers over time. Contrast this with hierarchies, where there is one communication channel for each manager except the root.

(2) We can have the problems be related. It may then be advantageous for managers to save partial results from their computation of one problem for the computation of the next problem.

(3) We can have the arrival of problems be stochastic. The scheduling of managers is complicated in Van Zandt (forthcoming), and it might be especially difficult to control queues and keep idle time low when arrivals are stochastic.

These are open questions that we do not pursue here. However, in Sections 2.4.3 and 2.4.4, we ask whether imposing stationarity leads to more regular hierarchies. Stationarity can be motivated by unmodeled communication costs that increase with the number of links between agents. Bolton and Dewatripont (1994) were the first to address this question, but we begin by examining the implications of stationarity for the Rad93 model.

2.4.3. Periodic Model with Stationarity Procedures. Suppose that we impose stationarity in the Rad93 model of computation. With stationarity, throughput cannot be increased through replication and so the throughput criterion has a strong effect on the set of efficient procedures.

Assume that managers in a stationary procedure may be idle between problems but are not idle in the middle of a problem. Let w_i be the number of cycles manager i is busy processing each cohort, which we call the manager's workload. Let $\bar{w}$ be the maximum workload. Then the throughput is $1/\bar{w}$. That is, the manager with the largest workload is the bottleneck that determines the throughput.

Fix the throughput θ. Suppose that n is a power of $1/\theta$, so that there is a uniform hierarchy with span $1/\theta$. We now show that this uniform hierarchy is efficient with respect to managerial costs and throughput. Whether managers are hourly or salaried, the only way to reduce managerial costs is to reduce the number of managers in the network. Since the workload in the uniform hierarchy was distributed evenly, the workload of at least one manager must go up after the number of managers is reduced. Hence, the throughput falls. The only way to increase the throughput is to decrease the average workload, but this requires additional managers and hence increases managerial costs.

However, uniform hierarchies are not the only ones that are efficient with respect to managerial costs and throughput. Any hierarchy in which the managers have equal workloads is efficient. For example, suppose $n = 36$. With 7 managers, we can attain a throughput of one problem per 6 cycles with any of the three networks shown in Figure 5. The bottom-left hierarchy is like a Rad93 efficient one-shot network, except that the data is distributed so that managers have equal workloads. The delay is only 9, compared to 12 for the other two hierarchies. Thus, if we also minimize delay, then this Rad93 hierarchy dominates the other two.

There is a general proposition behind this example (see Van Zandt 1996c for the proof).

Proposition 1. *If delay* d *and throughput* θ *can be achieved by a stationary hierarchy with* q *managers, and if*

$$\left\lceil \frac{q+n-1}{q} \right\rceil \geq \lfloor log_2 \, q \rfloor, \tag{3}$$

then there is a stationary Rad93-type hierarchy with q *managers and with delay of at most* d *and throughput of at least* θ.

This result does not mean that stationarity does not affect the regularity of hierarchies. A *Rad93-type* hierarchy is one in which the aggregation of partial results is the same as in the efficient one-shot Rad93 network (specifically, it is an MS network in Van Zandt forthcoming), but the raw data may be distributed unevenly among the managers. The data is distributed in the efficient stationary hierarchies in order to

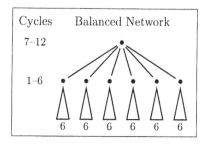

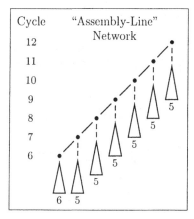

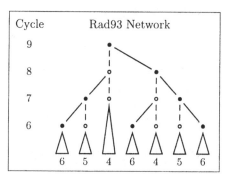

Figure 5. Three computation procedures with 7 managers and a throughput of 1/6, for $n = 36$ and the Rad93 model of computation. The Rad93 network has the shortest delay (9).

equalize the workloads of the managers. Since the upper-level managers have the most postprocessing operations, they also process the least amount of raw data. When the inequality (3) is not satisfied, some of the upper-level managers do not process any raw data at all.

2.4.4. Returns to Specialization. The model of computation in Bolton and Dewatripont (1994; henceforth BD94) explicitly focuses on the time it takes to read raw data or messages. In one interpretation of their model, a single manager (center) must read in all the data, because aggregation of information is impossible. However, it is possible to convert raw data to a format that makes it easier to read, because irrelevant information is omitted or because the data is rewritten in an efficient internal protocol. It takes one cycle to read in a raw datum and

$$d(m) = \lambda + d_r m$$

cycles to read a message with m transcribed data, where λ is an overhead cost of receiving information from a subordinate and d_r is the time it takes to read a transcribed datum ($d_r \leq 1$).

If the center does all the processing, then the center's workload and the delay are n. The center's workload can be reduced by decentralizing the processing of raw data. For example, if the center only reads transcribed data and if the center has s immediate subordinates, then the center's workload is $s\lambda + d_r n$. If the overhead of communicating with each subordinate is not too high (λ close to 0) and if reading transcribed data is easier than reading raw data ($d_r < 1$), then this workload is less than n. If $d_r = 1$ then we have a degenerate case; subordinates cannot decrease the workload of the center and hence information processing cannot be decentralized.

If the hierarchy has more than two tiers then some transcribed data passes through an intermediate manager before reaching the center. This relaying uses the intermediate manager's time but does not reduce the time it takes the center to read transcribed data. Hence, a two-tier hierarchy is sufficient for decentralizing the transcription of raw data. However, to achieve high throughput, each transcriber should have a small workload and hence many managers are needed to transcribe the data. In a two-tier hierarchy, all the transcribers report to the center. The communication overhead of λ per subordinate can be decentralized by adding more tiers to the hierarchy, so that there are many transcribers but the center has only a few subordinates. If $\lambda = 0$ then we again have a degenerate case; there is no communication overhead and hence efficient hierarchies have at most two tiers.

This model of computation can also be interpreted as a generalization of the Rad93 model of associative computation. If we drop the restriction in Rad93 on the size of the internal memory (this restriction has not been important so far), then the model of computation in Rad93 is isomorphic to the one in BD94, with $d_r = 0$ and $\lambda = 1$. If $d_r = 0$ and $\lambda < 1$, then BD94 differs from Rad93 only in that reading a raw datum is more time-consuming than reading an item communicated from another manager. However, if $d_r > 0$ then this cannot be a model of those associative operations, such as addition or comparisons, for which the output has the same informational size as each input.

In BD94, periodic computation is studied and a partial characterization is given of stationary networks that are efficient with respect to throughput and managerial costs but not to delay. The authors thus concentrate on the effect of the throughput criterion. We have motivated the importance of throughput by the assumption that the network must be stationary. The true motivation of BD94 is quite different, but we shall defer discussion of it.

In measuring managerial costs, the authors assume that the managers are hourly workers. With the Rad93 model of computation, the set of efficient stationary networks is the same whether managers are salaried or hourly workers, because all hierarchies with the same number of managers have the same number of operations. However, in the BD94 model of computation, the number of operations depends on how many managers data passes through, at least if $d_r > 0$.

In BD94, several results are presented that show that efficient networks tend to be more regular than Rad93 networks when $d_r > 0$. Here are some of these results.

(1) Proposition 4 of BD94 states that, for any manager, the size of the smallest message he receives is as large as the largest message that any of his subordinates receives. Note that the Rad93 networks do not satisfy this condition. For example, in the network in Figure 4, the root manager (manager 4) receives a message of size 8 from manager 3, while manager 6 receives a message of size 16 from manager 7. The condition is violated even when data is redistributed to equalize the workloads.

(2) Tiers are assigned so that managers who only process raw data are in the same tier, those whose subordinates only process raw data are in the next tier, and so on. Then managers in the bottom tier only send messages to managers in the next two tiers. The Rad93 networks do not satisfy this condition either.

(3) When a uniform hierarchy exists, it has strictly lower managerial costs than any other network with the same throughput. Thus, our Proposition 1 does not hold for their model of computation with $d_r > 0$. For example, suppose $d_r = \lambda = 1/12$. Then all the managers in the uniform hierarchy in Figure 5 have the same workload. The data will have to be redistributed to equalize the workloads in the other two networks, but let's first compare the number of operations as the networks are shown in the figure. The number of operations is n plus λ times the number of messages, plus d_r times the total size of the messages. The same amount of raw data is processed, and the same number of messages are sent, in the three networks. Differences are thus due to the size of the messages. In the uniform network, the total size of the messages is 36, in the Rad93 network the total is 61, and in the assembly-line network the total is 111. These differences become larger if we attempt to equalize the workloads, which involves shifting raw data from upper-level managers to lower-level managers. Hence, the Rad93 and assembly-line networks are strictly inferior to the uniform hierarchy.

Now let's examine the real story behind BD94's interest in throughput. The authors are actually looking for stationary networks that minimize the managerial costs per problem. This is roughly the design problem of an organization with a large flow of problems, where delay is not important and the organization can replicate stationary networks in order to attain the necessary throughput. If that were the end of the story then the best stationary network to replicate is the one with a single manager, since parallelization just introduces communication costs. However, BD94 assumes that the speed at which operations are executed in a stationary network increases with the network's throughput, because the throughput is the rate at which managers repeat the same operations; BD94 calls these productivity gains "returns to specialization." Thus, while parallelization increases communication costs, it also increases returns to specialization and so may result in a net decrease in resource costs. A necessary condition for a network to minimize managerial costs per problem is that it be efficient with respect to gross managerial costs and throughput.

3   Computation of Resource Allocations

In this section, we present and compare applications of three different information processing paradigms – team theory, decentralized batch processing, and decentralized real-time control – to the same decision problem: resource allocation without externalities. This is the most classic of all economic decision problems, and is fundamental in both nonmarket organizations such as firms and in the variety of market institutions.

3.1   Hierarchical Decomposition of Resource Allocations

We begin by stating the resource allocation problem and describing a hierarchical decomposition property.

Given a total quantity x_R of a resource, the problem is to choose an allocation $\{x_i\}_{i \in I}$ of the resource to a set I of n households, firms, divisions, shops, agencies or projects in order to solve

$$\min_{\{x_i\}_{i \in I}} \sum_{i \in I} C_i(x_i)$$

$$\text{subject to } \sum_{i \in I} x_i = x_R. \tag{4}$$

Here x_i is a transfer to agent i that could represent input, output, net trades or consumption. We assume that x_i is scalar to simplify notation, but there could instead be several resources that are allocated. We refer to C_i as i's cost function and we call each agent a shop, but we could equivalently have written this as a problem of maximizing the sum of utilities or profits. The cost, profit, or utility functions could reflect costs, sales, endowments, and preferences. The parameters in the problem are the shops' cost functions and the total resource vector. Assume that

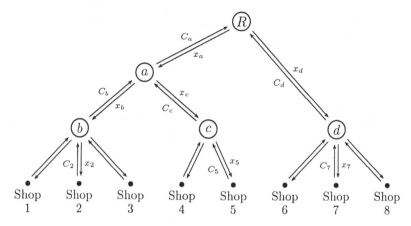

Figure 6. Hierarchical decomposition of the resource allocation problem without externalities. Cost functions are *aggregated* through an *upward* flow of information. Allocations are *disaggregated* through a *downward* flow of information.

allocating resources involves calculating the values of the shops' allocations.[17]

An important property of the resource allocation problem without externalities is that it can be hierarchically decomposed into similar (but smaller) problems whose solutions are independent. Consider the hierarchy in Figure 6. The terminal nodes are shops. Call the internal nodes managers. If manager c learns the cost functions of shops 4 and 5, he can allocate resources to these shops to minimize their total costs. He can also calculate the value of this minimization problem. For each amount x_c of resources manager c can allocate, let $C_c(x_c)$ be the minimized costs of the shops under him. Call this manager c's aggregate cost function. It is the lack of externalities that makes the function independent of resources allocated elsewhere in the hierarchy. Similarly, manager b can learn the cost functions of shops 1, 2, and 3 and calculate her aggregate cost function $C_b(x_b)$.

Now suppose manager a has an amount x_a of the resource to allocate to shops 1–5. He could learn the cost functions of shops 1–5 and allocate resources directly to these shops, and thereby also determine his aggregate cost function. Alternatively, he could learn his immediate subordinates' aggregate cost functions, C_b and C_c, and allocate resources to man-

[17] We thereby ignore the details of the physical distribution of resources, which is tied up with some subtle computational issues.

agers b and c in order to minimize the sum of their aggregate costs. Managers b and c then disaggregate their allocations by allocating the resources to their own immediate subordinates, as described previously. This resource allocation problem is such that the direct procedure and the indirect procedure result in the same allocations for the shops and the same aggregate cost function C_a for manager a.

For a general hierarchy $\{I, J, R, \{\Theta_j\}_{j \in J}\}$ as defined in Appendix A, the aggregate cost function C_j of manager $j \in J$ (whose direct subordinates are Θ_j and whose subordinate shops are θ_j) is given by

$$C_j(x_j) = \min_{\{x_i\}_{i \in \theta_j}} \sum_{i \in \theta_j} C_i(x_i)$$

subject to $\sum_{i \in \theta_j} x_i = x_j$.

The decomposition property means that

$$C_j(x_j) = \min_{\{x_k\}_{k \in \Theta_j}} \sum_{k \in \Theta_j} C_k(x_k)$$

subject to $\sum_{k \in \Theta_j} x_k = x_j$.

Furthermore,

$$C_j = \bigoplus_{i \in \theta_j} C_i = \bigoplus_{k \in \Theta_j} \left(\bigoplus_{i \in \theta_k} C_i \right) = \bigoplus_{k \in \Theta_j} C_k,$$

where $\oplus$ is the associative binary operation of aggregation of cost functions that was defined in Section 2.1.

This suggests the following hierarchical procedures for allocating resources. Starting at the bottom of the hierarchy, managers recursively calculate their aggregate cost functions and send these to their immediate superiors. Then, starting with the root manager, managers recursively allocate resources received from their immediate superiors to their immediate subordinates in order to minimize the total aggregate costs of their subordinates. The upward flow of cost functions and downward flow of resource allocations is also depicted in Figure 6.

Note that this decomposition of the resource allocation problem is quite different from the decomposition of functions into elementary operations. The latter is very fine-grained, and the elementary operations bear no resemblance to the overall decision problem. In contrast, the former is a coarse-grained decomposition that breaks the decision problem up into smaller recognizable decision problems. Organizational structure in terms of decision-making units that may contain many information processing agents is closely related to such coarse-grained decomposition of the firm's decision problem. There has been much research on such decomposition of decision problems and decentralization of decision making, beginning with Arrow and Hurwicz (1960) and Dantzig and Wolfe (1960); see Van Zandt (1996a) for a brief survey. Most of this literature has studied iterative mechanisms that are meant to be an alternative to the communication of entire cost functions that occurs here. However, the literature on aggregation/disaggregation methods (see Rogers et al. 1991 for a survey) in operations research does use such hierarchical decompositions of decision problems.

This hierarchical procedure yields the same allocations as the direct procedure in which a single manager allocates resources to the shops. However, there is no apparent advantage to the hierarchical procedure. We need to introduce computation and communication constraints so that hierarchical procedures permit advantageous decentralization of the information processing tasks.

3.2   Team Theory

3.2.1. Overview. Team theory, although not described in this way by Marschak and Radner (1972), is the design and analysis of perfect-recall extensive-form games in which the players have the same payoffs. Leaving aside for the moment what we mean by *design*, the *analysis* of a fixed game involves the characterization of the strategy profile that maximizes the expected payoff.[18] This is not conventional single-person decision theory in disguise, because if we treat all players as the same person then we obtain an extensive form (a decision tree) that may violate perfect recall. However, it truly differentiates itself from single-person statistical decision theory only when there is asymmetric and nonnested information about chance moves.

The simplest interesting class of problems is when there are n players who observe private signals about the state of nature and then simultaneously choose actions. This is a Bayesian game in which players have the same payoffs for every realization of the state and every action profile. The difference between this and a single-person static Bayesian decision problem is that, in the latter, the problem is to choose a plan (mapping from states to actions) subject to a single measurability constraint (the plan must be measurable with respect to the decision maker's information); in the former, the problem is to choose n plans and each must satisfy its own measurability constraint. The n-person problem

---

[18] This profile is one of the Nash equilibria, but there may be others, such as the Pareto inferior equilibria in coordination games.

can be reduced to a conventional single-person problem with a single measurability constraint only when all n players observe the same information.

A richer example is the resource allocation model studied in various forms in Radner (1986, originally published in 1972), Groves and Radner (1972), Arrow and Radner (1979), Groves and Hart (1982), and Groves (1983). The basic model in these papers has n production units controlled by production managers and a central office controlled by a resource manager. The profits of each production unit are a function of a local decision variable controlled by the unit's manager, of the amount of a resource received from the production manager, and of a local random parameter. The amount of the resource that can be allocated by the resource manager is a random parameter for unconstrained optimal decisions. The resource allocation should be a function of all the production unit's parameters and of the available resource, and the production managers should know their allocation before choosing their local decision variables. However, the extensive forms studied in the papers just listed do not allow such pooling of information. For example, the production managers may have to choose decision variables before learning the value of their resource allocations, or the resource manager may have to allocate resources based on incomplete information transmitted by the production units.

Since the players in such games have common interests, one may wonder why they do not first share their information. The answer is that such communication may be costly, and it may even be impossible to communicate fully and noiselessly. Here is where the design of the extensive form enters in. Changing the number of agents, the information that agents acquire, the communication between agents, and the control of action variables defines different multi-player extensive-form games for the same underlying decision problem.[19] These games differ not only in the maximum expected gross payoff that can be achieved but also in the costs of communication and information acquisition. The design of a team decision procedure involves not simply the specification of strategies for a fixed extensive form; it also involves the specification of the extensive form itself.[20]

---

[19] Given several extensive forms, it is possible to make these into subtrees of a grand extensive form in which there are initial nodes that choose one of the subtrees by specifying the pattern of communication and so forth. However, this is mixing up the design (which takes place on the initial nodes) and the implementation (which takes place in the subtrees) of the decision procedures.

[20] Much of the research that has studied organizational design has done so by comparing a few information structures or decision rules for a fixed set of agents. See, for example,

The sampling and communication costs that can be incorporated into team theory have more to do with bounded rationality than is often thought, which is why team theory appears in this survey. The cost of using information about the environment is not simply the cost of collecting the information, but also the human cost of processing and understanding the information. The cost of communication within an organization includes the receiver's processing cost and also the sender's cost of formulating the message (e.g., transferring information from the brain to paper). In a typical organization, these human processing costs are much larger than transmission costs, and so a model that includes these costs does capture some of the consequences of bounded rationality in team decision problems.

Although it is not necessary for a model to distinguish between information acquisition and transmission costs and information processing costs in order to claim that it is capturing the latter, it is possible for team theory models to make this distinction. For example, the cost of sampling or acquiring information does not depend on how many people use the information, whereas information processing costs do. This means that a model of a firm in which there is a cost for each manager that uses information is more accurate for information processing costs than for sampling costs. Another example is that the cost of transmitting ten messages is the same whether these all go to one person or whether each goes to a different person, but if there are bounds on the amount of information a single person can process (due to unmodeled constraints on the time that can elapse before decisions must be made or information becomes obsolete), then one person may not be able to process the ten messages even though ten people may be able to process one message each.

It is for this reason that it is possible to construct team theory models with an endogenous number of information processing agents. If there were an unboundedly rational agent, then it would be optimal to construct a team with just one such agent who receives any information that is acquired and who controls all actions. However, if agents are bounded in the amount of information they can process, then hiring more agents is a way to bring more information to bear on the decisions. This is exactly what happens in Geanakoplos and Milgrom (1991), which we study in Sections 3.2.2 and 3.2.3.

So far, we have presumed that team theory can incorporate only communication constraints and not computation constraints. It is possible to

Beckmann (1958), McGuire (1961), Radner (1961), Groves and Radner (1972), Cremer (1980), Aoki (1986), Marschak (1986), Radner (1986), and Itoh (1987). An exception is Geanakoplos and Milgrom (1991), studied in Sections 3.2.2 and 3.2.3.

impose computation constraints on strategies for a given extensive form, and this possibility is mentioned in Marschak and Radner (1972). However, team theory developed without such constraints and hence has had the principle of statistical optimality of strategies once the extensive form is specified, without further constraints on or costs imputed to strategies. After 40 years, it is best to leave the term "team theory" for this approach.[21] Nevertheless, as seen in Section 3.4.2, it is possible to use team theory as a tool for representing the structure of computation procedures in models with computation constraints.

3.2.2. Resource Allocation via Pure Disaggregation. Team theory can incorporate both implicit and explicit constraints on the information processing capacity of individual agents. As an example of implicit constraints, Cremer (1980) studies a quadratic version of the resource allocation problem and characterizes the optimal grouping of shops when resources can only be allocated within groups of a fixed size. The story is that any manager who allocates resources has the capacity to do so for only a fixed number of shops. As an example of explicit constraints, suppose that, in an extension of Cremer (1980), information about shops is available as noisy signals of the shops' cost parameters. A manager has the capacity to process a fixed number of signals, but can compute any statistically optimal decision rule conditional on this information. One could characterize how many shops should be assigned to each manager and which signals a manager should observe.

Geanakoplos and Milgrom (1991; henceforth GM91) is a resource allocation model incorporating explicit constraints roughly like those just described. However, rather than just looking at the allocations to groups of shops that are each coordinated by a single manager, GM91 considers hierarchical allocation procedures similar to those described in Section 3.1. Unlike the hierarchical procedures in that section, in which the hierarchies both aggregate costs and disaggregate resource allocations, the GM91 hierarchies only disaggregate allocations, and this downward flow of allocations is the only communication between the managers. Any information the managers acquire about shop costs, including aggregate cost information (if available), comes from external sources. Manager j is endowed with the capacity to acquire one information structure in a set Φ_j of feasible information structures, and receives a wage w_j. The organization design problem is to choose a set of managers, arrange them in a hierarchy, and select recursive informa-

---

[21] This term is sometimes used more generally for any group decision model without incentive problems, which would include all the articles discussed in this survey.

tion acquisition and allocation rules so as to minimize expected shop costs plus managerial costs.

Let's first illustrate how multi-tier hierarchies and the resulting decentralization of information processing and decision making allow the organization to bring more information to bear on the resource allocation problem. Suppose that, for any collection of shops, the aggregate cost function for those shops is exogenously available. However, each manager can only read three such cost functions. A single manager cannot allocate resources to nine shops without error because doing so would require reading nine cost functions. However, the organization can employ four managers, and arrange them in the top two tiers of a three-tier uniform hierarchy, such that each manager has a span of three. This hierarchy can allocate resources without error, because each manager must read only three cost or aggregate cost functions.

The general organization design problem is potentially very complicated, even for a fixed hierarchy. When a manager receives an allocation from her immediate superior, the allocation conveys some of her superior's information, and the manager must know her superior's information structure and decision rules in order to use this information optimally. Furthermore, when the manager allocates resources to her own immediate subordinates, she must consider what information her subordinates have and then take into account that her allocation conveys information and so affects her subordinates' decisions to acquire information. Even when the information structure is fixed and is such that each manager's information about shops in her division is a sufficient statistic for her superior's information about these shops, a manager's optimal decision depends on the information acquired by her subordinates. For example, other things equal, it may be better for a manager to allocate more resources to those immediate subordinates with the most information.

There are two features of GM91 that get around these complications. The first is that the authors recursively derive decision rules, starting at the bottom of the hierarchy, that would be statistically optimal if the allocation received by each manager were uninformative (even though the information structure thus generated may not have this property). The second is that the authors assume that the cost functions are quadratic:[22]

---

[22] We have dropped a constant term that does not affect the allocation problem. Furthermore, Cremer (1980), Aoki (1986), and Geanakoplos and Milgrom (1991) study the multi-good case, but this generalization is not important for GM91. Derivations of the multi-good versions of the formulas that appear in this section can be found in Geanakoplos and Milgrom (1991) and Van Zandt (1996c).

$$C_i(x_i, \gamma_i) = b_i(x_i - \gamma_i)^2, \tag{5}$$

where b_i is a known constant and γ_i is a random variable that is called shop i's cost parameter.

These quadratic cost functions have a very simple aggregation property. The aggregate cost function of division $j \in J$ is

$$C_j(x_j, \gamma_j) \equiv b_j(x_j - \gamma_j),$$

where

$$\gamma_j \equiv \sum_{i \in \theta_j} \gamma_i \quad \text{and} \quad b_j \equiv \left(\sum_{i \in \theta_j} b_i^{-1} \right)^{-1};$$

γ_j is called j's aggregate cost parameter. The decomposition of the aggregation of cost functions takes the following form:

$$\gamma_j = \sum_{k \in \Theta_j} \gamma_k \quad \text{and} \quad b_j = \left(\sum_{k \in \Theta_j} b_k^{-1} \right)^{-1}.$$

Consider first the decision rule of a manager $j \in J$ whose subordinates are all shops. Because j's decision rule presumes that j's allocation x_j is uninformative, the fact that there is a hierarchy above j is unimportant and the derivation of j's allocation rule and information acquisition rule is the same as if this were a single-person decision problem under uncertainty. Fix j's allocation x_j and information $\phi_j \in \Phi_j$ (ϕ_j is a random object). Then j's allocation rule $f_j(x_j, \phi_j)$ should solve

$$\min_{\{x_i\}_{i \in \theta_j}} E\left[\sum_{i \in \theta_j} b_i(x_i - \gamma_i)^2 \middle| \phi_j \right]$$

subject to $\sum_{i \in \theta_j} x_i = x_j. \tag{6}$

The solution is[23]

$$x_i^* = \hat{\gamma}_i^j + b_i^{-1} b_j (x_j - \hat{\gamma}_j^j), \tag{7}$$

where $\hat{\gamma}_i^j = E[\gamma_i | \phi_j]$ and $\hat{\gamma}_j^j = E[\gamma_j | \phi_j] = \sum_{i \in \theta_j} \hat{\gamma}_i^j$. The total realized costs for j's division are[24]

---

[23] This allocation rule is part of Proposition 1 in GM91 and is analogous to equation (A8) in Cremer (1980).

[24] Equation (8) is obtained by substituting the allocation rule (7) into each shop's cost function (5), summing over the shops, and simplifying; see Van Zandt (1996c) for details. This

$$\tilde{C}_j\left(x_j,\left\{\gamma_i,\hat{\gamma}_i^j\right\}_{i\in\theta_j}\right)=C_j\left(x_j,\gamma_j\right)+L_j\left(\left\{\gamma_i,\hat{\gamma}_i^j\right\}_{i\in\theta_j}\right) \qquad (8)$$

where

$$L_j\left(\left\{\gamma_i,\hat{\gamma}_i^j\right\}_{i\in\theta_j}\right)=-b_j\left(\gamma_j-\hat{\gamma}_j^j\right)^2+\sum_{i\in\theta_j}b_i\left(\gamma_i-\hat{\gamma}_i^j\right)^2. \qquad (9)$$

That is, it is equal to the full-information minimized cost $C_j(x_j,\gamma_j)$ for the division under j plus a loss L_j $(\{\gamma_i,\hat{\gamma}_i^j\}_{i\in\theta_j})$ due to j's prediction error.

From the decomposition (8), we see that:

(1) manager j chooses her information to minimize the expected loss $E[L_j(\cdot)]$, so this choice does not depend on the allocation that j receives (i.e., is state-independent);

(2) only $C_j(x_j,\gamma_j)$ is relevant to the decision problem of j's immediate superior and hence that manager need not draw inferences about j's choice of information or beliefs.

Therefore, recursively deriving the decision rules for each manager as in GM91, each manager $j\in J$ chooses an allocation to minimize the expected value of $\sum_{k\in\Theta_j}C_k(x_k,\gamma_k)$, and the solution is

$$x_k^*=\hat{\gamma}_k^j+b_k^{-1}b_j\left(x_j-\hat{\gamma}_j^j\right)$$

for $k\in\Theta_j$. As we recursively calculate the shop costs, we derive the full-information minimized costs (as in equation (8)) plus the sum of the losses from the prediction errors of the subordinate managers. The total shop costs for the whole organization are thus

$$b_R\left(x_R-\gamma_R\right)^2+\sum_{j\in J}L_j\left(\left\{\gamma_k,\hat{\gamma}_k^j\right\}_{k\in\Theta_j}\right), \qquad (10)$$

where

$$L_j\left(\left\{\gamma_k,\hat{\gamma}_k^j\right\}_{k\in\Theta_j}\right)=-b_j\left(\gamma_j-\hat{\gamma}_j^j\right)^2+\sum_{k\in\Theta_j}b_k\left(\gamma_k-\hat{\gamma}_k^j\right)^2. \qquad (11)$$

decomposition is similar to equation (9) in GM91 and equation (A12) in Cremer (1980), but GM91 and Cremer (1980) report *expected* costs conditional on ϕ_j. By solving instead for *realized* costs, we can solve the design problem recursively without having to assume that subordinates have as much information about their divisions as their superiors do. Hence, we can obtain the results in Proposition 5 of GM91 without their sufficiency condition.

The organization design problem is to specify a hierarchy and information acquisition for each manager to minimize the expected value of (10) plus the managerial wages.

In GM91, the expected shop costs are written as the difference between the no-information expected costs and the sum of the values of the managers' information. This is done as follows. Suppose that no manager has any information. Then $\hat{\gamma}_j^j = E[\gamma_j] \equiv \overline{\gamma}_j$ for all $j \in J$ and $\hat{\gamma}_k^j = E[\gamma_k] \equiv \overline{\gamma}_k$ for all $k \in \Theta_j$. Hence, manager j's loss is $L_j(\{\gamma_k, \overline{\gamma}_k\}_{k \in \Theta_j})$. Furthermore, the resulting statistically optimal allocation is the no-information allocation $x_i = \overline{\gamma}_i + b_i^{-1} b_R (x_R - \overline{\gamma}_R)$. Therefore,

$$b_R \left(x_R - \gamma_R \right)^2 + \sum_{j \in J} L_j \left(\left\{ \gamma_k, \overline{\gamma}_k \right\}_{k \in \Theta_j} \right) = \sum_{i \in J} b_i \left(\overline{\gamma}_i + b_i^{-1} b_R \left(x_R - \overline{\gamma}_R \right) - \gamma_i \right)^2.$$

(12)

Define the ex post value of manager j's information to be the difference

$$\tilde{v}_j \equiv L_j \left(\left\{ \gamma_k, \overline{\gamma}_k \right\}_{k \in \Theta_j} \right) - L_j \left(\left\{ \gamma_k, \hat{\gamma}_k^j \right\}_{k \in \Theta_j} \right)$$

between j's loss if j had no information and j's actual loss. Then the total shop costs (10) are equal to the left-hand side (LHS) of (12) minus $\sum_{j \in J} \tilde{v}_j$ or, equivalently, to the no-information total shop costs (RHS) of (12)) minus $\sum_{j \in J} \tilde{v}_j$. Let C_R^{ni} be the expected value of the no-information shop costs and let $v_j = E[\tilde{v}_j]$, which we call the *value* of j's information. Then the expected value of the total shop costs are equal to $C_R^{ni} - \sum_{j \in J} v_j$. A little algebra shows that

$$C_R^{ni} = b_R \left(x_R - \overline{\gamma}_R \right)^2 + \sum_{i \in I} b_i \mathrm{Var} \left(\gamma_i \right)$$

(13)

and

$$v_j = -b_j \mathrm{Var} \left(\hat{\gamma}_j^j \right) + \sum_{k \in \Theta_j} b_k \mathrm{Var} \left(\hat{\gamma}_k^j \right).$$

(14)

A necessary condition for optimality is that the *value of each manager*, which we define to be the change in expected shop cost when the manager is fired, be no less than the manager's wage. In this hypothetical firing of a manager, we assume that the information structure for the remaining managers is not modified, and that the fired manager's immediate subordinates receive allocations from the manager's immediate superior, if he has one. If the manager is instead the root, then the manager's subordinates become the root managers of independent organizations. Since the role of managers is to acquire information in order to allocate resources, we assume that independent firms get their zero-

Table 1. *Returns to Scale in the Geanakoplos and Milgrom (1991) Model*

Assumptions/Restrictions	Results
None	Increasing returns
Disaggregate information	Increasing returns
	Limits to integration
	Optimal hierarchies not balanced
Disaggregate information/Balanced hierarchies	Limits to firm size
Aggregate information	Increasing returns
	Optimal hierarchies can be uniform

information optimal allocation.[25] The value of a manager other than the root depends on the information her immediate superior has about her immediate subordinates' cost functions. An easily calculated upper bound on the value of a manager is the value v_j of the manager's information. Hence, a necessary condition for optimality is $v_j \geq w_j$.

3.2.3. *Returns to Scale.* The informationally integrated unit in GM91 is the hierarchy, and the size of this unit – for the purpose of characterizing returns to scale – is the number n of shops. In this section, an optimal hierarchy or firm size is one that minimizes per-unit costs (expected shop costs plus managerial costs). The information processing constraints in GM91 do not limit firm size without additional assumptions and regularity restrictions on hierarchies. The returns to scale for various cases are listed in Table 1.

Generally, there is no optimal firm size in GM91 because one can always merge two firms by making one a subsidiary of the other; this can reduce total expected costs but does not change the managerial costs. Specifically, the root manager of one firm is made a subordinate of any manager in the other firm. Even without acquiring information about the subsidiary, the immediate superior of the subsidiary can make advantageous transfers to the subsidiary based only on information about her own shops. For example, with quadratic costs, the manager equates the *expected* marginal costs of all her immediate subordinates, conditional on her information. In the absence of information about the subsidiary,

---

[25] Under symmetry assumptions, this means that the allocation to each firm is proportional to the firm's size.

the expected marginal cost of any transfers to the subsidiary is deterministic; however, the expected marginal cost of transfers to the manager's other immediate subordinates depends on the realization of her information.

The hierarchy that results from the merger just described is typically not balanced. We now characterize the returns to scale of balanced hierarchies. This involves analyzing the value of the root manager, which was calculated in the previous section.

We impose the following symmetry assumptions:

(1) $b_i = 1$ for all i;
(2) $\{\gamma_i\}_{i \in I}$ are independent and identically distributed (i.i.d.), with mean 0 and variance σ^2;
(3)   for any collection of shops, total resources are 0 (coordination involves only transfers between shops).

Recall that $n_j = |\theta_j|$ is the size of manager j's division. Since $b_i = 1$ for all i, $b_j = 1/n_j$. Under all three assumptions, the expected full information total shop costs are $E[b_R \gamma_R] = \sigma^2$, and are independent of firm size.

In GM91, attention is focused on the case where managers have access only to disaggregate information, i.e., noisy observations of individual shops' cost parameters. Formally, $\hat{\gamma}_i^j$ is independent of $\hat{\gamma}_{i'}^j$ for $i' \neq i$. It follows that $\mathrm{Var}(\hat{\gamma}_k^j) = \sum_{i \in \theta_k} \mathrm{Var}(\hat{\gamma}_i^j)$, and the value of manager j's information (from equation (14)) is

$$-\frac{1}{n_j} \sum_{i \in \theta_j} \mathrm{Var}\left(\hat{\gamma}_i^j\right) + \sum_{k \in \Theta_j} \frac{1}{n_k} \sum_{i \in \theta_k} \mathrm{Var}\left(\hat{\gamma}_i^j\right). \tag{15}$$

Let $n_j^{\min} = \min\{n_k \mid k \in \Theta_j\}$. Then the value (15) of j's information is at most

$$\frac{1}{n_j^{\min}} \sum_{i \in \theta_j} \mathrm{Var}\left(\hat{\gamma}_i^j\right). \tag{16}$$

We formalize the bounds on the managers' information processing capacity by assuming that there is an upper bound V^{bound}, which is uniform across managers, on $\sum_{i \in \theta_j} \mathrm{Var}(\hat{\gamma}_i^j)$. Then (16) is at most

$$V^{\mathrm{bound}} / n_j^{\min}. \tag{17}$$

Assume also that each manager's wage is equal to $w > 0$. For a hierarchy to be optimal, $v_j \geq w$. Since also $v_j \leq V^{\mathrm{bound}}/n_j^{\min}$,

$$n_j^{\min} < V^{\mathrm{bound}} / w. \tag{18}$$

Thus, when only disaggregate information is available, every manager must have at least one subordinate whose division is not too large; that is, every manager must be "close" to the operations of some shops. (See GM91, Cor. 3, for an example.)

Now bring in the restriction that hierarchies be balanced. This implies that each division reporting to the root manager is approximately the same size. It follows from (18) that there is a bound on the size of each such division for optimal balanced hierarchies. Hence, the number of immediate subordinates to the root manager grows unboundedly with firm size. The value, per immediate subordinate, of the root manager's information decreases to zero, since the total value is bounded by V^{bound}. Hence, for large firm sizes, the unit costs are almost the same as when the root manager is fired. It is then better to create separate firms by dividing the root's immediate subordinates among multiple root managers (if there is some number of immediate subordinates for which the value of each root's information exceeds her wage – otherwise, the upper level of management should be eliminated entirely). Hence, if hierarchies must be balanced then there is a bounded optimal firm size.

We know, however, that without the restriction that hierarchies be balanced, firm size is not bounded. Hence the optimal hierarchies are not balanced for large firms. For example, if each manager can observe, without error, the cost parameters of up to 5 shops, then the optimal hierarchy could look like the assembly-line network in Figure 5 (Section 2.4).

These results assume that only disaggregate cost information is available. As a comparison, here is an example showing that under another extreme assumption – that all aggregate cost functions are available – returns to scale can be increasing even for uniform hierarchies.

Recall the example in Section 3.2.2, in which each manager can observe the aggregate cost parameters of three immediate subordinates. Then q managers, organized in *any* hierarchy (including a uniform hierarchy) such that each has a span of 3, can solve without error the resource allocation problem for $2q + 1$ shops.[26] The expected total shop costs are then σ^2 and the managerial wages are qw. Unit costs are thus

$$\frac{\sigma^2 + qw}{2q + 1}.$$

---

[26] In any tree with q interior nodes that all have s children, there are a total of qs children, $q - 1$ of which are interior nodes. Hence, there are $q(s - 1) + 1$ terminal nodes.

If $w < 2\sigma^2$ then this decreases monotonically to $w/2$, and is always lower than the per-unit cost of σ^2 when no information is processed. This suggests that returns to scale are increasing.[27]

3.3   Batch Parallel Processing

The assumption that managers have access only to disaggregate information is rather severe in the GM91 model, because the hierarchy cannot aggregate cost information (whereas, in practice, information flowing up hierarchies is an important source of aggregate information for upper-level managers). On the other hand, the assumption that aggregate cost information is freely available is also unrealistic, because the aggregation of cost information is a complex task for agents who are supposedly boundedly rational. Rather than having to judge what is the appropriate assumption on the availability of aggregate information, it is more sound to explicitly model aggregation by the hierarchy. For this purpose, we must deviate from team theory and model the computation constraints of the individual information processing agents.

We begin by studying the batch processing of the resource allocation problem. Because we studied batch processing extensively in Section 2 in the context of associative computation, we do not need an overview here and will not repeat the topics explored in that section. Hence, for simplicity, we use a PRAM computation model. We first present an abstract decomposition of the problem into elementary operations (following the section on batch processing in Van Zandt 1996d) in order to illustrate the hierarchical aggregation of cost functions. In this case, resource allocations are calculated without error. Then we turn in Section 3.3.2 to a temporal quadratic model (based on Van Zandt 1996e) in order to derive a cost of delay and characterize returns to scale. This introduces a source of error due to the use of old information.

3.3.1. *Aggregation of Cost Functions.* In Section 2, the function to be computed was the aggregate of n items under an associative operation. Now the task is to calculate the function $f: \mathcal{C}^n \times \mathbb{R} \to \mathbb{R}^n$, where $\mathcal{C}$ is the set of potential cost functions and $f(\{C_i\}_{i \in I}, x_R)$ is the solution to the

---

[27] Here is a sketch of a complete proof. Conjecture an optimal balanced hierarchy (that minimizes unit costs). One can show that the root of this hierarchy acquires information about three of his s_R immediate subordinates. Gather s_R of these supposedly optimal hierarchies under a new root, and have this root acquire information about three of her subordinates. The value of this new root will be the same as the value of each of the old roots, which by assumption is greater than the wage. Hence, merging the hierarchies in this way reduces the unit cost.

Table 2. *Elementary Operations and Serial and Parallel Delay for the Resource Allocation Problem*

Calculation	Elementary operation	Number of operations	Parallel delay
$C_R = \oplus_{i \in I} C_i$	$f_1(C_A, C_B) = C_A \oplus C_B$	$n-1$	$\lceil \log_2 n \rceil$
$p_R = C'_R(x_R)$	$f_2(C, x) = C'(x)$	1	1
$\left\{ x_i = C_i'^{-1}(p_R) \right\}_{i \in I}$	$f_3(C, p) = C'^{-1}(p)$	n	1
Total:		$2n$	$2 + \lceil \log_2 n \rceil$

resource allocation problem (4) in Section 3.1. The data are the cost functions $\{C_i\}_{i \in I}$ and the available resource x_R.

Assume that $\mathcal{C}$ is a set of strictly convex, differentiable cost functions on which the associative operation $\oplus$ is well-defined and closed. We choose a decomposition of this problem into elementary operations that is just fine enough so that interesting decentralization of information processing is possible. The following elementary operations are sufficient:

$$f_1 : \mathcal{C}^2 \to \mathcal{C}, \qquad f_1(C_A, C_B) = C_A \oplus C_B,$$

$$f_2 : \mathcal{C} \times \mathbb{R} \to \mathbb{R}, \qquad f_2(C, x) = C'(x),$$

$$f_3 : \mathcal{C} \times \mathbb{R} \to \mathbb{R}, \qquad f_3(C, p) = C'^{-1}(p);$$

f can then be computed with the following algorithm, whose steps are listed in Table 2. (a) First, the aggregate cost function $C_R = \oplus_{i \in I} C_i$ is computed with $n - 1$ operations f_1. (b) Then the shadow price $p = C'_R(x)$ is computed with f_2. (c) Finally, for each shop i, $x_i = C_i'^{-1}(p)$ is computed with f_3; this sets shop i's allocation so that i's marginal cost is equal to the shadow price. There are n of these operations, for a total of $2n$ operations.

For notational simplicity, assume that each elementary operation takes one cycle. If a single agent performs the $2n$ operations sequentially, then the delay is $2n$. Suppose instead that the operations are decentralized. As described in Section 2.3, the PRAM has no communication costs and maximal decentralization is optimal (if it does not increase the number of operations). The aggregation of the cost functions is an associative computation and takes $\lceil \log_2 n \rceil$ cycles. The shadow price is calculated, which takes one cycle. Finally, the n operations $\{x_i = C'^{-1}_i(p_R)\}_{i \in I}$ can be performed concurrently, in one cycle. Hence, the total delay is $2 + \lceil \log_2 n \rceil$, which is lower than the delay with serial processing. This reduction in delay is the advantage of decentralization, just as in Section 2. If the computation model had communication costs, then decentralization would also increase administrative costs.

A richer and more sophisticated model of batch processing of the resource allocation problem is found in Friedman and Oren (1995). The decomposition of the problem into elementary operations is finer and is based on an iterative price – quantity mechanism. Each shop computes approximately optimal demands given a shadow price. The center, which is an office within which information processing is decentralized, aggregates this information and adjusts the shadow price. The procedure has the feature that it can be stopped at any point and yields a feasible allocation. The authors characterize the asymptotic complexity of the procedure, that is, how delay depends on the precision of the solution and the number of shops.

How do these decentralized procedures relate to Figure 6? We know that associative computation has a hierarchical structure, and hence the upward flow of information in that figure is consistent with the decentralized aggregation of cost functions. For example, if each manager in the hierarchy aggregates the cost functions of his subordinates, then C_R is computed in 4 cycles instead of the 7 cycles it would take a single manager to do so. However, the disaggregation of resource allocations through the same hierarchy that is shown in Figure 6 does not appear in the algorithm. Instead, once the root has calculated the shadow price p_R, the allocations of the shops are computed concurrently in one step. (One can imagine that the shadow price is sent to each shop, where a manager calculates the shop's demand given the shadow price.) If instead resources were disaggregated by the hierarchy, then at the very least the number of operations would increase by $|J| - 1$, where $|J|$ is the number of managers (one operation for calculating each manager's allocation given the shadow price); the delay would also increase if this disaggregation took place recursively.

Hence, this batch processing model explains the hierarchical aggregation of information, but not the hierarchically decentralized decision making seen in Figure 6. In contrast, GM91 explains the decentralized decision making but not the aggregation of information.

3.3.2. *Cost of Delay and Returns to Scale.* In Section 2, we considered the trade-off between delay and managerial costs in a batch processing model of associative computation. In Section 3.3.1, we also derived delay as a function of organization size in a batch processing model of resource allocation. To determine the optimal level of decentralization in such a batch processing model, or to determine how the computation constraints affect returns to scale, we need a measure of the cost of delay.

Delay, however, is not an input that an organization purchases. Instead, it is costly to the extent that it degrades the quality of decision making, because decisions are based on older information. To properly model the cost of delay, one must study dynamic decision problems in which the value of information declines over time or there is a cost to postponing action.

For example, consider a temporal version of the one-good resource allocation problem with quadratic costs presented in Section 3.2.2.[28] An amount x_R of a resource is to be allocated each period $t \in \mathbb{Z}$ to n shops. The cost of shop i at time t is

$$C\left(x_{it}, \gamma_{it}\right) = \left(x_{it} - \gamma_{it}\right)^2.$$

The budget constraint $\sum_{i \in I} x_{it} = x_R$ must be satisfied each period. Hence, there is no intertemporal allocation of resources. The intertemporal link is informational: Each period's allocation must be computed from past observations of the cost parameters.

Assume that the n processes $\{\{\gamma_{it}\}_{t=-\infty}^{\infty}\}_{i \in I}$ are i.i.d., and that each process $\{\gamma_{it}\}_{t=-\infty}^{\infty}$ is a stationary first-order autoregressive process with mean 0 and variance σ^2:

$$\gamma_{it} = \beta \gamma_{i,t-1} + W_{it},$$

where $|\beta| < 1$ and the noise terms W_{it} are independent over i and t and have mean zero. The computation model is a PRAM whose elementary operations are addition, subtraction, and multiplication. Assume that each operation takes one period.

The period-t allocation is computed by gathering the cost parameters in period $t - L_R$, where the lag L_R is yet to be specified, and calculating the statistically optimal allocation. Let $\phi_{Rt} = \{\gamma_{i,t-L_R}\}_{i=1}^n$ be the information with which the period-t allocation is calculated, and let $x_{Rt} = x_R$. The statistically optimal decision rule is given by equation (19) from the GM91 team theory model:

$$x_{it} = \hat{\gamma}_{it}^R + \frac{1}{n}\left(x_{Rt} - \hat{\gamma}_{Rt}^R\right) = \beta^d \gamma_{i,t-L_R} + \frac{1}{n}\left(x_{Rt} - \beta^{L_R} \gamma_{R,t-L_R}\right), \quad (19)$$

---

[28] We have switched from the abstract model with general cost functions to particular parametric cost functions because we now need to impose statistical assumptions on the evolution of the cost functions.

Table 3. *Computation of the Period-t Allocation*

Decision rule: $x_{it} = \beta^{L_R} \gamma_{i,t-L_R} + 1/n\left(x_{Rt} - \beta^{L_R}\gamma_{R,t-L_R}\right)$

			Operations		
Step	Input	Output	Type	#	Delay
(a)	$\left\{\gamma_{i,t} - L_R\right\}_{i \in \Theta_R}$	$\left\{\hat{\gamma}_{it}^R = \beta^{L_R}\gamma_{i,t-L_R}\right\}_{i \in I}$	MUL	n	1
(b)	$\left\{\hat{\gamma}_{it}^R\right\}_{i \in I}$	$\hat{\gamma}_{Rt}^R = \sum_{i \in I}\hat{\gamma}_{it}^R$	ADD	$n-1$	$\lceil \log_2 n \rceil$
(c)	$x_{Rt}, \hat{\gamma}_{Rt}^R$	$x_{Rt} - \hat{\gamma}_{Rt}^R$	SUB	1	1
(d)	$x_{Rt} - \hat{\gamma}_{Rt}^R$	$\Delta_t = (1/n)\left(x_{Rt} - \hat{\gamma}_{Rt}^R\right)$	MUL	1	1
(e)	$\left\{\hat{\gamma}_{it}^R\right\}_{i \in I}, \Delta_t$	$\left\{x_{it} = \hat{\gamma}_{it}^R + \Delta_t\right\}_{i \in I}$	ADD	n	1
Total:				$3n+1$	$4 + \lceil \log_2 n \rceil$

Note: The n multiplications in step (a) and the n additions in step (e) can be executed in parallel in just one period. The output from step (a) is used in step (b) but is also retained in memory for use in step (e).

where $\gamma_{Rt} = \sum_{i \in I}\gamma_{it}$ is the period-t aggregate cost parameter, $\hat{\gamma}_{it}^R = E[\gamma_{it} \mid \phi_{Rt}] = \beta^{L_R}\gamma_{i,t-L_R}$, and $\hat{\gamma}_{Rt}^R = E[\gamma_{Rt} \mid \phi_{Rt}] = \sum_{i \in I}\hat{\gamma}_{it}^R$. We then obtain the expected shop costs for each period, as a function of the lag L_R, from equations (13) and (14):

$$n\left(\bar{x}^2 + \sigma^2\right) - (n-1)\beta^{2L_R}\sigma^2,$$

where $\bar{x} = x_R/n$ is the per-capital available resource.

The lag L_R is given by the delay in computing (19). The operations, and the sequence in which they are performed, are listed in Table 3, which shows that $L_R = 4 + \lceil \log_2 n \rceil$ and that there are $3n+1$ operations.

The overall costs (expected shop costs plus administrative costs) for each period are thus[29]

$$n\left(\bar{x}^2 + \sigma^2\right) - (n-1)\beta^{L_R}\sigma^2 + w(3n+1). \tag{20}$$

---

[29] If the computation model had communication costs, then we would obtain a function $L_R(a,n)$ that gives delay as a function of the administrative costs a and the number of shops n. The organization design problem would involve choosing the level of administrative costs in order to minimize the overall costs.

Now we let the scale n of the organization vary, keeping fixed the per-unit available resource $\bar{x}$. To emphasize the dependence of the lag on n, write the lag as $L_R(n) = 4 + \lceil \log_2 n \rceil$. Suppose, as a polar case, that the wage is zero. The per-unit costs are then

$$\bar{x}^2 + \sigma^2 - \left(\frac{n-1}{n}\right)\beta^{2L_R(n)}\sigma^2,$$

which are equal to $\bar{x}^2 + \sigma^2$ both for $n = 1$ and as $n \to \infty$ (since $\lim_{n \to \infty} L_R(n) = \infty$). Thus, for intermediate organization sizes, the average cost is less than when the organization has a single shop for which no coordination of trades is possible, but asymptotically the average cost increases to that of an organization with a single shop. We then conclude that, even if the wage is zero, there is a firm size that minimizes the average costs. This is a robust result (with respect to the computation model) because it depends only on the fact that the delay increases unboundedly with the size of the organization.

This conclusion is similar to that of Keren and Levhari (1983), who do not derive a "cost of delay" as we have done here but instead assume an exogenous cost of delay. For example, suppose that a firm hires n workers at a constant wage and sells its output at a constant price, but has a production function $f(n)g(d)$ when the delay is d. Let $d(n)$ be the administrative delay with n workers. Assume that g is decreasing and $\lim_{d \to \infty} g(d) = 0$. Then, if f is linear and $\lim_{n \to \infty} d(n) = \infty$, the per-worker output decreases to zero as $n \to \infty$; this continues to hold for nonlinear f as long as $f(n)$ increases more slowly than $1/g(d(n))$.

3.4   *Real-Time Parallel Computation*

3.4.1. *Delay in Real-Time Computation.* The exercise in Section 3.3.2, in which we derived the cost of delay from a temporal decision problem, does not fully exploit the model on which it is based. We wrote down what is actually a real-time (on-line) control problem, meaning a temporal control problem and a computation model for computing decision rules. But information becomes available and decisions are made at multiple decision epochs, and the computation of decision rules must adapt to this temporal structure. In Section 3.3.2, we artificially restricted attention to decision rules that, in each period, use information of the same lag. However, potentially each decision can be computed from information of heterogeneous lags, in which case there is no single measure of delay and no "cost of delay function" that could then be pasted into the pure computation models such as those discussed in Sections 2 and 3.3.1.

Furthermore, we also assumed that decision rules were statistically optimal conditional on the information from which they were computed, and we did not determine endogenously the information used to compute decisions. We now consider several models that treat real-time decentralization information processing more fully.

Marschak (1986, originally published in 1972) studies several real-time adjustment processes for allocating resources and explores some of the costs of delay. Groves (1983) is a team-theory model with real-time decision making. Real-time decentralized computation was first used in the economic theory of organizations, with an endogenous number of agents and with a parallel processing computation model, by Radner and Van Zandt (1992) and Van Zandt and Radner (1996). The main focus of these two papers is to characterize returns to scale, but Van Zandt and Radner (1996) also explores various properties of real-time computation, such as the potential lack of statistical optimality and the endogenous selection of decision rules. The property we review in this section is that the decision-theoretic benefit of decentralization is ambiguous because there is no single measure of delay. This property also appears in Van Zandt (1996e), which is based on the resource allocation problem and is studied in Section 3.4.2. Another model of real-time decentralization information processing, not reviewed here, is Meagher (1996b), in which a firm forecasts demand in order to decide on the introduction of new products.

The decision problem in Van Zandt and Radner (1996) is to predict the sum of n discrete time stochastic processes $\{X_{it} \mid i = 1, \ldots, n\}$ in each period $t \in \mathbb{Z}$. For example, the organization may be a firm with a single plant that sets its output level in each period based on a prediction of the total demand of n stores or sales offices or of the average productivity of n shops or workers. The prediction in period t is computed from past realizations of the individual processes up through period $t - 1$.

Suppose that predictions are linear and the computation technology for addition is that of Radner (1993). Assume, for simplicity, that managers can add constants and multiply data by constants without delay, so that calculating an affine function of a list of data is computationally equivalent to summing the data. Suppose also that the length of a decision period equals the length of a computational cycle. Finally, suppose that $n = 4$.

Compare two policies, $\{A_t\}_{t \in \mathbb{Z}}$ and $\{B_t\}_{t \in \mathbb{Z}}$, which set the prediction in period t to an affine function of one observation of each of the four processes. For each $t \in \mathbb{Z}$, the four observations for A_t are processed sequentially by a single manager in periods $t - 4, \ldots, t - 1$. If the

Policies:

$$A_t = \alpha_0 + \alpha_1 X_{1,t-1} + \alpha_2 X_{2,t-2} + \alpha_3 X_{3,t-3} + \alpha_4 X_{4,t-4}$$
$$B_t = \beta_0 + \beta_1 X_{1,t-2} + \beta_2 X_{2,t-2} + \beta_3 X_{3,t-3} + \beta_4 X_{4,t-3}$$

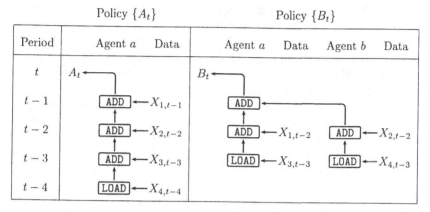

Figure 7. Two policies in Van Zandt and Radner (1996). Each decision in $\{A_t\}$ is computed by a single manager with four operations. Each decision in $\{B_t\}$ is computed by two managers with five operations. Because of decentralized information processing in $\{B_t\}$, the data have a smaller maximum lag than that of the data in $\{A_t\}$. However, the lags are not uniformly lower in $\{B_t\}$.

manager always processes the most recent observations, then the lags of the data are $\{1,2,3,4\}$. This is illustrated on the LHS of Figure 7. Note that there is no real decentralization or joint processing, because each decision is computed by a single manager.

In contrast, the policy $\{B_t\}_{t \in \mathbb{Z}}$ has decentralized information processing because each decision is computed by two managers. Each of the managers who compute B_t reads one observation in period $t-3$ and one in period $t-2$. The partial sums thus obtained at the end of period $t-2$ are aggregated by having one manager pass his sum to the other, who adds it to her own partial sum in period $t-1$, thereby computing the prediction for period t. If each manager always processes the most recent observation, then the lags of the data are $\{2,2,3,3\}$. This is illustrated on the RHS of Figure 7.

Because of the implicit communication cost in the Radner (1993) model, each decision requires an extra operation for $\{B_t\}$ compared to $\{A_t\}$. Therefore, as explained in Van Zandt and Radner (1996), four managers are needed to compute $\{A_t\}$ whereas five managers are needed to compute $\{B_t\}$. This is the resource cost of decentralization.

If we measured delay as in a batch processing model by the elapsed time from when the computation of a decision begins to when it ends, which would be appropriate if we required that each decision be calculated from data of homogeneous lags, then $\{A_t\}$ would have a delay of 4 whereas $\{B_t\}$ would have a delay of 3. The reduction in delay would be an unambiguous benefit of decentralization.

However, in this temporal learning problem, the speed-up is not unambiguous. The distribution $\{2,2,3,3\}$ of lags for $\{B_t\}$ does not dominate the distribution $\{1,2,3,4\}$ of lags for $\{A_t\}$, because $\{A_t\}$ uses both older data and more recent data than $\{B_t\}$.

This example illustrates a decision-theoretic cost of decentralization that can only be observed in a temporal learning problem: When a manager listens to a subordinate, the manager foregoes the opportunity to process very recent raw data (e.g., today's newspaper) and the foregone raw data can be more valuable than the subordinate's aggregated – but older – data (e.g., a summary of the newspapers from the previous seven days). Van Zandt and Radner (1996) provide an example in which there is never any decentralization, even if the cost of managers (the resource cost of decentralization) is zero, because of this decision-theoretic cost of delay.

3.4.2. *Real-Time Hierarchical Resource Allocation.* The decision problem in Radner and Van Zandt (1992) and Van Zandt and Radner (1996) involves a single prediction each period. This rules out decentralized decision making (having different decisions made at the same time computed from different information). Van Zandt (1996d,e) applies their methodology to the resource allocation problem, which does allow for multiple decisions and hence decentralized decision making. Van Zandt (1996d) presents the main message about the benefits of decentralized decision making in a real-time version of the abstract model in Section 3.3.1, and Van Zandt (1996e; henceforth VZ96) develops a model with quadratic costs, which amounts to an extension of the exercise in Section 3.3.2. We focus on VZ96 in order to compare it with GM91.

The decision problem in VZ96 is the temporal resource allocation problem with quadratic costs presented in Section 3.3.2, and the computation model is the PRAM presented there. This model is rich enough to represent a variety of market and nonmarket resource allocation mechanisms. However, VZ96 does not consider the full range of possible decision procedures but instead characterizes a restricted class of decision procedures that have hierarchical structures. The decision procedure in Section 3.3.2 is actually a special case of the ones considered by VZ96 and corresponds to a two-tier hierarchy without decentralized decision making. Hierarchies with more than two tiers in VZ96 exhibit decentralized decision making.

In most other economic models of hierarchies, the interior nodes represent individual managers. In contrast, in the hierarchies in VZ96, the interior nodes represent offices that contain many information processing agents. The hierarchical structure corresponds to decentralized decision making that takes the form of disaggregation of resource allocations. For example, the decision procedure in Section 3.3.2 corresponds to a two-tier hierarchy because there is no disaggregation of resource allocations. The leaves are the shops and the single managerial office is the root node. The operations in Table 3 are performed in parallel by multiple information processing agents (e.g., managers, clerks, and professionals) within this office. It is because of this macro approach to organizational structure that the model can be based on a PRAM instead of a computation model with communication costs. Such communication costs would be necessary to make determinate the micro structure of communication between individual information processing agents that is the basis for organizational structure in the literature on associative computation reviewed in Section 2.

The decision procedure in VZ96 that corresponds to a general hierarchy $\{I, J, R, \{\Theta_j\}_{j \in J}\}$ is related to the GM91 model as follows. For each period t, office j receives an allocation x_{jt} from its superior (or $x_{jt} = x_R$ if $j = R$) and calculates an allocation $\{x_{kt}\}_{k \in \Theta}$ for its immediate subordinates that satisfies $\sum_{k \in \Theta} x_{kt} = x_{jt}$. It is possible to determine the information ϕ_{jt} that j uses to compute $\{x_{kt}\}_{k \in \Theta}$. Note that ϕ_{jt} is a vector of random variables; its components are raw observations of the shops' cost parameters or partial results of other offices' computations. The decision procedures are constructed so that, in each period $t \in \mathbb{Z}$, the decision rules calculated by each office are team statistically optimal – that is, optimal in the GM91 model for this fixed hierarchy and the information structure $\{\phi_{jt}\}_{j \in J}$. Letting $\hat{\gamma}_{kt}^j = E[\gamma_{kt} \mid \phi_{jt}]$ and $\hat{\gamma}_{jt}^j = E[\gamma_{jt} \mid \phi_{jt}] = \sum_{k \in \Theta_j} \hat{\gamma}_{kt}^j$ for $j \in J$ and $k \in \Theta_j$, this means that

$$x_{kt} = \hat{\gamma}_{kt}^j + \frac{n_k}{n_j}\left(x_{jt} - \hat{\gamma}_{jt}^j\right). \tag{21}$$

Observe that the partial results of office j's calculations include $\{\hat{\gamma}_{jt}^j\}_{t \in \mathbb{Z}}$. This aggregate cost information is the information that j's immediate superior (if j is not the root) uses about j. (A shop's immediate superior uses the shop's cost parameters.) For each $t \in \mathbb{Z}$ and $j \in J$, the information ϕ_{jt} of each office and the procedure by which (21) is computed must

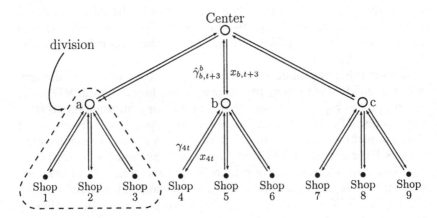

Figure 8. A three-tier hierarchy in Van Zandt (1996e), showing information flow in at beginning of period t.

be specified such that ϕ_{jt} and x_{jt} are available when office j uses them as inputs.

For example, consider a procedure that has the structure of a completely balanced three-tier hierarchy, as illustrated in Figure 8. We refer to each two-tier subtree as a division. Let s_2 be the span of the center, which is equal to the number of divisions. Let s_1 be the number of shops in each division. (Assume, to avoid some ceiling operations, that s_1 and s_2 are powers of 2.) Each division office allocates resources much like the center did in the two-tier hierarchy. That is, to allocate resources in period t, division office j collects the cost parameters of the shops in its division in period $t - L_1$ (where L_1 is yet to be specified) and then calculates the allocation that is statistically optimal in GM91. Then $\phi_{jt} = \{\gamma_{i,t-L_1}\}_{i \in \theta_j}$ and $\hat{\gamma}_{jt}^j = \beta^{L_2}\gamma_{i,t-L_1}$, and the calculation of (21) is just like the calculation of the center's decision rule in Section 3.3.2, except that the office's span is s_1 rather than n. Hence, from Table 3, we see that we can set $L_1 = 4 + \log_2 s_1$ and that office j has $3s_1 + 1$ operations per period.

The center allocates resources to the division using an analogous procedure. To allocate resources for period t, it collects the partial result $\{\hat{\gamma}_{j,t-L_2}^j\}_{j \in \Theta_R}$ from the divisions, where the lag L_2 is yet to be determined. It follows from the statistical assumptions that $\hat{\gamma}_{jt}^R = \beta^{L_2}\hat{\gamma}_{j,t-L_2}^j$ $(= \beta^{L_1+L_2}\gamma_{j,t-L_1-L_2})$ and so the calculation of (21) by the center is just like the calculation of the center's decision rule in Section 3.3.2, except the center's span is s_2 instead of n (note that the constant term n_j/n in (21) is equal to $1/s_2$). Hence, the center's delay is $4 + \log_2 s_2$ and the center has $3s_2 + 1$ operations per period.

This suggests that $L_2 = 4 + \log_2 s_2$, but first we need to examine the timing of the center's calculations. From Table 3, we can see both (i) that each division office j must know x_{jt} in period $t - 3$, and so the center must begin its calculations of the period-t allocation in period $t - 3 - (4 + \log_2 s_2)$; and (ii) that each division office j finishes calculating $\hat{\gamma}^j_{j,t-(4+\log_2 s_2)}$ by the end of period $t - 4 - (4 + \log_2 s_2)$. Therefore, in fact, $L_2 = 4 + \log_2 s_2$, but the center's calculations take place three periods earlier than if the center were just allocating resources directly to s_2 shops.

This three-tier hierarchy exhibits both the upward aggregation of cost information and the downward disaggregation of resource allocations that is observed in Figure 6. Although the model does not assign "authority" to any particular agents, it does divide the operations such that each node of the hierarchy calculates allocations for immediate subordinates. Decision making is decentralized not simply because of this but also because the different nodes of the hierarchy use different information, which is the hallmark of decentralized decision making in team theory. A division office j uses information about the cost parameters of the shops in its division from L_1 periods ago, and the center uses information about all the shops' cost parameters from $L_1 + L_2$ periods ago.

Compare the two-tier centralized hierarchy in Section 3.3.2 with this three-tier decentralized hierarchy. It might appear that the three-tier hierarchy has more decentralized aggregation of cost information; however, the hierarchical aggregation of cost information that is explicit in the three-tier hierarchy takes place within the central office of the two-tier hierarchy. The cumulative time spent aggregating cost parameters in the three-tier hierarchy is $\log_2 s_1 + \log_2 s_2$, which is equal to the aggregation delay of $\log_2 n$ in the two-tier hierarchy.

The true difference is that the center in the three-tier hierarchy, after calculating $\hat{\gamma}^R_{Rt}$, allocates resources to the division offices rather than directly to the shops. The advantage is that the division offices, when suballocating their allocations, can use the latest aggregate costs they have computed for their division, which are based on more recent data than that upon which their allocations are based. Each division uses information that is $4 + \log_2 s_1$ periods old, which is $\log_2 n - \log_2 s_1 = \log_2 s_2$ periods *more recent* than the information used by the center in the two-tier hierarchy.

We can define hierarchies with more than three tiers in which there is more decentralized decision making; the addition of each tier has the same kind of decision-theoretic benefit. There are two costs to the decentralized decision making that keep the optimal hierarchy from being a binary tree (which would be maximal decentralization within this class of hierarchical decision procedures).

The first cost is decision-theoretic. The central office in the three-tier hierarchy exploits the gains from trade between shops in different divisions. However, the center uses information whose cumulative lag is $L_1 + L_2 = (4 + \log_2 s_1) + (4 + \log_2 s_2) = 8 + \log_2 n$, which is four periods greater than the lag of the center's information in the two-tier hierarchy. Hence, some of these gains from trade are lost compared to the two-tier hierarchy.

The second cost is administrative. Recall that each division office has $3s_1 + 1$ operations per period and that the center has $3s_2 + 1$ operations per period. Then the total number of operations per period is

$$s_2\left(3s_1 + 1\right) + \left(3s_2 + 1\right) = 3n + 1 + 4s_2.$$

Thus, there are $4s_2$ more operations per period than in the two-tier hierarchy owing to the overhead from calculating resource allocations for the intermediate tier (roughly, due to operations (a) and (e) computed by the center and operations (c) and (d) by the intermediate offices).

The expected shop costs for hierarchies can be calculated using the formulas (13) and (14) from the GM91 model, just as we calculated the expected shop costs in Section 3.3.2. For example, since $\hat{\gamma}_{jt}^R = \beta^{L_1+L_2}\gamma_{j,t-L_1-L_2}$, the value of the center's information in the three-tier hierarchy is $(s_2 - 1)\beta^{2(L_1+L_2)}$ and the value of the information of each division is $(s_1 - 1)\beta^{2L_1}\sigma^2$. The overall costs (per-period expected shop costs plus administrative costs) are thus

$$n\left(\bar{x}^2 + \sigma^2\right) - \left(s_2 - 1\right)\beta^{2\left(L_1+L_2\right)}\sigma^2 - s_2\left(s_1 - 1\right)\beta^{2L_1}\sigma^2 + w\left(3n + 1 + 4s_2\right).$$

3.4.3. Returns to Scale. Real-time decentralized information processing is an appropriate paradigm for studying the impact of information processing constraints on returns to scale of organizations because (i) it is decision theoretic, (ii) it allows the information processing resources to increase with the scale of the organization, and (iii) it allows the decision procedures to depend endogenously on the size of the organization.

Van Zandt and Radner (1996) illustrate some of the advantages of this paradigm. The batch process model in Section 3.3.2 reaches the simple conclusion that the returns to scale are decreasing because delay increases inexorably with the size of the organization. Van Zandt and Radner (1996) find that the answer is not so simple. Recall that the decision problem in that paper is to predict the sum of a family of stochastic processes. Each process is assumed to be the sum of a common component (a stochastic process common to all the observed processes) and an idiosyncratic component (a stochastic process independent of all the other observed processes). Suppose that the idiosyncratic components are not serially correlated and hence are unpredictable. Then the problem is to predict just the common component. If the organization makes a prediction by taking a sample of each of the n processes on the same date, and then computes a linear function of the data, the increase in delay with n together with the ergodicity of the common process (which causes the value of information to decay over time) would imply that the per-unit loss converges, as the firm size increases, to the per-unit loss with no information. However, when the loss is a convex function of the per-unit error, any given prediction of the common component (e.g., conditional only on the past realizations of one process) leads to weakly decreasing per-unit loss as the scale of the decision problem increases. Hence, just by mimicking the sampling or computational policies of smaller firms (but scaling up the answer), larger firms can achieve lower per-unit costs (loss plus sampling or computational costs) than the smaller firms.

On the other hand, the effect of delay can cause returns to scale to be decreasing. Computational delay implies that there is a bound on how much information of a given lag can go into the computation of the decision in each period. This is not true in a benchmark sampling problem, in which data is costly but computation is not constrained, and as a result the returns to scale can be worse in the computation problem than in the sampling. For example, when the loss is a quadratic function of the error and the processes are statistically independent, returns to scale are constant in the sampling problem but decreasing with computational constraints (the per-unit loss converges to the per-unit loss when no information is processed).

Another principle that their results illustrate is the breakdown of replication arguments for proving nondecreasing returns to scale when there are computation constraints and organizations must be informationally integrated. For both cases in which the authors find nondecreasing returns to scale in the benchmark sampling problem but bounded optimal size of organizations in the computation problem, the proof for the sampling problem is based on a replication argument whereby large organizations can do no worse than several small organizations just by replicating the sampling policies of the small organizations. However, in the model with computation constraints, if a large organization replicates the computation procedures of several small organizations then it ends up with several predictions; these must be aggregated to produce a single prediction and the delay in doing so means that the large organization uses older information than the small organizations.

The returns to scale are also more subtle in the real-time resource allocation model of Section 3.4.2 than in the batch resource allocation model of Section 3.3.2. In the latter, or more generally in the real-time hierarchical model when the number of tiers is fixed, returns to scale are eventually decreasing even when the managerial wage is zero, just because of delay. (In hierarchies with more than two tiers, it is only the center's cumulative lag that increases inexorably with the size of the organization.)

However, when the number of tiers is not exogenously bounded, returns to scale are increasing if the managerial wage is zero. Just as in GM91, it is always possible to add a central office that coordinates independent hierarchies, and the value of this coordination is always positive. It is the ability to decentralize internally that allows large organizations to take advantage of potential gains from trade across many shops without losing the benefits of allocating resources based on recent information within small groups of shops.

However, when the wage is positive, there are again decreasing returns to scale. This is now because, although the value of the center's information is always positive, the value per immediate subordinate decreases to zero as the size of the organization increases. On the other hand, recall that the center's administrative costs per subordinate are roughly $3w$. Hence, in large organizations, the center's administrative costs exceed the value of its information processing and so it is better to divide the organization. The center has become too far removed from the daily operations owing to the cumulative information processing delay.

3.4.4. Comparison with the Team Theory Model. A quick glance reveals some superficial common elements of GM91 and VZ96. Both are based on a resource allocation problem with quadratic costs, and both emphasize hierarchical disaggregation of resource allocations.

The two models also have important links at a deep level. The benefit of decentralization is conceptually similar; in both models, decentralization allows lower-tier offices to allocate resources using good, specialized information about a small group of shops, while the upper tiers take advantage of gains from trade between these groups of shops. The notions of team decision rules and decentralized information in the GM91 are used to define hierarchically decomposed decision procedures in VZ96; moreover, VZ96 uses team decision rules that are statistically optimal in GM91 and hence uses their results both to derive the decision rules and to calculate the expected shop costs.

However, at an intermediate level, the two models are very different. In GM91, information acquisition is costly but individual computation is not constrained; in VZ96, information is available freely but individual computation is constrained. GM91 is static and VZ96 is dynamic. In GM91, each node is a manager, but in VZ96 each node is an office. In GM91, each office acquires information from external sources; in VZ96, each office acquires information from its subordinates, so that cost information is aggregated through an upward flow of information.

Furthermore, it is not possible to obtain GM91 as a reduced form of VZ96. One reason is that an office's administrative costs in VZ96 depend on the number of subordinates. Another is that an office's information in VZ96 depends on the structure of the hierarchy below it, since it acquires its information from its immediate subordinates.

These differences are reflected, for example, in the returns to scale of the two models. Recall the characterization of returns to scale of balanced hierarchies in GM91, which was reviewed in Section 3.2.3. Note that the shop's cost functions in a given period in VZ96 satisfy the assumptions in that section (i.i.d., $b_i = 1$, variance σ^2, mean 0). In completely balanced hierarchies in VZ96, the delay of an office in tier h, which has span s_h, is $L_h = 4 + \log_2 s_h$. The cumulative lag of the root's information is $\sum_{h=1}^{H} L_h = 4H + \log_2 n$ (since $\Pi_{h=1}^{H} s_h = n$). Thus, for $j \in \Theta_R$, we have $\hat{\gamma}_{jt}^R = \beta^{4H+\log_2 n} \gamma_{j,t-4H-\log_2 n}$. Then the value of the center's information is

$$
\left(s_R - 1\right)\beta^{2\left(4H + \log_2 n\right)}\sigma^2 = \left(s_R - 1\right)\beta^{2\log_2 s_R}\,\beta^{2\left(4H + \log_2 n/s_R\right)}\sigma^2. \tag{22}
$$

Suppose that we fixed the size n/s_R of each division subordinate to the root, but increase the number s_R of divisions and hence the scale of the organization. The term $\beta^{2(4H+\log_2 n/s_R)}$ in (22) is then fixed, and the value of $(s_R - 1)\beta^{2\log_2 s_R}$ increases unboundedly as long as $\beta > \sqrt{1/2}$. Thus, the assumption that $\sum_{i \in I} \mathrm{Var}(\hat{\gamma}_i^R)$ is bounded, which is needed in GM91 to obtain decreasing returns to scale, does not hold. For this reason, if the administrative cost of an office in VZ96 were independent of the number of subordinates, it would always be possible (if $\beta > \sqrt{1/2}$) to join together enough identical independent hierarchies of a fixed size under a center so that the value of the center's information processing exceeds the fixed costs. There would then be no bound on firm size. However, since actually the cost per immediate subordinate of the center is approximately constant, and since the value per subordinate of the center's information processing is

$$\left(\frac{s_R - 1}{s_R}\right)\beta^{2\left(4H + \log_2 n\right)}\sigma^2,$$

which decreases to zero as $n \to \infty$, there is a bounded size of an organization that minimizes the per-shop costs.

4   Questions Not Addressed

4.1   Markets versus Hierarchies

As emphasized by Williamson (1975, 1985), markets and bureaucracies are alternative and coexisting ways of organizing economic activities. Interest in the relative efficiency of markets and bureaucracies for calculating allocations of resources dates back at least to the debates about socialism from 1910 to 1940. An early consensus of that debate was that prices were necessarily part of efficient resource allocation mechanisms.[30] A later consensus was that the computation of the solutions to the planning problem, even using prices, was too large a task to be done centrally by a planning bureau.[31] Later, Taylor (1929), Lange (1936, 1937), Dickinson (1939), and others proposed iterative, decentralized price mechanisms in which the adjustment of prices was controlled by the planning bureau. Hayek (1940) and others contended that such mechanisms would be too cumbersome or slow. This discussion of planning mechanisms made the very interesting point that aggregating information about members of the economy and calculating optimal resource allocations was extremely complex, yet *completely missing was a discussion of how markets perform these calculations.*

Until recently, this gap has persisted in the formal study of communication and computational complexity of resource allocation mechanisms. The planning literature, the message-space literature, and team theory have all explicitly studied centrally directed mechanisms, or abstract mechanisms in which the calculation of allocations and the information processing loads of the agents are not modeled.[32]

The literature surveyed in this chapter is explicit in its modeling of information processing, but it has focused on bureaucratic organizations

---

[30] This is essentially the argument of both Barone (1935, originally published in 1908) and Mises (1951, originally published in 1922), although the former was proposing a price-based planning mechanism and the latter was claiming that price-based planning was not possible because of the lack of private ownership and exchange of the means of production. See also Hayek (1935) for details on the origin of these ideas.

[31] See Hayek (1940, pp. 125–6) for a summary.

[32] See Van Zandt (1996a) for a comparison of these approaches.

such as firms. There is also a large and rapidly growing literature on the dynamics of decentralized interaction between agents who are modeled as computing machines, including the literature on agent-based computational economics (see Tesfatsion 1996 for a survey) and multi-agent systems (see e.g. Youssefmir and Huberman 1995). For example, Axtell and Epstein (1996) is a model in which, through bilateral interaction, boundedly rational agents calculate a Pareto optimal allocation. It is possible to model markets and bureaucratic structures with the same information processing models and thereby compare their computational efficiency, but this has not yet been done.

4.2   Incentives

In organizations, information processing constraints create incentive problems and incentive problems create information processing requirements. If a firm's owner could effortlessly and directly control the workers of a firm, then there would be no managers whose incentives would be a problem. Instead, managers are delegated information processing tasks and decision making. This endogenously gives them privileged information, thereby creating hidden information problems. Information processing constraints lead not just to the delegation of one or more unrelated information processing tasks to one or more agents who do not communicate, but also to joint processing in which agents communicate to each other information that they may not communicate to the principal. Furthermore, their managerial tasks require effort but the managers' input and output are difficult to measure, thereby creating moral hazard problems. The incentive contracts typically proposed to solve these problems require information processing themselves. When these information processing tasks are decentralized, we must ensure that managers have the incentives to perform these computations correctly.

Models that study the interaction between information processing and incentive constraints allow the theory of incentives to move from the grand revelation mechanisms, in which all agents report to a principal, to more realistic organizational structures. This has been the theme of the hierarchical contracting literature, which includes Melumad et al. (1995), McAfee and McMillan (1995), and Mookherjee and Reichelstein (1995, 1996), and which has so far studied contracting in hierarchical organizations without much explicit modeling of the information processing constraints that lead to such structure. Mechanism design with communication constraints has also been studied in Green and Laffont (1986, 1987), Laffont and Martimort (1996), and Melumad et al. (1997).

Another theme of some recent papers, such as Aghion and Tirole (1997) and Chang and Harrington (1996), has been that organizational structure – through its effect the influence agents have on the organization's decisions – affects the incentives for these agents to acquire and process information.

4.3   Evolution of Organizations

The literature on organizations has so far mainly adopted a constrained optimal approach to bounded rationality. In this approach, the researcher specifies a computation, communication, or decision problem (with a performance criterion) along with a computation or communication technology (with a cost measure) and then characterizes the decision procedures (decision rules and computation or communication procedures) that are *optimal* taking into account the performance and information processing costs of the procedures. This is a natural approach to take in organization design.

For descriptive theories, constrained optimal procedures might approximate the behavior of organizations in very stationary environments, where many years of incremental learning and evolution can lead to good decision procedures even though the human hardware on which these procedures run is slow enough that the daily cost of (and delay in) implementing the procedures is significant. At the very least, the constrained optimal procedures provide an upper bound on the performance of an organization facing the given computational constraints. However, for complex or long-term decision problems that do not repeat themselves regularly, it is more important to explicitly specify and study evolutionary processes that are governed by selection rather than designed to constrained optimal. There are a few recent papers (including Jordan 1995 and Miller 1996) that take this approach, but they are not examined in this survey.

Appendix: Hierarchies

In this paper, a hierarchy is a rooted tree in which we define a node's *level* or *tier* to be the maximum distance from the node to one of the leaves inferior to the node. The leaves are thus all in tier 0; the root is in the highest tier H, which we call the height of the hierarchy; and the remaining interior nodes are in tiers $1, \ldots, H - 1$.

Throughout this survey, the interior nodes of a hierarchy represent *managers* or *offices*. In Section 2 (on associative computation), the leaves represent *data*, whereas in Section 3 (on the resource allocation

Table 4. *Notation for Hierarchies*

General	
J	Set of interior nodes (managers or offices), indexed $j \in J$
I	Set of leaves (data or shops), indexed $i \in I$
q	Number of interior nodes ($|J|$)
n	Number of leaves ($|I|$)
H	Height; tiers indexed $h \in \{0, \ldots, H\}$
R	Root ($R \in J$)
For each tier $h \in \{1, \ldots, H\}$	
J_h	Set of nodes in tier h
q_h	Number of nodes in tier h ($|J_h|$)
For each interior node $j \in J$	
Θ_j	Set of j's direct subordinates
s_j	Span of j ($|\Theta_j|$)
For each node $k \in I \cup J$	
θ_k	Set of leaves weakly inferior to k
n_k	Size of k's division ($|\theta_k|$)
h_k	Tier of node k (maximum distance from leaves)
Balanced and uniform hierarchies	
q_h	Number of nodes in tier $h \in [0, \ldots, H]$
s_h	Average span of the nodes in tier $h \in \{1, \ldots, H\}$ ($s_h = q_{h+1}/q_h$)
s	Average span of the interior nodes in a uniform hierarchy ($s = n^{1/H}$)

problem), the leaves represent *shops* or whatever are the ultimate recipients of resources or production orders. In both cases, a node's children are called its *immediate subordinates* and a node's parent is called its *immediate superior*. The notation for hierarchies is summarized in Table 4 and defined as follows.

A hierarchy is specified by $\{I, J, R, \{\Theta_j\}_{j \in J}\}$, where I is the set of data or shops, J is the set of managers or offices, $R \in I \cup J$ is the root, and Θ_j ($j \in J$) is manager j's immediate subordinates. Figure 9 shows a hierarchy in which $I = \{1, \ldots, 9\}$, $J = \{a, b, c, d, R\}$, and, for example, $\Theta_b = \{c, d\}$. For $k_1, k_2 \in I \cup J$, $k_1 > k_2$ (resp. $k_1 \geq k_2$) means that k_1 is (weakly) superior to k_2. Define also, for $j \in J$:

$$s_j \equiv |\Theta_j| \qquad = \text{span of manager or office } j;$$

$$\theta_j \equiv \{i \in I \mid i < j\} = \text{division } j;$$

$$n_j \equiv |\theta_j| \qquad = \text{size of division } j.$$

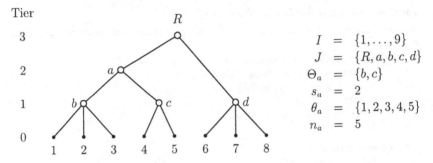

Figure 9. A hierarchy.

For example, in Figure 9, $s_a = 2$, $\theta_a = \{1, 2, 3, 4, 5\}$, and $n_a = 5$. By convention, $\theta_i = \{i\}$ and $n_i = 1$ for $i \in I$.

Furthermore, let $n = |I|$ be the number of data or shops (the *size* of the hierarchy), let $q = |J|$ be the number of managers or offices, and, for $h \in \{1, \ldots, H\}$, let J_h be the set of managers or offices in tier h and let $q_h = |J_h|$.

Here are some regularity properties that hierarchies can have.

(1) A hierarchy has no *skip-level reporting* if each immediate subordinate of any manager or office in tier h is in tier $h - 1$.[33]

(2) A hierarchy is *completely balanced* if it has no skip-level reporting and if all managers in the same tier have the same span. Completely balanced hierarchies are fully parameterized by the spans of the tiers and the height of the hierarchy.

(3) A hierarchy is *completely uniform* if it has no skip-level reporting and if all managers have the same span. Completely uniform hierarchies are fully parameterized by the height of the hierarchy or the common span of the managers.

These properties are illustrated in Figure 10. Note that the hierarchy in Figure 9 has none of these properties.

Completely balanced and completely uniform hierarchies are simple and are described by a few parameters. However, the definitions of completely balanced and completely uniform are restrictive. For example, unless n is a power of some integer, there are no completely uniform hierarchies with n terminal nodes. We circumvent these limitations in two ways. First, we will use the terms *balanced* and *uniform* for hierarchies that are almost completely balanced and almost completely uniform, respectively. Second, we will sometimes use continuous approximations,

---

[33] That is, if the path from the root to each leaf has the same length.

A hierarchy with skip-level reporting.

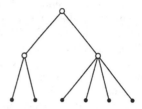

A hierarchy with no skip-level reporting that is not balanced.

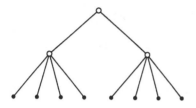

A balanced hierarchy that is not uniform. The root has a span of 2 and the managers in tier 1 have a span of 4.

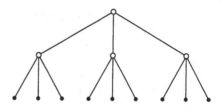

A uniform hierarchy. All managers have a span of 3.

Figure 10. Regularity properties of hierarchies.

meaning that we treat a manager's span or the number of managers in a tier as a continuous rather than a discrete variable. See Van Zandt (1995) for an analysis of the validity of such approximations and for more precise definitions of balanced and uniform hierarchies.

References

Aghion, P., and Tirole, J. (1997). Formal and real authority in organizations. *Journal of Political Economy*, 105, 1–29.

Aoki, M. (1986). Horizontal vs. vertical information structure of the firm. *American Economic Review*, 76, 971–83.

Arrow, K., and Hurwicz, L. (1960). Decentralization and computation in resource allocation. In R. W. Pfouts (ed.), *Essays in Economics and Econometrics* (pp. 34–104). Chapel Hill: University of North Carolina Press.

Arrow, K. J., and Radner, R. (1979). Allocation of resources in large teams. *Econometrica*, 47, 361–85.

Axtell, R., and Epstein, J. (1996). Distributed computation of optimal allocations through bilateral exchange. Brookings Institution, Washington, DC.

Baiman, S., Evans, J., and Noel, J. (1987). Optimal contracts with a utility-maximizing auditor. *Journal of Accounting Research*, 25, 217–44.

Baron, D., and Besanko, D. (1984). Regulation, asymmetric information and auditing. *RAND Journal of Economics*, 50, 447–70.

Barone, E. (1935). The ministry of production in the collectivist state. In F. A. v. Hayek (ed.), *Collectivist Economic Planning* (pp. 245–90). London: Routledge.

Beckmann, M. J. (1958). Decision and team problems in airline reservations. *Econometrica*, 26, 134–45.

(1983). *Tinbergen Lectures on Organization Theory*. Berlin: Springer.

Beggs, A. W. (1995). Queues and hierarchies. Wadham College, Oxford University, U.K.

Bolton, P., and Dewatripont, M. (1994). The firm as a communication network. *Quarterly Journal of Economics*, 109, 809–39.

Calvo, G., and Wellisz, S. (1980). Technology, entrepreneurs, and firm size. *Quarterly Journal of Economics*, 4, 663–77.

Chang, M.-H., and Harrington, J. E. (1996). Organizational structure and firm innovation. Department of Economics, Cleveland State University and John Hopkins University, Baltimore.

Cremer, J. (1980). A partial theory of the optimal organization. *Bell Journal of Economics*, 11, 683–93.

Culler, D., Karp, R., Patterson, D., Sahay, A., Schauser, K., Santos, E., Subramonian, R., and von Eicken, T. (1993). Log P: Towards a realistic model of parallel computation. Proceedings of the Fourth ACMSIGPLAN Symposium on Principles and Practice of Parallel Programming.

Dantzig, G. B., and Wolfe, P. (1960). Decomposition principles for linear program. *Operations Research*, 8, 101–11.

Demski, J., and Sappington, D. (1987). Hierarchical regulatory control. *RAND Journal of Economics*, 18, 77–97.

Dickinson, H. D. (1939). *Economics of Socialism*. Oxford: Oxford University Press.

Friedman, E. J., and Oren, S. S. (1995). The complexity of resource allocation and price mechanisms under bounded rationality. *Economic Theory*, 6, 225–50.

Geanakoplos, J., and Milgrom, P. (1991). A theory of hierarchies based on limited managerial attention. *Journal of the Japanese and International Economies*, 5, 205–25.

Gibbons, A., and Rytter, W. (1988). *Efficient Parallel Algorithms*. Cambridge University Press.

Green, J., and Laffont, J.-J. (1986). Incentive theory with data compression. In W. Heller, R. Starr, and D. Starrett (eds.), *Essays in Honor of K. J. Arrow*, vol. 3. Cambridge University Press.

(1987). Limited communication and incentive constraints. In T. Groves, R. Radner, and S. Reiter (eds.), *Information, Incentives, and Economic Mechanisms*. Minneapolis: University of Minnesota Press.

Groves, T. (1983). The usefulness of demand forecasts for team resource allocation in a dynamic environment. *Review of Economic Studies*, 50, 555–71.

Groves, T., and Hart, S. (1982). Efficiency of resource allocation by uninformed demand. *Econometrica*, 50, 1453–82.

Groves, T., and Radner, R. (1972). Allocation of resources in teams. *Journal of Economic Theory*, 4, 415–41.

Halpern, J. Y., and Moses, Y. (1990). Knowledge and common knowledge in a distributed environment. *Journal of the Association for Computing Machinery*, 37, 549–87.

Hayek, F. A. v. (1935). The nature and history of the problem. In F. A. v. Hayek (ed.), *Collectivist Economic Planning* (chap. 1). London: Routledge.

(1940). Socialist calculation: The competitive "solution." *Economica*, 7, 125–49.

Hong, L., and Page, S. (1995). Computation by teams of heterogeneous agents. Department of Economics, Syracuse University, and Division of Humanities and Social Sciences, California Institute of Technology, Pasadena.

Itoh, H. (1987). Information processing capacities of the firm. *Journal of the Japanese and International Economies*, 1, 299–326.

Jordan, J. (1995). Classification dynamics in the theory of decisions and organizations. Department of Economics, University of Minnesota, Minneapolis.

Keren, M., and Levhari, D. (1979). The optimum span of control in a pure hierarchy. *Management Science*, 11, 1162–72.

(1983). The internal organization of the firm and the shape of average costs. *Bell Journal of Economics*, 14, 474–86.

(1989). Decentralization, aggregation, control loss and costs in a hierarchical model of the firm. *Journal of Economic Behavior and Organization*, 11, 213–36.

Laffont, J.-J., and Martimort, D. (1996). Collusion and delegation. IDEI, Université de Toulouse I.

Lange, O. (1936). On the economic theory of socialism: Part one. *Review of Economic Studies*, 4, 53–71.

(1937). On the economic theory of socialism: Part two. *Review of Economic Studies*, 4, 123–42.

Malone, T. W., and Smith, S. A. (1988). Modeling the performance of organizational structures. *Operations Research*, 36, 421–36.

Marschak, T. (1986). Computation in organizations: The comparison of price mechanisms and other adjustment processes. In C. B. McGuire and R. Radner (eds.), *Decision and Organization* (pp. 237–81). Minneapolis: University of Minnesota Press.

Marschak, J., and Radner, R. (1972). *Economic Theory of Teams*. New Haven, CT: Yale University Press.

Marschak, T., and Reichelstein, S. (1995). Communication requirements for individual agents in networks and hierarchies. In J. Ledyard (ed.), *The Economics of Informational Decentralization: Complexity, Efficiency and Stability*. Boston: Kluwer.

(1996). Network mechanisms, informational efficiency, and hierarchies. Haas School of Business, University of California, Berkeley.

McAfee, R. P., and McMillan, J. (1995). Organizational diseconomies of scale. *Journal of Economics and Management Strategy*, 4, 399–426.

McGuire, C. B. (1961). Some team models of a sales organization. *Management Science*, 7, 101–30.

Meagher, K. J. (1996a). Efficient hierarchies: Equivalence under differing employment regimes. Department of Economics, Australian National University, Canberra.

(1996b). How to chase the market: An organizational and computational problem in decision making. Department of Economics, Australian National University, Canberra.

Meagher, K. J., and Van Zandt, T. (1998). Managerial costs for one-shot information processing. *Review of Economic Design*, 3 (forthcoming).

Melumad, N., Mookherjee, D., and Reichelstein, S. (1995). Hierarchical decentralization of incentive contracts. *RAND Journal of Economics*, 26, 654–72.

(1997). Contract complexity, incentives and the value of delegation. *Journal of Economics and Management Strategy*, 6, 257–89.

Miller, J. (1996). Evolving information processing organizations. Department of Social and Decision Sciences, Carnegie Mellon University, Pittsburgh.

Mises, L. v. (1951). *Socialism: An Economic and Sociological Analysis*. New Haven: Yale University Press.

Mookherjee, D., and Reichelstein, S. (1995). Incentives and coordination in hierarchies. Department of Economics, Boston University and Haas School of Business (UC Berkeley).

(1996). Budgeting and hierarchical control. Department of Economics, Boston University and Haas School of Business (UC Berkeley).

Mount, K., and Reiter, S. (1990). A model of computing with human agents. Discussion Paper no. 890, Center for Mathematical Studies in Economics and Management Science, Northwestern University, Evanston, IL.

(1998). A modular network model of bounded rationality. [Chapter 8 in this volume.]

Qian, Y. (1994). Incentives and loss of control in an optimal hierarchy. *Review of Economic Studies*, 61, 527–44.

Radner, R. (1961). *The Evaluation of Information in Organizations*, vol. 1. Berkeley: University of California Press.

(1986). Allocation of a scare resource under uncertainty: An example of a team. In C. B. McGuire and R. Radner (eds.), *Decision and Organization* (pp. 217–36). Minneapolis: University of Minnesota Press.

(1993). The organization of decentralized information processing. *Econometrica*, 62, 1109–46.

Radner, R., and Van Zandt, T. (1992). Information processing in firms and returns to scale. *Annales d'Economie et de Statistique*, 25/26, 265–98.

Reiter, S. (1996). Coordination and the structure of firms. MEDS, Northwestern University, Evanston, IL.

Rogers, D. F., Plante, R. D., Wong, R. T., and Evans, J. R. (1991). Aggregation and disaggregation techniques and methodology in optimization. *Operations Research*, 39, 553–82.

Rosen, S. (1982). Authority, control and the distribution of earnings. *Bell Journal of Economics*, 13, 311–23.

Taylor, F. M. (1929). The guidance of production in the socialist state. *American Economic Review*, 19, 1–8.

Tesfatsion, L. (1996). How economists can get a life. Department of Economics, Iowa State University.

Van Zandt, T. (1995). Continuous approximations in the study of hierarchies. *RAND Journal of Economics*, 26, 575–90.

(1996a). Decentralized information processing in the theory of organizations. In M. Sertel (ed.), *Contemporary Economic Development Reviewed, Volume 4: The Enterprise and its Environment*. London: MacMillan.

(1996b). Hidden information acquisition and static choice. *Theory and Decision*, 40, 235–47.

(1996c). Organizations with an endogenous number of information processing agents: Supplementary notes. Department of Economics, Princeton University.

(1996d). Real-time hierarchical resource allocation. Department of Economics, Princeton University.

(1996e). Real-time hierarchical resource allocation with quadratic costs. Department of Economics, Princeton University.

(forthcoming). The scheduling and organization of periodic associative computation: efficient networks. *Review of Economic Design*.

Van Zandt, T., and Radner, R. (1996). Real-time decentralized information processing and returns to scale. Department of Economics, Princeton University, and Stern School of Business, New York University.

Williamson, O. E. (1967). Hierarchical control and optimum firm size. *Journal of Political Economy*, 75, 123–38.

(1975). *Markets and Hierarchies, Analysis and Antitrust Implications*. New York: Free Press.

(1985). *The Economic Institutions of Capitalism*. New York: Free Press.

Youssefmir, M., and Huberman, B. A. (1995). Clustered volatility in multiagent dynamics. Dyamics of Computation Group, Xerox Palo Alto Research Center.

CHAPTER 8

A Modular Network Model of Bounded Rationality

Kenneth R. Mount and Stanley Reiter

Introduction

Many phenomena of economic behavior and economic institutions that are still not well understood might be better analyzed via theories that take into account limitations on the ability of humans to calculate and reason. It has been thought since the 1930s that limitations on information processing capabilities of individuals are fundamental to the existence, structure, and functioning of such economic organizations as firms (see, e.g., Kaldor 1934). If there were no restrictions on the ability of human beings to process information (i.e., to observe, communicate, and compute) then there would be no need for multi-person administrative organizations. Physical and technological limitations require that production involve sharing of tasks among many individuals. The efficiencies resulting from division of labor and specialization create a need for coordination of effort in production. In the absence of information processing limitations, decision making would not in itself require multi-person information processing. The complex internal structures of firms and other administrative organizations cannot be understood without recognizing that information processing tasks therein are distributed among individuals.

The distribution of information which arises in part as the result of limitations on human information processing also contributes to incentive problems, because it can create sources of private information. The analysis of incentives is usually done in game models, typically under the assumption that players are fully rational individuals. This kind of model has often led to new insights into strategic situations that were previously not well understood. If this were always or even generally the case then there would be little pressure to complicate the analysis by introducing considerations of bounded rationality. But often, indeed typically, solutions of repeated games of imperfect information consist of very large sets of equilibria in which any possible outcome is an equilibrium (the folk theorem). Rationalizing equilibria often involves complex strategic reasoning by the players. The combination of unsatisfactory results and perhaps unreasonable assumptions has led some game theorists to introduce limitations on the ability of a player to figure out his or her strategy (i.e., limitations on the rationality of players) and thereby reduce the size of the set of equilibria.[1]

Simon (1972, 1987) has advocated that economic theory take into account the boundedness of human rationality. This has stimulated explorations of organization via behavioral models rather than the rational behavior models based on optimization that are the norm in economic theory. On the other hand, Coase's (1937) hypothesis – that economic institutions are to be understood as optimal adaptations to constraints that limit the possibilities of contracting and exchange – remains the way most economists think about institutions and behavior. The transactions costs approach to institutions, specifically the firm, is in the spirit of this kind of theory, though it is not expressed in a formal model (cf. Williamson 1975).

To carry out the program indicated by Coase's principle, a theory of institutions should be one in which an institution or organization emerges as a solution of a constrained optimization problem. For this it is necessary to have a formal model of information processing, including computing, in which the relevant limitations can be expressed and their consequences analyzed. Information processing necessary to achieve coordinated economic action includes observation, communication, and computing. Communication among economic agents who know or can observe different parameters of the environment has been studied formally in the literature on decentralized mechanisms, starting with Arrow and Hurwicz (1959) and Hurwicz (1960), and in the literature on team theory. The literature on message-space theory in economics is surveyed in Marschak (1986) and in Hurwicz (1986). The same problem has been studied in computer science by Abelson (1980) and in the discrete case by Yao (1979) under the name "communication complexity." In contrast to the literature on communication, computation has received much less attention in economic theory.

The question is: How does one formalize limitations on rationality? A natural first step is to restrict attention to systematic reasoning, such as algorithmic processes as distinct from creative processes or leaps of intu-

---

[1] It should be noted that nonuniqueness of equilibrium is not always a bad thing. Models with unique solutions are not capable of explaining why different institutions or organizational forms coexist in the same environments. Matsuyama (1993) has emphasized this point.

itive thought. Having done that, it is natural to turn to computer science for guidance. The Turing machine model – and its finite memory version, the finite state sequential machine – or finite automaton are basic representations of algorithmic processes. The finite automaton model is perhaps the one that has received the most attention in economics, and has been particularly well-studied in game theory. Economists have applied the finite automaton model in a number of attempts to analyze the complexity of decision making and the functioning of economic organizations (cf. Futia 1977). The more recent applications of that model in game theory, especially in repeated games, seem to have been motivated by the problem of too many equilibria (Aumann 1981). Because strategies in a (repeated) game are functions from information to actions, restricting the number of states available to a player may restrict the set of strategies that are effectively available to that player, and therefore may restrict the set of equilibria of the game (see Neyman 1985, Abreu and Rubinstein 1988, and Rubinstein 1979, 1986).

Kalai and Stanford (1988) introduced a concept of complexity of a repeated game strategy which is defined independently of the concept of automaton. This concept, which classifies strategies into those whose complexity is n for each natural number n, permits restriction of the rationality of a player to be expressed by the condition that the only strategies available to a player are those whose complexity is at most n.[2]

The explorations in game theory using finite automata to model players captures some aspects of the complexity or the computational difficulty of a function or problem, but it seems that other aspects of computational difficulty that appear to be particularly important when human beings are doing the thinking or problem solving are not convincingly dealt with. One difficulty seems to be that the models involve a depth of reduction so fine that it seems unconvincing when applied to computations performed by human beings. Some investigators have turned to the "perceptron" (Minsky and Papert 1988), a kind of neural network (Hopfield 1982), as an alternative way of modeling computational limitations of players (see, e.g., Rubinstein 1993, Cho 1993a,b, and Cho and Li 1993).

Furthermore, another difficulty with applying the finite state automaton model more generally in economics is that the functions computed by them are discrete functions; that is, the domain and range of such a function are both discrete sets. This corresponds to the fact that the

---

[2] It turns out that the Kalai–Stanford complexity of a strategy is equal to the smallest number of states of a finite automaton that can compute that strategy.

inputs to a sequential machine are strings of symbols from a finite alphabet, such as $\{0, 1\}$, and so are the outputs. This poses no special difficulty in, for example, repeated games in which the stage game (the game being repeated) is a matrix game, but models in other economic settings commonly include functions whose domains and ranges are continua – for example, decision rules that describe behavior of consumers, whether or not strategic. The finite state sequential machine model cannot be applied directly to such functions.

The modular network model of computing is intended to permit analysis of computations performed by human beings (with or without the assistance of computing machines), to be applicable in standard economic models, to allow limitations on computing capabilities to be expressed formally, and to give some degree of control over the level of reduction of analysis required. This model was first proposed in Mount and Reiter (1982). Analysis of the model and its connections with standard models of computing are developed further in Mount and Reiter (1990), and some connections with models that study communication are examined in Mount and Reiter (1993). The modular network model is based on the neural network model of McCulloch and Pitts (1943) and Arbib (1969), and is an extension of that model in several respects. First, it permits computation with real numbers. Second, the set of elementary operations – which in the McCulloch–Pitts model are Boolean functions, including functions with thresholds – are permitted to be vector-valued functions of real variables. The set of elementary operations (functions) is a primitive of the model; that is, it can be specified by the modeler to suit the application in hand. The same is true of the topology of the network. Therefore, the level of reduction of analysis is controlled by the modeler in each application. These features facilitate the application of the model to human agents and to economic models. They also provide formal entities with which to express limitations on computing powers of individuals or other agents. Being a network model, the possibilities of parallel computation are readily expressed, and so is the dispersion of information. In economic terms the latter refers to the dispersion of information among agents (private information) or, in computing terms, to distributed memory.

When the alphabet is finite and the set of elementary operations consists of Boolean functions, the modular network model becomes equivalent to the finite automaton model in the sense that, for every such modular network, there is an equivalent finite automaton and vice versa. Furthermore, the complexity of a (continuous) function (of real variables) as measured in the modular network model (explained in what follows) is the limit of a sequence of complexities of finite approximations to that function as measured by finite (McCulloch–Pitts) networks, which, as we have said, are equivalent to finite automata.

A modular network is a model of the computation of a function (i.e., of an algorithm for computing a particular function) without regard to how that computation is further organized. In order to apply the model in the context of multi-person organizations, it is necessary to introduce additional structure. This is done by explicitly introducing computational resources to carry out the required computations, each computational agent being characterized by her set of elementary operations (computational capabilities) and by restrictions on the dispersion of initial information (who may observe what input variables or, in economic terms, environmental parameters). In that model, the problem addressed is how best to organize economic activity in a given environment. For example, given the specification of technological possibilities, in what organizational units ("firms") should production be organized, and how big should they be? This analysis is very briefly summarized in the last section of this paper (see also Reiter 1995).

The aim of this chapter is to provide an informal, intuitive presentation of the modular network model, emphasizing motivation and basic ideas. The exposition is aimed at communicating the model and the ideas embodied in it with a minimum of technical apparatus. We focus here on the use of modular networks to model computations carried out by a human being, illustrating the use of the model by examples. Formal definitions, theorems, and proofs can be found in Mount and Reiter (1982, 1993). Its use in a theory of the structure of firms can be found in Reiter (1995).

The recent work of Radner and of Van Zandt explores information processing within administrative organizations (firms). In Radner (1993), Radner and Van Zandt (1992), and Van Zandt and Radner (1995), the model of computing is one in which the elementary operations consist of binary associative operations on real numbers, such as addition of two numbers. The computational task facing the firm is to evaluate a given function at a given value of its multi-dimensional argument, using the processors available. The inputs to the function to be computed are available to any processor without restriction other than its capacity. In these features the model is a modular network model. However, they consider a problem in which a sequence of function evaluations must be made over time; in each of a succession of periods, a new "cohort" of values of the arguments of the function to be evaluated arrives at the input nodes of the network. The question addressed is how best to organize the sequence of computations when the costs of information processing depend on the time it takes to carry out the computation and the number of processors used. They also study returns to scale in such computations in relation to the problem of firm size and structure. Van Zandt (1995) has studied models in which the elementary operations are those carried out by simple computers called PRAMS.

Computing over the real numbers makes possible the use of classical mathematics. The modular network model and its analysis presented here (and in the references given) is related to certain classical problems in mathematics. In particular, the modular network model is related to Hilbert's thirteenth problem, and to the analysis of superpositions of functions carried out by Kolmogorov and Arnold. These connections are discussed in Section 5 (see also Blum, Shub, and Smale 1989).

There are nine sections in this chapter. Section 1 consists of a brief sketch of the modular network model of computing. Section 2 discusses the first of two examples of computing in which both humans and machines are elements of a network; Section 3 is the second of the examples in which both machines and humans are involved in a computation. Sections 4 introduces some simplifying assumptions that are used in Sections 5 and 6. Section 5 discusses the connection that the definition of complexity arising from the network model has with the mathematical studies of superposition (or function composition) and includes a statement of the Leontief–Abelson theorem. In some special circumstances one can determine uniquely, to within a special equivalence, a network that computes a given function in the least possible time. Section 6 gives an example of the construction of such a network for a special function of eight variables, and Section 7 discusses the selection of the modules of the network of Section 6 as the solutions of a system of equations. In Section 8 we analyze the complexity of computing the equilibrium price for an Edgeworth box economy. Section 9 concludes with a brief account of the application of the model of computing to a theory of the structure of organizations that process information for decision making.

1   The Modular Network Model of Computing

A modular network is specified by a set of *elementary operations*, and a *directed graph* (digraph) that shows constraints that the algorithm imposes on the order (partial) in which elementary operations can be performed. Some operations can be carried out in parallel, whereas others must follow a particular order. Viewed in another way, a *module* (embodying an elementary function) can be visualized as a black box with possibly many input lines and one output line, taking one unit of time to compute its output from its inputs. A *modular network*

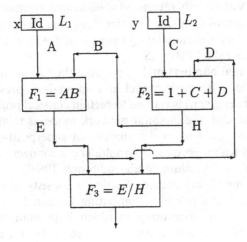

Figure 1

consists of modules wired together subject to the condition that each input wire of a module be connected to at most one output wire of a module.

An example is useful. The diagram in Figure 1 represents a (2,1)-network $\mathcal{C}$. The class $\mathcal{F}_{\mathcal{C}}$ of functions used in the network consists of four functions of the two real variables A and B:

$$\mathcal{F}_{\mathcal{C}} = \{A + B, AB, A/B, \text{identity function}\}.$$

Each vertex of the digraph that represents $\mathcal{C}$ is denoted by a box with a label that indicates the function assigned to that vertex. The vertices are labeled with upper-case letters (rather than lower-case) identifying the modules; L_1 and L_2 are the input vertices of the network, while the output vertex of the network is labeled F_3. Each arc of the digraph is labeled by a letter. We use the same labeling for a variable and for the arc that transmits the value from the module that outputs that variable to the one that receives it as an input (this is represented more precisely in Section 6).

We consider next how the $\mathcal{F}_{\mathcal{C}}$-network $\mathcal{C}$ computes. We have assumed that the output of a module f appears one unit of time after it receives its inputs. The *state of an $\mathcal{F}$-network* is an array whose entries are the states of the modules of the network in some prescribed order. We assume that the network is initially in some fixed state σ. A network with s input lines that is in state σ' acts on each s-tuple placed on the s input lines. If an s-tuple of values is placed on the network input lines, the

Table 1. *Table of States*

	L_1	L_2	F_1	F_2	F_3
σ	0	0	0	1	0
t					
0	x	y	0	1	0
1	x	y	x	$(1+y)$	0
2	x	y	$x(1+y)$	$(1+x+y)$	$x/(1+y)$
3	x	y	$x(1+x+y)$	$(1+x)(1+y)$	$\dfrac{x(1+y)}{(1+x+y)}$
4	x	y	$x(1+x)(1+y)$	$(1+y+x(1+x+y))$	$\dfrac{x(1+x+y)}{(1+x)(1+y)}$
5	x	y	$x(1+x+y+x^2+xy)$	$(1+y)(1+x+x^2)$	$\dfrac{x(1+x)(1+y)}{(1+y+x(1+x+y))}$

network will undergo a sequence of changes of state over time. (We assume that if the s-tuple of values on the input lines of the network is changed, the network returns to the fixed initial state σ for the start of the new computation.) As long as the values of the s-tuple on the network input lines remains unchanged, the values produced by the network at the network output vertices at the end of any interval of time are functions of the s-tuple on the network input lines.

Let the initial state in Figure 1 be σ. Assume that, in the initial state σ, the vertices L_1, L_2, F_1, F_2, F_3 have the values $0,0,0,1,0$, respectively. We represent the initial state σ by the row matrix (00010). Table 1 shows the sequence of changes of state over time as the network $\mathcal{C}$ computes.

Table 1 can be read as follows. The entry 0 in the column labeled F_1 and the row σ is the state of F_1 in the initial state σ of the network. The second row of Table 1 indicates the new state of the network at time $t = 0$. At that time, the input lines of the network are changed to the state in which input vertex L_1 has state x and input vertex L_2 has state y; that is, the values x and y are placed on the respective input lines at time 0. During the period from $t = 0$ to $t = 1$, the state of the network changes to a new state in which the state of F_1 is the value of the module $F_1(A, B) = AB$. Because, at $t = 0$, the line A has the value x and B has the value 1 (which is the initial state of the vertex F_2), it follows that F_1 changes to the state x at $t = 1$.

After four units of time (i.e., when $t = 4$, starting from the time that x and y were first placed on the network input lines), the output line F_3, corresponding to the module F_3, carries the value

$$h(x, y) = \frac{x(1 + x + y)}{(1 + x)(1 + y)},$$

and $t = 4$ is the earliest time at which this value appears on the output line of the network. The network $\mathcal{C}$ is said to compute the function h in four units of time.

Generally, a modular network $\mathcal{C}$ is said to *compute a function F in time t from initial state σ* if, for each sequence of values $(a_1, \ldots, a_p)$ assigned constantly to the network for t units of time, the value on the output lines of the network at time t is the function value $F(a_1, \ldots, a_p)$. Usually one is interested in the least time in which a network can compute a function.

It is clear that the least time needed to compute F depends both on the class of elementary operations allowed in the network and the topology of the digraph that represents the network.

As we have indicated, a module represents an elementary computation. The class of elementary functions is a *primitive* of the modular network model. That is, it plays the role of an undefined term in an axiomatic system, such as the term "commodity" in a general equilibrium system, say, as constructed by Debreu (1959). Thus, the set of elementary operations can be different in different applications of the model. For example, what is considered to be elementary may vary with the available means for computing. In some circumstances the basic arithmetic and logical operations may be taken to be the only elementary operations. In other circumstances – say, when the computing is to be done by a person equipped with a personal computer and a program for finding the roots of a polynomial of given degree p in n variables – then a user of the model might want to consider finding roots of such polynomials an elementary operation.

We may want to consider a class of algorithms rather than a particular one, for example, all algorithms corresponding to a neural network with one hidden layer and a given number of input modules. This is expressed by a constraint on the topology of the digraph. We also include the possibility that the functions assigned to the vertices of the digraph may be restricted. For example, in some cases the digraph is restricted to be a tree with the function assigned to the root required to be linear even when the set of elementary operations is not confined to linear modules. Another example is the set of restrictions that define modular networks that are simple perceptrons. These restrictions include both the topology of the network and the assignment of modules to vertices of the digraph. Thus, the structure of the allowable class of networks is also a primitive.

That the set of elementary functions is a primitive of the model gives the modeler control over the level of resolution of analyses done with the model. Once the set of elementary operations is specified, analysis of a function requires reduction of the computation to the level of elementary operations. For example, if the elementary operations are the basic logical and arithmetic operations on $\{0, 1\}$, then an algorithm for computation of a function must be expressed as a concatenation, perhaps with loops and branches, of binary operations. When computations are carried out by human beings in the context of an economic model, the level of reduction required by such an analysis can be impractically fine.

A commonly used notion of the complexity of a computation is the time it takes to carry it out. When an algorithm is represented in terms of sequence(s) of operations, the complexity of a function computed by that algorithm is related to the length of the longest such sequence or, alternatively, the average (in some sense) length of all sequences that might arise in the computation of the function. Since the objective is to find a model that allows computational limitations of human beings to be brought into the analysis, and since human beings can easily do some things that are difficult for computers to do (and vice versa), it seems desirable not to require that the elementary operations that are used to model computers also be used to model humans. This supports the idea of making the set of elementary operations a primitive.

The set of elementary functions provides the model with a formal way of expressing limitations on computational powers. The set of functions allowed to be modules might include, for example, Boolean functions, Heavyside or threshold functions, smooth functions, polynomials of no more than a specified degree, or real analytic functions. (For some purposes it is appropriate even to regard continuous functions as elementary.) In particular, the class of elementary operations can also formalize other limitations on computational abilities. For example, psychologists have pointed out that the number of things a person can pay attention to at the same time is limited (Miller 1956, Rosenblatt 1962). This limitation on computational powers can be expressed by the condition that an elementary operation can be a function of no more than a specified number of variables. Let $\mathcal{F}$ be the class of elementary operations. We call a modular network with elementary operations in the class $\mathcal{F}$ an $\mathcal{F}$-network. If the number of variables that an elementary function can have as arguments is restricted, say to r variables each of which can be at most d-dimensional (here we have in mind real variables), then we call the network an (r, d)-*network with modules in* $\mathcal{F}$. Where there is no ambiguity, we omit explicit reference to $\mathcal{F}$.

The *complexity* of a function relative to an $\mathcal{F}$-network is the minimum of the computing time required over all $\mathcal{F}$-networks that compute the given function. A function is *not computable* relative to $\mathcal{F}$ if there is no $\mathcal{F}$-network that computes it in finite time.

The extension of computation from integers and discrete functions to continuous variables and functions is a natural one. Limit theorems (Mount and Reiter 1990) confirm the intuition that computing with real numbers is an acceptable idealization of computing with integers, much as measurement with real numbers is an accepted idealization of measurement with rational numbers. These theorems tell us that the measure of complexity of a real-valued function f of real variables relative to (r, d)-networks with elementary operations $\mathcal{F}$ is a limit of measures of complexity, relative to finite (r, d)-networks, of discrete functions that approximate f. These results relate the extended notion of computing by (r, d)-networks to the finite state sequential machine model.

However, the model we have described so far is not yet adequate for representing directly some computations performed by humans. For that purpose we extend the model to include more abstract computations, provided that they can in a sense be reduced to computations with real variables. This is the purpose of introducing the idea of computing an *encoded version of a function*. The formal definition of this concept is presented in Section 3. For now we make do with an informal description that is sufficient for understanding the examples to follow. The idea is that a function to be computed may map a domain that is not a Euclidean space into another space, perhaps also not Euclidean. Human beings recognize or construct patterns, or other relationships, which generally are not presented as points of Euclidean spaces. For example, a set of points in the plane may be perceived as a two-dimensional representation of a box. Recognition of this visual pattern, a subset of Euclidean 2-space, can be thought of as computing a function that expresses the relation among the points in the subset that constitutes what is meant by saying it is a pattern – that is, a function whose value for that subset is the word "BOX." In such a case it may be possible to encode the more abstract domain and range of the function being computed in such a way as to transform the problem into one of computing a function between Euclidean spaces, and decoding the result. Figure 2 shows the scheme.

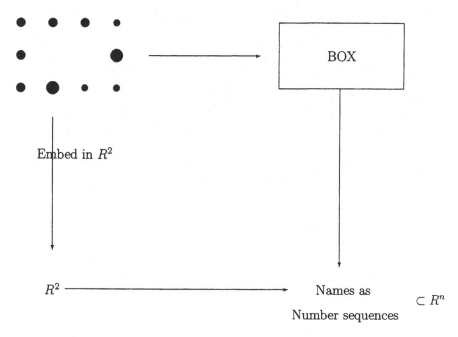

Figure 2

Before going further with the model, we take up two examples. These examples illustrate the application of the modular network model to computations performed by human beings and machines, and by human beings alone, and help clarify the ideas we have already discussed and that are subsequently presented in a more formal way.

2   Example I: Chernoff Faces

As a first example of the way in which humans and computers can interact to analyze complex information, we give an example in which the class of functions $\mathcal{F}$ used in the construction of an $\mathcal{F}$-network contains functions that are more easily evaluated by humans than by computers.

Human beings are good at seeing patterns. The ability to see patterns seems to depend on the structure and functioning of the human visual apparatus. Consequently, this ability applies to patterns in the space, or space-time, in which the visual system evolved, that is, in at most three or four dimensions (ignoring color).

On the other hand, situations arise in which we would like to detect patterns in high-dimensional data, say observations represented by points in R^k for k a positive integer much larger than 4. Computers are good at handling data of high dimensionality. Although there exist algorithmic processes, such as discriminant analysis or cluster analysis, for detecting patterns or regularities in some cases, we do not have pattern-recognizing algorithms that do as well as humans when restricted to low dimensions. Therefore, the idea of combining the power of computers to manipulate data with the ability of humans to see patterns is appealing. Indeed, the practice of making graphical representations of data as a way of bringing to bear the human visual system predates the electronic computer, and is widely used in physical, biological and social science, and mathematics, as well as in business and everyday affairs.

Chernoff (1973) introduced the idea of combining human beings and computers to detect patterns in a sample of observations of a relatively large number of variables. Specifically, he introduced the graphical representation of multi-dimensional data as *cartoon faces* drawn in two dimensions, and illustrated its use by two examples. These are:

(i)   a set of 8 measurements made on each of 87 fossils; and
(ii) a set of 53 observations of 12 variables taken from mineral analysis of a 4,500-foot core drilled from a Colorado mountain side.

The data are encoded as faces by a program that provides for up to 18 parameters that govern 18 features of a face. For example, one variable determines the horizontal distance between the eyes; another determines the height of the eyes; another determines the curvature of the arc that forms the mouth; and so forth. If the number of variables observed is $k \leq 18$, then $18 - k$ variables are fixed at some value and the remaining k variables determine the variable features of a face for each point observed. The computer prints out the set of faces, and a human being looks for a pattern in them. In the example with measurements made on fossils, the pattern sought was a classification of the fossils into groups of similar ones. In the second example, the observations were assumed to be generated by a multivariate stochastic process, and the problem was to detect a point in the time series of observations at which the process changed character.

Let

$$S \subset R^k, S = \left\{ x^1, \ldots, x^n \right\},$$

be the sample of n observations, each a k-dimensional point. Let η: $R^k \to R^2$ be a correspondence that assigns to k variables the subset of

R^2 that consists of the visual image encoding the variables. Set $\eta(x^1, \ldots, x^n) = (y^1, \ldots, y^n)$, where $y^i = \eta x^i$. (It is implicit in this notation that distinct points of S are assumed to be mapped to distinct subsets of R^2.) Thus, in Chernoff's first example $(k = 8)$, x^i is the vector of eight measurements made on the ith fossil and y^i is the cartoon face that encodes those measurements.

The problem is to classify the fossils, so we seek a partition of the set S or (correspondingly) a partition of the set $\{y^1, \ldots, y^n\}$. Because S has n elements, the number of nonempty subsets in a partition of S, and a fortiori in a partition of $\{y^1, \ldots, y^n\}$, is at most n. Therefore, a partition of S (or of $\{y^1, \ldots, y^n\}$) can be represented by characteristic functions as follows. Let $\xi \colon S \to \{0, 1\}^n$ where $\xi = (\xi_1, \ldots, \xi_n)$, let $\xi_i \colon S \to \{0, 1\}$, and define $Q_i = \{x \in S \mid \xi_i(x) = 1\} = \xi_i^{-1}(1) \subset S$. Then $Q = \{Q_1, \ldots, Q_r\}$ is a partition of S, where (possibly after a renumbering of the characteristic functions) Q_i is the ith nonempty subset defined by ξ. If we suppose that Y is the collection of all possible n-tuples of faces, then a partition

$$P = \{P_1, \ldots, P_r\}$$

of Y is defined by characteristic functions

$$\chi \colon Y \to \{0, 1\}^n,$$

where

$$\chi = (\chi_1, \ldots, \chi_n), \quad \chi_i \colon Y \to \{0, 1\},$$

and

$$P_i = \{y \in Y \mid \chi_i(y) = 1\} = \chi_i^{-1}(1) \subset Y.$$

Consider the entire computation as carried out by a machine. The machine would execute a program that embodied an algorithm for, say, a cluster analysis of S. The machine would compute a (vectorial) characteristic function ξ from inputs that consisted of the coordinates of the 8-dimensional points that characterize a fossil. An $\mathcal{F}$-network model would represent this computation in terms of the class of elementary operations $\mathcal{F}$.

Suppose on the other hand that, instead of doing a cluster analysis, a human being produced a partition of the set Y using as inputs the set Y of cartoon faces encoding S produced by the computer. We could view the human being as an agent capable of "computing χ directly." We would like our model to represent the entire computation – namely, the part that produces the cartoon faces (which is carried out by the machine) and the part that produces the classification of faces (carried out by the human being) – in a seamless way. In that case, even if there

$$S \xrightarrow{\ \xi=\mathrm{id}\chi\eta\ } \{0,1\}^n$$

$$\eta \downarrow \qquad\qquad \downarrow \mathrm{id}$$

$$Y \xrightarrow{\ \chi\ } \{0,1\}^n$$

Figure 3

were no algorithm for performing the required analysis on S, the function ξ could be defined as in Figure 3 and incorporated into the set $\mathcal{F}$. However, the time scale for elementary operations carried out by a person might be different from those carried out by a machine. We shall continue to assume that an elementary operation takes one unit of time.

For our purposes, Chernoff's second example differs from the first only in that the sets S and Y are ordered according to the time sequence of the observations and the functions ξ and χ are step functions, with the step at the point at which the stochastic process is deemed to change character.

3   Example II: Reading Handwriting

Another example of a computation that humans perform routinely and in many cases easily and yet is very difficult for computers is reading handwriting. The phrase "reading handwriting" can mean several different things. Here we take it to mean writing in noncursive form (i.e., printing) the (English) expressions indicated by a given sample of cursive script.

The translation of cursive script into printed form is still extremely difficult, complex, and problematic for machines, although it is routinely performed by literate persons (though not without error). An impressive example is the reading of physicians' prescriptions by pharmacists. Imagine a typesetter, a person or machine, who has before him (it) a manuscript (cursive statement) and a font of type, and whose task is to produce a sequence of type elements (upper- and lower-case letters, punctuation marks, and spaces) that correctly translate the cursive manuscript into printed form.

A cursive writing sample is a plane "curve," one that may have discontinuities (e.g., gaps between adjacent letters) due to the idiosyncrasies of handwriting of a particular person, or the normal spaces between words; it may have isolated points (e.g., the dot over the letter "i" or the full stop that marks the end of a sentence); it may also have crossing strokes, such as that for the letter "t."

We may consider these curves to be concatenations of elements of a finite-dimensional space consisting of conceivable finite samples of cursive script of no more than a given (unit) length. Thus we assume the writing to be constructed of some collection of curves capable of being represented by a subset of a finite-dimensional Euclidean space. Denote this space by C. (Other properties of curves that can be cursive writing samples, such as being of bounded variation or having uniform upper and lower bounds on the height of letters, could also be considered.) The space T of printed text consists of a null element as well as all finite strings over the alphabet made up of the font elements.

The act of reading a cursive statement may be represented by a function $\varrho: C \to T$. Typically, this function will be many-to-one. Unreadable cursive samples are mapped to the null element of T. (If it is useful to do so, the function ϱ may be assumed to depend on the person who writes, as well as on the person who reads, or both.)

First, however, we consider how a machine might perform this act of reading a given cursive writing sample. The curve that constitutes a cursive writing sample must be presented to the computer in a form the computer can accept. This may be done by a device like a scanner that converts the curve into a string of symbols from the alphabet recognized by the computer, or perhaps by a sensitive tablet on which the sample is written using some sort of stylus or light pen. The result of either of these input devices is an *encoded representation of the curve*. This may be as a graphic image or as an object specified by the equations that define the curve as a locus in 2-space, perhaps relative to some given coordinate system. Another possibility (which involves more information, however) is to describe the curve parametrically, by equations

$$x(t) = \phi_1(t), \quad y(t) = \phi_2(t), \quad t_1 \le t \le t_2,$$

where (x, y) denotes a point in the plane and t is in the interval between t_1 and t_2 in the real line. This representation, or a discrete approximation to it, might describe someone writing cursively on a sensitive tablet.

Given this input, the computer would need a program to process the input into the ASCII code for the string of font symbols that constitute the output desired. Because the task is a complex one for a computer, the program is likely to be long and perhaps likely to produce incorrect results on many writing samples. (In the present discussion we may regard an incorrect result as equivalent to infinite computing time, i.e., we would have to wait forever for the correct result. A more satisfactory approach would be to measure the degree to which the output approximates the correct result, but this seems too complicated for the present purpose.) The diagram in Figure 4 represents the situation.

$$
\begin{array}{ccc}
C & \xrightarrow{\;\rho\;} & T \\
e\downarrow & & \downarrow a \\
R^{l_1}\times\cdots\times R^{l_n} & \xrightarrow{\;f_\rho\;} & R^{l_1}\times\cdots\times R^{l_m}
\end{array}
$$

Figure 4

In Figure 4, the function $e\colon C \to R^{l_1} \times \cdots \times R^{l_n}$ is an encoding of the elements of C (i.e., cursive statements) into elements of $R^{l_1} \times \cdots \times R^{l_n}$. (Note that if the encoding is done by a device such as a scanner, the encoding may depend on the position of the cursive statement on the screen of the device. In that case the coding would not be unique unless the positioning of the cursive sample is standardized. We may either assume that this is the case, or define a set of transformations in the plane that leave the cursive sample invariant except for position and define the encoding to be the same for any element of the equivalence class so generated. Evaluating this equivalence relation describes something humans do regularly – e.g., in stabilizing the visual field – but it is a complex task for a machine.)

Furthermore, the function a in the diagram is an encoding of T in $R^{l_1} \times \cdots \times R^{l_n}$. The ASCII code for alphanumeric characters is an example. (Here the null element of T is mapped to any element of $R^{l_1} \times \cdots \times R^{l_n}$ that is not the image of any character.) The inverse of the encoding a, performed by a device such as a printer, would produce the final result, the translation of the cursive writing sample into a printed writing sample.

If the computer cannot read a cursive writing sample in one step then the function f_ρ would not be elementary for that computer – that is, not be in the set $\mathcal{F}$ consisting of the operations that are elementary for that computer. There would have to be a program written that computes f_ρ from the inputs using the operations that are elementary for that computer system.

The computation may be represented by an (r, d)-network, with modules from the class $\mathcal{F}$, that computes f_ρ. The complexity of f_ρ is likely to be very high, if indeed that function is at all computable relative to the modules in $\mathcal{F}$. If, for instance, the elementary operations consist of the arithmetic and logical operations, then a program that can read handwriting is likely to be long and involved, and the time required to compute f_ρ is likely to be long.

Consider next a person reading the cursive writing sample. That a person can read cursive script may be expressed by saying that the evaluation of the function ρ is an elementary operation for that person. That is, the person does it immediately or directly without any apparent intermediate steps, taking only a small (unit) interval of time per unit length of curve. Another way to describe this is that we do not analyze the process into steps that are internal to the reader.

Although the function ϱ is clearly a representation of the act of reading cursive writing, it is not in itself a useful model; it does not yet connect with any other model of computation, nor does there appear to be a way to use it in the analysis of economic models.

On the other hand, in modeling a person reading handwriting we may consider the function ϱ to be equivalent to the composition

$$\alpha^{-1} \circ f_\varrho \circ e \equiv \varrho \tag{E1}$$

in Figure 4. To say that a person can evaluate ϱ in one unit of time can be interpreted as saying that the composition (E1) can be evaluated in one unit of time. This amounts to saying that the function f_ϱ cannot take more than one unit of time. Hence it may be included as an elementary operation (i.e., a member of $\mathcal{F}$) in any application of the model in which a human being capable of reading cursive writing is among the computational resources.

For example, at the local drug store there is a pharmacist who reads the prescription form given to her by the customer, a form written by a physician in longhand. The pharmacist enters the prescription and other relevant information into a desktop computer by typing it on the keyboard. The computer processes this input according to its internal program, a computation representable by an (r, d)-network. The act of translating a unit length of the handwritten prescription into type (keystrokes) is elementary, and in the (r, d)-network model is formally seamless with the rest of the computation.

4   Analyzing the Complexity of a Function

With the preceding examples in mind, we now return to the modular network model. Specifically, we take up the question of how to use the modular network model to analyze the complexity of a function. In this, while we go into more detail, we make some simplifying assumptions in the interest of clarity. In particular, we take the concept of a directed graph as an intuitive one and do not give a mathematical definition; see Mount and Reiter (1990) for formal definitions of the concepts employed. Furthermore, we restrict the modules (elementary functions) to functions of at most r inputs, each of which is a d-dimensional vector; in fact, we take $r = 2$ and $d = 1$, restricting attention to elementary functions that are real-valued functions of at most two real variables. We also restrict attention to the computation of real-valued functions. Figure 1 showed a network that satisfies all these assumptions. Therefore,

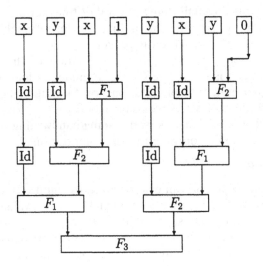

Figure 5

we may take the network shown in Figure 1 as a prototypical example. As seen in Table 1, that network computes many different functions from the same inputs as time increases. This property, which is inconvenient for analysis of the complexity of a function, is a result of the fact that the network in Figure 1 contains loops (i.e., its digraph contains cycles). However, if the function F to be analyzed is given then *a network C with loops that computes F in time t can be replaced by an equivalent network that computes F in time t, has the same modules as C (perhaps with the addition of projections and constants), and is free of loops.*

5   Modular Networks and Superpositions

The network in Figure 1 computes h (from the initial state shown in Table 1), so it is immediate from the graph that $h(x, y)$ can be written as

$$h(x, y) = F_3\left[F_1\left(x, F_2\left(y, F_1(x, 1)\right)\right), F_2\left(y, F_1\left(x, F_2(y, 0)\right)\right)\right]$$

for any x and y.

That is, h can be written as a *superposition* (composition) of the functions that are modules of the network that computes h. A network that is represented by a connected tree with a single root computes functions that are *superpositions* of the functions in $\mathcal{F}$ (i.e., superpositions of functions that are the modules of the network). Figure 5 shows such a network that computes h. The *depth of the superposition* – that is, the number of levels of functions used – is equal to the length of the tree. Furthermore, if the network inputs are constantly on the input lines for a time that exceeds the length of the tree, then the network output is constant for all times thereafter and the depth of superposition is the length of the tree.

Thus, we see that the complexity of a function F relative to (r, d)-networks with modules in the class $\mathcal{F}$ is equivalent to the minimum depth t such that F can be written as a superposition of functions from the class $\mathcal{F}$ with depth t. This formulation is useful for obtaining analytical conditions for a lower bound on the complexity of F when F is sufficiently smooth.

The complexity of F relative to (r, d)-networks with modules in $\mathcal{F}$ is related to a classical problem in mathematics: Hilbert's thirteenth problem (see Lorentz 1966). The essential substance of the problem is to decide whether a given function F of n variables can be written as a superposition of functions of fewer than n variables from a given class. It is implicit in the literature that the depth of the superposition expresses an intuitive notion of computational complexity.

When the functions in the superposition are restricted to be continuous and have fewer variables than F, Arnold and Kolmogorov have shown (cf. Lorentz 1966, p. 168; Vituskin 1961, Introduction) that F can always be written as a superposition of continuous functions of fewer variables. Indeed they have shown that each function of n variables can be written as a superposition of continuous functions of *two* variables. Furthermore, the depth of the superposition is bounded above by a constant that depends only on the number of variables of F. If, on the other hand, F is required to be smooth (i.e., continuously differentiable to some specified order), and if the functions used in the superposition are required to have the same degree of smoothness as F, then it is known that in general such a superposition representation cannot be guaranteed (cf. Lorentz 1966, Vituskin 1961).

Even if we reduce the class of functions and ask, as Hilbert did, whether an arbitrary analytic function of n variables can be written as a superposition of analytic functions of at most two variables, then an argument of Hilbert shows that the answer is No (see Lorentz 1966).

We may interpret these results as follows. The Arnold and Kolmogorov results suggest that there are *too many* continuous functions of two variables, and Hilbert's argument suggests that there are *too few* power series in two variables. Furthermore, in being too large, the class of continuous functions of two variables includes many functions that it would strain credulity to regard as elementary. On the other hand, real analytic functions of two variables can be considered as extensions or idealizations of arithmetic operations, especially if we restrict them to be truncated power series.

In any case, for the purpose of illustrating the analysis of complexity of functions, including the construction of minimal $(2,1)$-networks, we shall take the class $\mathcal{F}$ of elementary functions to consist of power series in two variables up to degree M. Specifically, we assume as follows.

A1 $\mathcal{F}$ consists of real analytic functions (power series) in two variables, truncated at degree M, with constant term identically zero and linear term not zero.

A2   The functions to be computed (i.e., whose complexity is to be analyzed) consist of real analytic functions of n variables that vanish at the origin. They are to be computed only up to degree M.

We then say that a function F can be computed in time T to degree M if it can be written, to degree M, as a superposition of length T of functions from $\mathcal{F}$ but not as a superposition of length $T-1$.

Are there conditions on the function F that inform us whether it can be written as a superposition of length T of functions from $\mathcal{F}$ but not as a superposition of length $T-1$? And further, how can we construct a superposition of length T for F or (equivalently) an (r,d)-network with modules in $\mathcal{F}$ that computes F in time T?

For this informal presentation we restrict attention to representing F as a superposition of analytic functions of two variables (see Mount and Reiter 1990 for a more general treatment). Accordingly, throughout this discussion the function F and the class of elementary functions $\mathcal{F}$ satisfy assumptions A1 and A2. We use the following theorem (Leontief 1947 and Abelson 1980). Although we apply the theorem here only to the special case defined by A1 and A2, we state the theorem in more general terms. We first state the theorem for a function $F: R^m \times R^n \to R$, and then illustrate in the special case how it can be used. We suppose that R^m has coordinates $x = (x_1, \ldots, x_m)$ and R^n has coordinates $y = (y_1, \ldots, y_n)$. In order to state the theorem, we define two matrices associated with the function F. These are:

$$BHF(x, y) = \begin{pmatrix} \partial F/\partial x_1 & \partial^2 F/\partial x_1 \partial y_1 & \cdots & \partial^2 F/\partial x_1 \partial y_n \\ \vdots & \vdots & \cdots & \vdots \\ \partial F/\partial x_m & \partial^2 F/\partial x_m \partial y_1 & \cdots & \partial^2 F/\partial x_m \partial y_n \end{pmatrix},$$

where $\underline{x} = (x_1, \ldots, x_m)$ and $\underline{y} = (y_1, \ldots y_n)$; and $BHF\ (\underline{y};\underline{x})$, constructed by interchanging $\underline{x}$ and $\underline{y}$ in the construction of the matrix $BHF\ (\underline{x};\underline{y})$.

The Leontief result (as used by Abelson 1980) implies: A necessary condition that a continuously differentiable function F can be written in the form $G(A(\underline{x}),\underline{y})$, where A is a function with continuous first derivatives in a neighborhood of a point $(\underline{a},\underline{b})$ with $\underline{a} = (a_1, \ldots, a_m)$ and $\underline{b} = (b_1, \ldots, b_n)$, is that the matrix $BHF\ (\underline{x};\underline{y})$ have rank at most 1. This rank condition is also a sufficient condition that F can be written in the form $G(A(\underline{x}),\underline{y})$ if F has nonvanishing first partials in the x_i at $(\underline{a},\underline{b})$.

Abelson used the necessary condition to analyze the information transfer of a multi-stage distributed computation of the function F. He analyzed the informational exchange requirements when two processors PX and PY compute the function $F(\underline{x},\underline{y})$ when only PX has the values x_i and only PY has the values y_j. He treated informational exchange as the communication of real number values. Abelson showed that if the matrix derived from $BHF\ (\underline{x};\underline{y})$ by deleting the first column has rank R, then each multi-stage distributed computation that computes F in a neighborhood of $(\underline{a},\underline{b})$ must have a total information transfer of at least R between the two processors.

Abelson's analysis of the communication required to compute a function given distributed information uses a submatrix of the bordered Hessian $BHF\ (\underline{x};\underline{y})$ and bounds the communication by a rank condition on a submatrix of the Hessian. We also use the matrix $BHF\ (\underline{x};\underline{y})$ and its twin $BHF\ (\underline{y};\underline{x})$ to analyze computational complexity. However, the rank conditions we require are not the same as Abelson's, and further we must analyze a *sequence* of such matrices derived from F.

Theorem (Leontief–Abelson).   *The function F equals $H(A(\underline{x}),B(\underline{y}))$ only if both matrices $BHF(\underline{x};\underline{y})$ and $BHF(\underline{y};\underline{x})$ have rank at most 1, and these rank conditions are also sufficient when first partials in x_i and in y_i are nonvanishing.* (A complete proof can be found in Mount and Reiter 1990.)

Suppose further that, in addition to satisfying the hypotheses of the theorem, F is a function of 2^N variables, that the linear part of F depends on all 2^N variables, and that (as assumed previously) $F(0, \ldots, 0) = 0$. It is easy to see that the shortest time in which F can possibly be computed is N. To see this, note that to compute the linear combination of the 2^N variables $x_i\ (j = 0, \ldots, 2^N - 1)$ that is the linear part of F in minimal time, using $(2, 1)$-modules in $\mathcal{F}$, one should compute as many of these as

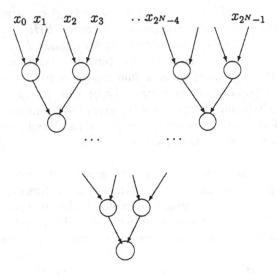

Figure 6

possible at the same time. This is done by the $(2,1)$-network shown in Figure 6, *a $(2,1)$-fan-in* of length N.

Now suppose that F (i.e., not just the linear part of F) can be computed up to degree M in the minimal time N. Then the graph of the $(2, 1)$-network that computes it must also be a fan-in of depth N. We need only specify the module assigned to each vertex of the fan-in in order to specify the network completely, that is, to write F as a superposition of functions in $\mathcal{F}$. We next show how to construct a proposed assignment. The Leontief–Abelson theorem can then be applied to verify that the assignment proposed can in fact be made.

6   Assigning Modules to the Vertices of the Fan-In

We begin by labeling the vertices of the fan-in. This is done as follows. If the vertex is a leaf (an input vertex) then it is labeled with the index of the variable that is input there. If the vertex is not an input vertex then it is labeled with an ordered pair. There are two cases.

(1)   The two inputs to the vertex v come from vertices labeled (i,j) and (k,l), respectively, where $i < k$. Then the label attached to v is (i,l).

(2)   The input lines of v are network input lines. Network input lines are labeled by the variables they carry. Thus, the inputs to v are

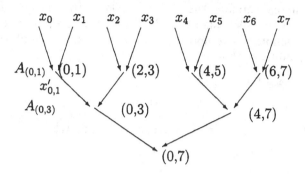

Figure 7

the variables in an adjacent pair (x_{2j}, x_{2j+1}) for some j in $0, \ldots,$ $2^{N-1} - 1$. In this case the vertex v has the label $(2j, 2j + 1)$.

This labeling is illustrated in Figure 7 for $N = 3$. The leaves are labeled in order from left to right, $0, 1, \ldots, 2^N - 1 = 0, 1, \ldots, 7$. The vertex whose inputs are x_0 and x_1 is labeled $(0, 1)$; the vertex whose inputs are the outputs of $(0, 1)$ and $(2, 3)$ is labeled $(0, 3)$; and so on. (There is no ambiguity in this labeling scheme, because if a vertex has inputs from vertices (i, j) and (k, l) then $i < k$ implies that $(i, l) \neq (i, j')$ for any vertex labeled (i, j').)

Under the assumptions we have made, a function F computed by a $(2, 1)$-network in minimal time determines the modules of the network essentially uniquely. The qualification "essentially" refers to the fact that the modules are determined up to an equivalence relation, according to which two functions are equivalent if they are the same except for changes of variables in the domain and range. This is defined more explicitly in what follows. In the interest of clarity and to minimize notational complexity, we illustrate the process of assigning modules for $N = 3$ using the tree in Figure 7. We suppose that $F: R^8 \to R$, where $F(x_0, \ldots, x_7)$ is computed by a network whose tree is shown in Figure 7 with modules in $\mathcal{F}$.

The module assigned to vertex (i, j) is denoted $A_{(i,j)}$. Consider first the vertex $(0, 1)$, which has as inputs the variables x_0 and x_1 and is therefore assigned the function $A_{(0,1)}$. Consider how the network evaluates F at the point $(x_0, x_1, 0, \ldots, 0)$. Because the functions $A_{(i,j)}$ in F have the property that $A_{(i,j)}[0, 0] = 0$, it follows that, at each vertex (i, j) such that $i \neq 0$, the output of the module assigned to that vertex must be 0. Furthermore, at each vertex $(0, j)$ where $j > 1$, only the left input line carries a value different from 0. Thus, each module $A_{(0,j)}$ where $j > 1$ acts like a (truncated) power series in one variable. Therefore, the composition of the modules from $A_{(0,3)}$ to the module assigned to the root acts like a power series in one variable. Denote this composition $h(z)$ (not to be confused with the function h of Table 1). Thus

$$h(z) = A_{(0,7)}\Big(A_{(0,3)}(z, 0), 0\Big).$$ (E2)

Write $F(x_0, x_1, 0, \ldots, 0) = F_{(0,1)}(x_0, x_1)$. Then

$$h\Big(A_{(0,1)}(x_0, x_1)\Big) = F\big(x_0, x_1, 0, \ldots, 0\big) = F_{(0,1)}\big(x_0, x_1\big).$$

Similarly, for $F(0, 0, x_2, x_3, 0, \ldots, 0) = F_{(2,3)}(x_2, x_3)$,

$$g\Big(A_{(2,3)}(x_2, x_3)\Big) = F_{(2,3)}\big(x_2, x_3\big),$$

where

$$g(z) = A_{(0,7)}\Big[A_{(0,3)}(z), 0\Big] = h(z).$$

The last equality is by equation (E2). Therefore,

$$h\Big(A_{(2,3)}(x_2, x_3)\Big) = F_{(2,3)}\big(x_2, x_3\big).$$

That is, the composition of the modules $A_{(0,j)}$, which is the function h, when composed with $A_{(0,1)}$ yields $F_{(0,1)}$ and yields $F_{(2,3)}$ when composed with $A_{(2,3)}$. Thus, if $h(z)$ is known and has an inverse, then we have determined both $A_{(0,1)}$ and $A_{(2,3)}$ from F once we know h. In the same way, the modules $A_{(4,5)}$ and $A_{(4,7)}$ can be assigned by using $F_{(4,5)}$ and $F_{(6,7)}$ defined analogously.

Next, define new variables $y_{i,j}$ by

$$y_{i,j} = A_{(i,j)}(x_i, x_j), \quad \text{where } (i, j) = (0, 1), (2, 3), (4, 5), \text{ or } (6, 7),$$

and consider the network shown in Figure 8.

The same process that was used to determine $A_{(0,1)}$ can be applied to the determination of $A_{(0,3)}$, using the function

$$G(y_{0,1}, y_{2,3}) = F(x_0, x_1, x_2, x_3, 0, \ldots, 0),$$

where $y_{0,1} = A_{(0,1)}(x_0, x_1)$ and $y_{2,3} = A_{(2,3)}(x_2, x_3)$. The other modules in Figure 8 can be assigned in the same way.

We consider next the extent to which the functions we have constructed are unique. Let us define an equivalence relation on real analytic functions of two real variables as follows.

Two (real analytic) functions $B(x, y)$ and $C(x, y)$ are *equivalent* if there are nonsingular (i.e., having nonzero linear terms) analytic functions u, k, l of one variable such that

$$B(x, y) = u\Big(C\big(k(x), l(y)\big)\Big).$$

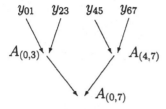

Figure 8

The constructions illustrated in Figures 7 and 8 indicate that if the function F can be computed by a superposition as in Figure 7, then the modules $A_{(i,j)}$ are unique to within equivalence; that is, they are equivalent to the functions $F_{(i,j)}$.

7   Determining the Modules by Solving Equations

We digress here to present a determination of the modules $A_{(0,j)}$ in Figure 7 that makes explicit use of the power series expressions for all the functions involved. This material can be skipped by readers who find the foregoing sufficiently explicit.

We assume that $M = 2$ – in other words, that F is to be computed up to degree 2 and the modules are power series truncated at degree 2. Then

$$F(x_0, \ldots, x_7) = \sum_{i=0}^{7} a_i x_i + \sum_{i=0}^{7} b_i x_i^2 + 2 \sum_{i=0\ldots7, j=0\ldots7, i<j} c_{i,j} x_i x_j.$$

Using the power series for F and the modules $A_{(0,j)}$, we have

$$F_{(0,1)}(x_0, x_1) = a_0 x_0 + a_1 x_1 + b_0 x_0^2 + b_1 x_1^2 + c_{0,1} x_0 x_1,$$

$$A_{(0,1)}(x_0, x_1) = \alpha_0 x_0 + \alpha_1 x_1 + \beta_0 x_0^2 + \beta_1 x_1^2 + \chi_{0,1} x_0 x_1,$$

$$A_{(0,3)}(y) = \alpha_0' y + \beta_0' y^2,$$

$$A_{(0,7)}(y', 0) = \alpha_0'' y' + \beta_0'' y'^2,$$

where

$$y = \alpha_0 x_0 + \alpha_1 x_1 + \beta_0 x_0^2 + \beta_1 x_1^2 + \chi_{0,1} x_0 x_1,$$

$$y^2 = \alpha_0^2 x_0^2 + 2\alpha_0 \alpha_1 x_0 x_1 + \alpha_1^2 x_1^2,$$

and hence

$$y' = A_{(0,3)}(y,0) = \alpha_0'\big(a_0 x_0 + a_1 x_1 + \beta_0 x_0^2 + \beta_1 x_1^2 + \chi_{0,1} x_0 x_1\big)$$
$$+ \beta_0'\big(a_0^2 x_0^2 + 2a_0 a_1 x_0 x_1 + a_1^2 x_1^2\big).$$

Using the expression for y' and calculating y'^2, we evaluate $A_{(0,7)}(y',0)$ to obtain

$$z = A_{(0,7)}(y',0)$$
$$= \alpha_0''\big(\alpha_0' a_0 x_0 + \alpha_0' a_1 x_1 + \big(\alpha_0' \beta_0 + \beta_0' a_0^2\big) x_0^2$$
$$+ \big(\alpha_0' \beta_1 + \beta_0' a_1^2\big) x_1^2 + \big(\alpha_0' \chi_{01} + 2\beta_0' a_0 a_1\big) x_0 x_1\big)$$
$$+ \beta_0''\Big(\big(\alpha_0' a_0\big)^2 x_0^2 + 2a_0 a_1 \big(\alpha_0'\big)^2 x_0 x_1 + \big(\alpha_0' a_1\big)^2 x_1^2\Big).$$

Because the superposition we have obtained is required to compute $F_{(0,1)}$, that is, because

$$F_{(0,1)}(x_0, x_1) = z \quad \text{for all } (x_0, x_1),$$

we may equate coefficients of like terms; this yields the following set of equations:

$$a_0 = \alpha_0'' \alpha_0' a_0,$$
$$a_1 = \alpha_0'' \alpha_0' a_1,$$
$$b_0 = \alpha_0''\big(\alpha_0' \beta_0 + \beta_0' a_0^2\big) + \beta_0''\big(\alpha_0' a_0\big)^2,$$
$$b_1 = \alpha_0''\big(\alpha_0' \beta_1 + \beta_0' a_1^2\big) + \beta_0''\big(\alpha_0' a_1\big)^2,$$
$$c_{01} = \alpha_0''\big(\alpha_0' \chi_{0,1} + 2\beta_0' a_0 a_1\big) + \beta_0''\Big(2a_0 a_1 \big(\alpha_0'\big)^2\Big). \tag{E3}$$

These are five equations in nine unknowns. We specify the values of four of the variables arbitrarily and solve for the remaining five. Thus, let

$$\alpha_0' = \alpha_0'' = \alpha_1' = \beta_0'' = 1. \tag{E4}$$

Then the equations (E3) reduce to

$$a_0 = \alpha_0, \quad a_1 = \alpha_1,$$
$$b_0 = \beta_0 + 2\alpha_0^2, \quad b_1 = \beta_1 + 2\alpha_1^2,$$
$$c_{0,1} = \chi_{0,1} + 4\alpha_0 \alpha_1,$$

or, equivalently, to

$$a_0 = \alpha_0, \quad a_1 = \alpha_1,$$
$$\beta_0 = b_0 - 2\alpha_0^2, \quad \beta_1 = b_1 - 2\alpha_1^2,$$
$$\chi_{0,1} = c_{0,1} - 4\alpha_0 \alpha_1. \tag{E5}$$

Equations (E4) and (E5) determine the modules $A_{(0,j)}$ for $j = 1, 3, 7$. To verify that these modules do in fact compute $F(x_0, x_1, 0, \ldots, 0)$, we substitute from (E4) and (E5) into (E2). Then the expression for z becomes

$$z = x_0 a_0 + x_1 a_1 + x_0^2 \left(b_0 - 2a_0^2 + 2a_0^2 \right)$$
$$+ x_1^2 \left(b_1 - 2a_1^2 + 2a_1^2 \right) + x_0 x_1 \left(c_{0,1} - 4a_0 a_1 + 4a_0 a_1 \right)$$
$$= a_0 x_0 + a_0 x_0 + b_0 x_0^2 + b_1 x_1^2 + c_{0,1} x_0 x_1$$
$$= F\left(x_0, x_1, 0, \ldots, 0 \right).$$

It should be noted that this algebraic method does not work for larger problems. We now return to the main line of exposition.

The process for determining the modules of the fan-in that computes F in the general case yields the following information about the expression of F as a superposition of functions in $\mathcal{F}$. Looking first at the root of the tree for F, we see that

$$F\left(x_0, \ldots, x_{2^N - 1} \right)$$
$$= H\left(F\left(x_0, \ldots, x_{2^{N-1}-1}, 0, \ldots, 0 \right), F\left(0, \ldots, 0, x_{2^{N-1}}, \ldots, x_{2^N-1} \right) \right),$$

where H is shorthand for $A_{(0, 2^N - 1)}$.

The function $F(x_0, \ldots, x_{2^{N-1}-1}, 0, \ldots, 0)$, or a function equivalent to it, is computed in minimal time by the subtree whose root is the vertex $(0, 2^{N-1} - 1)$. Similarly, the function $F(0, \ldots, 0, x_{2^{N-1}}, \ldots, x_{2^N-1})$, or a function equivalent to it, is computed in minimal time by the subtree whose root is the vertex $(2^{N-1}, 2^N - 1)$. In Figure 7 these are the subtrees with root $(0, 3)$ and $(4, 7)$, respectively.

Recall that the Leontief–Abelson theorem gives necessary and sufficient conditions for these computations. Therefore that theorem gives us two ways to verify whether the computation indicated in Figure 7 can actually be carried out, that is, whether the functions involved exist.

We illustrate the application of the theorem in a simple example.

8 Computing Equilibrium Price in an Edgeworth Box Economy

The function P to be computed gives the price as a function of the parameters characterizing the agents in a two-person, two-good exchange economy in which the utility functions of the agents are quadratic quasilinear. Denoting these parameters by (x, z) for agent 1 and by (x', z') for agent 2, the function P is given by

$$P\left(x, z, x', z' \right) = \frac{xz' - x'z}{x - x'}$$

(see Mount and Reiter 1982, p. 124, for the derivation of P). The function P is to be computed by a $(2,1)$-network whose inputs are the variables x, z, x', z' in some order. To avoid singularity, we make a coordinate translation to coordinates R, S, T, U, where

$$R = x - 1, \quad S = z, \quad T = x' + 1, \quad U = z'.$$

In the new coordinates,

$$P(R, S, T, U) = \frac{S + U + RU - ST}{2 + R - T}.$$

Here the number of variables is $2^N = 4$, so that $N = 2$. Hence a lower bound for the depth of $(2,1)$-networks that compute P is 2. If P is computable in time 2, then in terms of superpositions there must exist real analytic functions A', B', C', or A'', B'', C'', defined on a neighborhood of the origin in R^2, such that P can be written as

$$P(R, S, T, U) = C\big[A'(S, T), B'(R, U)\big] \tag{E6}$$

or

$$P(R, S, T, U) = C''\big[A''(R, T), B''(S, U)\big]. \tag{E7}$$

Consider the case in which P is given by equation (E6). The Leontief–Abelson theorem states that a necessary condition for the existence of A', B', C' satisfying (E6) is that the matrix

$$BHP(S, T; R, U)_{(0,0;0,0)} = \begin{pmatrix} \left(\dfrac{\partial P}{\partial S}\right)_{(0,0)} & \left(\dfrac{\partial^2 P}{\partial R\, \partial S}\right)_{(0,0)} & \left(\dfrac{\partial^2 P}{\partial S\, \partial U}\right)_{(0,0)} \\[2ex] \left(\dfrac{\partial P}{\partial T}\right)_{(0,0)} & \left(\dfrac{\partial^2 P}{\partial R\, \partial T}\right)_{(0,0)} & \left(\dfrac{\partial^2 P}{\partial U\, \partial T}\right)_{(0,0)} \end{pmatrix} \tag{E8}$$

have rank at most 1. But P, being real analytic, can be written in power series in the form

$$P = \big(S + U + RU - TS\big)\left(\sum_{j=0}^{\infty}(-1)^j\left(\frac{1}{2}\right)^{j+1}(T - R)^j\right)$$

$$= \left(\frac{1}{2}\right)\left[(S + U + RU - TS) + \frac{(S + U)(T - R)}{2}\right] + \theta,$$

where θ is a sum of monomials in R, S, T, U of degree at least 3. Evaluating the matrix in (E8), we see that

$$
BHP(S,T;R,U)_{(0,0;0,0)} = \begin{pmatrix} \dfrac{1}{2} & \dfrac{-1}{4} & 0 \\ 0 & 0 & \dfrac{1}{4} \end{pmatrix},
$$

which has rank 2.

We try next the possibility that

$$
P(R,S,T,U) = C''\big[A''(R,T),\, B''(S,U)\big].
$$

In this case the matrix BHP has the form

$$
BHP(S,T;R,U)_{(0,0;0,0)} = \begin{pmatrix} \left(\dfrac{\partial P}{\partial S}\right)_{(0,0)} & \left(\dfrac{\partial^2 P}{\partial R\,\partial S}\right)_{(0,0)} & \left(\dfrac{\partial^2 P}{\partial S\,\partial T}\right)_{(0,0)} \\ \left(\dfrac{\partial P}{\partial U}\right)_{(0,0)} & \left(\dfrac{\partial^2 P}{\partial R\,\partial U}\right)_{(0,0)} & \left(\dfrac{\partial^2 P}{\partial T\,\partial U}\right)_{(0,0)} \end{pmatrix}.
$$

When evaluated as before, this matrix is

$$
\begin{pmatrix} \dfrac{1}{2} & \dfrac{-1}{4} & \dfrac{-1}{4} \\ \dfrac{1}{2} & \dfrac{1}{4} & \dfrac{1}{4} \end{pmatrix},
$$

which has rank 2. Thus, the necessary condition of the Leontief–Abelson condition is not satisfied in either case. Therefore P cannot be computed in a neighborhood of the origin by a $(2,1)$-network with real analytic modules in *less* than three units of time from the inputs R,S,T,U. However, P clearly can be computed from R,S,T,U in three units of time.[3]

9   Concluding Remarks

The value of the modular network approach to modeling information processing will, as with other approaches, depend on results achieved with it. In this paper we have presented the basic ideas of the model and of the analysis of computational complexity in that model. We have also given two examples, Chernoff faces and reading handwriting, to illustrate its applicability to computing performed by human beings. Interesting as these applications may be, they are not applications to economics.

---

[3] A more complete analysis of this example is given in Mount and Reiter (1990). There the possible trade-off between communication in the form of message-space size and computational complexity is analyzed and the efficient frontier is derived.

Therefore, we conclude this paper with a very brief account of application of the model to a problem of economic theory, namely, a theory of the structure and size of organizational units, such as firms or divisions of firms. This discussion is necessarily brief; a full discussion would exceed the scope of this paper.

The problem addressed in Reiter (1995) is to construct a theory that carries out Coase's program, or principle, which is that economic institutions (such as firms) are optimal adaptations to certain constraints. As pointed out in the introduction of this chapter, firms typically have administrative or managerial structures in which information processing for decision making is shared among many people, the necessity for sharing arising from limitations on the information processing capacities of individuals. Therefore the theory is one that obtains the set of firms (or informationally independent organizational units) as solutions, not necessarily unique, of a constrained optimization problem. In that problem there should be:

(1)   a "variable" whose values correspond to different organizational units (e.g., different firms);
(2)   a set of constraints on this variable expressing technological possibilities and resource availability;
(3)   constraints on information processing; and
(4)   a criterion of performance that expresses the goals of action.

Incentive constraints on individuals and groups, which properly belong in the problem, are not addressed.

In order to solve the model we must find a subset of the set of possible firms that maximizes the criterion over the set of environments, subject to all the constraints.

Desired economic action is represented by a decision function, for example, a function that associates to each environment actions resulting in a Pareto optimal (or, alternatively, a profit maximizing) outcome. Information about the environment is distributed among agents. Coordination is defined in terms of the decision function, and the decision-making task is to compute the value of the decision function in each environment. The problem addressed is how best to organize decision making in these circumstances, taking account of the limitations on the information processing capabilities of individuals.

The information processing capabilities of an individual include:

(a)   conditions on the capability of the individual to observe environmental variables;

(b) the set of computational operations (modules) that are elementary for that individual (e.g., individual i may be capable of observing the value of a parameter x or of y but not both); and

(c) the ability to carry out at most one elementary operation in a unit of time.

A mode of organization in its informational aspect consists of:

(i) an algorithm for computing its decision function; and

(ii) an assignment to individual agents of the steps required to execute the algorithm.

An algorithm is modeled as a modular network. An assignment of the steps of the computation to individuals means that the module at each node of the digraph that represents the algorithm is assigned to an individual to carry out. The assignment of modules of the network to individuals must satisfy three conditions as follows:

(i) the assignment of input nodes to individuals must satisfy the constraints on what individuals may observe;

(ii) a module assigned to an individual must be one of her elementary operations;

(iii) the scheduling of execution of elementary operations in time must satisfy the condition that two or more operations assigned to the same individual cannot be carried out at the same time.

An assignment of a modular network to individual agents determines four characteristics on which information processing costs depend, each measured by a variable. These are: delay; communication; access to memory; and number of agents (processors) used.

The cost function is assumed to be linear in these variables. It is shown that cost minimization is achieved by efficient assignments, that is, assignments resulting in vectorially minimal (four-dimensional) vectors whose components are the arguments of the cost function.

Necessary and sufficient conditions for efficient assignments are derived, and algorithms are given for computing the set of efficient assignments. An efficient assignment of a modular network is represented by an efficient assigned directed acyclic graph – an EADAG. Thus, each EADAG represents an informationally efficient organization of the economic activity possible in the given class of environments. An EADAG may represent one or more informationally separate organizational units, depending on its structure. The idea behind the formal definition given in Reiter (1995) is that difficult coordination problems, described by the necessity to exchange a great deal of information among the individuals involved, require a highly integrated organization (one organizational unit), whereas other coordination problems can be handled with limited exchange of information. For example, in a two-person two-good exchange economy, individual preference relations may be very complicated, requiring an arbitrarily large number of parameters to specify, but the information that must be communicated between the two agents in order to achieve a Pareto outcome in each such environment can consist of just two numbers. If we were to represent this situation by a modular network describing the internal calculations needed to derive excess demands, as well as the calculations needed to find a market equilibrium, the solution EADAG would consist of two components: one corresponding to the internal calculations of each of the two economic agents. The internal communication in each component would increase with the number of parameters needed to specify the preference relations, while the number of variables that need to be transmitted between the components would be constant, independent of the number of parameters.

The model is applied to examples, showing circumstances in which the solution is one firm, with a bound on its size, and others in which it is two firms. Finally, some general results are discussed in which the prevalence of centralized or administrative rather than decentralized organization is related to the nature of the coordination problem presented by the class of environments to be organized.

References

H. Abelson (1980), *Lower Bounds on Information Transfer in Distributed Computations*, Journal of the Association for Computing Machinery 27: 384–92.

D. Abreu and A. Rubinstein (1988), *The Structure of Nash Equilibrium in Repeated Games with Finite Automata*, Econometrica 56: 1259–88.

M. A. Arbib (1969), *Theories of Abstract Automata*, Prentice-Hall, Englewood Cliffs, NJ.

K. J. Arrow and L. Hurwicz (1959), *On the Stability of the Competitive Equilibrium II*, Econometrica 27: 82–109.

R. J. Aumann (1981), *Survey of Repeated Games*, in *Essays in Game Theory and Mathematical Economics in Honor of Oskar Morgenstern*, Bibliographisches Institut, Mannheim, pp. 11–42.

L. Blum, M. Shub, and S. Smale (1989), *On a Theory of Computation and Complexity Over the Real Numbers: NP-Completeness, Recursive Functions and Universal Machines*, Bulletin of the American Mathematical Society 21: 1–46.

R. Coase (1937), *The Nature of the Firm*, Economica 4: 386–405.

H. Chernoff (1973), *The Use of Faces to Represent Points in 6-Dimensional Space Graphically*, *Journal of the American Statistical Association* 68: 361–8.

I. K. Cho (1993a), *Perceptrons Play Repeated Games with Imperfect Monitoring*, Mimeo, Department of Economics, University of Chicago.

I. K. Cho (1993b), *Perceptrons Play the Repeated Prisoner's Dilemma*, Mimeo, Department of Economics, University of Chicago.

I. K. Cho and H. Li (1993), *Complexity and Neural Network in Repeated Games*, Preprint, Department of Economics, University of Chicago.

G. Debreu (1959), *Theory of Value*, Wiley, New York.

C. Futia (1977), *The Complexity of Economic Decision Rules*, *Journal of Mathematical Economics* 4: 289–99.

J. J. Hopfield (1982), *Neural Networks and Physical Systems with Emergent Collective Computational Abilities*, *Proceedings of the National Academy of Science* 79: 2554–8.

L. Hurwicz (1960), *Optimality and Informational Efficiency in Resource Allocation Processes*, in *Mathematical Methods in the Social Sciences* (K. J. Arrow, S. Karlin, and P. Suppes, eds.), Stanford University Press.

L. Hurwicz (1986), *On Informational Decentralization and Efficiency*, in *Studies in Mathematical Economics* (S. Reiter, ed.), Mathematical Association of America, Washington, DC.

E. Kalai and W. Stanford (1988), *Finite Rationality and Interpersonal Complexity in Repeated Games*, *Econometrica* 56: 397–410.

N. Kaldor (1934), *The Equilibrium of the Firm*, *Economic Journal* 44: 70–80.

W. Leontief (1947), *A Note on the Interrelation of Subsets of Independent Variables of a Continuous Function with Continuous First Derivatives*, *Bulletin of the American Mathematical Society* 53: 343–50.

G. G. Lorentz (1966), *Approximation of Functions*, Holt, Rinehart and Winston, New York.

T. Marschak (1986), *Organizational Design*, in *Handbook of Mathematical Economics*, vol. II (K. J. Arrow and M. D. Intriligator, eds.), Elsevier, Amsterdam, pp. 1358–440.

K. Matsuyama (1993), *Toward an Economic Theory of Pattern Formation*, Discussion Paper no. 1079, Center for Mathematical Studies in Economics and Management Science, Northwestern University, Evanston, IL.

W. McCulloch and W. Pitts (1943), *A Logical Calculus of the Ideas Imminent in Nervous Activity*, *Bulletin of Mathematical Biophysics* 5: 115–33.

G. A. Miller (1956), *The Magic Number Seven, Plus or Minus Two: Some Limits on Our Capacity for Processing Information*, *Psychological Review* 63: 108.

M. L. Minsky and S. A. Papert (1988), *Perceptrons: An Introduction to Computational Geometry*, MIT Press, Cambridge, MA.

K. R. Mount and S. Reiter (1982), *Computation, Communication, and Performance in Resource Allocation*, Paper presented at the CEME–NBER Decentralization Seminar, University of Minnesota, Minneapolis.

K. R. Mount and S. Reiter (1990), *A Model of Computing with Human Agents*, Discussion Paper no. 890, Center for Mathematical Studies in Economics and Management Science, Northwestern University, Evanston, IL.

340   Kenneth R. Mount and Stanley Reiter

K. R. Mount and S. Reiter (1993), *Essential Revelation Mechanisms and Computational Complexity*, Discussion Paper no. 1047, Center for Mathematical Studies in Economics and Management Science, Northwestern University, Evanston, IL.

A. Neyman (1985), *Bounded Complexity Justifies Cooperation in the Finitely Repeated Prisoner's Dilemma*, Economic Letters 19: 227–9.

R. Radner (1993), *The Organization of Decentralized Information Processing*, Econometrica 62: 1109–46.

R. Radner and T. Van Zandt (1992), *Information Processing in Firms and Returns to Scale*, Annales d'Economie et la Statistique 25/26: 265–98.

S. Reiter (1995), *Coordination and the Structure of Firms*, Discussion Paper no. 1121, Center for Mathematical Studies in Economics and Management Science, Northwestern University, Evanston, IL.

F. Rosenblatt (1962), *Principles of Neurodynamics*, Spartan, Washington, DC.

A. Rubinstein (1979), *Equilibrium in Supergames with the Overtaking Criterion*, Journal of Economic Theory 21: 1–9.

A. Rubinstein (1986), *Finite Automata Play the Repeated Prisoner's Dilemma*, Journal of Economic Theory 39: 83–96.

A. Rubinstein (1993), *On Price Recognition and Computational Complexity in Monopolistic Model*, Journal of Political Economy 101: 473–84.

H. A. Simon (1972), *Theories of Bounded Rationality*, in *Decision and Organization* (C. B. McGuire and R. Radner, eds.) North-Holland, Amsterdam, pp. 161–76.

H. A. Simon (1987), *The Sciences of the Artificial*, 2nd ed., MIT Press, Cambridge, MA.

T. Van Zandt (1995), *Heirarchical Computation of the Resource Allocation Problem*, European Economic Review 39: 700–8.

T. Van Zandt and R. Radner (1995), *Information processing and returns to scale in a statistical decision problem*, Princeton University and AT&T Bell Laboratories.

A. G. Vituskin (1961), *Complexity of Tabulation Problems*, Pergamon, New York.

O. E. Williamson (1975), *Markets and Hierarchies, Analysis and Antitrust Implications*, New York, Free Press.

A. C. C. Yao (1979), *Some Complexity Questions Related to Distributed Computing*, Journal of the Association for Computing Machinery 22: 209–13.

Index